The Will of a People

The Will of a People

A Critical Anthology of Great African American Speeches

Edited with Introductions by
Richard W. Leeman and
Bernard K. Duffy

Southern Illinois University Press
Carbondale and Edwardsville

Library of Congress Cataloging-in-Publication Data
The will of a people: a critical anthology of great African American speeches / edited by Richard W. Leeman and Bernard K. Duffy.
p. cm.
Includes bibliographical references and index.
ISBN-13: 978-0-8093-3057-7 (pbk. : alk. paper)
ISBN-10: 0-8093-3057-1 (pbk. : alk. paper)
ISBN-13: 978-0-8093-9073-1 (ebook)
ISBN-10: 0-8093-9073-6 (ebook)
1. Speeches, addresses, etc., American—African American authors. 2. African Americans—History—Sources. 3. African American orators. I. Leeman, Richard W. II. Duffy, Bernard K.
PS663.N4W45 2011
815'.0080896073—dc23 2011016452

Printed on recycled paper.
The paper used in this publication meets the minimum requirements of American National Standard for Information Sciences—Permanence of Paper for Printed Library Materials, ANSI Z39.48-1992.

Our scholarship has been influenced by many teachers, mentors, and colleagues. Among these, we especially acknowledge Professors Jim St. Clair, Lyndrey Niles, Robert P. Newman, and Philip Wander, whose scholarly accomplishments and commitment to their students lit the path for our own professional lives. We dedicate this book to these four remarkable teachers.

Contents

Acknowledgments

Completing any book requires the cooperation of many people. An anthology would not be possible without the generosity of those who granted permissions to publish the speeches contained in this volume. Many authors, family members, and agents granted permissions gratis or at a reduced cost. We hope that their generosity will be amply repaid as new generations are inspired by the rich legacy of African American oratory. We are grateful for the assistance provided us by librarians and archivists and for the work of scholars who preceded us in heralding the importance of African American speakers and speeches in American history.

We thank Dr. Karl Kageff, editor-in-chief at Southern Illinois University Press, for graciously encouraging us to undertake this book; also project editor Wayne Larsen; copy editor Kathleen Kageff; and other talented professionals at the press, including Barbara Martin and Bridget Brown.

We are grateful to our students for reading draft material used in our classes and for their enthusiastic interest. Our respective institutions recognized the value of our study and provided as much support as possible in a crippled economy. Graduate students Kathy Taylor and Nicole Ramsey, at the University of North Carolina–Charlotte, helped us find and verify speech texts, track down rights holders, and secure permissions. Jill Fitzgerald at Cal Poly provided technical support. Gracious colleagues, including professors Shawn Long and Richard Besel, listened to our musings as the project took shape. Finally we thank our wives, professors Susan Duffy and Carol Leeman, and our children, Chris and Greg Leeman and Elizabeth Duffy, for their patience as we completed this project over the course of five years.

Introduction

Cicero maintained that there were fewer great orators than there were accomplished exemplars of other learned pursuits, such as poetry, art, or literature.[1] It might seem remarkable, then, that history has supplied so many African American orators who have been eloquent as well as influential, even in a society where legal discrimination and everyday prejudice have worked so pervasively against them. Today, few who have read such speakers would deny the richness, eloquence, and power of their speeches, although recognition of the historical and cultural significance of African American oratory is relatively recent. This volume assembles some of the finest of those orators and their orations. Within these pages, the reader will discover several foundational assumptions.

One assumption is that nothing substitutes for reading the speeches themselves. Although it is important to discuss the history that surrounds each speech, and to consider the illuminating and inventive rhetorical strategies and techniques employed by the speaker, the speech texts are the centerpiece of the volume. Although many of their persuasive appeals seem to speak to the ages, the speeches here are fascinating things because they represent a particular place and time. Orations are composed of the words selected by a particular speaker, designed to persuade a particular audience that hears the speech in a unique geographical and chronological context. Certainly the language and arguments selected often discernibly reflect the times in which the speaker lived. The orators of the nineteenth century, such as Maria W. Miller Stewart, Henry Highland Garnet, Frederick Douglass or Frances Ellen Watkins Harper, all employed more expansive vocabularies and more intricate sentences than those of more recent times. Stewart's 1832 "Why Sit Ye Here and Die?" and Harper's 1891 "Duty to Dependent Races" are far more leisurely productions than Barbara Jordan's 1974 "Watergate" speech or Marian Wright Edelman's 1995 "Children's Legislative Issues." Twentieth- and twenty-first-century speeches are more sharply phrased, almost percussive, affairs. More than vocabulary and sentence structure are in play, however. Speakers such as Frederick Douglass and Henry McNeal Turner regularly referenced Shakespeare, and embedding stanzas of poetry, if not an entire poem, within one's speech would not have surprised nineteenth-century audiences. Contemporary speakers, on the other hand, depend far more heavily on statistical and authoritative evidence.

While the speaker's style often reflects his or her time, each orator included here has a distinctive voice. The embodiment in words that each speaker gives to thoughts is as identifiable as the individual painter's pallet and the impasto created by his or her brushstrokes. Through the language, arguments, and structure of the speech, the orator comes alive against a now re-creatable historical scene. Sojourner Truth was unlettered, but her voice and intellect are acute, challenging her opponents at every turn. W. E. B. Du Bois is ever the scholar, while Stokely Carmichael (Kwame Ture)—no less intellectual than Du Bois—is a charismatic rapper. Ida B. Wells-Barnett sounds modern with her endless stream of numbers and examples, while Martin Luther King Jr.'s "I Have a Dream" harks back to an earlier era with his biblical, Shakespearian, and poetic references. King is the preacher as he takes his stand against the Vietnam War, while Shirley Anita St. Hill Chisholm is the consummate politician as she takes the same stand, citing the war proponents' words against themselves. Frances Ellen Watkins Harper is a poet and essayist, and her phrases are carefully crafted, often lyrical. Marcus Mosiah Garvey is a "street corner" speaker—reading his speeches does not fully capture their rhetorical power. Just as no two persons are identical, neither do two speakers' orations sound precisely the same. A part of us is always captured in our rhetorical choices. Through speeches such as those included in this work, the reader comes to know the speaker in a way he or she could not do by reading about the speaker. We are both united and distinguished by the means we use to edify and persuade. It is not an exaggeration to observe that an imprint of each orator's unique life is thus captured in the pages of this volume.

Speeches do not simply reflect the speakers and their times, however. They also tell us about the issues the speaker confronted and the audience who is addressed. Malcolm X speaks to an audience who, despite the stranglehold that Southern Democratic legislators were exerting upon Congress, felt that it had little choice but to affiliate with the Democratic Party. As he makes clear in "The Ballot or the Bullet," Malcolm X, in comparison with his audience, has no patience with a political loyalty that goes so unrewarded. Barbara Jordan is afraid that a part of her audience will discount her indictment of Richard Nixon as being politically motivated, and so she devotes the first portion of her speech to explaining why partisanship plays no role in her judgment of the president. One of the most fascinating dimensions of Henry Highland Garnet's speech is determining who his intended audience actually is. Is the audience the free African Americans who are attending the convention? The African American slaves to whom the speech is technically addressed? White abolitionists who have been preaching nonviolence? The Southern slave owners who should worry about the potential for more slave revolts? The same words have very different meanings depending upon which audience or audiences Garnet intends to persuade.

Orations are thus edifying historical documents; they record for us the nuances of an audience's experiences, attitudes, and beliefs. In the late nineteenth century, a Northern white audience would not accept an African American woman's testimony regarding lynching, so Ida B. Wells-Barnett draws her stories and evidence from the "mainstream," white newspapers. W. E. B. Du Bois implicitly references a speech by Elizabeth Cady Stanton as he addresses the organization for which she had served as president. Martin Luther King Jr. observes that the Constitution and Declaration of Independence gave African Americans a check that has come back marked insufficient funds, thereby exploiting the white stereotype of the African American's insolvency and thus earning sardonic laughter and applause from African Americans in his audience. Mary Church Terrell's speech is aptly named: "What It Means to Be Colored in the Capital of the United States." Her stories are replete with narrative devices to help her white listeners see Washington, DC—their own town—as it is experienced by African Americans.

Indeed, another foundational assumption is that, within these speeches, one can trace many of the ebbs and flows of American history. The various issues and developments in American race relations may all be found here. Jim Crow laws, discriminatory hiring, abolition, accommodation versus integration, lynching, the back-to-Africa movement, the civil rights movement, and desegregation—all are addressed in these orations. Many other features of the American historical landscape are also present, however. The early deification of George Washington, the evolving occupational choices for women, relations with Native Americans, American "manifest destiny," the industrial revolution, World War I and America's commitment to self-determination, the rise of the New Deal and government social programs, the Vietnam War, conscientious objectors, Nixon and Watergate, gay rights, immigration, and the rise of a mediated culture are just some elements of the historical scene from which these speeches draw. The speeches here do not simply reflect what it means to be an African American.

These are orations by Americans, and as such they embody in their concerns and arguments the issues and events that comprise American history. Yet these are still speeches by African Americans, and that, too, has historical and rhetorical import. A dimension of American life is represented in these speeches that could not be completely reconstructed or understood without them. Many of the speeches speak specifically to the needs and issues of race in America. Garnet and Douglass demand the abolition of slavery. Stewart, Harper, Washington, and Terrell argue for an end to prejudice and discrimination. Wells-Barnett attacks lynching. Turner, Du Bois, and King agitate for integration, voting rights, political rights, and human rights. Malcolm X and Stokely Carmichael seek social and economic equality as well. Marcus Garvey promotes pan-Africanism. Other speakers address topics that are not explicitly matters of "race relations," but it is notable that such orators do so from an African American perspective. Thus, Martin Luther King Jr. feels compelled to announce his controversial stand against the Vietnam War because US aggression in Southeast Asia contradicts his adherence to nonviolence. He also notes, however, that the Vietnam War is a particularly racial war because young African American men are disproportionately drafted, shipped abroad, and killed. Sojourner Truth addresses the legitimacy of women's rights but analogizes that right to the issue of abolition. Barbara Jordan speaks of a president's transgressions, locating the power of her indictment in her particular faith as an African American woman in the living Constitution. The orations included here give voice to a people's will, through the issues that are raised and how those issues are discussed.

And thus arises yet a third foundational assumption: that the speeches included here are uniquely African American, and that this element of the orator's identity is important. Such an assumption is advanced with some slight trepidation, for the terms "race" and "African American" are complex and subjective. From the "one drop" rule to the practice of "passing," the idea of race in American culture has been highly charged. Even the terminology has changed over the years—including African, black, colored, Negro, and African American—as the speeches in this volume demonstrate. While scholars and politicians may debate the essence of race, a singular fact about the speakers included here, however, is that they identified themselves with the African American community. W. E. B. Du Bois, of Dutch and African descent, was light-skinned enough to have "passed" had he chosen to do so, but he chose to attend and teach at historically black colleges and universities and devoted much of his life to leading the National Association for the Advancement of Colored People (NAACP). Barack Hussein Obama, raised by his white maternal family, has clearly embraced his identity as an African American. Mary Church Terrell was wealthy enough, and tempted, to remain in Europe, where race was not the social and political issue it was in America. She chose instead to return home to teach at the "colored" high school in Washington, DC, and served as president of the National Association of Colored Women. Marcus Garvey was proud of his Jamaican heritage, and his overarching cause was pan-Africanism, but his most important labors and most notable successes were located in the African American community in the United States.

But is the identity of the speaker as an African American uniquely important? We believe that it is. As we noted at the outset, African American orators have been prodigiously eloquent, although their eloquence does not always spring from exactly the same sources. Douglass, self-taught, read patriotic speeches and essays, which helped him learn the structure and style of traditional oratory, although his speeches are unique in many ways. Sojourner Truth draws upon the tradition of oral preaching and although she is eloquent, she does not consciously replicate the rhetorical devices passed down from classical writers. Yet, well-educated speakers such as Jesse Louis Jackson also are influenced by the same oral tradition in emphasizing cadence, rhythm, repetition, rhyme, and storytelling, as is Martin Luther King Jr., whose oratorical art is defined by his ability to felicitously and extemporaneously merge elements of his own and other people's most potent appeals. In much African American oratory one finds the undertones of the blues, as Taylor Branch said of King's famous "I Have a Dream" sequence: "[I]t expressed something that was neither pure rage nor pure joy, but the kind of universal transport that makes the blues sweet."[2] More than a matter of style, the blues is a way of expressing and contending with a shared cultural history, plight, and hope. Similarly, Henry Louis Gates and Nelly McKay have identified the African American discursive style as one that has leaned heavily on the vernacular as a rhetoric of challenge. Refusing to subscribe wholly to the white American's ethos and worldview, African Americans expressed in these vernacular forms their own ways of seeing the world, its history, and its meanings. The vernacular comprises, "[Ralph] Ellison said, nothing less than another instance of humanity's 'triumph over chaos.'"[3] Just as the speeches here illustrate, however, while some recurring rhetorical characteristics of African American oratory may be described, for every generalization there are multiple exceptions. The one observation that does not seem debatable, however, is that African Americans have given us many fine exemplars of eloquent oratory. Much of the eloquence one observes in African American oratory is grounded in the act of courageously telling truth to power. Stokely Carmichael and Malcolm X are two distinctive voices in this prophetic tradition.

The speeches collected here are often powerful, insightful, and moving. In part, this may be due to the oral tradition, rooted both in their African heritage and their American experience. African Americans have traditionally enjoyed only limited ability to control the channels of communication, such as newspapers, books, radio, television, and film. African American newspapers, for example, had difficulty surviving without the government and business printing contracts that sustained the white press. Despite his reputation and ability, four times Frederick Douglass started and was forced to abandon some variation of his *Rochester North Star.* As a mode of mass communication, however, public speaking has been far more affordable and accessible to African Americans. Platforms were provided for or created by African American orators, because their command of rhetoric and their messages were compelling and the issues important. Indeed, nineteenth-century speakers such as Douglass and Frances Watkins Harper were able to earn a living on the lecture circuit. Oratory was an important—perhaps the singularly most important—agency by which African Americans could produce social and political change, although speaking in the public forum created antagonism and risk for effective, controversial speakers.

Perhaps another reason we can identify so many eloquent African American speakers is because of the challenges they have confronted. The ideas that comprise the speeches in this work, for example, are large ones; they speak to the essence of our humanity. What is freedom? How does one merit freedom? What is equality of persons? What does the community owe its citizens? What do its citizens owe the community? How should a community work together for the greater good? What does it mean to be a nation? How should we care for the least of our brothers and sisters? Which wars are just, and which ones unjust? These are questions that, when answered, reaffirm the human charter and help mold our national and personal character. The words of the oppressed have helped define, expand, strengthen, and perpetuate freedom for all.

The power of these speeches does not, however, solely reside in the issues addressed and the questions answered. The orations included here are eloquent in part because they answer such fundamental questions by appealing to the best aspects of the American character: fairness, justice, tolerance, democracy, courage, and sacrifice. Whether in exultation, anger, or despair, African American orators have habitually spoken *for* freedom, not against it. They have spoken *for* equality and against denigrating the station of others in life. They have spoken *for* community, embracing the common good and envisioning a society that would be kinder, more prosperous, more caring, and inclusive. The idea of freedom is a case in point. African American orators, as represented in these pages, have traditionally avoided arguing for their freedom at the expense of others. They have not sought to gain their freedom by restricting that of another. Nor has their sensitivity been borne out of necessity, although they have certainly understood that an argument that supports freedom for one supports the same rights for all. Sojourner Truth and W. E. B. Du Bois, for example, elucidate the close relationship between rights for women and rights for African Americans. Du Bois also cautions his audience of white women against grounding their argument for voting rights in the complaint that men of other—implicitly inferior—races have already gained suffrage.

African American orators have thus argued on behalf of broader freedom for the whole community, not merely their own portion of it. Booker T. Washington spoke for many when he noted that oppression reduces the freedom of the oppressor as well as the oppressed. Nearly sixteen million hands will aid you in pulling the load, he tells white Southerners, or they will pull you down. Eight decades later, Jesse Louis Jackson delivered the same message to his audience: you cannot hold a man down in the ditch without remaining there yourself. Eliminating legal and de facto racial discrimination would not only free African Americans, it would provide the intellectual and moral space for white America to grow and prosper as well, proving the premise that the strength of a society can be measured by how fairly the least powerful members are treated.

And thus, although the speeches in this volume involve a variety of places and times and address a wide variety of issues—such as the expulsion of African American legislators, lynching, everyday life in Washington, DC, pan-Africanism, the Vietnam War, the impeachment of one president and the inauguration of another—there is also a common thread that weaves them together. The distinctive voices brought together on these pages speak in an expanding chorus that spans two hundred years of American life. Throughout this book, the reader will find an attention to the issues of justice, freedom, and equality. Those precious ideals, so firmly rooted in American culture, reach their apex in speeches such as the ones here.

So rich is the rhetorical tradition of African Americans, that many speeches could have been selected for inclusion in this volume but were not. Space, of course, imposed some limits on which, and how many, speeches were chosen. Some were not included due to an inability to secure permission to reprint them. Because the artifact is oral discourse, speech copyrights can be notoriously hard to identify and secure. Some of the orations that appear in this volume were selected because they are themselves famous—speeches recognized by name, such as Garnet's "Address to the Slaves of the United States," Douglass's "What to the American Slave Is the Fourth of July?," Truth's "A'n't I a Woman?," Washington's "Atlanta Compromise," King's "I Have a Dream," and Malcolm X's "The Ballot or the Bullet." Others were selected because they rank among the finest speeches delivered by an influential orator—for example, Turner's "I Claim the Rights of a Man," Harper's "Duty to Dependent Races," and Johns's "Rock Foundations." Still others are speeches that represent the larger body of work by a significant figure, such as Du Bois's "Disfranchisement" or Edelman's "Children's Legislative Issues." Other orations were selected for the significance of the occasion that they marked. Stewart's "Why Sit Ye Here and Die?" and Obama's "Inaugural Address" are two such speeches.It is fitting that this collection opens and closes with these two speeches—Stewart's and Obama's—for in some measure they represent the journey that African American orators have travelled as they have expressed the goals, ambitions, and dreams of their people. Maria Miller Stewart was unique for her time—a woman and an African American who dared to speak publically against the ills her people suffered. She spoke to the full range of those who comprised her audience: men and women, whites and blacks. For her temerity, she was hounded from the dais, and even from her home town of Boston. One hundred and seventy-seven years later, Barack Obama took the oath of office as President of the United States.

He was, obviously, also unique; the first African American to be elected president. His inaugural, like Maria Miller Stewart's speech so long ago, addressed an audience comprised of many different people from many different walks of life. Unlike Stewart, Obama was applauded for his oration, cheered on by many as he assumed the duties of president. In one regard these speeches represent continuity: the discrimination and prejudice about which Stewart spoke remain the backdrop against which Obama's election derived its historic meaning. Yet they also represent change. The ascendancy that was unimaginable in Stewart's time has been realized in the present.

In his landmark study *An American Dilemma*, published in 1944, Swedish sociologist Gunnar Myrdal wrote that race relations between African Americans and Euro-Americans constituted the overarching issue that had shaped America's past and would mold its future.[4] Neither the American nor the African American journey concludes with the presidency of Barack Obama, nor can this book include more than a representative sample of the many great orations that African Americans have delivered or will deliver in the future. We stand by our claim, however, that these are indeed great orations, characterized by the inspiration of their content, the artistry of their design, and the role they have played in American history, as they have given voice to the will of a people.

Maria W. Miller Stewart

Lecture, Delivered at the Franklin Hall (Why Sit Ye Here and Die?)

Maria W. Miller Stewart is generally regarded as the first American woman, of any race, to publicly address what was then termed a "promiscuous" audience, that is, an audience comprised of men and women. Women were permitted to preach to mixed audiences at meetings of the Society of Friends (Quakers), but the relatively rare public lectures that featured women speakers were generally understood to be acceptable only if delivered to exclusively female audiences. Similarly, racially mixed audiences were unusual, with segregation being the de facto practice in most cases with the exception of some church services, for which segregated seating was the norm. Maria Miller Stewart's lecturing in public, to racially mixed audiences comprised of males and females, did more than simply raise eyebrows, even in the then-liberal bastion of Boston.

Only the barest details are known about Stewart's early life. According to her pamphlet of essays, *Religion and the Pure Principles of Morality*, published in 1831, Maria Miller was born in Hartford, Connecticut, in 1803, and orphaned at the age of five. Shorn of her family, Maria was then "bound out" to an unnamed clergyman and his family. There she would complete various domestic chores in return for room, board, and, evidently, some schooling. She left the family in 1818, at the age of fifteen, and in 1826 married James Stewart, who died three years later. In 1831, she submitted a manuscript of essays to William Lloyd Garrison, the publisher of the *Liberator*. Garrison published excerpts in his paper but also printed the entire work as a pamphlet. In 1832, he published her second collection of essays, *Meditations from the Pen of Mrs. Maria W. Stewart*. On the basis of the popularity of her essays, in the spring of 1832 she was invited to deliver an address to the Afric-American Female Intelligence Society. That lecture primarily focused on evangelizing for Christianity and on challenging her audience of African American women to support each other in their endeavors to improve their position. The following fall, on September 21, 1832, Stewart delivered a lecture commonly titled "Why Sit Ye Here and Die" in Franklin Hall, the site of the monthly meetings for the New England Anti-Slavery Society.[1] Remarks contained within the text of Stewart's speech as well as historical tradition indicate that this was a "promiscuous" audience of males and females, African Americans and whites.[2] Rhetorical scholar Karyln Kohrs Campbell notes that the majority of readers of the *Liberator* were African American and concludes that, although racially mixed, Stewart's audience was probably comprised primarily of African Americans.[3]

"Why Sit Ye Here and Die?" is notable first for Stewart's employment of biblical verse. The opening stanzas of the speech are drawn from a story in the Second Book of Kings, in which four leprous men camped outside the besieged city of Jerusalem decide that, since either going into the city or staying where they are would mean certain death, they might as well go to the camp of the Aramaen army to beg for food. Arriving to find the army has fled in haste, the lepers not only fulfill God's prophecy through Elijah but are rewarded with great wealth and plentiful choice food. In this opening paragraph, Stewart powerfully challenges her audience. On its face, the speech is most directly a challenge to the African American portion of her audience. As discriminated against as the lepers of biblical times, even free African Americans, she observes throughout the speech, are materially and economically deprived in nineteenth-century America. By implication, her audience has nothing to lose by more aggressively asserting their rights and demanding redress of their grievances. Indeed, their reward for asserting themselves may be great wealth, and the assertion of their rights would enact God's will. On a different level, however, Stewart's admonition applies to the white members of her audience as well. In biblical terms, we are all lepers, and all must leave their sinful ways in order to fulfill God's will and enjoy His rewards. As she notes later in the speech, whites are prejudicial in the extreme against African Americans, and it is time for them to stop "sitting" in a way of life that means certain spiritual death.

Stewart's command of Old Testament verse is knowing and broad. In the course of this relatively brief speech she draws from the books of Second Kings, First Samuel, Joshua, Genesis, Second Samuel, Isaiah, Psalms,

Leviticus and Jeremiah. Three times she references the New Testament, calling upon a parable from the Gospel of Matthew, and citing verse from the epistles of James and Paul. Her reliance on the Old Testament is representative of abolitionists. The Old Testament, with a wrathful God of judgment, served their purposes well.[4] Stewart does not simply allude to the Bible, however. With only a single exception—her reference to the parable of the talents from the Gospel of Matthew—Stewart employs the Bible by weaving verse into the text of her speech. At times the verse is quoted verbatim, as when she commands: "Tell it not in Gath! publish it not in the streets of Askelon!" In other places, she adapts the verse to fit the point she is making, as when she observes that she is "as willing to die by the sword as the pestilence."

As with her opening citation of verse, Stewart's employment of the Bible is without exception rhetorically strategic. Lamenting the intellectual and spiritual barrenness that discrimination produces, she evokes Isaiah's description of God's punishment upon those nations that stood against him. They would be deserts, bringing forth "thorns and thistles," in stark contrast to the milk and honey of Canaan. Whites frequently and often literally characterized America as the new "Promised Land." Stewart's application of Isaiah is a strong warning that white prejudice and discrimination was turning that Promised Land into the desert of Arabia. Similarly, Stewart defends her decision to speak publicly—and thus endure all sorts of calumny—by calling to mind Psalm 69: "it is for [woman's] sake and yours that I have come forward and made myself a hissing and a reproach among the people." In other words, she chooses to endure the insults and threats because the cause of equal rights is a worthwhile one. Her choice of Psalm 69 to convey this thought is especially meaningful. In that psalm, the writer sings that he is being discriminated against without reason: "More in number than the hairs of my head are those who hate me without cause; many are those who would destroy me, my enemies who accuse me falsely. . . . I am the subject of gossip for those who sit in the gate, and the drunkards make songs about me."[5] In its conclusion, the psalm predicts that God's justice will be realized, particularly for those who have been discriminated against: "Let the oppressed see it and be glad; you who seek God, let your hearts revive. For the Lord hears the needy, and does not despise his own that are in bonds. . . . For God will save Zion and rebuild the cities of Judah; and his servants shall live there and possess it; and the children of his servants shall inherit it, and those who love his name shall live in it."[6] Her use of verse, then, not only defends her decision to put herself "forward" on behalf of a just cause, it reminds her white audience that the Bible promises that God will ultimately reward the oppressed, while it warns that He will cast out the oppressor.

Although references drawn from Biblical verse are found in all four of her speeches, "Why Sit Ye Here and Die" is notable for its prolific use of that rhetorical device. Certainly the Bible provided the moral foundation for many abolitionists' claims. Biblical appeals such as "How long, O Lord?"[7] or "God is no respecter of persons"[8] were common, intended to expose the hypocrisy of a nation that professed Christian doctrine while legalizing chattel slavery and Jim Crow discrimination. In this regard, Stewart is solidly within the abolitionist tradition. Her pronounced emphasis on citing the Bible, here in her second speech, however, may be rhetorically strategic in another way as well. Her first lecture had been delivered to the Afric-American Female Intelligence Society. That audience was, presumably, comprised solely of African American women. For this her second foray into public lecture, however, her audience was mixed, both by race and by gender. As an African American woman, Stewart's credibility would be suspect for three-quarters of the audience, even an audience that would be primarily abolitionist in sentiment. This was additionally true because Stewart was not delivering an abolitionist speech. Her address argued for the elimination of informal and legal discrimination, a position that was not embraced by all the abolitionists. By relying heavily on the Bible's authority, Stewart shifted the question of credibility from an African American woman to the word of God. To find her "not credible," the audience would have to deny the authority of the Bible. Her rhetorical risk was only this: to be persuasive she needed to incorporate the verses into her speech in ways that the audience found appropriate and learned. By all internal measures, Stewart did so. Her citation of verse was precise, drew from a variety of books in the Bible, did not appear strained, and wove complex rhetorical meanings between the biblical text and Stewart's message.

The second notable feature of Stewart's address is her manner of directly addressing the various constituencies of her audience. Her opening appeal—"why sit ye here and die?"—appears directed to the African Americans in her audience, while her second argument, analogizing the situation of free African Americans to those enslaved—appears aimed at enlightening the white members of her audience. At various turns, Stewart seeks to open whites' eyes to the oppressive nature of prejudice, while at other times encouraging African Americans to moral improvement or to lobbying the legislature for change. Stewart walks a delicate line here in a rhetorical balancing act that has been repeated by numerous African American orators and essayists. On the one hand, she seeks to encourage the African Americans in her audience to redouble their efforts to improve their lot in life. She thus urges African Americans to "turn their attention more assiduously to moral worth and intellectual improvement." "Moral" in this nineteenth-century context referred primarily to the development of philosophical refinements, that is, the pursuit of learning. Although there would be some broad implications in regard to one's moral or immoral behavior, Stewart's charge should not be understood through our twenty-first-century perspective as a condemnation of African Americans' moral conduct. She makes similar points for her nineteenth-century audience as well. As she declares later in the speech, taken as a "people, we are neither lazy nor idle," and whites need to understand African American conduct within the context of prejudice and discrimination: "Considering how little we have to excite or stimulate us, I am almost astonished that there are so many industrious and ambitious ones to be found."

Several times in her speech, Stewart returns to the theme that constant and arduous menial work for subsistence pay—or worse—is an intolerable evil. These are fetters that "bind the soul"; they are "chains of ignorance and poverty." Stewart references her own experience as a servant: "I have learnt, by bitter experience, that continual hard labor deadens the energies of the soul, and benumbs the faculties of the mind." Again, a careful balance must be struck. African Americans are willing to work—"I do not consider it derogatory, my friends, for persons to live out to service . . . and I would highly commend the performance of almost any thing for an honest living." However, "a miserable existence of servitude" does not permit a people to gain "literary acquirements" or "scientific knowledge." Twice Stewart makes appeals to the white women in her audience in this regard. She confides that she has "asked several individuals of my sex, who transact business for themselves," if they would hire African Americans to work for them. While the shop owners themselves disavow any personal prejudice, they refuse to hire African Americans because they would lose customers. "Such," she says, "is the powerful force of prejudice." Later in the speech, she asks the white females again to view life from the African American's perspective: "O, ye fairer sisters, whose hands are never soiled, whose nerves and muscles are never strained, go learn by experience!"

Stewart's lecture concludes with an extended exhortation directed towards the African American men in her audience. The passage is marked by various rhetorical turns and perspectives. She begins by addressing them "My beloved brethren" and invoking ties founded on their common Christianity, not ethnicity. Although earlier in the speech she condemned the white audience members for their prejudice, she now gives a positive nod to them as she challenges her last target: "so will it be vain for the advocates of freedom [white abolitionists] to spend their breath in our behalf, unless with united hearts and souls you make some mighty efforts to raise your sons and daughters from the horrible state of servitude and degradation in which they are placed." Stewart places the burden for the improvement of the race squarely upon the men: "it is upon you that woman depends." After thus marking African American men as the change agents who have not yet sufficiently acted to change, she follows with a passage that describes the lifespan of the African American man. This narrative, depicting how "smart, active, and energetic" young men, "with souls filled with ambitious fire" are beaten down by the oppression of prejudice until they are "aged sires . . . with their old wood-saws on their backs." On its surface, her portrayal challenges the men to fight for change that will allow them to live more profitable, fulfilling lives, but the story's moral—that African American men are victimized by the prejudice of the age—contains lessons for any of the audience's constituent members. It is a sympathetic portrayal, one that condemns the prejudice and discrimination of society, while redeeming its victims.

Yet Stewart again shifts the appeal directly back to African American men. There can be no excuses, she tells them, for failing to work toward improving their lot in society. Invoking the Pilgrims, she asks if those early colonists had said "the Britons have all the money and all the power, and we must continue their servants forever?" Hers is a gender-specific appeal, also. "It is upon you that woman depends," she tells them, "she can do but little besides using her influence." Stewart herself exemplifies that influence, through her decision to provide a public lecture on the topic. Thus, although Stewart acknowledges the economic and political reality, that the struggle for equal rights will largely fall upon African American men, by her willingness to speak publicly she enacts the responsibility that African American women have as well. They should use their influence—lobbying their white sisters for employment opportunities, castigating white men for their prejudice and discrimination, and encouraging African American men in their efforts. Women are "dependent," but not powerless, and by speaking publicly to an audience of mixed race and mixed gender, Stewart has expanded the range within which African American women are able to—and should—wield their influence.

Stewart delivered two more lectures in Boston during the following year, "An Address Delivered at the African Masonic Hall (African Rights and Liberty)" on February 27, 1833, and on September 23, 1833, "Mrs. Stewart's Farewell Address to Her Friends in the City of Boston (What If I Am a Woman?)."[9] The former lecture included significant passages in which Stewart castigated African American men for the wayward habits of many, and this may well be the speech that engendered the reported throwing of tomatoes at the speaker.[10] Throughout her brief speaking career, Stewart evidently endured much hostility, both formal and informal. Just as she noted in "Why Sit Ye Here and Die?"—that she had made of herself a "hissing and reproach"—so in her farewell address she made herself "contemptible in the eyes of many, that I might win some."[11] Her farewell address is a feminist discourse on behalf of women's rights, abilities, and responsibility to participate in public life through venues such as public lectures. Indeed, as rhetorical critic Karlyn Kohrs Campbell points out, Stewart's "brief career as a speaker illustrates the inevitable link between any rhetorical effort and the struggle for woman's rights."[12]

After her farewell address, Maria Miller Stewart left Boston, presumably to escape the barrage of criticism and verbal abuse to which she was subjected. In New York City, then Baltimore, and then Washington, DC, she took a series of low paying teaching posts in schools for African American youths. There is no evidence that she again took the public platform, even after other women, following her lead, had made the custom more widely accepted.[13] Although subsequent women speakers who appeared later in the century would draw stronger acclaim for their eloquence, Stewart's speeches demonstrated courage, learning, and intelligence. Self-taught, Stewart was a well-educated woman and the "high style" and "literary quality" of her speeches, such as "Why Sit Ye Here and Die?," reflected her intellect.[14] Moreover, just as the presence of the speaker herself, the speeches challenged her audience in fundamental, and fundamentally important, ways.

Lecture, Delivered at the Franklin Hall

(Why Sit Ye Here and Die?)

September 21, 1832
Boston, Massachusetts

Why sit ye here and die? If we say we will go to a foreign land, the famine and the pestilence are there, and there we shall die. If we sit here, we shall die. Come let us plead our cause before the whites: if they save us alive, we shall live—and if they kill us, we shall but die.[a]

Methinks I hear a spiritual interrogation—"Who shall go forward, and take off the reproach that is cast upon the people of color? Shall it be a woman?"[b] And my heart made this reply—"If it is thy will, be it even so, Lord Jesus!"

I have heard much respecting the horrors of slavery; but may Heaven forbid that the generality of my color throughout these United States should experience any more of its horrors than to be a servant of servants, or hewers of wood and drawers of water![c] Tell us no more of southern slavery; for with few exceptions, although I may be very erroneous in my opinion, yet I consider our condition but little better than that. Yet, after all, methinks there are no chains so galling as the chains of ignorance—no fetters so binding as those that bind the soul, and exclude it from the vast field of

a. 2 Kings 7:3–4: "Now there were four leprous men outside the city gate, who said to one another, "Why should we sit here until we die? If we say, 'Let us enter the city,' the famine is in the city and we shall die there; but if we sit here, we shall also die. Therefore, let us desert to the Aramean camp; if they spare our lives, we shall live; and if they kill us, we shall but die."

b. 1 Samuel 17:26: "David said to the men who stood by him, 'What shall be done for the man who kills this Philistine [Goliath], and takes away the reproach from Israel?'"

c. Joshua 9:23: "Now therefore you are cursed, and some of you shall always be slaves, hewers of wood and drawers of water for the house of my God."

useful and scientific knowledge. O, had I received the advantages of early education, my ideas would, ere now, have expanded far and wide; but, alas! I possess nothing but moral capability—no teachings but the teachings of the Holy Spirit.

I have asked several individuals of my sex, who transact business for themselves, if providing our girls were to give them the most satisfactory references, they would not be willing to grant them an equal opportunity with others? Their reply has been—for their own part, they had no objections; but as it was not the custom, were they to take them into their employ, they would be in danger of losing the public patronage.

And such is the powerful force of prejudice. Let our girls possess what amiable qualities of soul they may; let their characters be fair and spotless as innocence itself; let their natural taste and ingenuity be what they may; it is impossible for scarce an individual of them to rise above the condition of servants. Ah! Why is this cruel and unfeeling distinction? Is it merely because God has made our complexion to vary? If it be, O shame to soft, relenting humanity! "Tell it not in Gath! publish it not in the streets of Askelon!"[d] Yet, after all, methinks were the American free people of color to turn their attention more assiduously to moral worth and intellectual improvement, this would be the result: prejudice would gradually diminish, and the whites would be compelled to say, unloose those fetters!"Though black their skins as shades of night, / Their hearts are pure, their souls are white."[e]

Few white persons of either sex, who are calculated for anything else, are willing to spend their lives and bury their talents in performing mean, servile labor.[f] And such is the horrible idea that I entertain respecting a life of servitude, that if I conceived of there being no possibility of my rising above the condition of a servant, I would gladly hail death as a welcome messenger. O, horrible idea, indeed! to possess noble souls aspiring after high and honorable acquirements, yet confined by the chains of ignorance and poverty to lives of continual drudgery and toil. Neither do I know of any who have enriched themselves by spending their lives as house-domestics, washing windows, shaking carpets, brushing boots, or tending upon gentle-

d. 2 Samuel 1:20: "Tell it not in Gath, proclaim it not in the streets of Ashkelon; / or the daughters of the Philistines will rejoice, the daughters of the uncircumcised will exult."

e. A piece of self-written poetry first published in Stewart's *Religion and the Pure Principles of Morality*. For this speech, however, Stewart has three times substituted the pronoun "their" for "your," the latter of which appears in the original. Maria W. Stewart, *Productions of Maria W. Stewart* (Boston: Friends of Freedom and Virtue, 1835), 4.

f. Refers to the parable of the hidden talents, Matthew 25:14–30.

men's tables. I can but die but expressing my sentiments; and I am as willing to die by the sword as the pestilence;[g] for I am a true born American; your blood flows in my veins, and your spirit fires by breast.

I observed a piece in the *Liberator* a few months since, stating that the colonizationists had published a work respecting us, asserting that we were lazy and idle.[h] I confute them on that point. Take us generally as a people, we are neither lazy nor idle; and considering how little we have to excite or stimulate us, I am almost astonished that there are so many industrious and ambitious ones to be found; although I acknowledge, with extreme sorrow, that there are some who never were and never will be serviceable to society. And have you not a similar class among yourselves?

Again. It was asserted that we were "a ragged set, crying for liberty." I reply to it, the whites have so long and so loudly proclaimed the theme of equal rights and privileges, that our souls have caught the flame also, ragged as we are. As far as our merit deserves, we feel a common desire to rise above the condition of servants and drudges. I have learnt, by bitter experience, that continual hard labor deadens the energies of the soul, and benumbs the faculties of the mind; the ideas become confined, the mind barren, and, like the scorching sands of Arabia, produces nothing; or, like the uncultivated soil, brings forth thorns and thistles.[i]

Again, continual hard labor irritates our tempers and sours our dispositions; the whole system becomes worn out with toil and fatigue; nature herself becomes almost exhausted, and we care but little whether we live or die. It is true, that the free people of color throughout these United States are neither bought nor sold, nor under the lash of the cruel driver; many obtain a comfortable support; but few, if any, have an opportunity of becoming rich and independent; and the employments we most pursue are as unprofitable to us as the spider's web or the floating bubbles that vanish into

g. Ezekiel 7:15: "The sword is outside, pestilence and famine are inside; those in the field die by the sword; those in the city—famine and pestilence devour them." Leviticus 26:25. "I will bring the sword against you, executing vengeance for the covenant; and if you withdraw within your cities I will send pestilence among you, and you shall be delivered into enemy hands."

h. The colonization movement was primarily comprised of white Americans who perceived it as a solution to slavery. Some genuinely wished to transport purchased slaves back to Africa, others employed it as a tactic of delay, since it was inconceivable that enough slaves could be "purchased" so as to have even a modest impact on slavery in America. Some African Americans, such as Henry Highland Garnet, later participated in a "back-to-Africa" movement, sometimes called a "colonization" movement, but that organization was significantly different than the movement to which Stewart refers.

i. Isaiah 34:13: "Thorns shall grow over its strongholds, nettles and thistles in its fortresses. It shall be the haunt of jackals, an abode for ostriches."

air. As servants, we are respected; but let us presume to aspire any higher, our employer regards us no longer. And were it not that the King eternal has declared that Ethiopia shall stretch forth her hands unto God, I should indeed despair.[j]

I do not consider it derogatory, my friends, for persons to live out to service. There are many whose inclination leads them to aspire no higher; and I would highly commend the performance of almost any thing for an honest livelihood; but where constitutional strength is wanting, labor of this kind, in its mildest form, is painful. And doubtless many are the prayers that have ascended to Heaven from Afric's daughters for strength to perform their work. Oh, many are the tears that have been shed for the want of that strength! Most of our color have dragged out a miserable existence of servitude from the cradle to the grave. And what literary acquirements can be made, or useful knowledge derived, from either maps, books, or charts, by those who continually drudge from Monday morning until Sunday noon? O, ye fairer sisters, whose hands are never soiled, whose nerves and muscles are never strained, go learn by experience! Had we the opportunity that you have had, to improve our moral and mental faculties, what would have hindered our intellects from being as bright, and our manners from being as dignified as yours? Is not the workmanship as curious and complete? Have pity upon us, have pity upon us, O ye who have hearts to feel for others' woes; for the hand of God has touched us. Owing to the disadvantages under which we labor, there are many flowers among us that are "born to bloom unseen, / And waste their fragrance on the desert air."[k]

My beloved brethren, as Christ has died in vain for those who will not accept of offered mercy, so will it be vain for the advocates of freedom to spend their breath in our behalf, unless with united hearts and souls you make some mighty efforts to raise your sons and daughters from the horrible state of servitude and degradation in which they are placed. It is upon you that woman depends; she can do but little besides using her influence: and it is for her sake and yours that I have come forward and made myself a hissing and a reproach among the people[l]; for I am also one of the wretched and miserable daughters of the descendants of fallen Africa. Do you ask, why are you so wretched and miserable? I reply, look at many of the most worthy

j. Psalm 69: 31: "Let bronze be brought from Egypt; let Ethiopia hasten to stretch out its hands to God."

k. Thomas Gray, "Elegy Written in a Country Churchyard," 1751.

l. Psalm 69:7: "It is for your sake that I have borne reproach, that shame has covered my face."

and interesting of us doomed to spend our lives in gentlemen's kitchens. Look at our young men, smart, active, and energetic, with souls filled with ambitious fire; if they look forward, alas! what are their prospects? They can be nothing but the humblest laborers, on account of their dark complexions; hence many of them lose their ambition, and become worthless. Look at our middle-aged men, clad in their rusty plaids and coats; in winter, every cent they earn goes to buy their wood and pay their rents; their poor wives also toil beyond their strength, to help support their families. Look at our aged sires, whose heads are whitened with the frosts of seventy winters, with their old wood-saws on their backs. Alas, what keeps us so? Prejudice, ignorance, and poverty. But ah! methinks our oppression is soon to come to an end; yea, before the Majesty of heaven, our groans and cries have reached the ears of the Lord of Sabaoth.[m] As the prayers and tears of Christians will avail the finally impenitent nothing; neither will the prayers and tears of the friends of humanity avail us any thing, unless we possess a spirit of virtuous emulation within our breasts. Did the pilgrims, when they first landed on these shores, quietly compose themselves, and say, "the Britons have all the money and all the power, and we must continue their servants forever?" No; they first made powerful efforts to raise themselves, and then God raised up those illustrious patriots, Washington and Lafayette, to assist and defend them. And, my brethren, have you made a powerful effort? Have you prayed the Legislature for mercy's sake to grant you all the rights and privileges of free citizens, that your daughters may rise to that degree of respectability which true merit deserves, and your sons above the service situations which most of them fill.

m. Lord of Sabaoth: "Lord of hosts." Typically invoked to indicate God rescuing His people from dire, almost hopeless, circumstances. James 5:4: "Listen! The wages of the laborers who mowed your fields, which you kept back by fraud, cry out, and the cries of the harvesters have reached the ears of the Lord of hosts [Sabaoth]."

Henry Highland Garnet

An Address to the Slaves of the United States of America
(Speech to the National Convention of Colored Citizens)

Henry Highland Garnet and Frederick Douglass were widely considered by their contemporaries to be the two preeminent African American orators of the abolition period. Both Douglass and Garnet were fugitive slaves from the Eastern Shore of Maryland and had endured considerable hardships. From the very beginning of his speaking career, Garnet reveled in debate and excelled at producing fiery oratory that stirred his audiences. Even allowing for nineteenth-century observers' tendency towards exaggerated praise, it is clear that Garnet was an accomplished motivational speaker. Throughout his lifetime, he spoke on behalf of a variety of causes, including African and Haitian emigration, and his audiences often found themselves moved to act on behalf of those causes. Although by 1843 Garnet was already well known as an activist, his "Address to the Slaves of the United States of America" that year fully established his national fame for radical, exhortative speeches.

Born in 1815, Garnet and his family fled slavery in 1824 when he was nine years of age. Assisted by Quakers, the family relocated to New York City, where he enrolled in the African Free School. After some schooling, Garnet took employment as a deckhand, and in 1829, while he was away at sea, fugitive slave hunters broke into the family's home. His mother and father fled, while his sister was captured. Returning to discover the sudden dissolution of his family, Garnet shipped on with a schooner bound for Cuba. On that voyage, Garnet became ill, and his right leg swelled with infection. He again returned to New York, where he came under the tutelage of Theodore Wright, the minister of First Colored Presbyterian Church, who enrolled him as a student in the new Noyes Academy in New Hampshire. Shortly after its inception, the Noyes Academy was burned down by local citizens who objected to the presence of an integrated school in their town. At this time, Garnet's leg, which never fully healed, was amputated. Theodore Wright again encouraged Garnet to pursue his education and arranged for his enrollment in the Oneida Institute. There he completed a classical education, including instruction in Greek and Hebrew and upon graduation became a licensed Presbyterian minister, serving at the integrated First Presbyterian Church in Troy, New York. In 1843, he assumed the position of minister of Liberty Presbyterian Church, a missionary offshoot of his previous church.[1]

During this time, Garnet had become good friends with Gerrit Smith, a wealthy white abolitionist in western New York who was challenging William Lloyd Garrison's leadership of the abolitionist movement. Garrison, publisher of the *Liberator* and the best-known abolitionist of the time, argued that slavery could be ended only by "moral suasion"—that is, an appeal to the conscience of each individual. Garrison held that the Constitution was a proslavery document and that any participation in the US political system as it then existed would validate and legitimize the system of slavery. Garrison thus preached noninvolvement with the political process. In contrast, Gerrit Smith and others had become convinced that most of those who supported slavery would never be "persuaded" and that the pernicious institution could be abolished only when it became illegal. In 1842, they formed the Liberty Party, and Henry Highland Garnet supported that branch of the abolitionist movement enthusiastically.[2]

Before his "Address to the Slaves," 1843 had already been a busy year for Garnet. In March, he had addressed the Liberty Party Convention in Buffalo, New York, where he suggested that those African Americans, such as Frederick Douglass, who did not support the party were not being "true" to their race. In early August, Garnet similarly addressed the national Liberty Party Convention in New York City. Immediately thereafter, at a Colored Citizens and Their Friends Convention in the same city, Douglass publicly responded to Garnet, and from the convention floor, Garnet chided Douglass and the two became engaged in a heated argument.[3] Earlier in the summer of 1843, Charles Ray, Theodore Wright, and Henry Highland Garnet had called for a national Convention of Colored Citizens to be held in Buffalo, New York. On August 13, 1843, twenty-five delegates met to discuss the course of action that free African Americans should take in support of abolition. In addition to the African American delegates, there were some white observer/participants in the audience, including one who wrote an account of the convention and Garnet's "Address" for the *Cincinnati Daily Chronicle*. Also attending the convention was Frederick Douglass, at that time still a strong supporter of the Garrison faction of the abolition movement. Garnet spoke three times at the convention. On the first day, a day devoted primarily to prayer, Garnet delivered one of the two benedictions. On the second day, he gave an address that again enthusiastically endorsed the Liberty Party. On the third day, however, Garnet made a motion that a pamphlet be printed and distributed throughout the nation, and he delivered to the convention the content of that pamphlet in an address to which he would be forever linked. It was a radical speech that exhorted the slaves to rebel for their freedom. "Rather die freemen than live to be slaves," Garnet told them, and that was the sentiment repeated throughout the appeal.[4]

An exhortative speech—one designed less to convince and more to excite the audience to act—typically employs a variety of rhetorical devices. Exhortative speeches usually assume that the audience is already convinced of the *rightness* of the cause, but must be moved to act. Absolute claims that divide the question into either/or dualities and strong emotional appeals present the audience with a stark choice of either acting now or languishing forever. Figures of speech such as antithesis, hyperbole, and synecdoche efficiently communicate to the audience that strong action is needed immediately.[5] Rhetorical questions ask the audience what they are feeling, while moral imperatives tell them what to do. A model of exhortative discourse, Garnet's "Address to the Slaves" employs all of these in an effort, ironically, not so much to move the *slaves* to action but to move his immediate audience of free African Americans to action.

Because exhortative speakers assume an audience is already "convinced," but not yet committed to act, they describe the world in absolute terms, as a place of either/or, with the right path already clearly illuminated. Indeed, Garnet explicitly notes the limited scope of his speech: "We shall not attempt, in this short address, to present to the world all the dark catalogue of this nation's sins, which have been committed upon an innocent people." Alluding to the Old Testament pronouncement that God is "no respecter of persons," Garnett declares that the evil of slavery and the slave's right to physically resist are manifest, and do not need examination. "Brethren, it is as wrong for your lordly oppressors to keep you in slavery, as it was for the man thief to steal our ancestors from the coast of Africa. . . . The humblest peasant is as free in the sight of God as the proudest monarch that ever swayed a sceptre. Liberty is a spirit sent out from God, and like its great Author, is no respecter of persons." For exhortative speakers, such evil divides the world in two, with the good on one side sharply separated from the bad on the other. In that way, Garnet could bind free African Americans with their enslaved brethren. "While you have been oppressed," he says to the slaves, "we have also been partakers with you; nor can we be free while you are enslaved." A fugitive slave himself who had lost his family to bounty hunters, Garnet's declaration of the kinship between free and enslaved African Americans draws upon his experience rather than his poetic imagination.

Within this sharply divided moral universe, Garnet pays particular attention early in the speech to pointing out to slaves that they had been wronged. Not only is slavery evil, but it is an evil that has been directed towards and visited upon them in particular. Free African Americans mourned "your sorrows," he tells them, "earnestly hoping that before this day your sacred liberty would have been restored." Nor do the cruelties of slavery end at the grave but are instead "inherited" from the slaves by succeeding generations, who are as a result "cursed and ruined by American slavery." "Your intellect has been destroyed as much as possible," Garnet continues, "and every ray of light they have attempted to shut out from your minds." So all pervasive is the evil of slavery, that those who inflict it are themselves cursed: "The oppressors themselves have become involved in the ruin. They have become weak, sensual and rapacious—they have cursed you—they have cursed themselves—they have cursed the earth which they have trod."

To move an audience to act in unconventional and radical ways, the exhortative speaker generally employs strongly emotional appeals. In the main, Garnet's emotional appeals remind his audience of the injustices of slavery. "They buy and sell you as though you were brute beasts," he tells his audience. Their slave ancestors had been "doomed to unrequited toil and deep degradation," as are they, but his most emotional appeals concern the slave's family. Midway through the speech, he attacks this subject with a series of provocatively worded imperative sentences: "Look around you, and behold the bosoms of your loving wives heaving with untold agonies! Hear the cries of your poor children! Remember the stripes your fathers bore. Think of the torture and disgrace of your noble mothers. Think of your wretched sisters, loving virtue and purity, as they are driven into concubinage and are exposed to the unbridled lusts of incarnate devils." Twice in the speech he returns to that theme, including once in the conclusion.

Throughout the speech, his language, especially the verbs, adjectives, and epithets, underlines the emotional cruelty of slavery. Slavery afflicts, persecutes, crushes, curses, ruins, and dooms "with a fierceness which we might not expect to see in the fiends of hell." Slave owners are "soul thieves," who tear slaves' wives away, pamper their own lusts, and "steal the light which shines from the word of God. Slavery's evil injustice is diabolical, its wickedness tremendous, its burdens grievous, its sins dark, and its institutions nefarious. Garnet further magnifies the evil of slavery by personifying the institution itself. In nineteenth-century America, evil was often personified and described as an independent, malignant agent. Garnet's description of slavery is consistent with this notion of evil itself. "Slavery had stretched its dark wings of death over the land," Garnet recounts to his audience, "its throne is established, and now it reigns triumphant." Slavery had actively "fixed a deep gulf between you and us," he tells the slaves. This organic evil is independent of the "guilty wretches who maintained it." "The propagators of the system," he says, "very soon discovered its growing evil, and its tremendous wickedness." Caught in slavery's snare of avarice and lust, however, the slave owners could not and would not dismantle the system of evil. Ultimately, this animate form of evil is antithetical to God Himself: "But slavery sets all [God's commandments] at naught, and hurls defiance in the face of Jehovah."

Although Garnet relies most heavily upon describing the evils of slavery—as did most abolitionists—a very different emotional appeal comprised the last section of the body of his speech. In that passage, he tells the stories of four enslaved men who led rebellions: Denmark Veazie, Nathaniel Turner, Joseph Cinque, and Madison Washington. Here the emotion elicited is one of pride, as he casts the rebellions in terms of bravery and glory. "In the whole history of human efforts to overthrow slavery," he declares, "a more complicated and tremendous plan [than Veazie's] was never formed." Although Veazie's rebellion was not ultimately successful, "the guilty soul thieves were overwhelmed with fear" and talk about emancipation after this "one blast of the trumpet of freedom." Nathaniel Turner was "patriotic," and "future generations will remember him among the noble and the brave." Cinque, of *Amistad* fame, was successful in winning his freedom and that of the "ship load of his fellowmen" and now "sings of liberty on the sunny hills of Africa" and "feels himself as free as that king of the forest." Madison Washington was a "bright start of freedom" who had taken "his station in the constellation of true heroism." These were all, for Garnet, "noble men" who had brought pride to themselves and to all African Americans: "Those who have fallen in freedom's conflict, their memories will be cherished by the true hearted and the God fearing in all future generations; those who are living, their names are surrounded by a halo of glory." Garnet organizes this section beginning with the two "unsuccessful" revolts and finishing with the two successful ones, although he is careful to praise all acts of resistance, whether ultimately successful or not.

After calling for race pride in the glory and honor of those who had acted and struck for liberty, Garnet returns to his appeal to anger and outrage—with some appeal to guilt as well—in the conclusion of the speech: "But you are a patient people. You act as though, you were made for the special use of these devils. You act as though your daughters were born to pamper the lusts of your masters and overseers. And worse than all, you tamely submit while your lords tear your wives from your embraces and defile them before your eyes." By implication, Garnet's castigation of the slaves as a "patient people" in the face of that which demanded outrage and action extends to the free African Americans in his audience as well. Their reliance on moral suasion instead of forceful action demonstrates that they, too, are a "patient people" beyond all bounds of reason or morality.

Garnet's emotional appeals are designed for a single purpose: to urge his audience to stand up for good and act against evil. As with most exhortative speakers, Garnet wants his audience to act, and appeals to action are distributed throughout the oration. The opening of his speech foreshadows his later calls to action by noting that, "until this time," free African Americans had been "contented in sitting still and mourning over your sorrows." He proceeds to a brief narrative examining the history and evils of slavery, reaching a crescendo when he declares that slavery now "reigns triumphant" in the country, but that the oppressors have cursed themselves as well as the slaves through their actions. He then recalls the promise of the American Revolution, contrasting that struggle for freedom with the hollow promises that slavery would ultimately be repealed, and then concludes with his first declaration in favor of physical resistance. "When the power of Government returned to their hands, did they emancipate the slaves? No; they rather added new links to our chains. Were they ignorant of the principles of Liberty? Certainly they were not. The sentiments of their revolutionary orators fell in burning eloquence upon their hearts, and with one voice they cried, LIBERTY OR DEATH. Oh, what a sentence was that! It ran from soul to soul like electric fire, and nerved the arms of thousands to fight in the holy cause of Freedom. Among the diversity of opinions that are entertained in regard to physical resistance, there are but a few found to gainsay that stern declaration. We are among those who do not." From this point forward, Garnet's speech integrates calls for action with condemnation of inaction. "TO SUCH DEGRADATION (as that of American slavery)," he said, "IT IS SINFUL IN THE EXTREME FOR YOU TO MAKE VOLUNTARY SUBMISSION" (capitals in original). God, he claims, lays a "moral obligation" upon the slaves—and by extension, free African Americans, to physically resist. In language later echoed by Malcolm X, Garnet commands that "IT IS YOUR SOLEMN AND IMPERATIVE DUTY TO USE EVERY MEANS, BOTH MORAL, INTELLECTUAL, AND PHYSICAL, THAT PROMISES SUCCESS." In what may strike one as the height of impracticality, Garnet demonstrates the extreme urgency for action: "Go to your lordly enslavers," he instructs the slaves, "and tell them plainly, that you *are determined to be free*" (emphasis in original). He shortly follows that recommendation with what has endured as the most famous passage from his speech: "You had better all die—*die immediately*, than live slaves, and entail your wretchedness upon your posterity. If you would be free in this generation, here is your only hope. However much you and all of us may desire it, there is not much hope of redemption without the shedding of blood. If you must bleed, let it all come at once—rather *die freemen than live to be slaves*" (emphases in original). To rather "die freemen than live to be slaves" is repeated again in his peroration, as he also exhorts his audience to "Let your motto be resistance! *resistance!* RESISTANCE!" and to "remember that you are FOUR MILLIONS!" Significantly, at the close of his speech, Garnet moderates the kind of resistance he urged the slave to undertake. Rather than commanding them that they must be "going up" and confronting the slave owner directly, Garnet recommends that "what kind of resistance you had better make you must decide by the circumstances that surround you, and according to the suggestion of expediency." His call for *some* type of physical resistance and action remains categorical, however, as he declares that "no oppressed people have ever secured their liberty without resistance." While he leaves it to his audience to identify the proper form their resistance should take, the moral imperative *to* resist remained.

The convention's minutes record that the speech was greeted by silence, polite applause, and then more silence. Although Garnet had been demonstrative in his speech, his audience did not respond in kind. At this time still fully in the Garrison camp favoring moral suasion over political action, Frederick Douglass is recorded as opining that the speech focused "too much" on "physical force," and "would lead to insurrection." Douglass declared that, for himself, he wanted "no part in such an act." Garnet hotly responded that "maybe the slaves ought simply to ask for their liberty since the masters would surely let them have it." Douglass advanced a motion that rejected Garnet's call for rebellion, and that motion carried by one vote, 13–12. Contemporary newspaper coverage of the speech was divided. The *Emancipator* called the speech "true eloquence—the ridiculous, the pathetic, the indignant, all called into irresistible action." The *Cincinnati Daily Chronicle* reporter wrote that "it is enough to awaken every right-thinking mind to abhor the institution that would hold him [the speaker] or those like him in bondage." Unsurprisingly, Garrison's *Liberator* attacked the speech as "inflammatory," and the *Albany Argus* termed it a "dangerous document."[6] In cooperation with some of the other conventioneers, however, Garnet proceeded to publish the speech in pamphlet form, and it was widely distributed.

Following his 1843 address, Garnet continued to advance the antislavery cause, both in America and on a European tour. Garnet was also active in Republican Party politics and the emigration movement, and in 1858 he helped found the African Civilization Society, which advocated emigration to Africa as one means of escaping racial oppression and discrimination in America. In 1865, he became the first African American to speak in the Capitol building, delivering a memorial address to Abraham Lincoln before the House of Representatives. Appointed minister and consul general to Liberia in 1881, there Henry Highland Garnet died in 1882 after a long oratorical career as Presbyterian minister, abolitionist firebrand, and emigration enthusiast.

An Address to the Slaves of the United States of America

(Speech to the National Convention of Colored Citizens)

August 15, 1843
Buffalo, New York

Brethren and Fellow Citizens:—Your brethren of the North, East, and West have been accustomed to meet together in National Conventions, to sympathize with each other, and to weep over your unhappy condition. In these meetings we have addressed all classes of the free, but we have never, until this time, sent a word of consolation and advice to you. We have been contented in sitting still and mourning over your sorrows, earnestly hoping that before this day your sacred liberty would have been restored. But, we have hoped in vain. Years have rolled on, and tens of thousands have been borne on streams of blood and tears, to the shores of eternity. While you have been oppressed, we have also been partakers with you; nor can we be free while you are enslaved. We, therefore, write to you as being bound with you. Many of you are bound to us, not only by the ties of a common humanity, but we are connected by the more tender relations of parents, wives, husbands, children, brothers, and sisters, and friends. As such we most affectionately address you.

Slavery has fixed a deep gulf between you and us, and while it shuts out from you the relief and consolation which your friends would willingly render, it affects and persecutes you with a fierceness which we might not expect to see in the fiends of hell. But still the Almighty Father of mercies has left to us a glimmering ray of hope, which shines out like a lone star in a cloudy sky. Mankind are becoming wiser, and better—the oppressor's power is fading, and you, every day, are becoming better informed, and more numerous. Your grievances, brethren, are many. We shall not attempt, in this short address, to present to the world all the dark catalogue of this nation's sins, which have been committed upon an innocent people. Nor is it indeed necessary, for you feel them from day to day, and all the civilized world look upon them with amazement.

Two hundred and twenty seven years ago, the first of our injured race were brought to the shores of America. They came not with glad spirits to select their homes in the New World. They came not with their own consent, to find an unmolested enjoyment of the blessings of this fruitful soil. The first dealings they had with men calling themselves Christians, exhibited to them the worst features of corrupt and sordid hearts; and convinced them that no cruelty is too great, no villainy and no robbery too abhorrent for even enlightened men to perform, when influenced by avarice and lust. Neither did they come flying upon the wings of Liberty, to a land of freedom. But they came with broken hearts, from their beloved native land, and were doomed to unrequited toil and deep degradation. Nor did the evil of their bondage end at their emancipation by death. Succeeding generations inherited their chains, and millions have come from eternity into time, and have returned again to the world of spirits, cursed and ruined by American slavery.

The propagators of the system, or their immediate ancestors, very soon discovered its growing evil, and its tremendous wickedness, and secret promises were made to destroy it. The gross inconsistency of a people holding slaves, who had themselves "ferried o'er the wave" for freedom's sake, was too apparent to be entirely overlooked. The voice of Freedom cried, "Emancipate yourselves." Humanity supplicated with tears for the deliverance of the children of Africa. Wisdom urged her solemn plea. The bleeding captive pled his innocence, and pointed to Christianity who stood weeping at the cross. Jehovah frowned upon the nefarious institution, and thunderbolts, red with vengeance, struggled to leap forth to blast the guilty wretches who maintained it. But all was in vain. Slavery had stretched its dark wings of death over the land, the Church stood silently by the priests prophesied falsely, and the people loved to have it so. Its throne is established, and now it reigns triumphant.

Nearly three millions of your fellow citizens are prohibited by law and public opinion, (which in this country is stronger than law,) from reading the Book of Life. Your intellect has been destroyed as much as possible, and every ray of light they have attempted to shut out from your minds. The oppressors themselves have become involved in the ruin. They have become weak, sensual, and rapacious—they have cursed you—they have cursed themselves—they have cursed the earth which they have trod.

The colonists threw the blame upon England. They said that the mother country entailed the evil upon them, and that they would rid themselves of it if they could. The world thought they were sincere, and the philanthropic pitied them. But time soon tested their sincerity.

In a few years the colonists grew strong, and severed themselves from the British Government. Their independence was declared, and they took their station among the sovereign powers of the earth. The declaration was a glorious document. Sages admired it, and the patriotic of every nation reverenced the God-like sentiments which it contained. When the power of Government returned to their hands, did they emancipate the slaves? No; they rather added new links to our chains. Were they ignorant of the principles of Liberty? Certainly they were not. The sentiments of their revolutionary orators fell in burning eloquence upon their hearts, and with one voice they cried, Liberty or Death. Oh what a sentence was that! It ran from soul to soul like electric fire, and nerved the arm of thousands to fight in the holy cause of Freedom. Among the diversity of opinions that are entertained in regard to physical resistance, there are but a few found to gainsay that stern declaration. We are among those who do not. Slavery! How much misery is comprehended in that single word. What mind is there that does not shrink from its direful effects? Unless the image of God be obliterated from the soul, all men cherish the love of Liberty. The nice discerning political economist does not regard the sacred right more than the untutored African who roams in the wilds of Congo. Nor has the one more right to the full enjoyment of his freedom than the other. In every man's mind the good seeds of liberty are planted, and he who brings his fellow down so low, as to make him contented with a condition of slavery, commits the highest crime against God and man. Brethren, your oppressors aim to do this. They endeavor to make you as much like brutes as possible. When they have blinded the eyes of your mind—when they have shut out the light which shines from the Word of God—when they have embittered the sweet waters of life then, and not till then, has American slavery done its perfect work.

TO SUCH DEGRADATION IT IS SINFUL IN THE EXTREME FOR YOU TO MAKE VOLUNTARY SUBMISSION. The divine commandments you are in duty bound to reverence and obey. If you do not obey them, you will surely meet with the displeasure of the Almighty. He requires you to love him supremely, and your neighbor as yourself—to keep the Sabbath day holy—to search the Scriptures—and bring up your children with respect for his laws, and to worship no other God but him. But slavery sets all these at naught, and hurls defiance in the face of Jehovah. The forlorn condition in which you are placed, does not destroy your moral obligation to God. You are not certain of heaven, because you suffer yourselves to remain in a state of slavery, where you cannot obey the commandments of the Sovereign of the universe. If the ignorance of slavery is a passport to heaven, then it is a blessing, and no curse, and you should rather desire its perpetuity than its abolition. God will not receive slavery, nor ignorance, nor any other state of mind, for love and obedience to him. Your condition does not absolve you from your moral obligation. The diabolical injustice by which your liberties are cloven down, NEITHER GOD, NOR ANGELS, OR JUST MEN, COMMAND YOU TO SUFFER FOR A SINGLE MOMENT. THEREFORE IT IS YOUR SOLEMN AND IMPERATIVE DUTY TO USE EVERY MEANS, BOTH MORAL, INTELLECTUAL, AND PHYSICAL THAT PROMISES SUCCESS. If a band of heathen men should attempt to enslave a race of Christians, and to place their children under the influence of some false religion, surely Heaven would frown upon the men who would not resist such aggression, even to death. If, on the other hand, a band of Christians should attempt to enslave a race of heathen men, and to entail slavery upon them, and to keep them in heathenism in the midst of Christianity, the God of heaven would smile upon every effort which the injured might make to disenthrall themselves.

Brethren, it is as wrong for your lordly oppressors to keep you in slavery, as it was for the man thief to steal our ancestors from the coast of Africa. You should therefore now use the same manner of resistance, as would have been just in our ancestors when the bloody foot prints of the first remorseless soul thief was placed upon the shores of our fatherland. The humblest peasant is as free in the sight of God as the proudest monarch that ever swayed a sceptre. Liberty is a spirit sent out from God, and like its great Author, is no respecter of persons.

Brethren, the time has come when you must act for yourselves. It is an old and true saying that, "if hereditary bondmen would be free, they must themselves strike the blow." You can plead your own cause, and do the work of emancipation better than any others. The nations of the world are moving in the great cause of universal freedom, and some of them at least will, ere long, do you justice. The combined powers of Europe have placed their broad seal of disapprobation upon the African slave trade. But in the slaveholding parts of the United States, the trade is as brisk as ever. They buy and sell you as though you were brute beasts. The North has done much—her opinion of slavery in the abstract is known. But in regard to the South, we adopt the opinion of the *New York Evangelist*—We have advanced so far, that the cause apparently waits for a more effectual door to be thrown open than has been yet. We are about to point out that more effectual door. Look around you, and behold the bosoms of your loving wives heaving with untold agonies! Hear the cries of your poor children! Remember the stripes your fathers bore. Think of the torture and disgrace of your noble mothers. Think of your wretched sisters, loving virtue and purity, as they are driven into concubinage and are exposed to the unbridled lusts of incarnate devils. Think of the undying glory that hangs around the ancient name of Africa—and forget not that you are native born American citizens, and as such, you are justly entitled to all the rights that are granted to the freest. Think how many tears you have poured out upon the soil which you have cultivated with unrequited toil and enriched with your blood; and then go to your lordly enslavers and tell them plainly, that *you are determined to be free*. Appeal to their sense of justice, and tell them that they have no more right to oppress you, than you have to enslave them. Entreat them to remove the grievous burdens which they have imposed upon you, and to remunerate you for your labor. Promise them renewed diligence in the cultivation of the soil, if they will render to you an equivalent for your services. Point them to the increase of happiness and prosperity in the British West Indies since the Act of Emancipation. Tell them in language which they cannot misunderstand, of the exceeding sinfulness of slavery, and of a future judgment, and of the righteous retributions of an indignant God. Inform them that all you desire is FREEDOM, and that nothing else will suffice. Do this, and for ever after cease to toil for the heartless tyrants, who give you no other reward but stripes and abuse. If they then commence the work of death, they, and not you, will be responsible for the consequences. You had better all die—*die immediately*, than live slaves and entail your wretchedness upon your posterity. If you would be free in this generation, here is your only hope. However much you and all of us may desire it, there is not much hope of redemption without the shedding of blood. If you must bleed, let it all come at once—*rather die freemen, than live to be slaves*. It is impossible like the children of Israel, to make a grand exodus from the land of bondage. The Pharaohs are on both sides of the blood red waters! You cannot move en masse, to the dominions of the British Queen—nor can you pass through Florida and overrun Texas, and at last find peace in Mexico. The propagators of American slavery are spending their blood and treasure, that they may plant the black flag in the heart of Mexico and riot in the halls of the Montezumas. In the language of the Rev. Robert Hall,[a] when addressing the volunteers of Bristol, who were rushing forth to repel the invasion of Napoleon, who threatened to lay waste the fair homes of England, "Religion is too much interested in your behalf, not to shed over you her most gracious influences."

You will not be compelled to spend much time in order to become inured to hardships. From the first moment that you breathed the air of heaven, you have been accustomed to nothing else but hardships. The heroes of the American Revolution were never put upon harder fare than a peck of corn and a few herrings per week. You have not become enervated by the luxuries of life. Your sternest energies have been beaten out upon the anvil of severe trial. Slavery has done this, to make you subservient, to its own purposes; but it has done more than this, it has prepared you for any emergency. If you receive good treatment, it is what you could hardly expect; if you meet with pain, sorrow, and even death, these are the common lot of slaves.

Fellow men! Patient sufferers! behold your dearest rights crushed to the earth! See your sons murdered, and your wives, mothers and sisters doomed to prostitution. In the name of the merciful God, and by all that life is worth, let it no longer be a debatable question whether it is better to choose *Liberty* or *death*.

In 1822, Denmark Veazie,[b] of South Carolina, formed a plan for the liberation of his fellow men. In the whole history of human efforts to overthrow slavery, a more complicated and tremendous plan was never formed. He was betrayed by the treachery of his own people, and died a martyr to freedom. Many a brave hero fell, but history, faithful to her high trust, will transcribe his name on the same monument with Moses, Hampden,[c] Tell,[d] Bruce[e] and

a. Reverend Robert Hall (1764–1831): English Baptist minister who spoke and wrote on the religious view of contemporary political and social issues.

b. Denmark Vesey (1767?–1822): Born in the Caribbean and brought to South Carolina as a slave, Vesey (originally named Telemaque) purchased his freedom in 1799 from lottery winnings and worked thereafter as a carpenter. In 1816, he cofounded an AME church in Charleston. Although himself free, for several years prior to 1822 he plotted an organized slave insurrection, acquiring and hiding weapons and arranging the support of Haiti. Estimates of the number of slaves involved in the planning ran as high as nine thousand. The plot was discovered, and some 139 African Americans and four whites were arrested. Forty-seven, including Vesey, were executed.

c. John Hampden (1595–1643): Major figure of the English Revolution, staunch defender of Parliament's right to govern.

d. William Tell (circa 14th century): Legendary Swiss folk hero who resisted noble authority and helped lead the battle that established the Swiss Confederation. The historical accuracy of the Tell story has been debated.

e. Robert the Bruce, or Robert I of Scotland (1274–1349): Successfully led Scotland against England in the Wars for Scottish Independence.

Wallace,[f] Toussaint L'Ouverture,[g] Lafayette[h] and Washington. That tremendous movement shook the whole empire of slavery. The guilty soul thieves were overwhelmed with fear. It is a matter of fact, that at that time, and in consequence of the threatened revolution, the slave States talked strongly of emancipation. But they blew but one blast of the trumpet of freedom and then laid it aside. As these men became quiet, the slaveholders ceased to talk about emancipation; and now behold your condition today! Angels sigh over it, and humanity has long since exhausted her tears in weeping on your account!

The patriotic Nathaniel Turner[i] followed Denmark Veazie. He was goaded to desperation by wrong and injustice. By despotism, his name has been recorded on the list of infamy, and future generations will remember him among the noble and brave.

Next arose the immortal Joseph Cinque,[j] the hero of the Amistad. He was a native African, and by the help of God he emancipated a whole ship load of his fellow men on the high seas. And he now sings of liberty on the sunny hills of Africa and beneath his native palm trees, where he hears the lion roar and feels himself as free as that king of the forest.

Next arose Madison Washington[k] that bright star of freedom, and took his station in the constellation of true heroism. He was a slave on board the brig Creole, of Richmond, bound to New Orleans, that great slave mart, with

---

f. William Wallace (1272–1305): Scottish knight who led troops in several battles of the War for Scottish Independence. He was captured by the English and executed by Edward I for treason.

g. Francois-Dominique Toussaint L'Ouverture (1743–1803): A freed slave who led a successful revolution of slaves and freed Africans in Haiti against French control. Established a Haitian constitution and served as governor until the French defeated him in battle. As a condition of surrender, however, he insisted that the French guarantee that slavery would not be reestablished.

h. Gilbert du Motier, the Marquis de Lafayette (1757–1834): French noble who served as a commander in the American army during the American Revolution. He also served as the vice president of the Estates-General during the early phases of the French Revolution and there presented the "Declaration of the Rights of Man and of the Citizen."

i. Nathaniel Turner (1800–1831): A slave in Southampton, Virginia, who in 1831 led a rebellion of slaves, starting with a small group who travelled from plantation to plantation gathering followers and killing the white slave owners. By the end of the two day rebellion, he had gathered over fifty followers and killed over fifty whites.

j. Sengbe Pieh, or Joseph Cinque (1813–1879): A rice farmer from western Africa (modern day Sierra Leone) who was enslaved. Helped lead a revolt on the slave transport schooner *Amistad* as it was headed to Cuba. The ship sailed for two months before being landed in Long Island, New York. Cinque and his fellow slaves were found guilty of mutiny, but the case was appealed to the US Supreme Court, which found for Cinque. In 1842, Cinque and the others were returned to their homes in Africa.

k. Madison Washington: In 1841, led a slave rebellion on the *Creole*. Washington was the cook on the slave transport ship. He and eighteen other slaves took over the ship and sailed the vessel to Nassau in the Bahamas and freedom.

a hundred and four others. Nineteen struck for liberty or death. But one life was taken, and the whole were emancipated, and the vessel was carried into Nassau, New Providence.

Noble men! Those who have fallen in freedom's conflict, their memories will be cherished by the true hearted and the God fearing in all future generations; those who are living, their names are surrounded by a halo of glory.

Brethren, arise, arise! Strike for your lives and liberties. Now is the day and the hour. Let every slave throughout the land do this, and the days of slavery are numbered. You cannot be more oppressed than you have been—you cannot suffer greater cruelties than you have already. *Rather die freemen than live to be slaves.* Remember that you are FOUR MILLIONS!

It is in your power so to torment the God cursed slaveholders that they will be glad to let you go free. If the scale was turned, and black men were the masters and white men the slaves, every destructive agent and element would be employed to lay the oppressor low. Danger and death would hang over their heads day and night. Yes, the tyrants would meet with plagues more terrible than those of Pharaoh. But you are a patient people. You act as though, you were made for the special use of these devils. You act as though your daughters were born to pamper the lusts of your masters and overseers. And worse than all, you tamely submit while your lords tear your wives from your embraces and defile them before your eyes. In the name of God, we ask, are you men? Where is the blood of your fathers? Has it all run out of your veins? Awake, awake; millions of voices are calling you! Your dead fathers speak to you from their graves. Heaven, as with a voice of thunder, calls on you to arise from the dust.

Let your motto be resistance! *resistance!* RESISTANCE! No oppressed people have ever secured their liberty without resistance. What kind of resistance you had better make, you must decide by the circumstances that surround you, and according to the suggestion of expediency. Brethren, adieu! Trust in the living God. Labor for the peace of the human race, and remember that you are FOUR MILLIONS.

Sojourner Truth

A'n't I a Woman?
(Speech at the Women's Rights Convention)

Isabella, born a slave, renamed herself Sojourner Truth to reflect her calling as an itinerant preacher of the Christian gospel and the social gospel of racial and gender equality. As Sojourner Truth, she became one of the most colorful and remarkable orators of the nineteenth century. Collectively, her speeches fuse the reformist goals of liberating African Americans from slavery and liberating women from cultural oppression. Her voice, intellect, and commanding presence made Truth and her message unforgettable. Among her many speeches, the one she delivered at the Women's Rights Convention in 1851 is by far the best known, nothing short of an oratorical monument to her career, but ironically modern historians dispute the credibility of the most widely anthologized and quoted version.

Isabella's fame as an orator could not have been predicted from the humble circumstances of her birth. Her early biography is incomplete and inexact. She was the youngest of ten or twelve children of slaves owned by Johannis Hardenbergh, a colonel in the Revolutionary Army who, like other Dutch colonists, farmed land in Ulster County, New York.[1] A number Isabella's siblings were sold to other landowners, and upon the death of Colonel Hardenbergh's son, Isabella would be separated from her elderly parents to work as a slave in the household of John Neely. She spoke only the Dutch she had learned from her previous owners, and the Neelys spoke only English. The difficulties of communicating with Isabella resulted in frustration for her owners, who took out these frustrations on the slave. She was beaten by both the Neelys. Her back showed the ineradicable effects of a whipping inflicted upon her by her master for a reason she could not discern.[2] With the helpful intercession of her father, Isabella was sold again, first to a Dutch tavern owner and finally to another Dutch family, headed by John Dumont, in whose house Isabella lived for sixteen years. Though not with the capriciousness of the Neelys, John Dumont punished Isabella with beatings but also praised her for her hard work. Perniciously, Isabella, who was only twelve or thirteen when sold to the Dumonts, became the victim of sexual abuse by Dumont's wife, Sally, a fact that she refers to obliquely in the autobiography she dictated to Olive Gilbert.[3] Still, Isabella felt herself to be a part of the Dumont household and expressed affection for John Dumont, although not for Sally.

John Dumont arranged a marriage for Isabella to another of his slaves, Thomas. As a teenager she had also had a relationship with Robert, a slave on another farm, which was cut short by his owner, who forbade the union and brutally beat Robert into submission. Isabella bore five children and it is speculated that one might have been by Robert.

A New York State law emancipated all slaves by July 4, 1827, and Dumont had agreed to free her one year earlier than the law dictated. He later reneged on the promise, and Isabella struck her own bargain, leaving his household before the end of the year, but four or five months after the originally agreed-upon date.[4] She left for freedom carrying her baby with her, but leaving her other children, Elizabeth and Peter, behind. Isabella found sanctuary at the home of Isaac and Maria Van Wagenen, who persuaded Dumont to accept $25 for Isabella and $5 for her baby for a year.[5]

Isabella became a Methodist, and her new life as a freed slave was increasingly involved in religion. A schism existed between the New England and New York City Methodists. The New England Methodists, who were once committed to living a simple, but holy life, had grown more materialistic while the New York City Methodists subscribed to the earlier version of Methodism. Allying herself with the more staid version of Methodism, referred to as "perfectionism," Isabella dressed and lived austerely, and she abstained from drinking alcohol but continued to smoke for another forty years. Her actions and rhetoric are suffused with the strength that came from her Christian faith. As Nell Painter suggests: "More than anything else she did or said in her life, this ability to act with the support of a powerful supernatural force and to mine its extraordinary resources made Sojourner Truth a representative African-American woman."[6]

Isabella's strong religious beliefs also led her to join a religious sect, headed by Robert Matthews, "the Prophet Matthias." She met Matthias in 1832 and ultimately joined him on a commune, Zion Hill, in Westchester County, New York. Although Matthias, who claimed to be Christ, preached racial equality, he inflicted corporal punishment on Isabella. Isabella found contentment in the commune, however, and would have remained in the sect had Zion Hill not dissolved. Isabella was later drawn to the Millerites, who similarly had a father figure, William Miller. Miller preached an end-of-time doctrine that called upon members to proselytize as many people as possible before a fast-approaching day of judgment.[7] Through the Millerites, Isabella came to the Northampton Association for Education and Industry, a utopian commune in Massachusetts, where she thrived. There she found intellectual discussions and listened to lectures by abolitionists such as William Lloyd Garrison, Frederick Douglass, and Wendell Phillips. During this period of her life Isabella renamed herself Sojourner Truth. The metaphysical implications of "Truth" are obvious, the title "Sojourner," perhaps less so. It suggested her itinerancy, certainly, but also her belief in the imminence of the Second Coming that made life a brief sojourn.[8]

Within a few years, Truth became one of the best-known opponents of slavery and the subjugation of women. Part of the reason for her celebrity was the publication in 1850 of her autobiography, *The Narrative of Sojourner Truth: A Northern Slave*, dictated to Olive Gilbert, an educated white woman and fellow Millerite. Indirectly, the idea for the book came from Douglass, whose *Narrative of the Life of Frederick Douglass: An American Slave* had been published in 1845 and met with immediate commercial success.[9] Although Truth spoke widely and often, her famous speech at the Woman's Rights Convention at Akron, Ohio, on May 28, 1851, is a potent distillate of her wide-ranging speaking career.

Francis Gage, who presided at the meeting, held in a church, left a detailed account of Truth's speech. Unfortunately, the account was written twelve years after the event and is markedly different from more contemporaneous accounts.[10] Truth biographers Nell Painter and Carleton Mabee separately argue that Gage has lengthened and dramatized Truth's speech, to the point of inventing the four times repeated refrain "A'n't I a Woman," and other potent rhetorical appeals. Painter and Mabee also maintain that the audience and situation were not as Gage describes. Still, the Gage version of Truth's speech published in *The History of Woman Suffrage* is the most popular, if not the most accurate. Unfortunately, Truth had little way of monitoring the accuracy of media accounts of her speech; she was illiterate and spoke extemporaneously or impromptu.[11] In an era when important speeches were destined for print, and sometimes set in type before they were even delivered, most speakers could exert some control over what the newspapers and others reported; Truth could not.

According to Gage's evocative account, when Truth's presence at the meeting was observed, participants expressed concern about the mixing of the causes of abolition with the rights of women, for which the audience was said to be unprepared. Some implored Gage not to allow Truth to speak. Gage has it that Truth's speech was cast as a bold response to several comments critical of gender equality uttered by male preachers who attended the meeting. Responding to resolutions proposed by women delegates, the preachers chimed in with captious, but authoritatively pronounced, arguments that stunned the women. Superior intellect and the gender of Christ were cited as reasons for the privileged place of men. One minister argued that the story of Jesus gave no hint of the equality of women. One suggested that the inequality of women was confirmed by the sins attributed to the biblical Eve.

Gage maintains that just when the tide of the debate had seemed to turn against the women, Sojourner Truth rose from her seat on the pulpit steps. At a height of five feet eleven inches, an "Amazon form," according to Gage, Truth towered over most women in the audience. At this point, there were renewed pleas not to allow her to speak, or at least that is what Gage tells us. Carleton Mabee, who examined twenty-seven accounts of the Akron convention, claims that there is no evidence that the women objected to Truth speaking, and Painter even denies that Truth had been sitting on the pulpit steps.[12]

Gage, who published poetry and fiction, offers a fanciful vernacular version of Sojourner's speech with Truth's pronunciation replicated phonetically, for example, "Well chilern, whar dar is so much racket dar must be something out o'kilter."[13] Sojourner's nineteenth-century Dutch/English dialect is difficult to imagine and there is no way to confirm the accuracy of Gage's phonetic version. While adding what appears to be greater authenticity to Truth's speech, it seems to parody Truth and might actually misrepresent Truth's dialect in the direction of how African Americans spoke in South Carolina where Gage lived when she wrote her account. Newspaper versions of the address, including the one anthologized here, are expressed in conventional speech. We have chosen to anthologize Gage's version with the phonetic dialect as it usually appears in modern anthologies. There is no way to know what Sojourner's exact words were or how she spoke them. Historical evidence strongly suggests that Gage framed the history of the address to link antislavery and feminism more strongly, through the invention and repetition of "A'n't [Aren't] I a woman," for example.[14] Inevitably, an analysis of the Gage version of the speech is a comment on Gage's rhetorical invention as well as Truth's.

Truth's prickly speech is incisively logical. In the Gage version, Truth begins with an enthymeme based upon a rhetorical probability. "Well children, where there is so much racket there must be something out of kilter." She derives her conclusion from a generalization based upon experience, namely, the loud dispute suggests the existence of a problem. Her mode of expression, particularly her reference to the audience as children, makes the introduction seem like maternal chiding. Other versions of the speech do not include this passage. In Gage's version, Truth next warns that white men face a two-pronged threat from African American slaves in the South and white women in the North, while in the *Anti-Slavery Bugle* version, this warning is saved for the conclusion.[15]

According to Gage, Truth immediately turned to address one of the allegations made by men in the audience. "That man over there says that women need to be helped into carriages, and lifted over ditches, and to have the best place everywhere. Nobody ever helps me into carriages, or over mud-puddles, or gives me any best place. And a'n't I a woman?" The opponent of women's rights is, in other words, guilty of the logical fallacy of the excluded middle. If *all* women require the help of men, how is that *some* women—black women—are expected to fend for themselves? Truth thereby denies the truth of the patronizing major premise. All women do *not* need the assistance men.

Since the newspaper version of the speech does not contain, let alone repeat four times, "And a'n't I a woman?" we might be assessing Gage's intentions as much as Truth's. Mabee argues that Gage, an abolitionist and a women's rights advocate, had good reason to publish Truth's 1851 speech twelve years later during the Civil War when the cause of abolition had eclipsed that of women's rights. Truth personified the connection between the two causes, and Gage's repetition of "a'n't I a woman" vividly amplified that connection. Mabee also notes provocatively that compared to another popular article about Truth by Harriet Beecher Stowe that focuses upon Truth as black, Gage's article is less mentioned until the 1970s and 1980s, when linking the plight of women with that of African Americans became a common theme.[16]

Truth expands on the thought that she and other women are perfectly capable of taking care of themselves. She was not offered help, nor did she need it. "Look at me! Look at my arm! (and she bared her right arm to the shoulder, showing her tremendous muscular power). I have ploughed, and planted, and gathered into barns, and no man could head me! And a'n't I a woman?" In the Gage version, Truth spoke of bearing the lash and seeing her children sold into slavery. Truth's manifest physical capacity was matched by the emotional strength required of many African American women. "And when I cried out with my mother's grief, none but Jesus heard me! And a'n't I a woman?" To establish her ethos and play on the audience's sympathies, Truth speaks of having "borne thirteen children," while there is historical evidence of five. Gage, rather than Truth, is undoubtedly responsible for this deliberate exaggeration. It is poignantly true, however, that one of her children was "sold South" into slavery. For his return she fought valiantly and successfully in the courts.

In the wake of a forceful logical argument, it strikes a note of irony that Truth next grapples with the issue of the relative intelligence of men and women. "Then they talk about this thing in the head, what do they call it? ('Intellect,' whispered someone near.). That's it honey. What's that got to do with women's rights or negro's rights? If my cup won't hold but a pint, and yours holds a quart, wouldn't you be mean not to let me have my little half-measure full?" Here again, Truth selects the rhetorical path less taken. Women's rights speakers typically responded to the charge that women were less intelligent or capable than men by arguing that women had excelled in all the usual intellectual pursuits. Women, they pointed out through examples, had become doctors, lawyers, poets, authors, business owners, and even the Empress of Russia. Their argument here mirrored Truth's response to the charge that women were physically less able than men. Where Truth had responded that she, a woman, was as physically capable as any man, women's rights speakers usually responded to the intelligence argument by pointing out that women were as intellectually capable as any man.

In her response, however, Truth elects to shift the criteria by which the argument is to be settled. Rather than explicitly deny the fact of the claim—that women are less intelligent than men—Truth puts forward a disjunctive hypothetical ("If my cup won't hold but a pint") and then puts forward a standard that honoring one's rights is a question of character: "wouldn't you be mean not to let me have my little half-measure full?" Truth's argument is a clever rhetorical turn in which she carefully selects the argumentative ground on which she will engage her opponent. In a larger sense, the argument put forward by this illiterate, former slave is later repeated by a Harvard

PhD, W. E. B. Du Bois. In his speech "Disfranchisement," Du Bois argues that only through the complete enfranchisement of their rights can the "least" of a society's members develop to their full potential. Ironically, yet very possibly intentionally, Truth demonstrates the intellectual prowess of a woman, even as she chooses not to debate the fact of woman's intelligence with her opponent.

To the preacher's charge that Christ's importance in the Bible signals that men should have greater rights, Truth responded: "Where did your Christ come from? From God and a woman! Man had nothin' to do with him." Not the Bible itself, but how it was interpreted, revealed the implied status of women.

More difficult was an answer to the assertion that women were tainted Biblically by Eve's sin of tempting Adam. But, of course, in reviling Eve, the preacher had unwittingly given a great deal of credit to Eve. "If the first woman God ever made was strong enough to turn the world upside down all alone, these women together (and she glanced her eye over the platform) ought to be able to turn it back and get it right side up again." The rhetorical probability was flawlessly presented. Eve's sin was undeniable, but so also was her power.

These are textbook examples of arguments that borrow the premises of one's opponents' arguments to turn the tables against them. Though not formally schooled in rhetorical technique, Truth did not mince words in defeating her ideological foes. Gage reports that her speech met with sustained cheering. "She had taken us up in her strong arms and carried us safely over the slough of difficulty turning the whole tide in our favor. I have never in my life seen anything like the magical influence that subdued the mobbish spirit of the day."[17] In Gage's narrative, the women who had been fearful of the effect Truth, a former slave, might have on the cause of women came to realize that her intellectual and physical capacity gave powerful evidence of gender equality. Although Truth reminded her audience of her slave past and also played on the sympathies of the audience, the ethos she created focused on her innate power and tenacity.

As a performance, Truth's short speech was less a testament to her former slavery, and more a testament to her present strength. As she bared her arm for the audience—evocative, says Painter, of slave auctions—so did she bare her intellect, her rhetorical resourcefulness, and her moral resolve.[18] She addressed the objectors of women's rights with withering logic, but the real message of the speech was Truth herself—acerbic and uncompromising, while disarmingly genial and authentic. But these conclusions about Truth's persona are partly guided by the Gage version, whose credibility Painter and Mabee rightly question. Studies of numerous contemporaneous accounts of the speech make it difficult to believe the details of the story Gage narrates. The audience included many advocates of abolition including Gage, and the women in attendance are unlikely to have been the easily intimidated neophytes that Gage represents them as being. Nor, according to Mabee, was there any threat of "mobbish" opposition to the claims of women. Mabee also refutes the idea that white women did not want Truth to speak.[19] Without the hostility of white males and the apprehensions of white females in the audience, the speech might have been a good deal less dramatic or consequential than Gage makes it appear. But even the shorter version of the speech published in the *Anti-Slavery Bugle* provides reason to see the speech as important; the question "A'n't I a Woman?" is never posed, but Truth does proclaim "I *am* a woman's rights" (emphasis added). Although much less dramatic than "A'n't I a woman?" there is a clear correspondence between the two thoughts, as Suzanne Fitch and Roseann Mandziuk also note.[20] Gage may have drawn the ringing phrase from the abolitionist motto: "Am I not a woman and a sister?[21]

Frederick Douglass, the abolitionist and former slave whose sublimely eloquent speeches reflect his learning and formal command of language, viewed the illiterate Truth as a "genuine specimen of the uncultured Negro," but he clearly understood why white reformers would make her a celebrity. She was, he said, "a strange compound of wit and wisdom, of wild enthusiasm and flint-like common sense . . . [and] seemed to please herself and others best when she put her ideas in the oddest forms."[22] Although the version promulgated by Gage was probably embellished, "A'n't I a Woman" is a powerful representative anecdote, an archetypal story, so true symbolically that admiring students and scholars sometimes object to caviling about the accuracy of the details.[23] Though historically questionable, Gage's apocryphal version is memorable and moving. Accepting contemporary journalistic versions of Truth's speech as better approximations of what was actually said, and acknowledging Painter and Mabee's histories as more accurate than Gage's colorful recollection, makes neither Truth nor her speech any less remarkable or compelling. The speech has come to represent Truth, and while her lifetime struggle against oppression is irreducible to the words spoken on a single day, they are surely a testament to her tenacity and effectiveness as a civil rights advocate and feminist.

A'n't I a Woman?

(Speech at the Women's Rights Convention)

May 28, 1851
Akron, Ohio

Salem (Ohio) *Anti-Slavery Bugle* Version

One of the most unique and interesting speeches of the convention was made by Sojourner's Truth, an emancipated slave. It is impossible to transfer it to paper, or convey any adequate idea of the effect it produced upon the audience. Those only can appreciate it who saw her powerful form, her whole-souled, earnest gesture, and listened to her strong and truthful tones. She came forward to the platform and addressing the President said with great simplicity.

May I say a few words? Receiving an affirmative answer, she proceeded; I want to say a few words about this matter. I am a woman's rights [*sic*]. I have as much muscle as any man, and can do as much work as any man. I have plowed and reaped and husked and chopped and mowed, and can any man do more than that? I have heard much about the sexes being equal; I can carry as much as any man, and can eat as much too, if I can get it. I am strong as any man that is now.

As for intellect, all I can say is, if woman have a pint and man a quart—why can't she have her little pint full? You need not be afraid to give us our rights for fear we will take too much—for we won't take more than our pint'll hold.

The poor men seem to be all in confusion and don't know what to do. Why children, if you have woman's rights give it to her and you will feel better. You will have your own rights, and they won't be so much trouble.

I can't read, but I can hear. I have heard the Bible and have learned that Eve caused man to sin. Well if woman upset the world, do give her a chance to set it right side up again. The lady has spoken about Jesus, how he never spurned woman from him, and she was right. When Lazarus died, Mary and Martha came to him with faith and love and besought him to raise their brother. And Jesus wept—and Lazarus came forth. And how came Jesus into the world? Through God who created him and woman who bore him. Man, where is your part?

But the women are coming up blessed be God and a few of the men are coming up with them. But man is in a tight place, the poor slave is on him, woman is coming on him, and he is surely between a hawk and a buzzard.

History of Woman Suffrage Version

"Wall, chilern, whar dar is so much racket dar must be somethin' out o' kilter. I tink dat 'twixt de niggers of de Souf and de womin at de Norf, all talkin' 'bout rights, de white men will be in a fix pretty soon. But what's all dis here talkin' 'bout?"

"Dat man ober dar say dat womin needs to be helped into carriages, and lifted ober ditches, and to hab de best place everywhar. Nobody eber helps me into carriages, or ober mud-puddles, or gibs me any best place!" And raising herself to her full height, and her voice to a pitch like rolling thunders, she asked "And a'n't I a woman? Look at me! Look at me! Look at my arm! (and she bared her right arm to the shoulder, showing her tremendous muscular power). I have ploughed, and planted, and gathered into barns, and no man could head me! And a'n't I a woman? I could work as much and eat as much as a man—when I could get it—and bear de lash a well! And a'n't I a woman? I have borne thirteen chilern, and seen 'em mos' all sold off to slavery, and when I cried out with my mother's grief, none but Jesus heard me! And a'n't I a woman?"

"Den dey talks 'bout dis ting in de head; what dis dey call it?" ("Intellect," whispered some one near.) "Dat's it, honey. What's dat got to do wid womin's rights or nigger's rights? If my cup won't hold but a pint, and yourn holds a quart, wouldn't ye be mean not to let me have my little half-measure full?" And she pointed her significant finger, and sent a keen glance at the minister who had made the argument. The cheering was long and loud.

"Den dat little man in black dar, he say women can't have as much rights as men, 'cause Christ wan't a woman! Whar did your Christ come from?" Rolling thunder couldn't have stilled that crowd, as did those deep, wonderful tones, as she stood there with outstretched arms and eyes of fire. Raising her voice still louder, she repeated, "Whar did your Christ come from? From

God and a woman! Man had nothin' to do wid Him." Oh, what a rebuke that was to that little man.

Turning again to another objector, she took up the defense of Mother Eve. I can not follow her through it all. It was pointed, and witty, and solemn; eliciting at almost every sentence deafening applause; and she ended by asserting: "If de fust woman God ever made was strong enough to turn de world upside down all alone, dese women togedder (and she glanced her eye over the platform) ought to be able to turn it back, and get it right side up again! And now dey is asking to do it, de men better let 'em." Long-continued cheering greeted this. "Bleeged to ye for hearin' on me, and now old Sojourner han't got nothin' more to say."

Amid roars of applause, she returned to her corner, leaving more than one of us with streaming eyes, and hearts beating with gratitude. She had taken us up in her strong arms and carried us safely over the slough of difficulty turning the whole tide in our favor. I have never in my life seen anything like the magical influence that subdued the mobbish spirit of the day, and turned the sneers and jeers of an excited crowd into notes of respect and admiration. Hundreds rushed up to shake hands with her, and congratulate the glorious old mother, and bid her God-speed on her mission of "testifyin' agin concerning the wickedness of this 'ere people."

Frederick Douglass

What to the American Slave Is the Fourth of July?

There was not a more famous or more eloquent African American abolitionist than Frederick Douglass. Born a slave, the unacknowledged son of an unknown white father and an African American mother in Maryland, Douglass found his voice as an abolitionist and advocate of the equal rights of African Americans in Baltimore. He listened to and participated in debates among free blacks in the city, becoming a member of the East Baltimore Mental Improvement Society. At the age of twelve he had read Caleb Bingham's *The Columbian Orator*, a collection of patriotic works including essays and dialogues, used in school rooms early in the nineteenth century to develop literacy and an appreciation of eloquence and the importance of public discourse in a free republic. Bingham's book, which Douglass devoured soon after he had taught himself to read, had a profound and lasting impact upon him. Bingham particularly emphasized that speakers should employ a natural style of language and delivery, and he preached the importance of combining eloquence with content that merited eloquence, for example, the idea and ideal of liberty.[1] As an abolitionist orator, Douglass initially aligned himself with the radical views of William Lloyd Garrison, who claimed that the US Constitution immorally supported slavery and that slaves should be immediately emancipated.[2] Garrison ultimately came to believe that the only solution was disunion and secession.[3] The Garrisonians made significant inroads in persuading the American public of the immorality of slavery, but Douglass broke with the Garrisonians in 1847, although initially he continued to support their view of the Constitution. By 1850, Douglass thought differently, preferring to see the Constitution as embodying tenets of equality that, if properly interpreted, would lead Americans to abandon slavery.[4]

As an orator, Douglass quickly became a celebrity. The Massachusetts Anti-Slavery Society hired him as a paid lecturer, a position he held from 1841 until 1845. Abolitionists understood that life stories of fugitive slaves made compelling and credible persuasive appeals. Among the African American speakers who satisfied the public interest in the life of the slave, the uncommonly literate and eloquent Douglass rose to stardom. Early in his speaking career, he was particularly known for his "Slaveholder's Sermon," a scathing parody of white ministers' preaching to the plantation slaves.[5] So literate was Douglass, that rumors circulated that he was an imposter; such an educated speaker could not be a fugitive slave. To establish his bona fides, he published *Narrative of the Life of Frederick Douglass* in 1845. His increased fame brought increased danger that bounty hunters would seize him and return him to slavery, however, so Douglass sailed to Britain and, until 1847, lectured across the British Isles. He returned to the United States after reluctantly allowing British supporters to purchase his freedom so that he could continue his abolition work in America itself. A career as an editor and journalist followed, with publications such as *North Star, Frederick Douglass's Paper, Douglass Monthly*, and *New National Era*. The issues that concerned Douglass encompassed not only abolition but woman's rights, temperance, peace, and capital punishment.[6]

Douglass delivered "What to the American Slave is the Fourth of July?" as part of an 1852 Independence Day celebration at Corinthian Hall in Rochester, New York, the city where he had taken up residence after his return from Britain. The Rochester Ladies' Anti-Slavery Society invited Douglass to deliver the main address, and Douglass wished to speak on July 5, following a tradition in the New York State African American community. The audience was comprised of six hundred people who had paid the ticket price of twelve and a half cents each, the equivalent of $3.20 in current dollars.[7] Since many in Douglass's mostly white, immediate audience were abolitionists such as himself, in large measure he was "preaching to the choir." Among Garrisonian abolitionists, though, his antislavery interpretation of the Constitution would have been controversial. Before Douglass took the podium to address his audience, a clergyman first read the Declaration of Independence.[8] Douglass's speech, subdued and circumspect at the outset, abruptly turns to mordant criticism of the nation and, apparently, of his audience: "America is false to the past, false to the present, and solemnly binds herself to be false to the future. . . . I will not equivocate; I will not excuse."

As the speech unfolds, Douglass deliberately violates the norms of the occasion, but it is difficult to believe that his inviters might not have expected as much from the fiery thirty-four-year-old abolitionist. Surely, the immediate audience would have recognized the rhetorical artifice in his acutely uncomfortable question: "Do you mean, citizens, to mock me, by asking me to speak to-day?" The women abolitionists who invited Douglass would not have been surprised by the tension he deliberately creates between himself and his audience. As the editor of the *Frederick Douglass Papers* remarks, "Sarcasm, invective, and ridicule were constants in Douglass's orations."[9] Those who knew his reputation as an abolitionist speaker would have been disappointed had his speech lacked the firebrand qualities that had made him a sought-after orator. Douglass's ironic treatment of his subject might have been a thrillingly provocative oratorical strategy, but it is difficult to believe that an audience of abolitionist sympathizers would have found it personally offensive. The implied audience to whom Douglass directs his criticism served as a foil for his charge of mockery, and a critical component of the rhetorical drama he created.

Customarily, ceremonial (or epideictic) speeches take noncontroversial themes, the praise or blame of what is acknowledged as praiseworthy or blameworthy. Although belonging to the epideictic genre, this speech does not fulfill the conventional purpose of a Fourth of July address—to praise America and its institutions among Americans. Its praise is reserved for the sacrifices made and the risks taken by the Founders on behalf of liberty, and even that praise serves to heighten Douglass's argument of blame—that Americans in the present were guilty of the sin of hypocrisy for accepting the institution of slavery in their midst. Douglass, though a free man, assumes the position of a representative of African Americans callously enslaved in a nation dedicated to liberty, and the position of free Northern African Americans accorded, at best, only second-class citizenship. Indeed, if Douglass were speaking only on behalf of abolition, the irony of the speech would be less meaningful. Although Douglass appears to criticize his immediate audience, the people he wishes to make most uncomfortable with his criticisms are the larger audience that would read his carefully burnished speech in print. He reveals as much in saying midway through the speech: "O! had I the ability and could I reach the nation's ear." A journalist, Douglass well understood both the power of the printed word and the power of committing an act of oratorical defiance that would make his speech newsworthy. Northern journalists were known to describe Douglass in terms ranging from "'saucy negro,' 'the impudent negro,' 'an impertinent black vagabond,' [to] 'that black disgrace to human nature.'"[10]

The main body of the speech is divided into two broad sections, the first praising the Founders, and the second criticizing the present generation for not acting in the same spirit of liberty as their forebears. Douglass begins the speech by lowering expectations about his speech, a nineteenth-century rhetorical custom he regularly followed: "I evince no elaborate preparation nor grace my speech with a high sounding exordium. With little experience and less learning, I have been able to throw my thoughts hastily and imperfectly together."[11] In reality, Douglass had departed from his normal practice of extemporaneous and impromptu speaking and had spent fully three weeks preparing the speech.[12] Despite Douglass's claims to the contrary, the exordium, or introduction, that follows *is* distinctly "high-sounding" and replete with carefully contemplated, if not sometimes labored, metaphors. He speaks of a nation as a "great stream" that might "rise in quiet and stately majesty and inundate the land, refreshing and fertilizing the earth with [its] mysterious properties," but warns that it might "rise in wrath and fury" or that the river "may dry up, and leave nothing behind but a withered branch, and the unsightly rock, to howl in the abyss-sweeping wind, the sad tale of departed glory. As with rivers so with nations." Although easy to overlook as a rhetorical embellishment, this carefully constructed metaphor contains the central idea of the speech. Douglass saw that to live, the nation must continue to renew itself from the same sources that had created it—the idea of equality in the Declaration of Independence and the idea of liberty in the Constitution. Douglass's hydrological metaphor sounds the same chords as "a Nation conceived in Liberty," tested by the Civil War (the "wrath and fury" in Douglass's metaphor) and destined for "a new birth of freedom" that Lincoln would memorably envision eleven years later in the Gettysburg Address.[13]

In narrating the nation's birth, Douglass celebrates the deeds of *your* fathers, not *his*. With each successive use of "you" and "your," Douglass coils the spring of an invective that is released in the major portion of the speech focused upon the present and the future. He tendentiously describes the circumstances that led to the nation's foundation based upon the principle of liberty: "Oppression makes a wise man mad. Your fathers were wise men, and if they did not go mad, they became restive under this treatment." After many paragraphs in which Douglass distances himself from his audience by referring repeatedly to "your fathers," he breaks the tension of this deliberate alienation from the audience: "Fellow citizens, I am not wanting in respect for the fathers of this republic. . . . The point from which I am compelled to view them is not, certainly, the most favorable; and yet I cannot contemplate their great deeds with less than admiration. . . . I will unite with you to honor their memory." While Douglass cannot but admire the impulses toward liberty of the Founding Fathers, he reminds his audience that as a former slave and disenfranchised citizen, his perspective is at a great remove from theirs, and that his admiration is less filial than intellectual. The "causes which led to this anniversary" is a "branch of knowledge in which you feel, perhaps, a much deeper interest than your speaker." Douglass has only half-fulfilled the purposes of a Fourth of July speech, which was in the nineteenth century a most important ritual in American patriotism. His narrative metes out praise but is underlain by a grim and glowering detachment from the object of praise.

Douglass's caveats and self-conscious, ironic positioning in the historical section of the speech prepare the ground for his discussion of the present problem. "My business," he says, "if I have any here to-day, is with the present." Circumspect historical narrative and personal distancing give way to imperatives, exhortations, and embarrassing questions: "You have no right to wear out and waste the hard-earned fame of your fathers to cover your indolence," thunders Douglass. "What have I, or those I represent, to do with your national independence?" He presses the irony of his being asked to speak when he is "not included within the pale of this glorious anniversary": "*You* may rejoice, *I* must mourn." Douglass invokes the image of his former bondage to press the irony of his delivering a speech celebrating independence: "To drag a man in fetters into the grand illuminated temple of liberty, and call upon him to join you in joyous anthems, were inhuman mockery and sacrilegious irony. Do you mean, citizens, to mock me, asking me to speak to-day?" Douglass's question and the metaphor of the manacled African American in the "temple of liberty" might seem melodramatic and unwarranted. There is a double irony here since Douglass was not a slave, nor was he being physically forced, as a slave might be, to speak that day. Yet, like all African Americans who lived in the United States in 1852, including those, such as himself, who were nominally free, Douglass was fettered by the Jim Crow discriminatory practices of the North reflecting the same racial prejudice that made slavery possible. Even many abolitionists, although opposed to slavery, supported such discrimination. As John Lucaites observes: "Douglass came to recognize the latent, if well-intentioned, racist paternalism that underscored the efforts of many white abolitionists like Garrison. He thus came relatively quickly to the conclusion that the social and political implications of such racism were even more significant than the problem of slavery, for they pervaded not only the plantation, but the world of the free black as well."[14]

Irony is not merely a stylistic device in this speech; it is a strategic response, a refrain that thunders from deep within the speech. "At a time like this, scorching irony, not convincing argument, is needed. O! had I the ability and could I reach the Nation's ear, I would, to-day, pour out a fiery stream of biting ridicule, blasting reproach, withering sarcasm, and stern rebuke." Although coyly denying his broader influence, he uses the interest of reaching a much larger audience to justify his use of "scorching irony." In this section, Douglass employs the rhetorical trope of *paralipsis*, arguing points that he claims are so obvious that they do not require argument—that the slave is a man, that slavery is wrong. He reasons, for example, that if slaves are not men, there would not be laws in the South forbidding their education. Seeking to prove undeniably the wrongfulness of slavery, he presents a litany of specific wrongs that slavery has produced, among which are: "to make men brutes, to rob them of their liberty, to work them without wages, . . . to beat them with sticks, to flay their flesh with the lash, to load their limbs with irons, to hunt them with dogs, to sell them at auction, [and] to sunder their families."

Another aspect of the present is the internal slave trade, which Douglass describes in haunting detail. He contrasts the slave with the mandrover, the "inhuman wretch who drives" the pitiable "sad procession" of shackled slaves to the Baltimore pier to sail to the New Orleans slave market and ultimately to the cotton fields and sugar mills of the Deep South. As if describing a tableau that he creates with image-laden language, Douglass moves from one detail of the tableau to the next: "There, see the old man with locks thinned and gray. Cast one glance, if you please, upon that young mother, whose shoulders are bare to the scorching sun, her briny tears falling on the brow of the babe in her arms." The appeals are auditory as well as visual; Douglass describes the "chain rattles" and the crack of the slave whip, the anguished scream of a young woman flayed.[15]

Douglass maintains that the Fugitive Slave Law essentially nationalized slavery. The law made it possible for an African America man living in the

North to be consigned to slavery in the South upon the testimony of two witnesses. He questions why the churches have not publicly criticized this law. Religion, he says, should not be simply a "form of worship" but a vital principle requiring active "benevolence, justice, love and good will towards man." It should offer support and protection to blacks who fear deportation to the South. Most prominent ministers, North and South, he claims, cling to the idea "that we ought to obey man's law before the law of God." In his Second Inaugural Address, Lincoln would echo Douglass's thoughts about the sin of silence in the face of evil. Lincoln saw the Civil War theologically as God's punishment to the South for having slavery and to the North for allowing it. In the climax of this section, Douglass warns ominously and presciently that the existence of slavery would damage the nation. He set before the audience's eyes the image of slavery as a lurking, parasitic beast. "Oh! be warned! be warned! A horrible reptile is coiled up in your nation's bosom; the venomous creature is nursing at the tender breast of your youthful republic; *for the love of God, tear it away.*" In less than ten years the reptile would spring forth in civil war wherein 603,000 American lives were lost.

Finally, Douglass comes to the question of the Constitution. Whether the Constitution was a proslavery or an antislavery document was hotly debated by abolitionists.[16] In the early years of his abolitionist career, Douglass had taken the view of his compatriot William Lloyd Garrison, that the Constitution was a proslavery document, and argued that position in a formal debate in 1850, although he had earlier wavered in that belief, maintaining in 1849 that "I am satisfied that if strictly 'construed according to its reading,' it is not a pro-slavery instrument." He admitted, however, that the framers had made it a proslavery instrument.[17] Breaking with Garrison in May of 1851, Douglass came to espouse the views of "political abolitionists" such as Gerrit Smith, who argued that the Constitution understood outside of its historical circumstances, opposed slavery.[18] If that proposition were true, then political action could be used to bring about its abolition.

In the Fourth of July oration, Douglass attempts to redeem the nation's founders from the charge that in writing the Constitution they conceived a document that both affirmed liberty and slavery. He argues: "If the Constitution were intended to be, by its framers and adopters, a slave-holding instrument, why neither *slavery, slaveholding,* nor *slave* can anywhere be found in it." Douglass argues a literalist interpretation of the Constitution: "Now, take the constitution according to its plain reading, and I defy the presentation of a single pro-slavery clause in it." He then declares that it is a right, if not an obligation, for "every American citizen . . . to form an opinion of the constitution, and to propagate that opinion, and to use all honorable means to make his opinion the prevailing one." Douglass sees the correct understanding of the Constitution as a vehicle by which to expand the idea of liberty to include African Americans, to keep the "great stream" from drying up. Surely this is his aim, although he leaves the "full and fair discussion," of the subject for a later time.

In his conclusion, Douglass returns to the Declaration of Independence and its "great principles." He also expresses faith in the future and in the promise that technology and commerce will make known American social evils that formerly could be hidden: "Oceans no longer divide, but link nations together. . . . Space is comparatively annihilated. . . . No abuse, no outrage whether in taste, sport or avarice, can now hide itself from the all-pervading light." The conclusion offers further ironies. Although opposed to William Lloyd Garrison's views on the Constitution, Douglass concludes with a five-stanza poem, written by Garrison, "The Triumph of Freedom." Douglass had spoken earlier of slaves "whose chains . . . are . . . rendered more intolerable by the jubilee shouts that reach them." Garrison's paean anticipates "the year of jubilee," but in contrast to the celebration of American liberty that Douglass had acknowledged and then scorned as hypocritical, the heartfelt jubilee the poem prophesies would occur when the "oppress'd" "wear the yoke of tyranny like brutes no more." Unlike the American Fourth of July, this is the celebration to which Douglass could lift his voice in unqualified support.

What to the American Slave Is the Fourth of July?

July 5, 1852
Rochester, New York

Mr. President, Friends and Fellow Citizens: He who could address this audience without a quailing sensation, has stronger nerves than I have. I do not remember ever to have appeared as a speaker before any assembly more shrinkingly, nor with greater distrust of my ability, than I do this day. A feeling has crept over me, quite unfavorable to the exercise of my limited powers of speech. The task before me is one which requires much previous thought and study for its proper performance. I know that apologies of this sort are generally considered flat and unmeaning. I trust, however, that mine will not be so considered. Should I seem at ease, my appearance would much misrepresent me. The little experience I have had in addressing public meetings, in country schoolhouses, avails me nothing on the present occasion.

The papers and placards say, that I am to deliver a 4th of July oration. This certainly, sounds large, and out of the common way, for me. It is true that I have often had the privilege to speak in this beautiful Hall, and to address many who now honor me with their presence. But neither their familiar faces, nor the perfect gage I think I have of Corinthian Hall, seems to free me from embarrassment.

The fact is, ladies and gentlemen, the distance between this platform and the slave plantation, from which I escaped, is considerable—and the difficulties to be overcome in getting from the latter to the former, are by no means slight. That I am here to-day is, to me, a matter of astonishment as well as of gratitude. You will not, therefore, be surprised, if in what I have to say, I evince no elaborate preparation, nor grace my speech with any high sounding exordium.[a] With little experience and with less learning, I have been able to throw my thoughts hastily and imperfectly together; and trusting to your patient and generous indulgence, I will proceed to lay them before you.

This, for the purpose of this celebration, is the 4th of July. It is the birthday of your National Independence, and of your political freedom. This, to you, is what the Passover was to the emancipated people of God. It carries your minds back to the day, and to the act of your great deliverance; and to the signs, and to the wonders, associated with that act, and that day. This celebration also marks the beginning of another year of your national life; and reminds you that the Republic of America is now 76 years old. I am glad, fellow-citizens, that your nation is so young. Seventy-six years, though a good old age for a man, is but a mere speck in the life of a nation. Three score years and ten is the allotted time for individual men; but nations number their years by thousands. According to this fact, you are, even now, only in the beginning of your national career, still lingering in the period of childhood. I repeat, I am glad this is so. There is hope in the thought, and hope is much needed, under the dark clouds which lower above the horizon. The eye of the reformer is met with angry flashes, portending disastrous times; but his heart may well beat lighter at the thought that America is young, and that she is still in the impressible[b] stage of her existence. May he not hope that high lessons of wisdom, of justice and of truth, will yet give direction to her destiny? Were the nation older, the patriot's heart might be sadder, and the reformer's brow heavier. Its future might be shrouded in gloom, and the hope of its prophets go out in sorrow. There is consolation in the thought, that America is young.—Great streams are not easily turned from channels, worn deep in the course of ages. They may sometimes rise in quiet and stately majesty, and inundate the land, refreshing and fertilizing the earth with their mysterious properties. They may also rise in wrath and fury, and bear away, on their angry waves, the accumulated wealth of years of toil and hardship. They, however, gradually flow back to the same old channel, and flow on as serenely as ever. But, while the river may not be turned aside, it may dry up, and leave nothing behind but the withered branch, and the unsightly rock, to howl in the abyss-sweeping wind, the sad tale of departed glory. As with rivers so with nations.

Fellow-citizens, I shall not presume to dwell at length on the associations that cluster about this day. The simple story of it is that, 76 years ago, the

a. Exordium: The beginning or introduction of a speech.
b. Impressible: Susceptible of an impression being made.

people of this country were British subjects. The style and title of your "sovereign people" (in which you now glory) was not then born. You were under the British Crown. Your fathers esteemed the English Government as the home government; and England as the fatherland. This home government, you know, although a considerable distance from your home, did, in the exercise of its parental prerogatives, impose upon its colonial children, such restraints, burdens and limitations, as, in its mature judgment, it deemed wise, right and proper.

But, your fathers, who had not adopted the fashionable idea of this day, of the infallibility of government, and the absolute character of its acts, presumed to differ from the home government in respect to the wisdom and the justice of some of those burdens and restraints. They went so far in their excitement as to pronounce the measures of government unjust, unreasonable, and oppressive, and altogether such as ought not to be quietly submitted to. I scarcely need say, fellow citizens, that my opinion of those measures fully accords with that of your fathers. Such a declaration of agreement on my part would not be worth much to anybody. It would, certainly, prove nothing, as to what part I might have taken, had I lived during the great controversy of 1776. To say *now* that America was right, and England wrong, is exceedingly easy. Everybody can say it; the dastard, not less than the noble brave, can flippantly discant[c] on the tyranny of England towards the American Colonies. It is fashionable to do so; but there was a time when to pronounce against England, and in favor of the cause of the colonies, tried men's souls.[d] They who did so were accounted in their day, plotters of mischief, agitators and rebels, dangerous men. To side with the right, against the wrong, with the weak against the strong, and with the oppressed against the oppressor! *here* lies the merit, and the one which, of all others, seems unfashionable in our day. The cause of liberty may be stabbed by the men who glory in the deeds of your fathers. But, to proceed.

Feeling themselves harshly and unjustly treated by the home government, your fathers, like men of honesty, and men of spirit, earnestly sought redress. They petitioned and remonstrated; they did so in a decorous, respectful, and loyal manner. Their conduct was wholly unexceptionable. This, however, did not answer the purpose. They saw themselves treated with sovereign indifference, coldness and scorn. Yet they persevered. They were not the men to look back.

c. Discant: A form of liturgical singing.
d. "These are the times that try men's souls," from Thomas Paine, *The American Crisis*.

As the sheet anchor[e] takes a firmer hold, when the ship is tossed by the storm, so did the cause of your fathers grow stronger, as it breasted the chilling blasts of kingly displeasure. The greatest and best of British statesmen admitted its justice, and the loftiest eloquence of the British Senate came to its support. But, with that blindness which seems to be the unvarying characteristic of tyrants, since Pharaoh and his hosts were drowned in the Red Sea,[f] the British Government persisted in the exactions complained of.

The madness of this course, we believe, is admitted now, even by England; but we fear the lesson is wholly lost on our present ruler.

Oppression makes a wise man mad. Your fathers were wise men, and if they did not go mad, they became restive under this treatment. They felt themselves the victims of grievous wrongs, wholly incurable in their colonial capacity. With brave men there is always a remedy for oppression. Just here, the idea of a total separation of the colonies from the crown was born! It was a startling idea, much more so, than we, at this distance of time, regard it. The timid and the prudent (as has been intimated) of that day, were, of course, shocked and alarmed by it.

Such people lived then, had lived before, and will, probably, ever have a place on this planet; and their course, in respect to any great change, (no matter how great the good to be attained, or the wrong to be redressed by it), may be calculated with as much precision as can be the course of the stars. They hate all changes, but silver, gold and copper change! Of this sort of change they are always strongly in favor.

These people were called Tories in the days of your fathers; and the appellation, probably, conveyed the same idea that is meant by a more modern, though a somewhat less euphonious term, which we often find in our papers, applied to some of our old politicians.

Their opposition to the then dangerous thought was earnest and powerful; but, amid all their terror and affrighted vociferations against it, the alarming and revolutionary idea moved on, and the country with it.

On the 2nd of July, 1776, the old Continental Congress, to the dismay of the lovers of ease, and the worshipers of property, clothed that dreadful idea with all the authority of national sanction. They did so in the form of a resolution; and as we seldom hit upon resolutions, drawn up in our day whose transparency is at all equal to this, it may refresh your minds and help my story if I read it.

e. Sheet anchor: A large, additional anchor designed for emergency situations.
f. Exodus 14:26–28.

Resolved: That these united colonies are, and of right, ought to be free and Independent States; that they are absolved from all allegiance to the British Crown; and that all political connection between them and the State of Great Britain *is* and ought to be, dissolved.

Citizens, your fathers made good that resolution. They succeeded; and to-day you reap the fruits of their success. The freedom gained is yours; and you, therefore, may properly celebrate this anniversary. The 4th of July is the first great fact in your nation's history—the very ring-bolt in the chain of your yet undeveloped destiny.

Pride and patriotism, not less than gratitude, prompt you to celebrate and to hold it in perpetual remembrance. I have said that the Declaration of Independence is the RINGBOLT to the chain of your nation's destiny; so, indeed, I regard it. The principles contained in that instrument are saving principles. Stand by those principles, be true to them on all occasions, in all places, against all foes, and at whatever cost.

From the round top of your ship of state, dark and threatening clouds may be seen. Heavy billows, like mountains in the distance, disclose to the leeward huge forms of flinty rocks! That *bolt* drawn, that *chain* broken, and all is lost. *Cling to this day—cling to it*, and to its principles, with the grasp of a storm-tossed mariner to a spar at midnight.

The coming into being of a nation, in any circumstances, is an interesting event. But, besides general considerations, there were peculiar circumstances which make the advent of this republic an event of special attractiveness.

The whole scene, as I look back to it, was simple, dignified and sublime.

The population of the country, at the time, stood at the insignificant number of three millions. The country was poor in the munitions of war. The population was weak and scattered, and the country a wilderness unsubdued. There were then no means of concert and combination, such as exist now. Neither steam nor lightning had then been reduced to order and discipline. From the Potomac to the Delaware was a journey of many days. Under these, and innumerable other disadvantages, your fathers declared for liberty and independence and triumphed.

Fellow Citizens, I am not wanting in respect for the fathers of this republic. The signers of the Declaration of Independence were brave men. They were great men too—great enough to give fame to a great age. It does not often happen to a nation to raise, at one time, such a number of truly great men. The point from which I am compelled to view them is not, certainly, the most favorable; and yet I cannot contemplate their great deeds with less than admiration. They were statesmen, patriots and heroes, and for the good they did, and the principles they contended for, I will unite with you to honor their memory.

They loved their country better than their own private interests; and, though this is not the highest form of human excellence, all will concede that it is a rare virtue, and that when it is exhibited, it ought to command respect. He who will, intelligently, lay down his life for his country, is a man whom it is not in human nature to despise. Your fathers staked their lives, their fortunes, and their sacred honor, on the cause of their country. In their admiration of liberty, they lost sight of all other interests.

They were peace men; but they preferred revolution to peaceful submission to bondage. They were quiet men; but they did not shrink from agitating against oppression. They showed forbearance; but that they knew its limits. They believed in order; but not in the order of tyranny. With them, nothing was "*settled*" that was not right. With them, justice, liberty and humanity were "*final*;" not slavery and oppression. You may well cherish the memory of such men. They were great in their day and generation. Their solid manhood stands out the more as we contrast it with these degenerate times.

How circumspect, exact and proportionate were all their movements! How unlike the politicians of an hour! Their statesmanship looked beyond the passing moment, and stretched away in strength into the distant future. They seized upon eternal principles, and set a glorious example in their defense. Mark them!

Fully appreciating the hardship to be encountered, firmly believing in the right of their cause, honorably inviting the scrutiny of an on-looking world, reverently appealing to heaven to attest their sincerity, soundly comprehending the solemn responsibility they were about to assume, wisely measuring the terrible odds against them, your fathers, the fathers of this republic, did, most deliberately, under the inspiration of a glorious patriotism, and with a sublime faith in the great principles of justice and freedom, lay deep the corner-stone of the national superstructure, which has risen and still rises in grandeur around you.

Of this fundamental work, this day is the anniversary. Our eyes are met with demonstrations of joyous enthusiasm. Banners and pennants wave exultingly on the breeze. The din of business, too, is hushed. Even Mammon seems to have quitted his grasp on this day. The ear-piercing fife and the stirring drum unite their accents with the ascending peal of a thousand church bells. Prayers are made, hymns are sung, and sermons are preached in honor of this day; while the quick martial tramp of a great and multitudinous nation, echoed back by all the hills, valleys and mountains of a vast continent, bespeak the occasion one of thrilling and universal interests—a nation's jubilee.

Friends and citizens, I need not enter further into the causes which led to this anniversary. Many of you understand them better than I do. You could instruct me in regard to them. That is a branch of knowledge in which you feel, perhaps, a much deeper interest than your speaker. The causes which led to the separation of the colonies from the British crown have never lacked for a tongue. They have all been taught in your common schools, narrated at your firesides, unfolded from your pulpits, and thundered from your legislative halls, and are as familiar to you as household words. They form the staple of your national poetry and eloquence.

I remember also that as a people Americans are remarkably familiar with all facts which make in their own favor. This is esteemed by some as a national trait—perhaps a national weakness. It is a fact, that whatever makes for the wealth or for the reputation of Americans, and can be had *cheap*! will be found by Americans. I shall not be charged with slandering Americans if I say I think the American side of any question may be safely left in American hands.

I leave, therefore, the great deeds of your fathers to other gentlemen whose claim to have been regularly descended will be less likely to be disputed than mine!

The Present

My business, if I have any here to-day, is with the present. The accepted time with God and his cause is the ever-living now.

> Trust no future, however pleasant,
>   Let the dead past bury its dead;
> Act, act in the living present,
>   Heart within, and God overhead.[g]

We have to do with the past only as we can make it useful to the present and to the future. To all inspiring motives, to noble deeds which can be gained from the past, we are welcome. But now is the time, the important time. Your fathers have lived, died, and have done their work, and have

g. Henry Wadsworth Longfellow, "A Psalm of Life."

done much of it well. You live and must die, and you must do your work. You have no right to enjoy a child's share in the labor of your fathers, unless your children are to be blest by your labors. You have no right to wear out and waste the hard-earned fame of your fathers to cover your indolence. Sydney Smith[h] tells us that men seldom eulogize the wisdom and virtues of their fathers, but to excuse some folly or wickedness of their own. This truth is not a doubtful one. There are illustrations of it near and remote, ancient and modern. It was fashionable, hundreds of years ago, for the children of Jacob to boast, we have "Abraham to our father," when they had long lost Abraham's faith and spirit.[i] That people contented themselves under the shadow of Abraham's great name, while they repudiated the deeds which made his name great. Need I remind you that a similar thing is being done all over this country to-day? Need I tell you that the Jews are not the only people who built the tombs of the prophets, and garnished the sepulchres of the righteous? Washington could not die till he had broken the chains of his slaves. Yet his monument is built up by the price of human blood, and the traders in the bodies and souls of men, shout—"We have Washington to *our father*."—Alas! that it should be so; yet so it is. "The evil that men do, lives after them, / The good is oft' interred with their bones."[j]

Fellow-citizens, pardon me, allow me to ask, why am I called upon to speak here to-day? What have I, or those I represent, to do with your national independence? Are the great principles of political freedom and of natural justice, embodied in that Declaration of Independence, extended to us? and am I, therefore, called upon to bring our humble offering to the national altar, and to confess the benefits and express devout gratitude for the blessings resulting from your independence to us?

Would to God, both for your sakes and ours, that an affirmative answer could be truthfully returned to these questions! Then would my task be light, and my burden easy and delightful. For *who* is there so cold, that a nation's sympathy could not warm him? Who so obdurate and dead to the claims of gratitude, that would not thankfully acknowledge such priceless benefits? Who so stolid and selfish, that would not give his voice to swell the hallelujahs of a nation's jubilee, when the chains of servitude had been

h. Sidney Smith (1771–1846). Anglican clergyman and writer who published anthologies of his sermons.

i. Matthew 3:8–9: "Therefore bear fruits worthy of repentance, and do not think to say to yourselves, 'We have Abraham as our father.' For I say to you that God is able to raise up children to Abraham from these stones." Also Luke 3:8.

j. William Shakespeare, *Julius Caesar*, from Mark Anthony's eulogy of Caesar.

torn from his limbs? I am not that man. In a case like that, the dumb might eloquently speak, and the "lame man leap as an hart."[k]

But, such is not the state of the case. I say it with a sad sense of the disparity between us. I am not included within the pale of this glorious anniversary! Your high independence only reveals the immeasurable distance between us. The blessings in which you, this day, rejoice, are not enjoyed in common. The rich inheritance of justice, liberty, prosperity and independence, bequeathed by your fathers, is shared by you, not by me. The sunlight that brought life and healing to you, has brought stripes and death to me. This Fourth of July is *yours*, not *mine*. *You* may rejoice, *I* must mourn. To drag a man in fetters into the grand illuminated temple of liberty, and call upon him to join you in joyous anthems, were inhuman mockery and sacrilegious irony. Do you mean, citizens, to mock me, by asking me to speak to-day? If so, there is a parallel to your conduct. And let me warn you that it is dangerous to copy the example of a nation whose crimes, towering up to heaven, were thrown down by the breath of the Almighty, burying that nation in irrecoverable ruin! I can to-day take up the plaintive lament of a peeled and woe-smitten people!

"By the rivers of Babylon, there we sat down. Yea! we wept when we remembered Zion. We hanged our harps upon the willows in the midst thereof. For there, they that carried us away captive, required of us a song; and they who wasted us required of us mirth, saying, Sing us one of the songs of Zion. How can we sing the Lord's song in a strange land? If I forget thee, O Jerusalem, let my right hand forget her cunning. If I do not remember thee, let my tongue cleave to the roof of my mouth."[l]

Fellow-citizens; above your national, tumultuous joy, I hear the mournful wail of millions! whose chains, heavy and grievous yesterday, are, to-day, rendered more intolerable by the jubilee shouts that reach them. If I do forget, if I do not faithfully remember those bleeding children of sorrow this day, "may my right hand forget her cunning, and may my tongue cleave to the roof of my mouth!" To forget them, to pass lightly over their wrongs, and to chime in with the popular theme, would be treason most scandalous and shocking, and would make me a reproach before God and the world.

k. Isaiah 35:4–6: "Say to those who are fearful-hearted, 'Be strong, do not fear! Behold, your God will come with vengeance, with the recompense of God; He will come and save you.' Then the eyes of the blind shall be opened and the ears of the deaf shall be unstopped. Then the lame man shall leap as a hart, and the tongue of the dumb sing." A hart is a deer.

l. Psalm 137:1–6.

My subject, then fellow-citizens, is AMERICAN SLAVERY. I shall see, this day, and its popular characteristics, from the slave's point of view. Standing, there, identified with the American bondman, making his wrongs mine, I do not hesitate to declare, with all my soul, that the character and conduct of this nation never looked blacker to me than on this 4th of July! Whether we turn to the declarations of the past, or to the professions of the present, the conduct of the nation seems equally hideous and revolting. America is false to the past, false to the present, and solemnly binds herself to be false to the future. Standing with God and the crushed and bleeding slave on this occasion, I will, in the name of humanity which is outraged, in the name of liberty which is fettered, in the name of the constitution and the Bible, which are disregarded and trampled upon, dare to call in question and to denounce, with all the emphasis I can command, everything that serves to perpetuate slavery—the great sin and shame of America! "I will not equivocate; I will not excuse;" I will use the severest language I can command; and yet not one word shall escape me that any man, whose judgment is not blinded by prejudice, or who is not at heart a slaveholder, shall not confess to be right and just.

But I fancy I hear some one of my audience say, it is just in this circumstance that you and your brother abolitionists fail to make a favorable impression on the public mind. Would you argue more, and denounce less, would you persuade more, and rebuke less, your cause would be much more likely to succeed. But, I submit, where all is plain there is nothing to be argued. What point in the anti-slavery creed would you have me argue? On what branch of the subject do the people of this country need light? Must I undertake to prove that the slave is a man? That point is conceded already. Nobody doubts it. The slaveholders themselves acknowledge it in the enactment of laws for their government. They acknowledge it when they punish disobedience on the part of the slave. There are seventy-two crimes in the State of Virginia, which, if committed by a black man, (no matter how ignorant he be), subject him to the punishment of death; while only two of the same crimes will subject a white man to the like punishment.—What is this but the acknowledgement that the slave is a moral, intellectual and responsible being?—The manhood of the slave is conceded. It is admitted in the fact that Southern statute books are covered with enactments forbidding, under severe fines and penalties, the teaching of the slave to read or to write.—When you can point to any such laws, in reference to the beasts of the field, then I may consent to argue the manhood of the slave. When the dogs in your streets, when the fowls of the air, when the cattle on your hills, when the fish of the sea, and the reptiles that crawl, shall be unable to distinguish the slave from a brute, then will I argue with you that the slave is a man!

For the present, it is enough to affirm the equal manhood of the Negro race. Is it not astonishing that, while we are ploughing, planting and reaping, using all kinds of mechanical tools, erecting houses, constructing bridges, building ships, working in metals of brass, iron, copper, silver and gold; that, while we are reading, writing and cyphering, acting as clerks, merchants and secretaries, having among us lawyers, doctors, ministers, poets, authors, editors, orators and teachers; that, while we are engaged in all manner of enterprises common to other men, digging gold in California, capturing the whale in the Pacific, feeding sheep and cattle on the hill-side, living, moving, acting, thinking, planning, living in families as husbands, wives and children, and, above all, confessing and worshipping the Christian's God, and looking hopefully for life and immortality beyond the grave, we are called upon to prove that we are men!

Would you have me argue that man is entitled to liberty? that he is the rightful owner of his own body? You have already declared it. Must I argue the wrongfulness of slavery? Is that a question for Republicans? Is it to be settled by the rules of logic and argumentation, as a matter beset with great difficulty, involving a doubtful application of the principle of justice, hard to be understood? How should I look to-day, in the presence of Americans, dividing, and subdividing a discourse, to show that men have a natural right to freedom? speaking of it relatively, and positively, negatively, and affirmatively. To do so, would be to make myself ridiculous, and to offer an insult to your understanding. There is not a man beneath the canopy of heaven, that does not know that slavery is wrong *for him*.

What, am I to argue that it is wrong to make men brutes, to rob them of their liberty, to work them without wages, to keep them ignorant of their relations to their fellow men, to beat them with sticks, to flay their flesh with the lash, to load their limbs with irons, to hunt them with dogs, to sell them at auction, to sunder their families, to knock out their teeth, to burn their flesh, to starve them into obedience and submission to their masters? Must I argue that a system thus marked with blood and stained with pollution is *wrong*? No! I will not. I have better employments for my time and strength than such arguments would imply.

What, then, remains to be argued? Is it that slavery is not divine; that God did not establish it; that our doctors of divinity are mistaken? There is blasphemy in the thought. That which is inhuman, cannot be divine! *Who can reason on such a proposition?* They that can, may; I cannot. The time for such argument is past.

At a time like this, scorching irony, not convincing argument, is needed. O! had I the ability, and could I reach the nation's ear, I would, to-day, pour out a fiery stream of biting ridicule, blasting reproach, withering sarcasm, and stern rebuke. For it is not light that is needed, but fire; it is not the gentle shower, but thunder. We need the storm, the whirlwind, and the earthquake. The feeling of the nation must be quickened; the conscience of the nation must be roused; the propriety of the nation must be startled; the hypocrisy of the nation must be exposed; and its crimes against God and man must be proclaimed and denounced.

What, to the American slave, is your Fourth of July? I answer: a day that reveals to him, more than all other days in the year, the gross injustice and cruelty to which he is the constant victim. To him, your celebration is a sham; your boasted liberty, an unholy license; your national greatness, swelling vanity; your sounds of rejoicing are empty and heartless; your denunciations of tyrants, brass fronted impudence; your shouts of liberty and equality, hollow mockery; your prayers and hymns, your sermons and thanksgivings, with all your religious parade, and solemnity, are, to him, mere bombast, fraud, deception, impiety, and hypocrisy—a thin veil to cover up crimes which would disgrace a nation of savages. There is not a nation on the earth guilty of practices, more shocking and bloody, than are the people of these United States, at this very hour.

Go where you may, search where you will, roam through all the monarchies and despotisms of the old world, travel through South America, search out every abuse, and when you have found the last, lay your facts by the side of the everyday practices of this nation, and you will say with me, that, for revolting barbarity and shameless hypocrisy, America reigns without a rival.

The Internal Slave Trade

Take the American slave-trade, which, we are told by the papers, is especially prosperous just now. Ex-Senator Benton[m] tells us that the price of men was never higher than now. He mentions the fact to show that slavery is in no danger. This trade is one of the peculiarities of American institutions. It is carried on in all the large towns and cities in one-half of this confederacy;

m. Thomas Hart Benton (1782–1858): US senator from Missouri, editor of the *Enquirer*, and strong proponent of the westward expansion of the United States.

and millions are pocketed every year, by dealers in this horrid traffic. In several states, this trade is a chief source of wealth. It is called (in contradistinction to the foreign slave-trade) "*the internal slave trade.*" It is, probably, called so, too, in order to divert from it the horror with which the foreign slave-trade is contemplated. That trade has long since been denounced by this government, as piracy. It has been denounced with burning words, from the high places of the nation, as an execrable traffic. To arrest it, to put an end to it, this nation keeps a squadron, at immense cost, on the coast of Africa. Everywhere, in this country, it is safe to speak of this foreign slave-trade, as a most inhuman traffic, opposed alike to the laws of God and of man. The duty to extirpate and destroy it, is admitted even by our doctors of divinity. In order to put an end to it, some of these last have consented that their colored brethren (nominally free) should leave this country, and establish themselves on the western coast of Africa! It is, however, a notable fact that, while so much execration is poured out by Americans upon those engaged in the foreign slave-trade, the men engaged in the slave-trade between the states pass without condemnation, and their business is deemed honorable.

Behold the practical operation of this internal slave-trade, the American slave-trade, sustained by American politics and America religion. Here you will see men and women reared like swine for the market. You know what is a swine-drover? I will show you a man-drover. They inhabit all our Southern States. They perambulate the country, and crowd the highways of the nation, with droves of human stock. You will see one of these human flesh-jobbers, armed with pistol, whip and bowie-knife, driving a company of a hundred men, women, and children, from the Potomac to the slave market at New Orleans. These wretched people are to be sold singly, or in lots, to suit purchasers. They are food for the cotton-field, and the deadly sugar-mill. Mark the sad procession, as it moves wearily along, and the inhuman wretch who drives them. Hear his savage yells and his blood-chilling oaths, as he hurries on his affrighted captives! There, see the old man, with locks thinned and gray. Cast one glance, if you please, upon that young mother, whose shoulders are bare to the scorching sun, her briny tears falling on the brow of the babe in her arms. See, too, that girl of thirteen, weeping, *yes*! weeping, as she thinks of the mother from whom she has been torn! The drove moves tardily. Heat and sorrow have nearly consumed their strength; suddenly you hear a quick snap, like the discharge of a rifle; the fetters clank, and the chain rattles simultaneously; your ears are saluted with a scream, that seems to have torn its way to the center of your soul! The crack you heard, was the sound of the slave-whip; the scream you heard, was from the woman you saw with the babe. Her speed had faltered under the weight of her child and her chains! that gash on her shoulder tells her to move on. Follow the drove to New Orleans. Attend the auction; see men examined like horses; see the forms of women rudely and brutally exposed to the shocking gaze of American slave-buyers. See this drove sold and separated forever; and never forget the deep, sad sobs that arose from that scattered multitude. Tell me citizens, WHERE, under the sun, you can witness a spectacle more fiendish and shocking. Yet this is but a glance at the American slave-trade, as it exists, at this moment, in the ruling part of the United States.

I was born amid such sights and scenes. To me the American slave-trade is a terrible reality. When a child, my soul was often pierced with a sense of its horrors. I lived on Philpot Street, Fell's Point, Baltimore, and have watched from the wharves, the slave ships in the Basin, anchored from the shore, with their cargoes of human flesh, waiting for favorable winds to waft them down the Chesapeake. There was, at that time, a grand slave mart kept at the head of Pratt Street, by Austin Woldfolk. His agents were sent into every town and county in Maryland, announcing their arrival, through the papers, and on flaming "*hand-bills*" headed "CASH FOR NEGROES." These men were generally well dressed men, and very captivating in their manners. Ever ready to drink, to treat, and to gamble. The fate of many a slave has depended upon the turn of a single card; and many a child has been snatched from the arms of its mother by bargains arranged in a state of brutal drunkenness.

The flesh-mongers gather up their victims by dozens, and drive them, chained, to the general depot at Baltimore. When a sufficient number have been collected here, a ship is chartered, for the purpose of conveying the forlorn crew to Mobile, or to New Orleans. From the slave prison to the ship, they are usually driven in the darkness of night; for since the antislavery agitation, a certain caution is observed.

In the deep, still darkness of midnight I have been often aroused by the dead heavy footsteps, and the piteous cries of the chained gangs that passed our door. The anguish of my boyish heart was intense; and I was often consoled, when speaking to my mistress in the morning, to hear her say that the custom was very wicked; that she hated to hear the rattle of the chains, and the heart-rending cries. I was glad to find one who sympathized with me in my horror.

Fellow-citizens, this murderous traffic is, to-day, in active operation in this boasted republic. In the solitude of my spirit, I see clouds of dust raised on the highways of the South; I see the bleeding footsteps; I hear the doleful wail of fettered humanity, on the way to the slave markets, where the victims are to be sold like *horses*, *sheep* and *swine*, knocked off to the highest bidder. There I see the tenderest ties ruthlessly broken, to gratify the lust, caprice and rapacity of the buyers and sellers of men. My soul sickens at the sight.

> Is this the land your Fathers loved,
> The freedom which they toiled to win?
> Is this the earth whereon they moved?
> Are these the graves they slumber in?[n]

But a still more inhuman, disgraceful, and scandalous state of things remains to be presented. By an act of the American Congress, not yet two years old, slavery has been nationalized in its most horrible and revolting form.[o] By that act, Mason & Dixon's line has been obliterated; New York has become as Virginia; and the power to hold, hunt, and sell men, women, and children as slaves remains no longer a mere state institution, but is now an institution of the whole United States. The power is co-extensive with the Star-Spangled Banner and American Christianity. Where these go, may also go the merciless slave-hunter. Where these are, man is not sacred. He is a bird for the sportsman's gun. By that most foul and fiendish of all human decrees, the liberty and person of every man are put in peril. Your broad republican domain is hunting ground for men. Not for thieves and robbers, enemies of society, merely, but for men guilty of no crime. Your lawmakers have commanded all good citizens to engage in this hellish sport. Your President, your Secretary of State, your *lords*, *nobles* and ecclesiastics enforce, as a duty you owe to your free and glorious country, and to your God, that you do this accursed thing. Not fewer than forty Americans have, within the past two years, been hunted down and, without a moment's warning, hurried away in chains, and consigned to slavery and excruciating torture. Some of these have had wives and children, dependent on them for bread; but of this, no account was made. The right of the hunter to his prey stands superior to the right of marriage, and to *all* rights in this republic, the rights of God included! For black men there are neither law, justice, humanity, nor religion. The Fugitive Slave *Law* makes MERCY TO THEM A CRIME; and bribes the judge who tries them. AN AMERICAN JUDGE GETS TEN DOLLARS FOR EVERY VICTIM HE CONSIGNS to slavery, and five, when he fails to do so.

n. John Greenleaf Whittier, "Stanzas for the Times."
o. The Fugitive Slave Law.

The oath of any two villains is sufficient, under this hell-black enactment, to send the most pious and exemplary black man into the remorseless jaws of slavery! His own testimony is nothing. He can bring no witnesses for himself. The minister of American justice is bound by the law to hear but *one* side; and *that* side, is the side of the oppressor. Let this damning fact be perpetually told. Let it be thundered around the world, that, in tyrant-killing, king-hating, people-loving, democratic, Christian America, the seats of justice are filled with judges, who hold their offices under an open and palpable *bribe*, and are bound, in deciding in the case of a man's liberty, *to hear only his accusers*!

In glaring violation of justice, in shameless disregard of the forms of administering law, in cunning arrangement to entrap the defenseless, and in diabolical intent, this Fugitive Slave Law stands alone in the annals of tyrannical legislation. I doubt if there be another nation on the globe, having the brass and the baseness to put such a law on the statute-book. If any man in this assembly thinks differently from me in this matter, and feels able to disprove my statements, I will gladly confront him at any suitable time and place he may select.

Religious Liberty

I take this law to be one of the grossest infringements of Christian Liberty, and, if the churches and ministers of our country were not stupidly blind, or most wickedly indifferent, they, too, would so regard it.

At the very moment that they are thanking God for the enjoyment of civil and religious liberty, and for the right to worship God according to the dictates of their own consciences, they are utterly silent in respect to a law which robs religion of its chief significance, and makes it utterly worthless to a world lying in wickedness. Did this law concern the "*mint, anise* and *cummin*"[p]—abridge the right to sing psalms, to partake of the sacrament, or to engage in any of the ceremonies of religion, it would be smitten by the thunder of a *thousand* pulpits. A general shout would go up from the church, demanding *repeal, repeal, instant repeal!* And it would go hard with that politician who presumed to solicit the votes of the people without inscribing this motto on his banner. Further, if this demand were not complied with,

p. Matthew 23:23: "Woe to you, scribes and Pharisees, hypocrites! For you pay tithe of mint and anise and cummin, and have neglected the weightier matters of the law: justice and mercy and faith."

another Scotland would be added to the history of religious liberty, and the stern old Covenanters would be thrown into the shade. A John Knox[q] would be seen at every church door, and heard from every pulpit, and Fillmore[r] would have no more quarter than was shown by Knox, to the beautiful, but treacherous queen Mary of Scotland.[s]—The fact that the church of our country, (with fractional exceptions), does not esteem "the Fugitive Slave Law" as a declaration of war against religious liberty, implies that that church regards religion simply as a form of worship, an empty ceremony, and not a vital principle, requiring active benevolence, justice, love and good will towards man. It esteems sacrifice above mercy; psalm-singing above right doing; solemn meetings above practical righteousness. A worship that can be conducted by persons who refuse to give shelter to the houseless, to give bread to the hungry, clothing to the naked, and who enjoin obedience to a law forbidding these acts of mercy, is a curse, not a blessing to mankind. The Bible addresses all such persons as "scribes, Pharisees, hypocrites, who pay tithe of *mint*, *anise*, and *cummin*, and have omitted the weightier matters of the law, judgment, mercy and faith."[t]

The Church Responsible

But the church of this country is not only indifferent to the wrongs of thee slave, it actually takes sides with the oppressors. It has made itself the bulwark of American slavery, and the shield of American slave-hunters. Many of its most eloquent Divines, who stand as the very lights of the church, have shamelessly given the sanction of religion and the Bible to the whole slave system.—They have taught that man may, properly, be a slave; that the relation of master and slave is ordained of God; that to send back an escaped bondman to his master is clearly the duty of all the followers of the Lord Jesus Christ; and this horrible blasphemy is palmed off upon the world for Christianity.

q. John Knox (1510–1572): Scottish clergyman, a leader of the Protestant Reformation and a founder of Presbyterianism. Knox frequently preached against Mary, Queen of Scots, who officially allowed Protestantism but, as a devout Catholic, was viewed by many Scottish Catholics as a monarch who would restore Roman Catholicism as the state religion.

r. Millard Fillmore (1800–1874): President of the United States, 1850–1853.

s. Mary I of Scotland, or Mary, Queen of Scots (1542–1587): Mary officially permitted adherence to Protestantism but, as a devout Catholic, was viewed by many Scottish Catholics, and English Catholics, to be a monarch who would restore Roman Catholicism as the state religion.

t. Matthew 23:23.

For my part, I would say, Welcome infidelity! welcome atheism! welcome anything—in preference to the gospel, *as preached by those divines.* They convert the very name of religion into an engine of tyranny, and barbarous cruelty, and serve to confirm more infidels, in this age, than all the infidel writings of Thomas Paine,[u] Voltaire,[v] and Bolingbroke,[w] put together, have done! These ministers make religion a cold and flinty-hearted thing, having neither principles of right action, nor bowels of compassion. They strip the love of God of its beauty, and leave the throng of religion a huge, horrible, repulsive form. It is a religion for oppressors, tyrants, man-stealers, and *thugs*. It is not that "*pure and undefiled religion*" which is from above, and which is "*first pure, then peaceable, easy to be entreated*, full of mercy and good fruits, *without partiality and without hypocrisy.*"[x] But a religion which favors the rich against the poor; which exalts the proud above the humble; which divides mankind into two classes, tyrants and slaves; which says to the man in chains, stay there; and to the oppressor, oppress on; it is a religion which may be professed and enjoyed by all the robbers and enslavers of mankind; it makes God a respecter of persons, denies his fatherhood of the race, and tramples in the dust the great truth of the brotherhood of man. All this we affirm to be true of the popular church, and the popular worship of our land and nation—a religion, a church, and a worship which, on the authority of inspired wisdom, we pronounce to be an abomination in the sight of God. In the language of Isaiah, the American church might be well addressed, "Bring no more vain ablations; incense is an abomination unto me: the new moons and Sabbaths, the calling of assemblies, I cannot away with; it is iniquity, even the solemn meeting. Your new moons, and your appointed feasts my soul hateth. They are a trouble to me; I am weary to bear them; and when ye spread forth your hands I will hide mine eyes from you. Yea! when ye make many prayers, I will not hear. YOUR HANDS ARE FULL OF BLOOD; cease to

---

u. Thomas Paine (1737–1809): Author of *Common Sense* and *The American Crisis*, both written in support of the American Revolution. Paine also wrote in support of the French Revolution and, in *The Age of Reason*, wrote in support of deism, a philosophy which supports a belief in a supreme being through reason, but not through faith or revelation. As such, it is generally perceived as opposed to organized religion.

v. Francois-Marie Arouet, pen name, Voltaire (1694–1778): Noted French author and philosopher. Like Paine, Voltaire was a deist and well known for his sharp attacks on organized religion.

w. Henry St. John Bolingbroke (1678–1751): English philosopher and deist.

x. James 3:17: "But the wisdom that is from above is first pure, then peaceable, gentle, willing to yield, full of mercy and good fruits, without partiality and without hypocrisy."

do evil, learn to do well; seek judgment; relieve the oppressed; judge for the fatherless; plead for the widow."[y]

The American church is guilty, when viewed in connection with what it is doing to uphold slavery; but it is superlatively guilty when viewed in connection with its ability to abolish slavery.

The sin of which it is guilty is one of omission as well as of commission. Albert Barnes[z] but uttered what the common sense of every man at all observant of the actual state of the case will receive as truth, when he declared that "There is no power out of the church that could sustain slavery an hour, if it were not sustained in it."[aa]

Let the religious press, the pulpit, the Sunday school, the conference meeting, the great ecclesiastical, missionary, Bible and tract associations of the land array their immense powers against slavery and slave-holding; and the whole system of crime and blood would be scattered to the winds; and that they do not do this involves them in the most awful responsibility of which the mind can conceive.

In prosecuting the anti-slavery enterprise, we have been asked to spare the church, to spare the ministry; but *how*, we ask, could such a thing be done? We are met on the threshold of our efforts for the redemption of the slave, by the church and ministry of the country, in battle arrayed against us; and we are compelled to fight or flee. From *what* quarter, I beg to know, has proceeded a fire so deadly upon our ranks, during the last two years, as from the Northern pulpit? As the champions of oppressors, the chosen men of American theology have appeared—men, honored for their so-called piety, and their real learning. The Lords of Buffalo, the Springs of New York, the Lathrops of Auburn, the Coxes and Spencers of Brooklyn, the Gannets and Sharps of Boston, the Deweys of Washington,[ab] and other great religious lights of the land, have, in utter denial of the authority of *Him*, by whom they professed to be called to the ministry, deliberately taught us, against

y. Isaiah 1:13–17.

z. Albert Barnes (1798–1870): Popular Presbyterian minister and theologian, author of *Notes on the New Testament* and *An Inquiry into the Scriptural Views of Slavery.*

aa. Albert Barnes, *An Inquiry into the Scriptural Views of Slavery* (Philadelphia: Perkins and Purves, 1846), 383.

ab. Some of the references are obscure, but Douglass seems to be including proslavery ministers, such as the Revs. John King Lord and Nathan Lord, in this list, as well as ministers who opposed slavery but advocated supporting the government, such as the Revs. Samuel H. Cox and Ezra Gannett.

the example or the Hebrews and against the remonstrance of the Apostles, they teach "*that we ought to obey man's law before the law of God.*"

My spirit wearies of such blasphemy; and how such men can be supported, as the "standing types and representatives of Jesus Christ," is a mystery which I leave others to penetrate. In speaking of the American church, however, let it be distinctly understood that I mean the *great mass* of the religious organizations of our land. There are exceptions, and I thank God that there are. Noble men may be found, scattered all over these Northern States, of whom Henry Ward Beecher of Brooklyn, Samuel J. May of Syracuse, and my esteemed friend [Rev. R. R. Raymond] on the platform, are shining examples[ac]; and let me say further, that upon these men lies the duty to inspire our ranks with high religious faith and zeal, and to cheer us on in the great mission of the slave's redemption from his chains.

Religion in England and Religion in America

One is struck with the difference between the attitude of the American church towards the anti-slavery movement, and that occupied by the churches in England towards a similar movement in that country. There, the church, true to its mission of ameliorating, elevating, and improving the condition of mankind, came forward promptly, bound up the wounds of the West Indian slave, and restored him to his liberty. There, the question of emancipation was a high religious question. It was demanded, in the name of humanity, and according to the law of the living God. The Sharps, the Clarksons, the Wilberforces, the Buxtons, and Burchells and the Knibbs, were alike famous for their piety, and for their philanthropy.[ad] The anti-slavery movement *there* was not an anti-church movement, for the reason that the church took its full share in prosecuting that movement: and the anti-slavery movement in this country will cease to be an anti-church movement, when the church of this country shall assume a favorable instead of a hostile position towards that movement.

ac. Henry Ward Beecher (1813–1887), Congregationalist minister, and Samuel J. May (1797–1871), Unitarian minister, were both famous staunch abolitionists. Rev. Raymond is more obscure, although he is mentioned in several abolitionist accounts, e.g., he was a member of the Syracuse Vigilance Committee, which was formed for the purpose of opposing enforcement of the Fugitive Slave Law (*Syracuse Standard* 14 Oct. 1850.)

ad. Granville Sharp (1735–1813), Thomas Clarkson (1760–1846), William Wilberforce (1759–1833), Sir Thomas Fowell Buxton (1786–1846), Thomas Burchell (1799–1846), and William Knibb (1803–1845) were British ministers, politicians, and reformers whose work culminated in the British Slavery Abolition Act 1833.

Americans! your republican politics, not less than your republican religion, are flagrantly inconsistent. You boast of your love of liberty, your superior civilization, and your pure Christianity, while the whole political power of the nation (as embodied in the two great political parties) is solemnly pledged to support and perpetuate the enslavement of three millions of your countrymen. You hurl your anathemas at the crowned headed tyrants of Russia and Austria, and pride yourselves on your Democratic institutions, while you yourselves consent to be the mere *tools* and *body-guards* of the tyrants of Virginia and Carolina. You invite to your shores fugitives of oppression from abroad, honor them with banquets, greet them with ovations, cheer them, toast them, salute them, protect them, and pour out your money to them like water; but the fugitives from your own land you advertise, hunt, arrest, shoot and kill. You glory in your refinement and your universal education yet you maintain a system as barbarous and dreadful as ever stained the character of a nation—a system begun in avarice, supported in pride, and perpetuated in cruelty. You shed tears over fallen Hungary, and make the sad story of her wrongs the theme of your poets, statesmen and orators, till your gallant sons are ready to fly to arms to vindicate her cause against her oppressors; but, in regard to the ten thousand wrongs of the American slave, you would enforce the strictest silence, and would hail him as an enemy of the nation who dares to make those wrongs the subject of public discourse! You are all on fire at the mention of liberty for France or for Ireland; but are as cold as an iceberg at the thought of liberty for the enslaved of America.—You discourse eloquently on the dignity of labor; yet, you sustain a system which, in its very essence, casts a stigma upon labor. You can bare your bosom to the storm of British artillery to throw off a threepenny tax on tea; and yet wring the last hard-earned farthing from the grasp of the black laborers of your country. You profess to believe "that, of one blood, God made all nations of men to dwell on the face of all the earth,"[ae] and hath commanded all men, everywhere to love one another; yet you notoriously hate, (and glory in your hatred), all men whose skins are not colored like your own. You declare, before the world, and are understood by the world to declare, that you "*hold these truths to be self evident, that all men are created equal; and are endowed by their Creator with certain inalienable rights; and that, among these are, life, liberty, and the pursuit of*

ae. Acts 17:26. Douglass was probably wise to edit the passage: "And He has made from one blood every nation of men to dwell on all the face of the earth, and has determined their preappointed times and the boundaries of their habitation."

happiness;" and yet, you hold securely, in a bondage which, according to your own Thomas Jefferson, "*is worse than ages of that which your fathers rose in rebellion to oppose,*" *a seventh part* of the inhabitants of your country.[af]

Fellow-citizens! I will not enlarge further on your national inconsistencies. The existence of slavery in this country brands your republicanism as a sham, your humanity as a base pretence, and your Christianity as a lie. It destroys your moral power abroad; it corrupts your politicians at home. It saps the foundation of religion; it makes your name a hissing, and a by word to a mocking earth. It is the antagonistic force in your government, the only thing that seriously disturbs and endangers your *Union*. It fetters your progress; it is the enemy of improvement, the deadly foe of education; it fosters pride; it breeds insolence; it promotes vice; it shelters crime; it is a curse to the earth that supports it; and yet, you cling to it, as if it were the sheet anchor of all your hopes. Oh! be warned! be warned! a horrible reptile is coiled up in your nation's bosom; the venomous creature is nursing at the tender breast of your youthful republic; *for the love of God, tear away*, and fling from you the hideous monster, and *let the weight of twenty millions crush and destroy it forever*!

The Constitution

But it is answered in reply to all this, that precisely what I have now denounced is, in fact, guaranteed and sanctioned by the Constitution of the United States; that the right to hold and to hunt slaves is a part of that Constitution framed by the illustrious Fathers of this Republic.

Then, I dare to affirm, notwithstanding all I have said before, your fathers stooped, basely stooped.

> To palter with us in a double sense:
> And keep the word of promise to the ear,
> But break it to the heart.[ag]

And instead of being the honest men I have before declared them to be, they were the veriest imposters that ever practiced on mankind. *This* is the inevitable conclusion, and from it there is no escape. But I differ from those

---

af. Letter from Thomas Jefferson to Jean Nicholas Demeunier, 24 Jan. 1786: "What a stupendous, what an incomprehensible machine is man! Who can endure toil, famine, stripes, imprisonment & death itself in vindication of his own liberty, and the next moment . . . inflict on his fellow men a bondage, one hour of which is fraught with more misery than ages of that which he rose in rebellion to oppose."

ag. William Shakespeare, *Macbeth*.

who charge this baseness on the framers of the Constitution of the United States. *It is a slander upon their memory*, at least, so I believe. There is not time now to argue the constitutional question at length—nor have I the ability to discuss it as it ought to be discussed. The subject has been handled with masterly power by Lysander Spooner, Esq., by William Goodell, by Samuel E. Sewall, Esq., and last, though not least, by Gerrit Smith, Esq.[ah] These gentlemen have, as I think, fully and clearly vindicated the Constitution from any design to support slavery for an hour.

Fellow-citizens! there is no matter in respect to which, the people of the North have allowed themselves to be so ruinously imposed upon, as that of the pro-slavery character of the Constitution. In *that* instrument I hold there is neither warrant, license, nor sanction of the hateful thing; but, interpreted as it *ought* to be interpreted, the Constitution is a GLORIOUS LIBERTY DOCUMENT. Read its preamble, consider its purposes. Is slavery among them? Is it at the gateway? or is it in the temple? It is neither. While I do not intend to argue this question on the present occasion, let me ask, if it be not somewhat singular that, if the Constitution were intended to be, by its framers and adopters, a slave-holding instrument, why neither *slavery*, *slaveholding*, nor *slave* can anywhere be found in it. What would be thought of an instrument, drawn up, legally drawn up, for the purpose of entitling the city of Rochester to a track of land, in which no mention of land was made? Now, there are certain rules of interpretation, for the proper understanding of all legal instruments. These rules are well established. They are plain, common-sense rules, such as you and I, and all of us, can understand and apply, without having passed years in the study of law. I scout the idea that the question of the constitutionality or unconstitutionality of slavery is not a question for the people. I hold that every American citizen has a right to form an opinion of the constitution, and to propagate that opinion, and to use all honorable means to make his opinion the prevailing one. Without this right, the liberty of an American citizen would be as insecure as that of a Frenchman. Ex-Vice-President Dallas[ai] tells us that the constitution is an object to which no

ah. Lysander Spooner (1808–1887) was the author of *The Un-Constitutionality of Slavery* (1840); Willimar Goodell (1792–1878) was a founder of the New York State Anti-Slavery Society, the American Anti-Slavery Society, and the Liberty Party; Samuel E. Sewall (1799–1888) was a lawyer and leader in the Liberty Party; and Gerrit Smith (1797–1874) was a wealthy philanthropist and supporter of the abolition movement and in 1848, 1852, and 1856, the presidential nominee of the Liberty Party.

ai. George Mifflin Dallas (1792–1864): Democratic US senator from Pennsylvania and vice president under James K. Polk.

American mind can be too attentive, and no American heart too devoted. He further says, the constitution, in its words, is plain and intelligible, and is meant for the home-bred, unsophisticated understandings of our fellow-citizens. Senator Berrien[aj] tell us that the Constitution is the fundamental law, that which controls all others. The charter of our liberties, which every citizen has a personal interest in understanding thoroughly. The testimony of Senator Breese,[ak] Lewis Cass,[al] and many others that might be named, who are everywhere esteemed as sound lawyers, so regard the constitution. I take it, therefore, that it is not presumption in a private citizen to form an opinion of that instrument.

Now, take the constitution according to its plain reading, and I defy the presentation of a single pro-slavery clause in it. On the other hand it will be found to contain principles and purposes, entirely hostile to the existence of slavery.

I have detained my audience entirely too long already. At some future period I will gladly avail myself of an opportunity to give this subject a full and fair discussion.

Allow me to say, in conclusion, notwithstanding the dark picture I have this day presented of the state of the nation, I do not despair of this country. There are forces in operation, which must inevitably work the downfall of slavery. "The arm of the Lord is not shortened,"[am] and the doom of slavery is certain. I, therefore, leave off where I began, with *hope*. While drawing encouragement from the Declaration of Independence, the great principles it contains, and the genius of American Institutions, my spirit is also cheered by the obvious tendencies of the age. Nations do not now stand in the same relation to each other that they did ages ago. No nation can now shut itself up from the surrounding world, and trot round in the same old path of its fathers without interference. The time *was* when such could be done. Long established customs of hurtful character could formerly fence themselves in, and do their evil work with social impunity. Knowledge was then confined

aj. John MacPherson Berrien (1781–1856): US senator from Georgia, first as a member of the Democratic Party and then as a Whig. Also served as Attorney General under Andrew Jackson.
ak. Sidney Breese (1800–1878): Judge and Democratic US senator from Illinois.
al. Lewis Cass (1782–1866): Democratic US senator from Michigan and Democratic presidential nominee in 1848.
am. Isaiah 59:1–2: "Behold, the Lord's hand is not shortened, that it cannot save, nor His ear heavy, that it cannot hear. But your iniquities have separated you from your God; and your sins have hidden His face from you, so that He will not hear."

and enjoyed by the privileged few, and the multitude walked on in mental darkness. But a change has now come over the affairs of mankind. Walled cities and empires have become unfashionable. The arm of commerce has borne away the gates of the strong city. Intelligence is penetrating the darkest corners of the globe. It makes its pathway over and under the sea, as well as on the earth. Wind, steam, and lightning are its chartered agents. Oceans no longer divide, but link nations together. From Boston to London is now a holiday excursion. Space is comparatively annihilated.—Thoughts expressed on one side of the Atlantic, are distinctly heard on the other.

The far-off and almost fabulous Pacific rolls in grandeur at our feet. The Celestial Empire, the mystery of ages, is being solved. The fiat of the Almighty, "Let there be Light,"[an] has not yet spent its force. No abuse, no outrage whether in taste, sport or avarice, can now hide itself from the all-pervading light. The iron shoe, and crippled foot of China must be seen, in contrast with nature. *Africa must rise and put on her yet unwoven garment. "Ethiopia shall stretch out her hand unto God."*[ao] In the fervent aspirations of William Lloyd Garrison,[ap] I say, and let every heart join in saying it:

God speed the year of jubilee
  The wide world o'er
When from their galling chains set free,
Th' oppress'd shall vilely bend the knee,
And wear the yoke of tyranny
  Like brutes no more.
That year will come, and freedom's reign,
To man his plundered fights again
Restore.

God speed the day when human blood
  Shall cease to flow!
In every clime be understood,
The claims of human brotherhood,
And each return for evil, good,
  Not blow for blow;

an. Genesis 1:3.
ao. Psalm 68:31.
ap. William Lloyd Garrison (1805–1879): Leading abolitionist, editor of the *Liberator*, and a founder of the American Anti-Slavery Society.

That day will come all feuds to end.
And change into a faithful friend
        Each foe.

God speed the hour, the glorious hour,
        When none on earth
Shall exercise a lordly power,
Nor in a tyrant's presence cower;
But all to manhood's stature tower,
        By equal birth!
That hour will come, to each, to all,
And from his prison-house, the thrall
        Go forth.

Until that year, day, hour, arrive,
With head, and heart, and hand I'll strive,
To break the rod, and rend the gyve,[aq]
The spoiler of his prey deprive—
        So witness Heaven!
And never from my chosen post,
Whate'er the peril or the cost,
        Be driven.[ar]

aq. A shackle, or a fetter.
ar. William Lloyd Garrison, "The Triumph of Freedom."

Henry McNeal Turner

I Claim the Rights of a Man
(Speech to the Georgia State Legislature)

Bishop Henry McNeal Turner carried controversy with him wherever he went. His prodigious intellect and forceful personality enabled him to combat adversity throughout his life. Iconoclastic and proud, he experienced a stinging rejection during the summer of 1868. Participating in the Georgia Constitutional Convention of 1867, he had helped white Georgians become reconstituted in the Union. In April of the following year, he and thirty-one other African Americans were elected to the state legislature. That legislature, controlled by conservative white Democrats, soon voted to expel the black members from the legislature because, the white members argued, the newly adopted constitution had no specific provision that granted African Americans the "right to hold office."

On September 3, 1868, at only thirty-four years of age the recognized leader of the black delegation, Bishop Turner delivered the final speech by an African American protesting the impending expulsion. In what historian John Dittmer calls "the most powerful speech of his career," Turner categorically denounced the white Democrats.[1] Other scholars, too, identify this speech as among the best and most influential of his career.[2] Rhetorical scholar Melbourne Cummings writes that the speech marked a turning point in Turner's discourse, inaugurating a "theme that runs throughout Turner's subsequent rhetoric" of black nationalism.[3] From this point forward, she argues, Turner's essays and speeches are "filled with the hopelessness of Blacks in the United States and the reasons for their dejection."[4]

Henry McNeal Turner had been born a free black in South Carolina in 1834. His grandfather had secured his freedom before the Revolution by arguing in court that he was a descendant of African royalty. A British law prohibited the enslavement of royalty, and thus Turner's grandfather was emancipated. Despite their free status, however, Turner's family was poor and lived in almost the same circumstances as slaves. In his youth, Turner was compelled to work the plantation cotton fields, where he labored alongside enslaved blacks and was treated as one by the overseer. The laws prohibiting the teaching of slaves applied to free blacks as well, and so Turner studied secretly, becoming literate only under the threat of prosecution. Shortly after his twentieth birthday, he was hired as an itinerant preacher by the white-controlled Methodist Church. Provided with traveling papers by the church, Turner toured the "black belt" states, preaching to African American congregations organized by the slave owners and local white churches. Despite his documentation, however, Turner traveled under the constant possibility that he would be arrested as a troublemaker or enslaved under some spurious charge.[5]

By 1858, Turner had become disillusioned with the segregated and discriminatory practices of the Methodist Church and so migrated to Baltimore, where he joined the African Methodist Episcopal (AME) Church. There he studied Latin, Greek, Hebrew, and theology at Trinity College, and he expanded his education further through wide reading and informal study. For example, in order to teach himself anatomy, he attended many nighttime dissections of cadavers at the local medical school. In 1860 he was ordained a deacon in the AME Church, and in 1862 he was assigned to Union Bethel Church in Washington, DC, at that time the largest AME Church in the city. During the Civil War, Abraham Lincoln appointed him the first black US Army chaplain, and in that capacity he participated in several battles.[6]

After the war, Turner obtained an appointment with the Freedmen's Bureau and moved to Georgia. Once more disillusioned by racist practices within an institution, Turner resigned his appointment and went to work again full-time for the AME Church. Prior to the Civil War, the AME Church had been banned in the South. As presiding elder and superintendent, Turner's job was to establish and organize the church. So well did he perform this task that for decades after, Georgia had the largest AME membership in the South. Again Turner's work was dangerous. Southern whites were suspicious of blacks organizing themselves into institutions of any kind, and during this period he often traveled with armed guards. No sooner had Turner organized Georgia for the AME Church than he was asked to help organize it for the Republican Party. Well-connected and highly respected, Turner helped create a structure for the Republican Party within the African American community and was subsequently a leading figure in Georgia's Constitutional Convention of 1867. That convention, charged with writing a state constitution consistent with Congress's Reconstruction laws, was heavily boycotted by conservative white Democrats. White politicians did not want to be forever tainted by having participated in a political act that publicly acquiesced to the hated Yankees and simultaneously acknowledged the citizenship rights of African Americans.[7]

At the Constitutional Convention, Turner distinguished himself by graciously encouraging accommodation with white Georgia political leaders. He helped fight for full citizenship rights for all white Southerners and agreed to an educational test and poll tax regarding suffrage. He also supported legislation that protected property rights, all in an effort to extend the olive branch to conservative whites and thereby reunify the state. In the newly elected legislature, however, it became clear that accommodation was a failed strategy. In the early days of the legislature, Turner and other black legislators introduced progressive legislation that included legal protection for sharecroppers, financial support of black institutions of higher education, an eight-hour work day, the chartering of black cooperative stock companies, and an end to the convict lease system. Not only were these proposals voted down, but white Republicans failed to support this problack legislation, and Turner himself came under attack personally. By the end of the summer 1868, the Georgia State Legislature was considering a resolution to expel its African American members. Speaking last among the African American legislators, in a speech designed as a judgment rather than as one to convince the audience, Bishop Turner spoke his mind and laid bare his frustrations.

Turner begins his speech by declaring that he is not interested in persuading the white legislators. Some of his African American colleagues had tried to do so, he says, taking "occasion to appeal to the sympathies of the Members," but it had reminded him of "slaves begging under the lash." Undoubtedly recalling some of his own accommodation at the Constitutional Convention, Turner previews the purpose of his speech: "I am here to demand my rights, and to hurl thunderbolts at the men who would dare to cross the threshold of my manhood." His was to be a speech of fire and brimstone, not tender appeals. In an analogy that condemns rather than invites, Turner observes that one must "Fight the Devil with fire," and so, if his rhetoric judges his opponents rather than tries to woo them, he wishes the "gentlemen to understand that it is but fighting them with their own weapon."

Turner's suggestion that his opponents are the devil merely foreshadows his more frontal attacks on their character and their reasoning. "The Anglo-Saxon race," he tells them within the first several minutes of the speech, "is a most surprising one. No man has ever been more deceived in that race than I have been for the last three weeks. I was not aware that there was in the character of that race so much cowardice, or so much pusillanimity. The treachery which has been exhibited in it by gentlemen belonging to that race has shaken my confidence in it more than anything that has come under my observation from the day of my birth." He compares the Democratic oligarchy, the former slaveholders who still control politics in the South, to the royal family of France. "Such Democrats as we are having in this State," he says, "come pretty well under the description of the Bourbons by Napoleon Bonaparte, who said that they never originated a new idea, nor ever forgot an old one." Later in the speech he compares those same leaders to the Pharaoh in the Bible, and later again to the Devil. They are messengers who would "quibble" with every detail of an idea, and at the end he declares that they were "wicked."

He several times offers his audience a challenge. Part way through the speech, he says that if the state legislators submit the question to the US Congress, he would abide by the latter's decision. Indeed, he continues, if the Democrats reconvened the state Constitutional Convention and put to them the issue of African Americans' rights to elective office, he would abide by the convention's decision. Of course, the Democratic state legislature would not do so, for both of those bodies were Republican controlled. That was precisely Turner's point: the Democrats were interpreting the actions of those Republican bodies for their own prejudice and convenience, and not out of political principle. Returning to the argument that African Americans were ignorant, evidently raised by Representative Scott from Floyd, Georgia, Turner directly challenges his opponent to a contest: "I would pledge myself to do this, however: To take the Holy Bible and read it in as many different languages as he will. If *he* reads it in English, *I* will do it; if *he* reads it in Latin, *I* will do the same; if in Greek, *I* will read it in that language, too; and if in Hebrew, *I* will meet *him*, also, there. It can scarcely, then, be upon the plea of ignorance that he would debar me from the exercise of political rights." Surely Turner knew that nothing would enrage the prejudiced mind more than this bold challenge. Surely he understood that many of the whites in his audience would despise him for expressing it, exposing as it did their hypocrisy and intellectual cowardice.

However, while Turner quickly begins "hurling thunderbolts" in the speech, his address does follow a general progression from rebuttal to judgment. That is, although he suggests several times in the opening paragraphs that he does not care whether he actually changes the minds of his opponents, he still presents well-developed refutations to their arguments. Several times he asks, "What is the question at issue?" and after thus framing the discussion, he constructs a logical response to his opponents' charges. Could they sit in judgment of his manhood? That is a matter for God. Whose legislature is this? The Constitutional Convention's, a body in which African Americans, not white Democrats, had participated. Is Turner a man? Using medical evidence, he counters the often-made claim that a black person and the orangutan have more in common than do whites and blacks. What had the African race accomplished? Among other achievements they had taught military tactics to Napoleon and theology to St. Augustine.

Turner's denial of every argument his opponents made leads at times to some refutations that may sound odd to the modern ear. A common charge against African Americans was that, freshly emancipated from slavery, they sought elective office for which they were ill-suited. Even today, a common myth is that African Americans, corrupt and inexperienced, controlled elective government in the South during Reconstruction. In fact, however, African Americans never constituted a majority in any state legislature, and the only African American governor during that era was Governor Pinchback of Louisiana, who had been elected lieutenant governor and assumed the governorship for forty-one days upon the removal from office of the sitting governor. The record also indicates that there was little corruption by African American officeholders and that, to the extent that they were allowed to manage governmental affairs, they did so ably. Still, for whites Southerners, the charge that African Americans were trying to be "above their raising" was a persuasive appeal, and so Turner begins his rebuttal by denying its veracity. African Americans had "never wanted office," he responds. Indeed he tries to turn the argument against his opponents. The idea of holding office had been placed there by "the white man." Nor was it the "carpet-baggers, either, nor Yankees nor scalawags, but the high-bred and dignified Democracy [Democrats] of the South" who had encouraged blacks to seek office. However, just as Turner almost sounds as if he does not want African Americans to hold office, he moves the argument along by referring to a second, more prominent argument that his opponents had made: that Congress's Reconstruction measures had only specified that African Americans be allowed the right to vote, not that they be allowed to hold office. Yet African Americans already served in office at the national level, Turner points out, and had even been considered for the position of ambassador, and "is it not a great deal better office than any seat held in this body?"

Throughout the speech Turner occasionally pauses from his refutation to castigate his audience, as when he belittles the office they hold as members of the Georgia State Legislature. Or, in another passage, he begins by analyzing Congress's intention in passing the Reconstruction measures and concludes that section with a declaration of his rights.

> If Congress has simply given me merely sufficient civil and political rights to make me a mere political slave for Democrats, or anybody else—giving them the opportunity of jumping on my back, in order to leap into political power—I do not thank Congress for it. Never, so help me, God, shall I be a political slave. I am not speaking for those colored men who sit with me in this House, nor do I say that they endorse my sentiments, but assisting Mr. Lincoln to take me out of servile slavery, did not intend to put me and my race into *political* slavery. If they did, let them take away my ballot—I do not want it, and shall not have it. I don't want to be a mere tool of that sort. I have been a slave long enough.

This highly quotable passage has become "vintage Turner," characterizing his intransigent spurning of political compromise that does not fully respect him as a citizen and a person. Having compromised himself severely during the Constitutional Convention the preceding year; he refused ever to do so again.

The middle part of the speech is a fascinating legal and historical treatise, as he cites Madison, Jefferson, Washington, Lafayette, a congressional memorial from 1794, Judge Lumpkin of Georgia, Irwin's Code of Georgia, Bouvier's *Law Dictionary*, the Roman historian Tacitus, and the Georgia charter of Queen Elizabeth to John Hawkins. The Framers did not intend the Constitution to institutionalize slavery, he insists, and he documents that claim more specifically than most nineteenth-century speakers did. Slavery had never been specifically legalized in the United States, he says, and he cites Constitutional and judicial authorities in that regard. Finally, he points out, whites had been slaves in Roman times but had benefited because the Romans, like the Muslims and other historical peoples, had treated their emancipated slaves with far more dignity and rights than the supposedly Christian Southerners accorded African Americans in the reconstructed South. Turner's discourse on the history and legality of slavery is all the more remarkable because it comes from a man who had been largely self-educated and whose limited formal training was in theology and languages, not history and law. Further, Turner's erudition and wisdom belies his youthful age.

After his legal analysis, Turner unleashes a jeremiad, a type of speech that judges and condemns an audience while seeking a renewal of abandoned values, in this case the inborn equality of all persons, rather than seeking to convince the audience of new ideas. He foreshadows this turn to judgment and condemnation earlier in the speech as he alternately castigates, challenges, and refutes his opponents. Significantly, the turning point comes with a personal remark. Alluding to his compromises in the Constitutional Convention, Turner observes that "no man in Georgia has been more conservative than I." He continues: "'Anything to please the white folks' has been my motto." He then publicly disavows any such future compromises: "I can assure you, however, Mr. Speaker, that I have had quite enough, and to spare, of such 'conservatism.'" This passage, short though it is, has overtones of religious confession and redemption. Turner acknowledges his secular sin—that he had forsaken his people and his true convictions in an attempt to secure some partial gains—and he renounces any temptation to commit that sin again. Once he has thus purified himself, he possesses the full moral standing necessary to condemn his "fellow" sinners—the Southern Democrats—and his condemnation was merciless.

The expulsion, he says, is not a "thrust at me" but at the Bible and at God himself. It is poor thanks for having built up the country, worked the fields, and garnered the harvests for 250 years. Denied the fruits of their labors, African Americans were only demanding their political rights, and even those were being denied them: "You have all the elements of superiority on your side; you have our money and your own; you have our education and your own; and you have our land and your own, too. . . . It is extraordinary that a race such as yours, professing gallantry, and chivalry, and education, and superiority, living in a land where ringing chimes call child and sire to the Church of God . . . that, with all these advantages on your side, you can make war upon the poor defenseless black man." "You may expel us, gentlemen," Turner warns, "but I firmly believe that you will some day repent it." He continues in a defiant vein, saying that he will tell his fellow African Americans that, although they should pay their taxes and be good citizens in most regards, they should "never lift a finger nor raise a hand in defense of Georgia, unless Georgia acknowledges that you are men, and invests you with the rights pertaining to manhood." Turner is reconciled to the knowledge that he cannot sway his audience, but he can condemn them and warn them. "Go on with your oppressions," he concedes, "Babylon fell. Where is Greece? Where is Nineveh? and where is Rome, the mistress Empire of the world? Why is it that she stands, today, in broken fragments throughout Europe? Because oppression killed her." "We are a persecuted people," he again declares, and "good men in all nations have been persecuted; but the persecutors have been handed down to posterity with shame and ignominy." So it would be with the South, and Turner vows to do his part to insure posterity's condemnation. "So help me, God," he avers, "I will go through all the length and breadth of the land" to tell those of his race about the injustice being committed that day.

The speech ends as a fully evolved jeremiad against his audience, complete with his calling upon God for the ultimate, harsh judgment of his opponents: "You may expel us, gentlemen, by your votes, today; but, while you do it, remember that there is a just God in Heaven, whose All-Seeing Eye beholds alike the acts of the oppressor and the oppressed, and who, despite the machinations of the wicked, never fails to vindicate the cause of Justice, and the sanctity of His own handiwork." After the vote of expulsion, Turner led the entire African American delegation to the legislature out of the hall. In an unmistakably Biblical gesture, as he exited he paused to turn and defiantly scrape the mud from his boots.[8]

That Turner's speech was designed to condemn his audience, rather than to persuade them, is evident in the arguments and language he chose. In most of Turner's other speeches, he used richly metaphorical language to plane the edges of his thoughts. His appeals were to generalized principles and ideas, to metaphysical and religious beliefs. In other words, he regularly met his nineteenth-century audiences' expectation that platform oratory would be literate and erudite discourse, and Turner relished opportunities to display the level of education that an African American could attain, and largely through self-education at that. He was himself an example of the equality he claimed for all African Americans. In "I Claim the Rights of a Man," however, Turner's charges are direct and plain, and his language pointed and piquant. "I am here to demand my rights," he says. "This objection, sir, is an unheard of monopoly of power." Or as he queries his audience on his humanity: "Am I a man? Have I a soul to save, as you have? Am I susceptible of eternal development as you are? . . . Have black men ever exhibited bravery, as white men have done?" In this speech to the Georgia State Legislature, Turner still spins some intricate sentences and inserts the occasional word that few but the highly educated would recognize. Generally, however, the language of the speech utilizes his direct, challenging style. He had come to condemn his audience, not enlighten or entertain them.

Speeches are commonly thought of as intending persuasion for all who hear them, but Turner's address illustrates that great speeches need not be persuasive to their immediate audience. True, Turner provides extensive reasoning as to why the expulsion of the black members was illegal and unjustified, but those arguments seem more a declaration of truths to be pronounced for the nation and posterity than an attempt to change the hearts and minds of the white legislators. He insults his audience, he challenges them, he belittles them, and he condemns them. After a period of political compromise, he is announcing his permanent departure from the path of accommodation, and he held to that promise. The Georgia State Legislature did indeed vote to expel its African American members, although they were reinstated the subsequent year by the US Congress. Turner, however, did not run for reelection, instead returning to his work with the AME Church.

In the last part of the century and into the beginning of the next, Bishop Henry McNeal Turner was known primarily for his advocacy of black nationalism and emigration to Africa, and his harsh denunciations of the United States.[9] When asked, in 1902, whether African Americans would be able to attain to the American type of civilization, he responded that "such being the barbarous condition of the United States, and the low order of civilization which controls its institutions where right and justice should sit enthroned, I see nothing for the Negro to attain unto in this country." The roots of that response lay in large part in his 1868 classic address of judgment and condemnation, "I Claim the Rights of a Man." Thirty-four years later, he was still being compelled to claim those self-same rights.[10]

I Claim the Rights of a Man

(Speech to the Georgia State Legislature)

September 3, 1868
Atlanta, Georgia

Mr. Speaker: Before proceeding to argue this question upon its intrinsic merits, I wish the Members of this House to understand the position that I take. I hold that I am a member of this body. Therefore, sir, I shall neither fawn nor cringe before any party, nor stoop to beg them for my rights. Some of my colored fellow-members, in the course of their remarks, took occasion to appeal to the sympathies of Members on the opposite side, and to eulogize their character for magnanimity. It reminds me very much, sir, of slaves begging under the lash. I am here to demand my rights, and to hurl thunderbolts at the men who would dare to cross the threshold of my manhood. There is an old aphorism which says, "Fight the Devil with fire," and if I should observe the rule in this instance, I wish gentlemen to understand that it is but fighting them with their own weapon.

The scene presented in this House, to-day, is one unparalleled in the history of the world. From this day, back to the day when God breathed the breath of life into Adam, no analogy for it can be found. Never, in the history of the world, has a man been arraigned before a body clothed with legislative, judicial or executive functions, charged with the offence of being of a darker hue that his fellow-men. I know that questions have been before the Courts of this country, and of other countries, involving topics not altogether dissimilar to that which is being discussed here to-day. But, sir, never, in all the history of the great nations of this world, never before—has a man been arraigned, charged with an offence committed by the God of Heaven Himself. Cases may be found where men have been deprived of their rights for crimes and misdemeanors; but it has remained for the State of Georgia, in the very heart of the nineteenth century, to call a man before the bar, and there charge him with an act for which he is no more responsible than for the head which he carries on his shoulders. The Anglo-Saxon race, sir, is a most surprising one. No man has ever been more deceived in that race than I have been for the last three weeks. I was not aware that there was in the character of that race so much cowardice, or so much pusillanimity.[a] The treachery which has been exhibited in it by gentlemen belonging to that race has shaken my confidence in it more than anything that has come under my observation from the day of my birth.

What is the question at issue? Why, sir, this Assembly, to-day, is discussing and deliberating on a matter upon which Angels would tremble to sit in judgment; there is not a Cherubim that sits around God's Eternal Throne, to-day, that would not tremble—even were an order issued by the Supreme God Himself—to come down here and sit in judgment of my manhood. Gentlemen may look at this question in whatever light they choose, and with just as much indifference as they may think proper to assume, but I tell you, sir, that this is a question which will not die today. This even shall be remembered by posterity for ages yet to come, and while the sun shall continue to climb the hills of heaven.

Whose Legislature is this? Is it a white man's Legislature, or is it a black man's Legislature? Who voted for the Constitutional Convention, in obedience to the mandate of the Congress of the United States? Who first rallied around the standard of Reconstruction? Who set the ball of loyalty rolling in the State of Georgia? And whose voice was heard on the hills and in the valleys of this State? It was the voice of the brawny-armed Negro, with the few humanitarian-hearted white men who came to our assistance. I claim the honor, sir, of having been the instrument of convincing hundreds—yea, thousands—of white men, that to reconstruct under the measures of the United States Congress was the safest and the best course for the interest of the State.

Let us look at some facts in connection with this matter. Did half of the white men of Georgia vote for this legislature? Did not the great bulk of them fight, with all their strength, the Constitution under which we are acting? And did they not fight against the organization of this Legislature? And further, sir, did they not vote against it? Yes, sir! And there are persons in this Legislature, today, who are ready to spit their poison in my face,

a. Pusillanimity: Cowardice.

while they themselves opposed, with all their power, the ratification of this Constitution. They question my right to a seat in this body, to represent the people whose legal votes elected me. This objection, sir, is an unheard of monopoly of power. No analogy can be found for it, except it be the case of a man who should go into my house, take possession of my wife and children, and then tell me to walk out. I stand very much in the position of a criminal before your bar, because I dare to be the exponent of the views of those who sent me here. Or, in other words, we are told that if black men want to speak, they must speak through white trumpets; if black men want their sentiments expressed, they must be adulterated and sent through white messengers, who will quibble, and equivocate, and evade, as rapidly as the pendulum of a clock. If this be not done, then the black men have committed an outrage, and the Representatives must be denied the right to represent their constituents.

The great question, sir, is this: Am I a man? If I am such, I claim the rights of a man. Am I not a man, because I happen to be of a darker hue than honorable gentlemen around me? Let me see whether I am or not. I want to convince the House, today, that I am entitled to my seat here. A certain gentleman has argued that the Negro was a mere development similar to the ourang-outang or chimpanzee, but it so happens that, when a Negro is examined, physiologically, phrenologically[b] and anatomically, and, I may say, physiognomically,[c] he is found to be the same as persons of different color. I would like to ask any gentleman on this floor, where is the analogy? Do you find me a quadruped, or do you find me a man? Do you find three bones less in my back than in that of the white man? Do you find less organs in the brain? If you know nothing of this, I do; for I have helped to dissect fifty men, black and white, and I assert that by the time you take off the mucous pigment—the color of the skin—you cannot, to save your life, distinguish between the black man and the white. Am I a man? Have I a soul to save, as you have? Am I susceptible of eternal development, as you are? Can I learn all the arts and sciences that you can—has it ever been demonstrated in the history of the world? Have black men ever exhibited bravery, as white men have done? Have they ever been in the professions! Have they not as good articulative organs as you? Some people argue that there is a very close similarity between the larynx of the Negro and the larynx of the ourang-outang. Why, sir, there is not so much similarity between them as there is between

b. Phrenology (antiquated): The study of the physical aspects of the brain.
c. Physignomony: Related to the study of physique.

the larynx of the man and that of the dog, and this fact I dare any Member of this House to dispute. God saw fit to vary everything in nature. There are no two men alike—no two voices alike—no two trees alike. God has weaved and tissued variety and versatility throughout the boundless space of his creation. Because God saw fit to make some red, and some white, and some black, and some brown, are we to sit here in judgment upon what God has seen fit to do? As well might one play with the thunderbolts of heaven as with that creature that bears God's image—God's photograph.

The question is asked: "What is it that the Negro race has done?" Well, Mr. Speaker, all I have to say upon the subject is this: that if we are the class of people that we are generally represented to be, I hold that we are a very great people. It is generally considered that we are the Children of Canaan, and that the curse of a father rests upon our heads, and has rested, all through history.[d] Sir, I deny that the curse of Noah has anything to do with the Negro. We are not the Children of Canaan; and if we were sir, where should we stand? Let us look a little into history. Melchisedeck was a Canaanite; all the Phoenicians—all those inventors of the arts and sciences—were the posterity of Canaan; but, sir, the Negro is not.[e] We are the children of Cush, and Canaan's curse has nothing whatever to do with the Negro.[f] If we belong to that race, Ham belonged to it, under whose instructions Napoleon Bonaparte[g] studies military tactics. If we belong to that race, St. Augustine[h] belonged to it. Who was it that laid the foundation of the great Reformation? Martin Luther,[i] who lit the light of Gospel Truth—a light that will never go out until the sun shall rise to set no more; and, long ere then, democratic principles will have found their level in the regions of Pluto and of Proserpine.[j]

The Negro is here charged with holding office. Why, sir, the Negro never wanted office. I recollect that when we wanted candidates for the Constitutional Convention, we went from door to door in the "Negro belt," and

d. The Curse of Ham, also called the Curse of Canaan, derives from Genesis 9:20–27, in which Noah curses the descendants of Ham's youngest son, Canaan, to be "slaves" to the descendants of his other two sons, Shem and Japheth. In nineteenth-century America, slave owners often used the passage to justify slavery, claiming that Africans were the descendants of Ham and his son Canaan.

e. Melchizidek: King of Salem and priest of God Most High, he blesses Abraham and receives a tithe from him in Genesis 14:18–20.

f. Cush was the eldest son of Ham. Genesis 10:6–14.

g. Napoleon Bonaparte (1769–1821): Emperor of France, 1804–1814.

h. St. Augustine (354–430): Bishop of Hippo, located in modern-day Algeria. Famous theologian of the early Christian church and author of *Confessions* and *The City of God*.

i. Martin Luther (1483–1546): Roman Catholic clergyman and leader of the Protestant Reformation.

j. In Roman mythology, Pluto and his wife, Proserpine, are the god and goddess of the underworld.

begged white men to run. Some promised to do so; and yet, on the very day of election, many of them first made known their determination not to comply with their promises. They told black men, everywhere, that they would rather see *them* run; and it was this encouragement of the white men that induced the colored man to place his name upon the ticket as a candidate for the Convention. In many instances, these white men voted for us. We did not want them, nor ask them, to do it. All we wanted them to do was, to stand still and allow us to walk up to the polls and deposit our ballots. They would not come here themselves, but would insist on sending us. Ben. Hill[k] told them it was a nigger affair, and advised them to stay away from the polls—a piece of advice which they took very liberal advantage of. If the "niggers" had "office on the brain," it was the white man that put it there—not carpet-baggers, either, nor Yankees, nor scalawags, but the high-bred and dignified Democracy of the South.[l] And, if any one is to blame for having Negroes in these Legislative Halls—if blame attaches to it at all—it is the Democratic party. Now, however, a change has come over the spirit of their dream. They want to turn the "nigger" out; and, to support their argument, they say that the black man is debarred from holding office by the Reconstruction measures of Congress. Let me tell them one thing for their information. Black men have held office, and are now holding under the United States Government. Andrew Johnson, President of the United States, in 1865, commissioned me as United States Chaplain, and I would have been Chaplain today, had I not resigned—not desiring to hold office any longer. Let the Democratic party, then go to Mr. Johnson, and ask him why he commissioned a Negro to that position? And if they inquire further, they will ascertain that black men have been commissioned as Lieutenants, Captains, Majors, Brevet Colonels, Surgeons, and other offices of trust and responsibility, under the United States Government. Black men, today, in Washington City, hold positions as clerks, and the only reason why Mr. Langston[m] is not at this time a Consul Diplomat o[r] Minister Plenipotentiary in some foreign country, is because he would not be corrupted by President Johnson and made to subscribe to

k. Benjamin Harvey Hill (1823–1882): A Whig member of the Georgia legislature prior to the Civil War, he spoke against secession in 1861. He ultimately voted for secession, however, and was elected to the Confederate Senate. He spoke vigorously against Reconstruction in 1867. He was later elected representative to the US Congress (1875–1877) and then a US senator (1877–1882).

l. By "Democracy" he means the Democratic Party of the South.

m. Probably refers to John Mercer Langston (1829–1897), the first dean of the Howard Law School and in 1888 elected US congressman from Virginia.

his wicked designs. Is not that an office, and is it not a great deal better office than any seat held in this body?

The honorable gentleman from Whitfield (Mr. Shumate), when arguing this question a day or two ago, put forth the proposition that to be a Representative was not to be an officer—"it was a privilege that citizens had a right to enjoy." There are his words. It was not an office; it was a "privilege." Every gentleman here knows that he denied that to be a representative was to be an officer. Now, he is recognized as a leader of the Democratic party in this House, and generally cooks victuals for them to eat; makes that remarkable declaration, and how are you, gentlemen on the other side of the House, because I am an officer, when one of your great lights gave that I am *not* an officer? If you deny my right—the right of my constituents to have representation here—because it is a "privilege," then, sir, I will show you that I have as many privileges as the whitest man on this floor. If I am not permitted to occupy a seat here, for this purpose of representing my constituents, I want to know how the white men can be permitted to do so? How can a white man represent a colored constituency, if a colored man cannot do it? The great argument is: "Oh, we have inherited" this, that and the other. Now, I want the gentlemen to come down to cool, common sense. Is the created greater than the Creator? Is man greater than God? It is very strange, if a white man occupy on this floor *a seat created by colored votes*, and a black man cannot do it. Why, gentlemen, it is the most short-sighted reasoning in the world. A man can see better than that with half an eye: and even if he had no eye at all, he could forge one, as the Cyclops did, or punch one with his finger, which would enable him to see through that.

It is said that Congress never gave us the right to hold office. I want to know, sir, if the Reconstruction measures did not base their action on the ground that no distinction should be made on account of race, color, or previous condition! Was not that the grand fulcrum on which they rested? And did not every reconstructed State have to reconstruct on the idea that no discrimination, in any sense of the term, should be made? There is not a man here who will dare say, "No." If Congress has simply given me merely sufficient civil and political rights to make me a mere political slave for Democrats, or anybody else—giving them the opportunity of jumping on my back, in order to leap into political power—I do not thank Congress for it. Never, so help me, God, shall I be a political slave. I am not speaking for those colored men who sit with me in this House, nor do I say that they endorse my sentiments (cries from the colored Members, "We Do!), but assisting Mr. Lincoln to take me out of servile slavery, did not intend to put me and my race into *political* slavery. If they did, let them take away my ballot—I do not want it, and shall not have it. (Several colored Members: "Nor we!") I don't want to be a mere tool of that sort. I have been a slave long enough.

I tell you what I would be willing to do: I am willing that the question should be submitted to Congress for an explanation as to what was meant in the passage of their Reconstruction measures, and of the Constitutional Amendment. Let the Democratic party in this House pass a Resolution giving this subject that direction, and I shall be content. I dare you, gentlemen, to do it. Come up to the question openly, whether it meant that the Negro might hold office, or whether it meant that he should merely have the right to vote. If you are honest men, you will do it. If, however, you will not do that, I would make another proposition: Call together, again, the Convention that framed the Constitution under which we are acting; let them take a vote upon the subject, and I am willing to abide their decision.

In the course of this discussion, a good deal of reference has been made to the Constitution. I am as much a man as anybody else. I hold that that document is neither proscripted, or has it ever, in the first instance, sanctioned slavery.

The Constitution says that any person escaping from service in one State, and going to another, shall, on demand, be given up. What has been the clause under which the Democratic fire-eaters have maintained that that document sanctioned slavery in man. I shall show you that it meant no such thing. It was placed there, according to Mr. Madison,[n] altogether for a different purpose. In the Convention that drafted the Constitution, Mr. Madison declared, he "thought it wrong to admit in the Constitution the idea that there could be property in men." On motion of Mr. Randolph,[o] the word "SERVITUDE" was struck out, and "service" unanimously inserted—the former being thought to express the condition of SLAVES, and the latter the obligation of free person(s).[p]

Now, if you can, make anything out of that that you find in it. It comes from one of the fathers of the Constitution. Sir, I want the gentleman to

n. James Madison (1751–1836): Principal author of the US Constitution and later the fourth president of the United States (1809–1815).

o. Edmund Randolph (1753–1813): Member of the Constitutional Convention, later governor of Virginia and the second US secretary of state.

p. Turner footnotes the reference as 3rd Mad. Pap., 1429 and 1569.

know that that Constitution, as Mr. Alexander N. Stephens[q] said, I think, in 1854, so far as slavery is concerned, is neutral. He said, that if slavery existed in Georgia, it existed under the Constitution and by the authority of the Constitution; that if slavery did not exist in Pennsylvania, or in New York, *it was equally under the Constitution.*

That is a distinct avowal that the Constitution was neutral, and it is the opinion of a man who is acknowledged to be a man of great mind and large acquaintance with political affairs. Again: the Constitution of the United States has the following clause: "This Constitution, and *all laws made in pursuance thereof*, shall be the supreme law of the land."

Every law, therefore, which is passed under the Constitution of the United States, is a portion of the supreme law of the land, and you are bound to obey it.

But gentlemen say that the Democrats did not pass the Reconstruction measures. I know they did not. Such Democrats as we are having in this State come pretty well under the description given of the Bourbons[r] by Napoleon Bonaparte, who said that they never originated a new idea, nor ever forgot an old one. They certainly never would pass such measures. Did the Revolutionary Fathers intend to perpetuate slavery? Many say they did; I say they did not. What was meant by the clause which states that no bill of attainder or *ex-post facto* law shall be passed? I will tell you what I believe the Revolutionary Fathers meant: I believe it was intended to put a clause there which should eventually work out the emancipation of the slaves. It was not intended that because the father had served in slavery the curse should descend.

One of the strongest objections to the negro holding office is based upon the fact that he has been a slave, and had no rights; but the Fathers of this country framed a Constitution and Laws, whose spirit and letter condemn this everlasting proscription of the negro.

Let us take, for example, an extract from a memorial sent to Congress in 1794. It was written by a Committee of which Dr. Rush[s] was Chairman, and is signed by such men as Samuel Adams, John Adams, Isaac Law, Stephen

q. Alexander Stephens (1812–1883): Vice president of the Confederate States, he was subsequently elected to the Georgia State Legislature in 1868 and was a Democratic member of the legislature Bishop Turner was addressing.

r. The House of Bourbon was the royal family that ruled France from 1589 to 1792 and then was restored to power from 1815 to 1830.

s. Benjamin Rush (174–1813): Pennsylvania physician, member of the Continental Congress and signer of the Declaration of Independence.

Hopkins, and a host of other prominent gentlemen.[t] This memorial says: "Many reasons concur in persuading us to abolish slavery in our country. It is inconsistent with the safety of the liberties of the United States. Freedom and slavery cannot long exist together."[u] Let it be remembered that some of the gentlemen who signed this memorial had been Presidents of the United States. It is also well known that General Washington, in his will, earnestly expresses a desire that all his slaves should receive their freedom upon the death of his wife. He says: "Upon the decease of my wife, it is my will and desire that all the slaves held by me in my own right should receive their freedom. And I do most pointedly and solemnly enjoin on my Executors to see that the clause regarding my slaves, and every part thereof, be religiously fulfilled." Did *he* intend to perpetuate slavery or negro proscription? What says he, when writing to General Lafayette?[v]—"There is not a man living" who "wishes more sincerely than I do, to see a plan adopted for the abolition of slavery, but there is only one plan by which it can be accomplished. That is by legislative authority, and this, so far as my suffrage will go, shall not be wanting." General Lafayette once said: "I never thought, when I was fighting for America, that I was fighting to perpetuate slavery. I never should have drawn my sword in her defense, if I suspected such a thing." Jefferson says: "And can the liberties of the nation be thought secure, when we have removed the only firm basis—the conviction of the minds of the people that liberty is the gift of God? Indeed, I tremble for my country, "when I reflect that God is just, and that injustice cannot last forever."[w] I could quote from such men for days and weeks together, to show the spirit that was in them upon this subject, if I thought it necessary to my cause.We are told that we have no right to hold office, because it was never conferred upon us by "specific enactment." *Were we ever made slaves by specific enactment?* I hold, sir, that there never was a law passed in this country, from its foundation

t. Samuel Adams (1722–1803) organized the revolutionary Committees of Correspondence and was member of the Continental Congress and signer of the Declaration of Independence; John Adams (1735–1826), member of the Continental Congress, helped draft the Declaration of Independence and was second president of the United States; Stephen Hopkins (1707–1785) was chief justice and governor of Rhode Island colony, member of the Continental Congress, and signer of the Declaration of Independence.

u. From the *Minutes of the Proceedings of a Convention of Delegates from the Abolition Societies*, held in Philadelphia, 1794.

v. Gilbert du Motier, or the Marquis de La Fayette (1757–1834): French national who served as a commander in the American army in the Revolution. He later participated in the French Revolution, although he was imprisoned by the Jacobins. He was released by Napoleon and served in the French government until his death in 1834.

w. Thomas Jefferson, *Notes on the State of Virginia*, 1781.

to the Emancipation, which enacted us slaves. Even the great Mr. Calhoun said: "I doubt whether there is a single State in the South that *ever enacted them slaves.*"[x] If, then, you have no law enacting me a slave, how can you question my right to my freedom? Judge Lumpkin,[y] one of the ablest jurists that Georgia ever had, said that there never was any positive law in the State of Georgia that forbade negroes from testifying in Courts; "and they are," said he, "only debarred by their ignorance and ignoble status." Neither did Queen Elizabeth,[z] when she gave to Sir John Hawkins[aa] a charter to bring negroes to this country, give him that right with any other understanding than that no violence or force should be used therefore; and she never intended that they should be anything more than apprentices. Mr. Madison, in speaking upon the subject of jury-trials for negroes, says; "Proof would have to be brought forward that slavery was established by preexisting laws;" "and," said he, "it will be impossible to comply with such a request, *for no such law could be produced.*" Why, then, do gentlemen clamor for proof of our being free "by virtue of specific enactment?" Show me any specific law of Georgia, or of the United States, that enacted black men to be slaves, and I will then tell you that, before we can enjoy our rights as free men, such law must be repealed.

I stand hero today, sir, pleading for ninety thousand black men—voters—of Georgia; and I shall stand and plead the cause of my race until God, in His providence, shall see proper to take me hence. I trust that He will give me strength to stand, and power to accomplish the simple justice that I see for them.

Why did your forefathers come to this country? Did they not flee from oppression? They came to free themselves from the chains of tyranny, and to escape from under the heel of the Autocrat. Why, sir, in England, for centuries together, men—and white men at that—wore metal collars around their necks, bearing, in graven characters, the names by which they were known. Your great and noble race were sold in the slave-marts of Rome. The Irish, also, held many white slaves, until 1172; and even Queen Elizabeth,

x. John C. Calhoun (1782–1850): South Carolina senator and vice president of the United States, 1829–1833. Outspoken supporter of slavery and states' rights. The quotation is cited in J. D. B. De Bow, *The Industrial Resources, etc. of the Southern and Western States*, (New Orleans: De Bow's Reviews, 1852), 2:389.

y. Wilson Lumpkin (1783–1870): Governor of Georgia, 1831–1835.

z. Queen Elizabeth I of England (1533–1603).

aa. John Hawkins (1532–1595): Slave trader of the sixteenth century. Generally regarded as the first merchant to sail the "Triangular Trade," running between Africa, the New World, and Europe.

in her day, had to send a deputation to inquire into the condition of such white slaves as had been born in England. King Alfred the Great,[ab] in his time, provided that for seven years' work the slave should be set free. And, going back to more ancient and more valuable authority, did not God himself when he had brought the Children of Israel out of Egypt, say unto then: "Remember that you were slaves in Egypt?" I say to you, white men, today, that the great deliverance of the recent past is not altogether dissimilar to the great deliverance of ancient times. Your Democratic party may be aptly said to represent Pharaoh; the North to represent one of the walls, and the South the other. Between these two great walls the black man passes out to freedom, while your Democratic party—the Pharaoh of today—follows us with hasty strides and lowering visage.[ac]

The gentleman from Floyd (Mr. Scott) went down amid the chambers of the dead, and waked up the musty decision of Judge Taney in the Dred Scott case.[ad] Why, the very right on which he denied citizenship to Dred Scott, was, that if he were a citizen, he would be a free man, and invested with all rights of citizenship. The Constitution says that "All persons born or naturalized in the United States, and resident in this State, are hereby declared citizens of this State; and no law shall be made or enforced that shall abridge the privileges or immunities of citizens of the United States, or of this States, or deny to any person within its jurisdiction the equal protection of its laws."[ae]

For what purpose was this clause inserted in that Constitution? It was placed there, sir, to protect the rights of every man—the Heaven-granted, inalienable, unrestricted rights of mine, and of my race. Great God, if I had the voice of seven thunders, today, I would make the ends of the earth to hear me. The Code of Laws known as Irwin's Code of Georgia,[af] clearly states the rights of citizens. Section 1648 is as follows: "Among the rights of citizens are the enjoyment of personal security, of personal liberty, private property and the disposition thereof, the elective franchise, the right to hold office, to appeal to the Courts, to testify as a witness, to perform any civil function, and to keep and bear arms."

ab. King Alfred the Great of England (849–899).

ac. References the Hebrews' crossing of the Red Sea while Moses parted the waters. Exodus 13:14–14:29.

ad. *Dred Scott v. Sandford*: The United States Supreme court decision, written by Chief Justice Roger Taney, which held that a slave was not a citizen under the Constitution and could not sue in federal court.

ae. Fourteenth Amendment of the United States Constitution.

af. The Code of Laws (1861, 1867) for the State of Georgia: Compiled by David Irwin and known informally as "Irwin's Code of Laws."

Section 1649 of the same Code says: "All citizens are entitled to the exercise of their right as such, unless specially prohibited by law."

I would like to ascertain, Mr. Speaker, what prohibition has been put upon me, or upon my race, and what can be put upon it, under the provision of the Constitution, which would deprive us of holding office. The Constitution of Georgia, Article 2, Section 2, says that, "Every male person who has been born or naturalized, or who has legally declared his intention to became a citizen of the United States, twenty years old or upward, who shall have resided in this State six months preceding the election, and shall have resided thirty days in the county in which he offers to vote, and shall have paid all taxes which may have been required of him, and which he may have had an opportunity of paying, agreeably to law, for the year next preceding the election (except as hereinafter provided), shall be declared an elector; and every male citizen of the United States, of the age aforesaid (except as hereinafter provided), who may be a resident of the State at the time of the adoption of this Constitution, shall be deemed an elector, and shall have all the rights of an elector as aforesaid."

Now let me read to you the meaning of the word "citizen," as given by Mr. Bouvier in his Law Dictionary[ag]: "In American law, one who, under the Constitution and Laws of the United States, has a right to vote for Representatives in Congress and other public officers, and who is qualified to fill offices in the gift of the people. Any white person born in the United States or naturalised person born out of the same, "who has not lost his right as such." Now, sir, I claim to be a citizen, I claim to be an elector, and I claim to be entitled to hold office.

We have heard a good deal said about Greece and Rome, and the great nations of antiquity, and of such great men as Socrates, Seneca, Aristotle, Plato, Herodotus, Horace, and Homer. Well, I make a reference or two to these times and nations. A freedman among the Romans was nothing more than, in the time of slavery in this country, a free negro would be. He could not come in contact with the citizen upon an equal footing, but when the Empire came under the sway of Constantine,[ah] he provided that all slaves who were made free upon account of meritorious conduct should be enfranchised. Go back, then, Georgians, to the days of Constantine, and learn from him a lesson of wisdom. In the days of Justinian, too, provision was

ag. Bouvier's *Law Dictionary*, first published in 1839, was a highly regarded legal dictionary among American lawyers.

ah. Emperor Constantine I of Rome (272–337): First Roman emperor who converted to Christianity.

made that every slave who was made free should be enfranchised and made a full citizen of Rome. The celebrated Roman writer, Horace,[ai] boasted that he was the son of a freedman; and I would remind you, also, that one of the Emperors and rulers of Rome had a slave mother. Another provision of those times was, that a slave could become free and a citizen by the consent of six thousand other citizens. Now, sir, even following the example o£ Rome, am I not a citizen? Have not more than six thousand white citizens voted me my rights as such? And have not forty thousand white citizens voted for the Constitution which grants me my rights as such?

We learn soma peculiar points in regard to slavery from many of the writers of ancient times. Tacitus,[aj] for instance, tells us that, amongst the ancient Germans, if, in gaming, the slave should win, the master became his property and slave, while he became master. Mohammed[ak] gave political rights to all slaves who defended his religion; and so, indeed, in general, did the Crusaders; and the Popes of Rome used to teach their flocks that all men were the Lord's freemen. St. Jerome[al] once remarked that a man's right to enfranchisement existed in his knowledge of the truth. I might quote for hours from such authorities as those upon the rights which rested in, and were acquired by, the slaves of old, but I deem it unnecessary to do so at this time.

These colored men, who are unable to express themselves with all the clearness and dignity, and force of rhetorical eloquence, are laughed at in derision by the Democracy of the country. It reminds me very much of the man who looked at himself in a mirror, and, imagining that he "was addressing another person, exclaimed: "My God, how ugly you are!" (Laughter.) Those gentlemen do not consider for a moment the dreadful hardships—which these people have endured, and especially those who in any way endeavored to acquire an education.

For myself, sir, I was raised in the cotton field of South Carolina, and, in order to prepare myself for usefulness, as well to myself as to my race, I determined to devote my spare hours to study. When the overseer retired at night to his comfortable couch, I sat and read, and thought, and studied, until I heard him blow his horn in the morning. He frequently told me, with an oath, that if he discovered me attempting to learn that he would whip

ai. Horace (Quintus Horatius Flaccus, 65 B.C.E. to 8 B.C.E.): Famed for his poetry.
aj. Tacitus (56–117): Roman historian, author of the *Annals* and the *Histories*.
ak. Mohammed (570–632): Founder of Islam.
al. St. Jerome (347–420): Highly regarded theologian of the early Christian church.

me to death, and I have no doubt he would have done so, if he had found an opportunity. I prayed to Almighty God to assist me, and He did, and I thank Him with my whole heart and soul.

Personally, I have the highest regard for the gentleman from Floyd (Mr. Scott), but I need scarcely say that I heartily despise the political sentiments which he holds. I would pledge myself to do this, however: To take the Holy Bible and read it in as many different languages as he will. If *he* reads it in English, *I* will do it; if *he* reads it in Latin, *I* will do the same; if in Greek, *I* will read it in that language, also, and if in Hebrew, *I* will meet *him*, also, there. It can scarcely, then, be upon the plea of ignorance that he would debar me from the exercise of political rights.

I must now direct your attention to a point which shows the intention of the framers of the Constitution of Georgia, which you have sworn to support. In the "Proceedings of the Constitutional Convention," which framed this Constitution, I find, under date of March 3d, 1868, that, on motion of Mr. Akerman, the report of the Judiciary Committee, on the subject of the qualifications of parson a for membership to the first General Assembly, after the ratification and adoption of the Constitution, was taken up, and without amendment, adopted.—That report is as follows: "*Be it ordained by the people of Georgia, in Convention assembled*, That the persons eligible as members of the General Assembly, at the first election held under the Constitution framed by this Convention, shall be citizens of the United States who shall have been inhabitants of this state for six months, and of the district or county for which they shall be elected for three months next preceding such election, and who, in the case of Senators, shall have attained the age of twenty-five years, and, in the case of Representatives, the age of twenty-one years, at the time of such election."

Gentlemen will observe the word "inhabitant" in that Ordinance; and it was put there especially, in order that no question could arise as to who were eligible to fill the positions of Senator and Representative.

So far as I am personally concerned, no man in Georgia has been more conservative than I. "Anything to please the white folks" has been my motto; and so closely have I adhered to that course, that many among my own party have classed me as a Democrat. One of the leaders of the Republican party in Georgia has not been at all favorable to me for some time back, because he believed that I was too "conservative" for a Republican. I can assure you, however, Mr. Speaker, that I have had quite enough, and to spare, of such "conservatism."

The "conservative" element has pursued a somewhat erratic course in the reconstruction of Georgia. In several instances—as, for instance, in Houston county—they placed negroes on their tickets for county offices, and *elected* them, too, and *they are holding* office today. And this policy is perfectly consistent with the doctrine taught, in public and in private, by the great lights of Democracy, all through the last canvass. They objected to the Constitution, "because," said they, "it confers upon niggers the right to hold office." Even Mr. Alexander H. Stephens—one of the greatest men, if not *the greatest* man, in the South, today, and one for whom I have the utmost respect—in a conversation that I had with him before the Legislature convened (Governor Brown's[am] Marietta speech being one of the topics under consideration very generally throughout the State at that time), said: "Governor Brown says that the black man cannot hold office under that Constitution, but he knows that he can."

But, Mr. Speaker, I do not regard this movement as a thrust at me. It is a thrust at the Bible—a thrust at the God of the Universe, for making a man and not finishing him; it is simply calling the Great Jehovah a fool. Why, sir, though we are not white, we have accomplished much. We have pioneered civilization here; we have built up your country; we have worked in your fields, and garnered your harvests, for two hundred and fifty years! And what do we ask of you in return? Do we ask you for compensation for the sweat our fathers bore for you—for the tears you have caused, and the hearts you have broken, and the lives you have curtailed, and the blood you have spilled? Do we ask retaliation? We ask it not. We are willing to let the dead past bury its dead; but we ask you, now for our RIGHTS. You have all the elements of superiority upon your side; you have our money and your own; you have our education and your own; and you have our land and your own, too. We, who number hundreds of thousands in Georgia, including our wives and families, with not a foot of land to call our own—strangers in the land of our birth; without money, without education, without aid, without a roof to cover us while we live, nor sufficient clay to cover us when we die! It is extraordinary that a race such as yours, professing gallantry, and chivalry, and education, and superiority, living in a land where ringing chimes call child and sire to the Church of God—a land where Bibles are read and Gospel truths are spoken, and where courts of justice are presumed to exist; it is extraordinary, I say, that, with all these advantages on your

am. Joseph E. Brown (1821–1894): Governor of Georgia from 1856 to 1865.

side, you can make war upon the poor defenseless black man. You know we have no money, no railroads, no telegraphs, no advantages of any sort, and yet all manner of injustice is placed upon us. You know that the black people of this country acknowledge you as their superiors, by virtue of your education and advantages.

There was a Resolution passed here at the early part of this session stating that all persons who were in their seats were eligible thereto. What are gentlemen going to do, with that Resolution staring them in the face? Your children and my children will read that Resolution, and they will be astonished that persons, claiming to be men, with souls and consciences, should, contrary to the express provision of that Resolution, turn the colored man out of his seat in this Hall. Another Resolution came before this House, a short time ago, praying Congress to remove all political disabilities from the white people of Georgia. I stood up in my place here, sir, and advocated that Resolution, and advised all colored Members to do the same, and almost every one of them voted for it. We were willing to give the white a man every right which he ever rightfully possessed, and, were there forty negroes in this country to one white man, I would have precisely the same feeling, and act precisely the same way. The action of the House reminds me very much of a couple of lines of verse which we occasionally read: "When the Devil was sick, the Devil a saint would be; / When the Devil was well, the Devil a saint was he."[an] When this House was "sick" with fear for the safety of the seats of ineligible Democrats, they were all very gracious and polite. But, when the Resolution was passed, declaring, in the face of facts, that all who were in their seats were eligible, then the foot was raised which was to trample on the poor negro, and that, too, "by those who claim bravery and chivalry."

You may expel us, gentleman, but I firmly believe that you will some day repent it. The black man cannot protect a country, if the country doesn't protect him; and if, tomorrow, a war should arise, I would not raise a musket to defend a country where my manhood is denied. The fashionable way in Georgia, when hard work is to be done, is, for the white man to sit at his ease, while the black man does the work; but, sir, I will say this much to the colored men of Georgia, as if I should be killed in this campaign, I may have no opportunity of telling them at any other time: Never lift a finger nor raise a hand in defense of Georgia, unless Georgia acknowledges that you are men, and invests you with the rights pertaining to manhood. Pay your

an. Lines of poetry/proverbs dating from medieval times.

taxes, however, obey all orders from your employers, take good counsel from friends, work faithfully, earn an honest living, and show, by your conduct, that you can be good citizens.

I want to take your memories back to 1862. In that year, the Emperor of Russia,[ao] with one stroke of his pen, freed twenty-two millions of serfs. What did Russia do, then? Did she draw lines of distinction between those who had been serfs and her other citizens? No! That noble Prince, upon whose realm the sun never sets, after having freed these serfs, invested them with all the political rights enjoyed by his other subjects. America boasts of being the most enlightened, intelligent and enterprising nation in the world, and many people look upon Russia as not altogether perfectly civilized. But, look at what Russia has done for her slaves; there were twenty-two millions of them, while there are but four millions of us in the whole South, and only half a million in Georgia. If the action is taken in this House that is contemplated today, I will call a colored Convention, and I will say to my friends: Let us send North for carpet-baggers[ap] and Yankees, and let us send to Europe and all over the world for immigrants, and when they come here, we will give them every vote we have, and send them to the Legislature, in preference to sending a Georgian there.

Go on with your oppressions. Babylon[aq] fell. Where is Greece? Where is Ninevah?[ar] and where is Rome, the mistress Empire of the world? Why is it that she stands, today, in broken fragments throughout Europe? Because oppression killed her. Every act that we commit is like a bounding ball. If you curse a man, that curse rebounds upon you; and when you bless a man, the blessing returns to you: and when you oppress a man, the oppression, also will rebound. Where have you ever heard of four millions of freemen being governed by laws, and yet have no hand in their making? Search the records of the world, and you will find no example. "Governments derive their just powers from the consent of the governed." How dare you to make laws by which to try me and my wife and children, and deny me a voice in the making of these laws? I knew you can establish a monarchy, an autocracy, an oligarchy, or any other kind of an "ocracy" that you please; and that you

ao. Emperor Alexander II of Russia (1818–1881): Signed the law emancipating the Russian serfs in 1861.

ap. Carpet-baggers: Northerners who came South after the Civil War in order to profit from Reconstruction and the postwar economic recovery.

aq. Babylon: Ancient empire located in modern day Iraq, especially prominent in the seventh and sixth centuries B.C.E.

ar. Ninevah: A great Assyrian city of Biblical times, especially in the seventh century B.C.E.

can declare whom you please to be sovereign; but tell me, sir, how you can clothe me with more power than another, where all are sovereigns alike? How can you say you have a Republican form of Government, when you make such distinction and enact such proscriptive laws?

Gentlemen talk a good deal about the negroes "building no monuments." I can tell the gentlemen one thing; that is, that we could have built monuments of fire while the war was in progress. We could have fired your woods, your barns and fences, and called you home. Did we do it? No, sir! And God grant that the negro may never do it, or do anything else that would destroy the good opinion of his friends. No epithet is sufficiently opprobrious for us now. I say, sir, that we have built a monument of docility, of obedience, of respect, and of self-control, that will endure longer than the Pyramids of Egypt.

We are a persecuted people. Luther was persecuted; Galileo was persecuted; good men in all nations have been persecuted; but the persecutors have been handed down to posterity with shame and ignominy. If you pass this Bill, you will never get Congress to pardon or enfranchise another rebel in your lives. You are going to fix an everlasting disfranchisement upon Mr. Toombs[as] and the other leading men of Georgia. You may think you are doing yourselves honor by expelling us from this House; but when we go, we will do as Wickliffe[at] and as Latimer[au] did. We will light a torch of truth that will never be extinguished—the impression that will run through the country, as people picture in their mind's eye these poor black men, in all parts of this Southern country, pleading for their rights. When you expel us, you make us forever your political foes, and you will never find a black man to vote a Democratic ticket again; for, so help me, God, I will go through all the length and breadth of the land, where a man of my race is to be found, and advise him to beware of the Democratic party. Justice is the great doctrine taught in the Bible. God's Eternal Justice is founded upon

as. Robert Toombs (1810–1885): US senator from Georgia, Confederate general, and Secretary of State for the Confederacy.

at. John Wycliffe (1328–1384): Early English dissident from the Roman Catholic Church. Argued for the Bible to be translated into the vernacular, and translated the Bible into English. Shortly after his death, Wycliffe's remains were exhumed and burned.

au. Hugh Latimer (1487–1555): English cleric and reformer. Although he argued for Protestant reform, he also clashed with Henry VIII over his divorces. Latimer was burned at the stake during Mary I's reign, as she attempted to restore Catholicism to England. Reportedly, his last words were "we shall this day light such a candle, by God's grace, in England, as I trust shall never be put out."

Truth, and the man who steps from Justice steps from Truth, and cannot make his principles to prevail.

I have now, Mr. Speaker, said all that my physical condition will allow me to say. Weak and ill, though I am, I could not sit passively here and see the sacred rights of my race destroyed at one blow. We are in a position somewhat similar to that of the famous "Light Brigade," of which Tennyson says, they had

Cannon to right of them,
Cannon to left of them,
Cannon in front of them,
Volleyed and thundered.[av]

I hope our poor, down-trodden race may act well and wisely through this period of trial, and that they will exercise patience and discretion under all circumstances.

You may expel us, gentlemen, by your votes, today; but, while you do it, remember that there is a just God in Heaven, whose All-Seeing Eye beholds alike the acts of the oppressor and the oppressed, and who, despite the machinations of the wicked, never fails to vindicate the cause of Justice, and the sanctity of His own handiwork.

av. From "The Charge of the Light Brigade," by Alfred Lord Tennyson.

Frederick Douglass

Oration on the Occasion of the Dedication of the Lincoln Monument

On April 14, 1876, eleven years after the assassination of Abraham Lincoln, Frederick Douglass delivered the featured address at the ceremony marking the unveiling of the Lincoln Monument in Washington, DC. The monument, built by funds raised by freedmen, was the first national memorial to the late president. The estimated crowd of twenty-five thousand included dignitaries such as President Ulysses S. Grant, his cabinet, US congressmen, and Supreme Court justices but was predominantly composed of African Americans.[1] The occasion required an epideictic speech, one that praised and honored the martyred president, and as the preeminent African American orator of the day, active in Republican Party politics at the national level, Frederick Douglass was the logical choice to present it. Yet Douglass had also been a vocal critic of Lincoln during the war. A traditional ceremonial speech, filled with sweeping praise, superlatives, and generalities, would not have been credible. Douglass instead focused narrowly on Lincoln's accomplishment of emancipation of the slaves, thus fashioning a speech that praised the president's deeds while diplomatically neglecting a detailed account of the man himself. Douglass's address is a case study of cultivating community without insisting upon unanimity.

From the beginning of Lincoln's first campaign for president, Douglass had been publicly critical of the politician from Illinois. The Republican Party's 1860 campaign slogan—"No More Slave States"—was too timid for Douglass, and until the eleventh hour of the campaign, Douglass endorsed Gerrit Smith, the Abolition Party candidate. In October 1860, Douglass was still arguing that ten thousand votes for Smith were worth more than two million for Lincoln, and he denounced Lincoln's assurance to the South that a Republican president would not interfere with the institution of slavery in those states where it existed.[2] As the Southern states seceded and the Civil War ensued, Douglass was critical that Lincoln moved too slowly to declare that the war was an antislavery war, that Lincoln countermanded some of his generals who declared slaves emancipated in their military districts, and that he blocked their attempts to begin raising African American regiments.[3] For each step forward that Lincoln took—for example, allowing escaped slaves to be treated as contraband of war or outlawing slavery in the District of Columbia—it seemed to Douglass that Lincoln took one step back. When in the summer of 1862 Lincoln finally decided upon an Emancipation Proclamation, he did not publicly issue it until September, it did not take effect until January 1, 1863, and it only applied to those areas "still in rebellion"—that is, those places the Federal Government did not control. While Douglass privately fretted that Lincoln would be politically pressured to rescind the proclamation, he publicly proclaimed his confidence that Lincoln, once decided, would be steadfast in his decision. Even as he wanted more, Douglass understood the symbolic importance of the proclamation, as it finally declared the war to be a conflict fought, at least in part, against the institution of slavery.[4]

Although he supported the Emancipation Proclamation, Douglass remained critical of Lincoln's presidency. Lincoln long delayed the formation of African American regiments for the Union Army. Douglass understood the importance of having African Americans fight for—and thus "earn"—their freedom, because he foresaw the civil rights issues that would continue even after the war itself was concluded. When Lincoln finally authorized the creation of African American units, those troops were paid a lower scale than white soldiers—$7 a month as compared to $13 a month. Significantly, the $7 amount was the standard pay scale for a laborer—a strong message that African American troops were not "really" soldiers but were manual laborers for the army. African American troops received inferior training and equipment and when captured by Confederates, were turned over to state governments, prosecuted under the slave statutes, and then frequently tortured and killed. Douglass publicly petitioned Lincoln to retaliate against Confederate treatment of African American soldiers, but Lincoln steadfastly refused to do so. That refusal, wrote Douglass, made Lincoln as guilty as Jefferson Davis of the crimes committed against the African American soldiers. In the summer of 1863, although he had been one of the most vocal supporters of African American enlistment, he ceased his recruiting efforts.[5] After meeting with Lincoln personally, and receiving assurances that such second-class treatment would ultimately cease, Douglass chose to continue recruiting African American troops, but in the summer of 1864, he again chose to support the Abolition Party's candidate over Abraham Lincoln. Only after the Democratic Party nominated General George McClellan as its candidate—a man whose personality and politics Douglass loathed—did Douglass again pragmatically switch his support to Lincoln.

Douglass met three times with Abraham Lincoln, including the evening of Lincoln's Second Inaugural Address, shortly before the president's assassination. From Douglass's accounts, it is apparent that he liked Lincoln personally. He wrote at the time that Lincoln himself seemed devoid of prejudice and that he was one of the few white men Douglass had met who related to him as an equal. But while he liked Lincoln the man, he chafed at Lincoln's caution. Ironically, however, in his "Oration at the Dedication of the Lincoln Monument," Douglass chose *not* to praise Lincoln the man but instead spoke of Lincoln's deeds, holding that, ultimately, it was what Lincoln *did* that made him honorable.

As he stood to address the crowd on April 14, 1876, Douglass was clearly aware of the ceremonial demands of the situation. Such oratory demands that the speaker generalize about the collective values and sentiments of the audience. He begins the speech, for example, by noting the occasion that has brought them together, without, however, immediately naming the occasion. By this conspicuous omission, he tacitly notes the audience's shared sentiment and motivation: "I warmly congratulate you upon the highly interesting object which has caused you to assemble in such numbers and spirit as you have to-day." Only at the end of his extended introduction does he expressly enunciate the point of the gathering and the speech: "in a word, we are here to express, as best we may, by appropriate forms and ceremonies, our grateful sense of the vast, high, and pre-eminent services rendered to ourselves, to our race, to our country, and to the whole world by Abraham Lincoln." Although focused on the present occasion, Douglass understood that, in an encomium, the present necessarily serves as a lens through which the speaker filters the past and anticipates the future. "In view, then, of the past, the present, and the future," Douglass says, emphasizing the importance of the time, "with the long and dark history of our bondage behind us, and with liberty, progress, and enlightenment before us, I again congratulate you upon this auspicious day and hour." Time is a recurring issue in this speech: "the sentiment that brings us here to-day"; "For the first time in the history of our people, and in the history of the whole American people"; "in what we have said and done to-day"; "ours is no new-born zeal and devotion—merely a thing of this moment"; "there is little necessity on this occasion to speak at length and critically of this great and good man." Ultimately, the convergence of past, present, and future in this speech of praise leads to the enunciation of eternal principles. Douglass not only implies such eternal pronouncements, he explicitly references them: "Fellow-citizens, whatever else in this world may be partial, unjust, and uncertain, time, time! is impartial, just and certain in its action."

In addition to his sensitivity to time, Douglass is clearly aware of the need to praise the man to whose memory the monument had been raised. Four times Douglass congratulates the crowd upon its "assembling" on such an occasion and for the creation of the monument. Lincoln's services to "ourselves, to our race, to our country, and to the whole world" were "vast, high, and pre-eminent." The occasion is one of "high worship;" the dedication of a monument to the "exalted character and great works of Abraham Lincoln, the first martyr President of the United States." He concludes by naming Lincoln "our friend and liberator," and declaring that Lincoln's memory "will be precious forever." Later in the speech, Douglass includes a prosaic passage praising Lincoln as the "plebeian," the rail-splitter from the frontier cabin who "brought his strong common sense, sharpened in the school of adversity, to bear upon the question" of the rebellion.

Such moments of praise for Lincoln, although fitting the demands of the ceremony, provide only a partial picture of Douglass's address. Through most of the speech, Douglass strategically qualifies his praise of Lincoln and the moment. Unable to deliver an unqualified speech of praise and still remain true to his beliefs as well as his record, Douglass carefully dilutes his praise so that it satisfies the exigence of the occasion although he risks the impression of circumspection. Douglass not only remains true to his beliefs, but ultimately delivers a more powerful epideictic message.

From the very beginning of the speech, Douglass reduces the need to provide unqualified praise by dividing his audience in two: black and white. He starts with appellations that recognize the two audiences—"Friends and Fellow-Citizens"—the former, more endearing term unites him with the many African Americans present at the ceremony, while the second, more distant term acknowledges the political dignitaries and other whites who are present. In his opening enthusiasm for the "fact" of the gathering, his longest expression of congratulations dwells on the racial mixture of the audience. "I cannot forget," he remarks to the audience, "that no such demonstration would have been tolerated here twenty years ago. The spirit of slavery and barbarism, which still lingers to blight and destroy in some dark and distant parts of our country, would have made our assembling here the signal and excuse for opening upon us all the flood-gates of wrath and violence." Yet, the mere assembling of whites and blacks in a common place does not unite them as one audience. One sentence later, Douglass remarks on the distinctions between the two races: "I refer to the past not in malice, for this is no day for malice; but simply to place more distinctly in front the gratifying and glorious change which has come both to our white fellow-citizens and ourselves, and to congratulate all upon the contrast between now and then; the new dispensation of freedom with its thousand blessings to both races, and the old dispensation of slavery with its ten thousand evils to both races—white and black." Though he acknowledges the two audiences' differences, Douglass also illuminates their common bonds—the blessings brought to both races by the new dispensation of freedom, and the evils on both wrought by the institution of slavery. Douglass recognizes that the blessings and evils to both races are distinct, even though the cause (freedom, slavery) and the general product (blessings, evils) are the same. He thus succeeds in creating community, despite differentiating between the blacks and whites who constitute its members. That differentiation is critical as he begins to develop the major points of the speech.

A second critical point posited by Douglass in his introduction is the location of praise and value in the doing of a thing. In this instance, Douglass would undoubtedly agree with pragmatist William James that "action may not bring happiness, but there is no happiness without action." While many epideictic addresses rightly laud transcendent principles—freedom, justice, equality—Douglass points to the very act of *doing* as an important accomplishment. The assembling of the audience is a praiseworthy act, the fact of the monument itself is laudable, and when he mentions Lincoln in the introduction, it is Lincoln's "services" that he praises, not the character of the man himself. The concluding lines of the introduction of the speech note the presence of the congressmen, justices, president, and cabinet and calls them as witnesses to the fact of the monument, a fact that demonstrates that "we, the colored people, newly emancipated and rejoicing in our blood-bought freedom, near the close of the first century in the life of this Republic, have now and here unveiled, set apart, and dedicated a monument of enduring granite and bronze, in every line, feature, and figure of which the men of this generation may read, and those of after-coming generations may read, something of the exalted character and great works of Abraham Lincoln, the first martyr President of the United States." This theme—that the mere fact of "doing" can, of itself, be praiseworthy—becomes a central motif of the speech as Douglass focuses primarily on what Lincoln "did," and less on how he did it or on his character.

Immediately upon the conclusion of his introduction, Douglass elaborates upon these two points—the dual nature of the audience and the honor found in deeds done. He begins with a reflexive nod to his perception that, although Lincoln merits honor, it is not because he had fully identified with blacks; and Douglass uses this note to establish his theme. "It must be admitted," Douglass intones, "truth compels me to admit, even here in the presence of the monument we have erected to his memory, Abraham Lincoln was not, in the fullest sense of the word, either our man or our model." Douglass remarks that there was no mistaking that, "in his interests, in his associations, in his habits of thought, and in his prejudices," Abraham Lincoln was "a white man." Douglass notes that Lincoln did not assertively seek to end slavery, but rather its extension into the territories. "The race to which we belong," Douglass averred, "were not the special objects of his consideration." Lincoln's opposition to slavery was instead primarily rooted in a desire to preserve America. To his "white fellow-citizens," Douglass remarks that "you are the children of Abraham Lincoln. We are at best only his step-children, children by adoption, children by force of circumstances and necessity." Yet Douglass claims that the freedmen's monument, a memorial erected by the step-children rather than the children, is fully justified as the first monument to Lincoln because of what Lincoln *did*: "for while Abraham Lincoln saved for you a country, he delivered us from a bondage, according to Jefferson, one hour of which was worse than ages of the oppression your fathers rose in rebellion to oppose." To fulfill the requirements of the occasion, Douglas needs to draw attention to Lincoln's acts and their consequences, while subordinating the principles underlying the acts or the arguments that are used to justify them. Douglass thus preserves his status as a spokesman for African Americans, particularly those who had risen from slavery. In fact, Douglass makes of himself a more credible advocate by acknowledging the criticism of Lincoln.

Throughout the Civil War, Douglass says, African Americans fully understood both the limitations and the importance of Abraham Lincoln.

"Our faith in him was often taxed and strained to the uttermost," he notes, "but it never failed." Using a *time-oriented* anaphora of "when he," Douglass recites a litany of Lincoln's faults—his urging of the repatriation of blacks to Africa, his slowness to bring African Americans into the military, his revocation of General Fremont's Proclamation of Emancipation—and admits that "we were at times grieved, stunned, and greatly bewildered, but our hearts believed while they ached and bled." In Lincoln, he says, they perceived the "head of a great movement" but also left African Americans perplexed as to "when he" would act, although inevitably pressing on until slavery was abolished. Douglass thus extends his theme that Lincoln was flawed, but, despite those flaws, deserves praise for what he accomplished. Douglass follows the recitation of Lincoln's faults with a corresponding litany of what Lincoln *did*, employing an anaphora of "under his rule" that provide a counterbalance to the negative anaphora that focused on what had occurred in the past.

> [U]nder his rule, and in due time, about as soon after all as the country could tolerate the strange spectacle, we saw our brave sons and brothers laying off the rags of bondage, and being clothed all over in the blue uniforms of the soldiers of the United States; under his rule we saw two hundred thousand of our dark and dusky people responding to the call of Abraham Lincoln, and with muskets on their shoulders, and eagles on their buttons, timing their high footsteps to liberty and union under the national flag; under his rule we saw the independence of the black republic of Hayti [*sic*], the special object of slaveholding aversion and horror, fully recognized, and her minister, a colored gentleman, duly received here in the city of Washington; under his rule we saw the internal slave-trade, which so long disgraced the nation, abolished and slavery abolished in the District of Columbia; under his rule we saw for the first time the law enforced against the foreign slave-trade, and the first slave-trader hanged like any other pirate or murderer; under his rule, assisted by the greatest captain of our age, and his inspiration, we saw the Confederate States, based upon the idea that our race must be slaves, and slaves forever, battered to pieces and scattered to the four winds; under his rule, and in the fullness of time, we saw Abraham Lincoln, after giving the slave-holders three months' race in which to save their hateful slave system, penning the immortal paper, which, though special in its language was general in its principles and effect, making slavery forever impossible in the United States.

Douglass concludes the litany by summing up his criticism of Lincoln's temporizing versus praise for the president's ultimate deeds: "Though we waited long, we saw all this and more."

Throughout the remainder of the speech, Douglass returns to this theme that frankly acknowledges Lincoln's flaws while emphasizing the fact of the progress that was made. He reminds his audience of the emotions they had experienced as a result of his actions. "Can any colored man," he asks, "ever forget the night which followed the first day of January, 1863?" He reminds them of the contrast between Lincoln and his predecessor, James Buchanan: "Timid men said before Mr. Lincoln's inauguration, that we had seen the last President of the United States." He recalls, too, the "fourteenth day of April, 1865," the date of Lincoln's assassination.

Perhaps the most artful, and explicitly laudatory, of the passages that balance his portrayal of Lincoln occurs three-quarters of the way through the speech. He begins with an honest, reflexive assessment of Lincoln, referencing the start of the body of the speech in which he had declared that Lincoln belonged to the "white man": "I have said that President Lincoln was a white man, and shared the prejudices common to his countrymen towards the colored race." Yet this "unfriendly feeling on his part" was "one element of his wonderful success" in bringing the "loyal American people" through the Civil War. Douglass candidly reiterates that Lincoln's priority was not to save the black race: "His great mission was to accomplish two things: first, to save his country from dismemberment and ruin; and second, to free his country from the great crime of slavery." Douglass acknowledges the pragmatic calculus Lincoln had employed: "Had he put the abolition of slavery before the salvation of the Union, he would have inevitably driven from him a powerful class of American people and rendered resistance to rebellion impossible." Noticeably, Douglass's grammatical construction ignores the question of whether Lincoln was forced by circumstance to prioritize union over abolition or whether he did so out of prejudice. Douglass's grammar instead emphasizes the point of fact: had the priorities been different, the desired result (abolition of slavery), would have been jeopardized. Douglass concludes with an antithesis that again unites praise with frank assessment: "Viewed from the genuine abolition ground, Mr. Lincoln seemed tardy, cold, dull, and indifferent; but measuring him by the sentiment of his country, a sentiment he was bound as a statesman to consult, he was swift, zealous, radical, and determined."Douglass follows this eloquent passage that weighed Lincoln's character against his deeds with a rhetorically intriguing section that seeks directly, if only partially, to redeem Lincoln's character. Reminding his audience of the previously established prejudice that Lincoln shared with the majority of his fellow white citizens, Douglass avers that "it is hardly necessary to say that in his heart of hearts he loathed and hated slavery." In the preceding paragraph as elsewhere, Douglass had dismissed concerns about Lincoln's prejudice as less important than what he accomplished. Pulled perhaps by the demands of the epideictic moment, Douglass is unwilling wholly to reject considerations of Lincoln's character. Yet Douglass accomplishes this end not by asking the audience to rely on his own characterizations of Lincoln, but by asking them to listen to Lincoln's eloquent words. The judgment, then, comes from the audience itself and therefore has greater effect. Douglass quotes a beautifully cast and rightly famous passage from Lincoln's Second Inaugural Address: "Fondly do we hope, fervently do we pray, that this mighty scourge of war shall soon pass away, yet if God wills it continue till all the wealth piled by two hundred years of bondage shall have been wasted, and each drop of blood drawn by the lash shall have been paid for by one drawn by the sword, the judgments of the Lord are true and righteous altogether."[6] Yet, following this passage, which clearly implies praise of Lincoln's character, Douglass again reminds his audience of Lincoln's pragmatism, with yet another set of antitheses that eloquently place Lincoln's accomplishments within the context of his time: "He was assailed by Abolitionists; he was assailed by slave-holders; he was assailed by the men who were for peace at any price; he was assailed by those who were for a more vigorous prosecution of the war; he was assailed for *not* making the war an abolition war; and he was most bitterly assailed for *making* the war an abolition war" (emphasis ours). Significantly, in this passage, Douglass reminds his audience not only of Lincoln's deeds, but of his own. Douglass, his contemporaries would certainly recall, was one of the abolitionists who had assailed Lincoln to press the war vigorously and to make it an abolition war. Implicitly, Douglass admits his own past criticisms—just criticisms—of Lincoln's prejudice and pragmatic conservatism, but he also generously acknowledges the difficult political waters that Lincoln had been negotiating. Tellingly, through language choices and climactic structure, Douglass chooses to emphasize that Lincoln was "most bitterly assailed" for his actions by those who *opposed* abolition. Douglass thus invokes the rhetorical commonplace that the enemy of my enemy is my friend.

Fittingly for this unique epideictic speech that focused less on the character of the honored and more upon his deeds, Douglass concludes equivocally by turning the audience's attention away from Lincoln's deeds and towards their own. Like Lincoln, they are to be congratulated on doing the right thing; that the monument honoring Lincoln is perhaps most meaningful as a monument to *them*. On the surface ignoring the white dignitaries present, he singles out the African American portion of the audience, saying: "We have done a good work for our race to-day" by honoring "the memory of our friend and liberator." Drawing attention to the continued prejudice of the day, Douglass tells the audience that "When now it shall be said that the colored man is soulless, that he has no appreciation of benefits or benefactors; when the foul reproach of ingratitude is hurled at us, and it is attempted to scourge us beyond the range of human brotherhood, we may calmly point to the monument we have this day erected to the memory of Abraham Lincoln." Douglass understands that the prejudice he discerns in Lincoln's politics continues in the hearts of most of the white audience present. Though he focuses on Lincoln's deeds, Douglass's speech is also transcendent. He reminds the audience of both races that in the presence of widespread prejudice, it is most worthwhile to attend to those deeds which yield justice, regardless of the purity of the doer's motivation. Douglass invites his audience to dwell not on the flawed character of humanity, but upon those actions that make the world a more just place for those living in it. By attending to those changes around which the community could unite, he advances a notion of community even in the midst of tremendous social change and continuing prejudice. He honors just deeds even while acknowledging continued problems of principle.

The speech met with immediate acclaim. It was twice excerpted in the *New York Times*, once on the 15th of April and then again a week later on the 22nd.[7] Although the second excerpt was longer than the first, both included a key portion of Douglass's mixed epideictic, including the observation that Lincoln was preeminently the white man's president and as such could not be unequivocally praised by blacks, yet his accomplishments on their behalf warranted the erection of the monument. Later that year, the speech was published in Washington, DC, by Gibson Brothers publishers, as well as in St. Louis. The Gibson Brothers edition also included an appendix that described the other events of the day as well as facsimiles of Douglass's handwritten draft of the speech.[8] Even today, this model of restrained praise draws popular attention. On appropriate occasions, journalists and congressmen take note of the speech Douglass delivered, in large part because it serves as a metonymic reduction of the personal and professional relationship between the two men.[9] Although little studied in scholarly circles, it remains a model of constructing an epideictic speech that includes a candid appraisal of the flaws found in what, or who, is being honored.

Oration on the Occasion of the Dedication of the Lincoln Monument

April 14, 1876
Washington, DC

Friends and Fellow Citizens: I warmly congratulate you upon the highly interesting object which has caused you to assemble in such numbers and spirit as you have to-day. This occasion is in some respects remarkable. Wise and thoughtful men of our race, who shall come after us, and study the lesson of our history in the United States; who shall survey the long and dreary spaces over which we have travelled; who shall count the links in the great chain of events by which we have reached our present position, will make a note of this occasion; they will think of it and speak of it with a sense of manly pride and complacency.

I congratulate you, also, upon the very favorable circumstances in which we meet to-day. They are high, inspiring, and uncommon. They lend grace, glory, and significance to the object for which we have met. Nowhere else in this great country, with its uncounted towns and cities, unlimited wealth, and immeasurable territory extending from sea to sea, could conditions be found more favorable to the success of this occasion than here.

We stand to-day at the national centre to perform something like a national act—an act which is to go into history; and we are here where every pulsation of the national heart can be heard, felt, and reciprocated. A thousand wires, fed with thought and winged with lightning, put us in instantaneous communication with the loyal and true men all over this country.

Few facts could better illustrate the vast and wonderful change which has taken place in our condition as a people than the fact of our assembling here for the purpose we have to-day. Harmless, beautiful, proper, and praiseworthy as this demonstration is, I cannot forget that no such demonstration would have been tolerated here twenty years ago. The spirit of slavery and barbarism, which still lingers to blight and destroy in some dark and distant parts of our country, would have made our assembling here the signal and excuse for opening upon us all the flood-gates of wrath and violence. That we are here in peace to-day is a compliment and a credit to American civilization, and a prophecy of still greater national enlightenment and progress in the future. I refer to the past not in malice, for this is no day for malice; but simply to place more distinctly in front the gratifying and glorious change which has come both to our white fellow-citizens and ourselves, and to congratulate all upon the contrast between now and then; the new dispensation of freedom with its thousand blessings to both races, and the old dispensation of slavery with its ten thousand evils to both races—white and black. In view, then, of the past, the present, and the future, with the long and dark history of our bondage behind us, and with liberty, progress, and enlightenment before us, I again congratulate you upon this auspicious day and hour.

Friends and fellow-citizens, the story of our presence here is soon and easily told. We are here in the District of Columbia, here in the city of Washington, the most luminous point of American territory; a city recently transformed and made beautiful in its body and in its spirit; we are here in the place where the ablest and best men of the country are sent to devise the policy, enact the laws, and shape the destiny of the Republic; we are here, with the stately pillars and majestic dome of the Capitol of the nation looking down upon us; we are here, with the broad earth freshly adorned with the foliage and flowers of spring for our church, and all races, colors, and conditions of men for our congregation—in a word, we are here to express, as best we may, by appropriate forms and ceremonies, our grateful sense of the vast, high, and pre-eminent services rendered to ourselves, to our race, to our country, and to the whole world by Abraham Lincoln.

The sentiment that brings us here to-day is one of the noblest that can stir and thrill the human heart. It has crowned and made glorious the high places of all civilized nations with the grandest and most enduring works of art, designed to illustrate the characters and perpetuate the memories of great public men. It is the sentiment which from year to year adorns with fragrant and beautiful flowers the graves of our loyal, brave, and patriotic soldiers who fell in defence of the Union and liberty. It is the sentiment of gratitude and appreciation, which often, in presence of many who hear me, has filled yonder heights of Arlington with the eloquence of eulogy and the sublime enthusiasm of poetry and song; a sentiment which can never die while the Republic lives.

For the first time in the history of our people, and in the history of the whole American people, we join in this high worship, and march conspicuously in the line of this time-honored custom. First things are always interesting, and this is one of our first things. It is the first time that, in this form and manner, we have sought to do honor to an American great man, however deserving and illustrious. I commend the fact to notice; let it be told in every part of the Republic; let men of all parties and opinions hear it; let those who despise us, not less than those who respect us, know that now and here, in the spirit of liberty, loyalty, and gratitude, let it be known everywhere, and by everybody who takes an interest in human progress and in the amelioration of the condition of mankind, that, in the presence and with the approval of the members of the American House of Representatives, reflecting the general sentiment of the country; that in the presence of that august body, the American Senate, representing the highest intelligence and the calmest judgment of the country; in presence of the Supreme Court and Chief-Justice of the United States, to whose decisions we all patriotically bow; in the presence and under the steady eye of the honored and trusted President of the United States with the members of his wise and patriotic Cabinet, we, the colored people, newly emancipated and rejoicing in our blood-bought freedom, near the close of the first century in the life of this Republic, have now and here unveiled, set apart, and dedicated a monument of enduring granite and bronze, in every line, feature, and figure of which the men of this generation may read, and those of after-coming generations may read, something of the exalted character and great works of Abraham Lincoln, the first martyr President of the United States

Fellow-citizens, in what we have said and done to-day, and in what we may say and do hereafter, we disclaim everything like arrogance and assumption. We claim for ourselves no superior devotion to the character, history, and memory of the illustrious name whose monument we have here dedicated to-day. We fully comprehend the relation of Abraham Lincoln both to ourselves and to the white people of the United States. Truth is proper and beautiful at all times and in all places, and it is never more proper and beautiful in any case than when speaking of a great public man whose example is likely to be commended for honor and imitation long after his departure to the solemn shades the silent continents of eternity. It must be admitted, truth compels me to admit, even here in the presence of the monument we have erected to his memory, Abraham Lincoln was not, in the fullest sense of the word, either our man or our model. In his interests, in his associations, in his habits of thought, and in his prejudices, he was a white man.

He was pre-eminently the white man's President, entirely devoted to the welfare of white men. He was ready and willing at any time during the first years of his administration to deny, postpone, and sacrifice the rights of humanity in the colored people to promote the welfare of the white people of this country. In all his education and feeling he was an American of the Americans. He came into the Presidential chair upon one principle alone, namely, opposition to the extension of slavery. His arguments in furtherance of this policy had their motive and mainspring in his patriotic devotion to the interests of his own race. To protect, defend, and perpetuate slavery in the States where it existed Abraham Lincoln was not less ready than any other President to draw the sword of the nation. He was ready to execute all the supposed constitutional guarantees of the United States Constitution in favor of the slave system anywhere inside the slave States. He was willing to pursue, recapture, and send back the fugitive slave to his master, and to suppress a slave rising for liberty, though his guilty master were already in arms against the Government. The race to which we belong were not the special objects of his consideration. Knowing this, I concede to you, my white fellow- citizens, a pre-eminence in this worship at once full and supreme. First, midst, and last, you and yours were the objects of his deepest affection and his most earnest solicitude. You are the children of Abraham Lincoln. We are at best only his step-children; children by adoption, children by force of circumstances and necessity. To you it especially belongs to sound his praises, to preserve and perpetuate his memory, to multiply his statues, to hang his pictures high upon your walls, and commend his example, for to you he was a great and glorious friend and benefactor. Instead of supplanting you at this altar, we would exhort you to build high his monuments; let them be of the most costly material, of the most cunning workmanship; let their forms be symmetrical, beautiful, and perfect; let their bases be upon solid rocks, and their summits lean against the unchanging blue, overhanging sky, and let them endure forever! But while in the abundance of your wealth, and in the fullness of your just and patriotic devotion, you do all this, we entreat you to despise not the humble offering we this day unveil to view; for while Abraham Lincoln saved for you a country, he delivered us from a bondage, according to Jefferson, one hour of which was worse than ages of the oppression your fathers rose in rebellion to oppose.

Fellow-citizens, ours is no new-born zeal and devotion—merely a thing of this moment. The name of Abraham Lincoln was near and dear to our hearts in the darkest and most perilous hours of the Republic. We were no more ashamed of him when shrouded in clouds of darkness, of doubt, and defeat than when we saw him crowned with victory, honor, and glory. Our faith in him was often taxed and strained to the uttermost, but it never failed. When he tarried long in the mountain; when he strangely told us that we were the cause of the war; when he still more strangely told us to leave the land in which we were born; when he refused to employ our arms in defence of the Union; when, after accepting our services as colored soldiers, he refused to retaliate our murder and torture as colored prisoners; when he told us he would save the Union if he could with slavery; when he revoked the Proclamation of Emancipation of General Fremont[a]; when he refused to remove the popular commander of the Army of the Potomac,[b] in the days of its inaction and defeat, who was more zealous in his efforts to protect slavery than to suppress rebellion; when we saw all this, and more, we were at times grieved, stunned, and greatly bewildered; but our hearts believed while they ached and bled. Nor was this, even at that time, a blind and unreasoning superstition. Despite the mist and haze that surrounded him; despite the tumult, the hurry, and confusion of the hour, we were able to take a comprehensive view of Abraham Lincoln, and to make reasonable allowance for the circumstances of his position. We saw him, measured him, and estimated him; not by stray utterances to injudicious and tedious delegations, who often tried his patience; not by isolated facts torn from their connection; not by any partial and imperfect glimpses, caught at inopportune moments; but by a broad survey, in the light of the stern logic of great events, and in view of that divinity which shapes our ends, rough hew them how we will, we came to the conclusion that the hour and the man of our redemption had somehow met in the person of Abraham Lincoln. It mattered little to us what language he might employ on special occasions; it mattered little to us, when we fully knew him, whether he was swift or slow in his movements; it was enough for us that Abraham Lincoln was at the head of a great movement, and was in living and earnest sympathy with that

a. John C. Fremont (1813–1890): In 1856, he was the first presidential candidate of the Free Soil (later, Republican) Party. As a Union Army general he issued an order emancipating the slaves in Missouri in 1861, an order that Lincoln countermanded.

b. Refers to General George B. McClellan (1826–1885). In 1864, McClellan ran as the Democratic presidential nominee in opposition to Lincoln.

movement, which, in the nature of things, must go on until slavery should be utterly and forever abolished in the United States.

When, therefore, it shall be asked what we have to do with the memory of Abraham Lincoln, or what Abraham Lincoln had to do with us, the answer is ready, full, and complete. Though he loved Caesar less than Rome,[c] though the Union was more to him than our freedom or our future, under his wise and beneficent rule we saw ourselves gradually lifted from the depths of slavery to the heights of liberty and manhood; under his wise and beneficent rule, and by measures approved and vigorously pressed by him, we saw that the handwriting of ages, in the form of prejudice and proscription, was rapidly fading away from the face of our whole country; under his rule, and in due time, about as soon after all as the country could tolerate the strange spectacle, we saw our brave sons and brothers laying off the rags of bondage, and being clothed all over in the blue uniforms of the soldiers of the United States; under his rule we saw two hundred thousand of our dark and dusky people responding to the call of Abraham Lincoln, and with muskets on their shoulders, and eagles on their buttons, timing their high footsteps to liberty and union under the national flag; under his rule we saw the independence of the black republic of Hayti, the special object of slave-holding aversion and horror, fully recognized, and her minister, a colored gentleman, duly received here in the city of Washington; under his rule we saw the internal slave-trade, which so long disgraced the nation, abolished, and slavery abolished in the District of Columbia; under his rule we saw for the first time the law enforced against the foreign slave-trade, and the first slave-trader hanged like any other pirate or murderer; under his rule, assisted by the greatest captain of our age, and his inspiration, we saw the Confederate States, based upon the idea that our race must be slaves, and slaves forever, battered to pieces and scattered to the four winds; under his rule, and in the fullness of time, we saw Abraham Lincoln, after giving the slave-holders three months' race in which to save their hateful slave system, penning the immortal paper, which, though special in its language, was general in its principles and effect, making slavery forever impossible in the United States. Though we waited long, we saw all this and more.

Can any colored man, or any white man friendly to the freedom of all men, ever forget the night which followed the first day of January, 1863, when the world was to see if Abraham Lincoln would prove to be as good as his

c. "Not that I loved Caesar less, but that I loved Rome more": Brutus, in William Shakespeare's *Julius Caesar.*

word? I shall never forget that memorable night, when in a distant city I waited and watched at a public meeting, with three thousand others not less anxious than myself, for the word of deliverance which we have hear read to-day. Nor shall I ever forget the outburst of joy and thanksgiving that rent the air when the lightning brought to us the emancipation proclamation. In that happy hour we forgot all delay, and forgot all tardiness, forgot that the President had bribed the rebels to lay down their arms by a promise to withhold the bolt which would smite the slave-system with destruction; and we were thenceforward willing to allow the President all the latitude of time, phraseology, and every honorable device that statesmanship might require for the achievement of a great and beneficent measure of liberty and progress.

Fellow-citizens, there is little necessity on this occasion to speak at length and critically of this great and good man, and of his high mission in the world. That ground has been fully occupied and completely covered both here and elsewhere. The whole field of fact and fancy has been gleaned and garnered. Any man can say things that are true of Abraham Lincoln, but no man can say anything that is new of Abraham Lincoln. His personal traits and public acts are better known to the American people than are those of any other man of his age. He was a mystery to no man who saw him and heard him. Though high in position, the humblest could approach him and feel at home in his presence. Though deep, he was transparent; though strong, he was gentle; though decided and pronounced in his convictions, he was tolerant toward those who differed from him, and patient under reproaches. Even those who only knew him through his public utterance obtained a tolerable clear idea of his character and his personality. The image of the man went out with his words, and those who read them, knew him.

I have said that President Lincoln was a white man, and shared the prejudices common to his countrymen towards the colored race. Looking back to his times and to the condition of his country, we are compelled to admit that this unfriendly feeling on his part may be safely set down as one element of his wonderful success in organizing the loyal American people for the tremendous conflict before them, and bringing them safely through that conflict. His great mission was to accomplish two things: first, to save his country from dismemberment and ruin; and second, to free his country from the great crime of slavery. To do one or the other, or both, he must have the earnest sympathy and the powerful co-operation of his loyal fellow-countrymen. Without this primary and essential condition to success his efforts must have been vain and utterly fruitless. Had he put the abolition of slavery before the salvation of the Union, he would have inevitably driven from him a powerful class of the American people and rendered resistance to rebellion impossible. Viewed from the genuine abolition ground, Mr. Lincoln seemed tardy, cold, dull, and indifferent; but measuring him by the sentiment of his country, a sentiment he was bound as a statesman to consult, he was swift, zealous, radical, and determined.

Though Mr. Lincoln shared the prejudices of his white fellow-countrymen against the negro, it is hardly necessary to say that in his heart of hearts he loathed and hated slavery. The man who could say, "Fondly do we hope, fervently do we pray, that this mighty scourge of war shall soon pass away, yet if God wills it continue till all the wealth piled by two hundred years of bondage shall have been wasted, and each drop of blood drawn by the lash shall have been paid for by one drawn by the sword, the judgments of the Lord are true and righteous altogether,"[d] gives all needed proof of his feeling on the subject of slavery. He was willing, while the South was loyal, that it should have its pound of flesh, because he thought that it was so nominated in the bond; but farther than this no earthly power could make him go.

Fellow-citizens, whatever else in this world may be partial, unjust, and uncertain, time, time! is impartial, just, and certain in its action. In the realm of mind, as well as in the realm of matter, it is a great worker, and often works wonders. The honest and comprehensive statesman, clearly discerning the needs of his country, and earnestly endeavoring to do his whole duty, though covered and blistered with reproaches, may safely leave his course to the silent judgment of time. Few great public men have ever been the victims of fiercer denunciation than Abraham Lincoln was during his administration. He was often wounded in the house of his friends. Reproaches came thick and fast upon him from within and from without, and from opposite quarters. He was assailed by Abolitionists; he was assailed by slave-holders; he was assailed by the men who were for peace at any price; he was assailed by those who were for a more vigorous prosecution of the war; he was assailed for not making the war an abolition war; and he was most bitterly assailed for making the war an abolition war.But now behold the change: the judgment of the present hour, that taking him for all in all, measuring the tremendous magnitude of the work before him, considering the necessary means to ends, and surveying the end from the beginning, infinite wisdom has seldom sent any man into the world better fitted for his mission than

d. A close paraphrase of a portion of Lincoln's Second Inaugural Address.

Abraham Lincoln. His birth, his training, and his natural endowments, both mental and physical, were strongly in his favor. Born and reared among the lowly, a stranger to wealth and luxury, compelled to grapple single handed with the flintiest hardships of life, from tender youth to sturdy manhood, he grew strong in the manly and heroic qualities demanded by the great mission to which he was called by the votes of his countrymen. The hard condition of his early life, which would have depressed and broken down weaker men, only gave greater life, vigor, and buoyancy to the heroic spirit of Abraham Lincoln. He was ready for any kind and any quality of work. What other young men dreaded in the shape of toil, he took hold of with the utmost cheerfulness.

> A spade, a rake, a hoe,
> A pick-axe, or a bill;
> A hook to reap, a scythe to mow,
> A flail,[e] or what you will.[f]

All day long he could split heavy rails in the woods, and half the night long he could study his English Grammar by the uncertain flare and glare of the light made by a pine-knot. He was at home on the land with his axe, with his maul, with gluts, and his wedges; and he was equally at home on water, with his oars, with his poles, with his planks, and with his boat-hooks. And whether in his flat-boat on the Mississippi river, or at the fireside of his frontier cabin, he was a man of work. A son of toil himself, he was linked in brotherly sympathy with the sons of toil in every loyal part of the Republic. This very fact gave him tremendous power with the American people, and materially contributed not only to selecting him to the Presidency, but in sustaining his administration of the Government.

Upon his inauguration as President of the United States, an office, even where assumed under the most favorable conditions, fitted to tax and strain the largest abilities, Abraham Lincoln was met by a tremendous crisis. He was called upon not merely to administer the Government, but to decide, in the face of terrible odds, the fate of the Republic.

A formidable rebellion rose in his path before him; the Union was already practically dissolved; his country was torn and rent asunder at the centre. Hostile armies were already organized against the Republic, armed with the munitions of war which the Republic had provided for its own defence.

e. A flail: A hand-held threshing instrument.
f. Thomas Hood, "The Lay of the Laborer."

The tremendous question for him to decide was whether his country should survive the crisis and flourish, or be dismembered and perish. His predecessor in office had already decided the question in favor of national dismemberment, by denying to it the right of self-defence and self-preservation—a right which belongs to the meanest insect.

Happily for the country, happily for you and for me, the judgment of James Buchanan,[g] the patrician, was not the judgment of Abraham Lincoln, the plebeian. He brought his strong common sense, sharpened in the school of adversity, to bear upon the question. He did not hesitate, he did not doubt, he did not falter; but at once resolved that at whatever peril, at whatever cost, the union of the States should be preserved. A patriot himself, his faith was strong and unwavering in the patriotism of his countrymen. Timid men said before Mr. Lincoln's inauguration, that we had seen the last President of the United States. A voice in influential quarters said "Let the Union slide."[h] Some said that a Union maintained by the sword was worthless. Others said a rebellion of 8,000,000 cannot be suppressed; but in the midst of all this tumult and timidity, and against all this, Abraham Lincoln was clear in his duty, and had an oath in heaven. He calmly and bravely heard the voice of doubt and fear all around him; but he had an oath in heaven, and there was not power enough on the earth to make this honest boatman, backwoodsman, and broad-handed splitter of rails evade or violate that sacred oath. He had not been schooled in the ethics of slavery; his plain life had favored his love of truth. He had not been taught that treason and perjury were the proof of honor and honesty. His moral training was against his saying one thing when he meant another. The trust which Abraham Lincoln had in himself and in the people was surprising and grand, but it was also enlightened and well founded. He knew the American people better than they knew themselves, and his truth was based upon this knowledge.

Fellow-citizens, the fourteenth day of April, 1865, of which this is the eleventh anniversary, is now and will ever remain a memorable day in the annals of this Republic. It was on the evening of this day, while a fierce and sanguinary rebellion was in the last stages of its desolating power; while its

g. James B. Buchanan (1791–1868): Democratic president of the United States immediately preceding Abraham Lincoln. Buchanan was much criticized for the four-month period of inactivity between Lincoln's election and his inauguration, as the Southern states seceded from the Union.

h. Refers to a controversial statement allegedly uttered by Representative Nathaniel Banks of Massachusetts. The statement was at the center of the debate surrounding Banks's election as Speaker of the House of Representatives in 1855. See "XXXIV Congress—First Session," *New York Times*, 25 Dec. 1855.

armies were broken and scattered before the invincible armies of Grant and Sherman[i]; while a great nation, torn and rent by war, was already beginning to raise to the skies loud anthems of joy at the dawn of peace, it was startled, amazed, and overwhelmed by the crowning crime of slavery—the assassination of Abraham Lincoln. It was a new crime, a pure act of malice. No purpose of the rebellion was to be served by it. It was the simple gratification of a hell-black spirit of revenge. But it has done good after all. It has filled the country with a deeper abhorrence of slavery and a deeper love for the great liberator.

Had Abraham Lincoln died from any of the numerous ills to which flesh is heir; had he reached that good old age of which his vigorous constitution and his temperate habits gave promise; had he been permitted to see the end of his great work; had the solemn curtain of death come down but gradually—we should still have been smitten with a heavy grief, and treasured his name lovingly. But dying as he did die, by the red hand of violence, killed, assassinated, taken off without warning, not because of personal hate—for no man who knew Abraham Lincoln could hate him—but because of his fidelity to union and liberty, he is doubly dear to us, and his memory will be precious forever.

Fellow-citizens, I end, as I began, with congratulations. We have done a good work for our race to-day. In doing honor to the memory of our friend and liberator, we have been doing highest honors to ourselves and those who come after us; we have been fastening our-selves to a name and fame imperishable and immortal; we have also been defending ourselves from a blighting scandal. When now it shall be said that the colored man is soulless, that he has no appreciation of benefits or benefactors; when the foul reproach of ingratitude is hurled at us, and it is attempted to scourge us beyond the range of human brotherhood, we may calmly point to the monument we have this day erected to the memory of Abraham Lincoln.

i. Union Army Generals Ulysses S. Grant (1822–1885) and William Tecumseh Sherman (1820–1891).

Frances Ellen Watkins Harper

Duty to Dependent Races
(Speech to the National Council of Women of the United States)

Poet, author, lecturer, and reformer, Frances Ellen Watkins Harper was one of the most influential African American women of the mid- to late nineteenth century. Highly regarded for her oratorical poetry and poetic oratory, Harper spoke on behalf of abolition, civil rights, women's rights, and temperance.[1] "Duty to Dependent Races," a speech delivered in support of equal rights for African Americans to the reform-minded and activist National Council of Women, represents Harper's work at its finest. The speech is simultaneously logical and pointedly argued while expressed in a style that is highly polished. That speeches such as these, powerful and rhetorically strategic, could not mobilize stronger support for African American rights from the women's reform movement explains the frustration that many African American women felt when working with their white sisters for women's rights.

Frances Ellen Watkins was born a free black in the city of Baltimore in 1825. Orphaned at the age of three, she was reared by her aunt and uncle, William Watkins. The latter ran William Watkins Academy for Negro Youth and was a leader in the African American intellectual community of Baltimore, including the East Baltimore Improvement Society, a group whose meetings Frederick Douglass attended while a working as a slave at the shipyards. In her uncle's school, Frances studied the Bible, the classics, and elocution. She went to work as a domestic at the age of thirteen, and in her employer's home was provided full access to the family library. Drawing upon this combination of formal and informal education, in 1846, Frances Watkins published her first book of poetry, *Forest Leaves*, at the age of twenty-one. In

1850, with the passage of the Fugitive Slave Law of 1850, Frances moved north and began teaching school. In 1854, she published her second volume of poetry, *Poems on Miscellaneous Subjects*, and left teaching to become a paid lecturer for the Maine Anti-Slavery Society. Such lecturers were typically provided with a small beginning stipend and a travel itinerary of towns and venues at which to speak. From there, they were expected to support themselves financially through receipts at the door, passing the collection plate, or relying upon the generosity of local abolitionists. A noted essayist and poet, Frances Watkins was such a successful lecturer that she was not only able to support herself, but could contribute liberally to the Underground Railroad.[2] At one point, she asked that she be allowed to help personally with the transportation of fugitive slaves, but William Still responded that Watkins's financial contributions were so important to the organization that he requested she continue her labors in that field.[3] In 1860, Frances married Fenton Harper and retired from the lecture circuit, after which the couple purchased a farm in Columbus, Ohio, largely from her earnings.[4]

When Fenton Harper died in 1864, the farm was sold involuntarily to pay off outstanding debts—since the bank assumed that a widow could not financially afford the loan—and Frances moved with her daughter to New England, where she continued her writing and resumed her lecture tours. In the latter half of the century, she published one novel (*Iola Leroy; or, Shadows Uplifted*, 1892) and multiple volumes of poetry (*Sketches of Southern Life*, 1872; *Moses: A Story of the Nile*, 1889; *The Sparrow's Fall and Other Poems*, 1894; and *Atlanta Offerings: Poems*, 1895). Her speeches on her lecture tours during these years generally focused on either "moral law"—covering topics such as moral improvement, temperance, thrift, and industry—or "political law"—including universal suffrage for African Americans and women as well as full equal rights under the law.[5]

In addition to her writing and lecturing, Harper served as a member of and often an officer in a variety of leading women's organizations of the day, such as the Woman's Christian Temperance Union (WCTU), Congress of Colored Women in the United States, the National Council of Negro Women, and the American Equal Rights Association. The audience for "Duty to Dependent Races" is one such organization—the National Council of Women in the United States. Growing out of the International Council of Women conference held in 1888, reform-minded women in America decided to form a National Council of Women of the United States (NCW). Led by Frances Willard, the president of the WCTU, this confederation of officers representing a variety of women's organizations sought to increase their influence through the umbrella organization of the NCW. Although the specific reforms advanced varied according to the individual member or reform society, the organization was broadly committed to improving the rights of the disenfranchised and the well-being of all Americans. In 1891, at the first Triennial Meeting of the NCW, Harper spoke on behalf of African Americans during the section of the program entitled "Duty to Dependent Races."[6]

The introduction to Harper's speech is a model of public speaking. With a direct style typical of her oratory, Harper opens the speech by challenging the title of her talk that the organization had imposed, and thus confronts one of the audience's fundamental assumptions: that African Americans were a "dependent" race who needed to supplicate themselves in order to be "given" their rights. Not only does Harper draw from the title of her speech, but she does so in terms with which the audience—largely committed to women's rights—could fully identify. Men had long suggested that women needed to "ask" that equal rights be given to them, and many women's suffrage speakers had put forward that the argument needed to be reversed—women did not need to *ask* for their rights, men needed instead to recognize the rights to which women were inherently entitled. Harper advances the same thesis on behalf of African Americans and in support of that thesis, enumerates three claims around which the body of the speech is to be developed: the claim upon the nation for justice (equal rights), upon the government for protection, and upon the Christian citizens of the nation for goodwill.

Interestingly, the body of Harper's speech substantially reverses the first and second of these claims, although it is a reversal that allows the speech to build logically from the minimal claim that a government should protect its citizens' lives to the last, more expansive claim that Christians have an obligation to treat all people with charity and goodwill. Intertwined throughout is the middle claim that the American nation owes its citizens of color equal justice and liberty under the law. In content, Harper's speech echoes the antebellum claims of the abolitionist—that as an institution, slavery violated fundamental notions of government, the American ideal, and the principles of Christianity. In 1891, her arguments would have resonated with this audience of reform-minded women, no matter whether they had come of age during the antebellum reform-era or had participated in one of the postwar reform movements.

Harper's arguments emphasize reason, with a particularly marked use of passages that first frame the issue or problem to be solved, followed by maxims, or assumed universal principles, by which the nation's answer to the issue should be guided. For example, she describes the issue of lynching as a problem that separates the United States from all other civilized nations: "Outside of America, I know of no other civilized country, Catholic, Protestant, or even Mahometan [*sic*], where men are still lynched, murdered, and even burned for real or supposed crimes." In another passage, Harper identifies a common argument raised by supporters of the status quo as the problem to be solved: "Am I here met with the objection that the negro is poor and ignorant, and the greatest amount of land, capital, and intelligence is possessed by the white race, and that in a number of States negro suffrage means negro supremacy?" Harper then employs maxims that provide the grounds for solving the issue. "A government which can protect and defend its citizens from wrong and outrage and does not is vicious," she claims, while "a government which would do it and cannot is weak; and where human life is insecure through either weakness or viciousness in the administration of law, there must be a lack of justice, and where this is wanting nothing can make up the deficiency." Or again, "But there are some rights more precious than the rights of property or the claims of superior intelligence; they are the rights of life and liberty and to these the poorest and humblest man has just as much right as the richest and most influential man in the country." Maxims are powerful rhetorical tools when an audience understands them to be immediately and universally true, and believes their invocation appropriate to the situation. Further, maxims, or aphorisms, not only provide the major premises for deductive arguments, but when used well they vest the speaker with added credibility; that is, the speaker appears sage, perceptively understanding the larger principles at play in a situation. Just so, Harper's formulation regarding government protection; it places her audience of white American women in a difficult dilemma. Is the United States government vicious, because it could prevent lynching but does not? Or is the government weak, because it wishes to protect the victims of lynching but cannot? It must be one or the other. Her audience would prefer to believe that the US government was neither vicious nor weak. However, the psychological dissonance that Harper creates forces the conclusion that the American government should act vigorously and immediately to prevent the lynching of its citizens.

When separated from the text itself, the maxims employed by a speaker often reveal much about the orator's core beliefs, and Harper is no exception. Throughout the middle portion of her speech, her maxims particularly center on the issues of rights and the relationship of those rights to the socio-economic conditions of poverty and ignorance. Secondarily, her maxims argue that the country has a responsibility to improve the welfare of its poorer and more neglected citizens.

> "But there are some rights more precious than the rights of property or the claims of superior intelligence: they are the rights of life and liberty, and to these the poorest and humblest man has just as much right as the richest and most influential man in the country."
>
> "Ignorance and poverty are conditions which men outgrow."
>
> "No child can be blamed because he was born in the midst of squalor, poverty and ignorance, but society is criminal if it permits him to grow up without proper efforts for ameliorating his condition."

In their content, these maxims sound very modern indeed.

In the final section of Harper's speech, addressing the obligation of the United States as a Christian nation, her maxims are even more plentiful, posited one after another, and Biblical in origin.

> "And I, if I be lifted up, will draw all men to me."
>
> "It is better for a man that a millstone were hanged about his neck, and he were drowned in the depths of the sea, than that he should offend one of these little ones that believe in me."
>
> "If ye have respect of persons ye commit sin."
>
> "There is neither Greek nor Jew, circumcision nor uncircumcision, Scythian nor Barbarian, bond nor free, but Christ is all, and in all."

As Harper's list of Biblical maxims lengthens, she effectively conveys the message that in its principles—expressed as maxims—the Bible stands in direct contradiction to American policy regarding African Americans. To the extent that the supporters of segregation, lynching, and discrimination attempted a Biblical justification, their arguments were by necessity more sophistic and pedantic. In contrast, Harper's Biblical maxims are simple and direct, and immediately comprehended as condemning the practices of segregation and lynching as immoral and unchristian.

From this final section, Harper smoothly makes the transition into her peroration, in which continues her focus on the duties of a Christian nation while subtly recalling the earlier sections regarding the nation's duty to protect its citizens' lives and liberties. She refers to "American" Christianity and broadly references the "politicians" fretfully asking: "What shall we do with the weaker races?" She then invokes a final Biblical maxim, followed by the concluding thesis of her speech: "I hold that Jesus Christ answered that question nearly two thousand years since. 'Whatsoever ye would that men should do to you, do you even so to them.' When his religion fully permeates our civilization, and moulds our national life, the drink traffic will be abolished, the Indian question answered, and the negro problem solved." Harper's speech, replete with maxims, has thus come full circle, drawing on established maxims to create one final maxim of its own: the concluding sentence of her speech.

Among other rhetorical devices, Harper particularly employs clear organization as well as a series of pointed maxims in constructing her well-reasoned, well-argued speech. However, "Duty to Dependent Races," like many of her speeches, is notable not only for the care with which she develops her arguments, but also for the poetic language that distinguish the oration. Throughout the speech, the imagery, word choice, and sentence construction combine to make this poetic, but not necessarily florid, oratory.

Surveying Harper's choice of words in the speech, her strong verbs and adjectives particularly evidence a poetic mind at work. Harper's active metaphors create movement and help the audience visualize her points: justice is "trampled" upon, pity "bestowed," a people are in danger of being "dashed," fields "drenched" with blood, mountains were "heaved up," and vales have been "crowned" with fertility. Vivid adjectives are slightly less plentifully used, but still present, especially the closer the speech approaches its conclusion: "noble enthusiasm," "the crimson hand of war," "uplifting power," "degrading influence," and "fretful controversy."

Harper makes pronounced use of imagery in her speech. Similes, for example, convey her message poetically: men "scattered their wealth like chaff," "schools have sprung up like wells in the desert dust," and "I think of organized Christianity as a stream ploughing through different strata of earth, and partaking of the nature of the soil through which it percolates." Harper's metaphors also evoke rich poetic comparisons: for example the perversions of Christianity "are the shadow that has followed its sunshine and hindered its unfulfilled mission." In vivid imagery, Harper describes through personification "a degenerate Christianity sitting by the dishonored tomb of American slavery and remaining amid the graves of the dead past still virtually says to millions of God's poor children: 'Stand by thyself. Come not near me, for I am whiter than thou.'" Or, making the argument that a nation built on injustice cannot long endure, she proposes that "a man might just as well attempt to play with the thunderbolts of heaven and expect to escape unscathed, as for a nation to trample on justice and right and evade the divine penalty." Harper's passage on the progress of African Americans after the Civil War is representative. After positing two maxims—that rights of life and liberty are more precious than property or claims of superior intelligence, and that "ignorance and poverty are conditions which men outgrow"—Harper poetically introduces the gains made by African Americans: "Since the sealed volume was opened by the crimson hand of war, in spite of entailed ignorance, poverty, opposition and a heritage of scorn, schools have sprung up like wells in the desert." The ensuing list of gains is recited more prosaically—two million have learned to read; African Americans are now journalists; have earned college diplomas, created orphanages, and accumulated wealth. Her poetic turns are neatly assimilated into her speech, rather than overwhelming it.

Harper has several such notable poetic passages, particularly in those places where she employs parallel grammatical constructions, either of comparison (isocolon) or contrast (antithesis): for example, "As long as there are such cases as moral irresponsibility, mental imbecility; as long as Potiphar's wife stands in the world's pillory of shame, no man should be deprived of life or liberty without due process of law"; and "It is the pride of Caste which opposes the spirit of Christ." Perhaps her most poetic rhetorical moment occurs in the middle of the speech. Examining the charge that African Americans are poor and ignorant—and therefore not qualified to exercise the right to vote—Harper poses a rhetorical question to which she immediately posts a vivid reply: "It is said that the negro is ignorant. But why is he ignorant? It comes with ill grace from a man who has put out my eyes to make a parade of my blindness—to reproach me for my poverty when he has wronged me of my money." The understated "ill grace" contrasts sharply with the paradoxical "parade" (almost comical) "of my blindness" (tragic), while the metaphor of blindness sharply conveys the full effect of lack of education (ignorance). The poetic and rhetorical effect is further heightened by the pair of antitheses that reverse each other in their grammatical structure[7] ("a man who has put out my eyes to make a parade of my blindness—to reproach me for my poverty when he has wronged me of my money"). In this passage, Harper as poetic orator is in full force. It is revealing that this highly poetic moment occurs in the middle of her speech. Speakers generally reserve their most poetic expressions for the peroration, as they move towards a climactic conclusion, and Harper's language in her final section and her conclusion are indeed more heavily poetic than the body of the speech. Yet to place her most poetic and ironic line in the middle of the speech—where by its content it does indeed belong—is indicative of her practice to make her poetry work in service of her argument, rather than append her poetic language artificially.

It is hard to determine what effect Harper's speech may have had. The presentations of the NCW were published, but not the discussions or resolutions that may have followed. In 1893, the WCTU, for which Harper was an officer, and Frances Willard, president of the NCW, was also president, passed an antilynching resolution. That resolution was controversial, however, because its wording did as much to condone lynching by validating the alleged concerns about rape as it did to condemn the lawlessness of lynching. Vigorously challenged by Ida B. Wells-Barnett, in 1894, Willard and the WCTU amended its antilynching resolution with one that unequivocally condemned lynching. That resolution was renewed annually until the passage of the Eighteenth Amendment, when the nature of the WCTU as an organization changed dramatically.[8]

Although Harper was a respected African American voice in a number of predominantly white women's organizations such as the NCW and WCTU, she ultimately drifted away from those organizations. In part, that may have been because of advancing age. Towards the end of her life, her daughter became infirm and Frances Harper became her caregiver. Most biographers agree, however, that like many African American women, she became discouraged by the lack of support that even progressive-minded women's organizations such as the WCTU or the National Suffrage Association gave to African American reform issues such as segregation and lynching. Still, "Duty to Dependent Races" stands as a masterpiece of poetic oratory, and is quintessentially Harper. The speech excels in its prose—clearly organized, carefully reasoned—as well as in its poetic imagery and language. It is not surprising that in her day and throughout her life, Frances Ellen Watkins Harper was a highly respected and often listened-to voice of African Americans generally, and of African American women particularly.

Duty to Dependent Races

(Speech to the National Council of Women of the United States)

February 3, 1891
Washington, DC

While Miss Fletcher has advocated the cause of the Indian and negro under the caption of Dependent Races, I deem it a privilege to present the negro, not as a mere dependent asking for Northern sympathy or Southern compassion, but as a member of the body politic who has a claim upon the nation for justice, simple justice, which is the right of every race, upon the government for protection, which is the rightful claim of every citizen, and upon our common Christianity for the best influences which can be exerted for peace on earth and good-will to men.

Our first claim upon the nation and government is the claim for protection to human life. That claim should lie at the basis of our civilization, not simply in theory but in fact. Outside of America, I know of no other civilized country, Catholic, Protestant, or even Mahometan, where men are still lynched, murdered, and even burned for real or supposed crimes. As long as there are such cases as moral irresponsibility, mental imbecility; as long as Potiphar's wife[a] stands in the world's pillory of shame, no man should be deprived of life or liberty without due process of law. A government which has power to tax a man in peace, and draft him in war, should have power to defend his life in the hour of peril. A government which can protect and defend its citizens from wrong and outrage and does not is vicious. A government which would do it and cannot is weak; and where human life is insecure through either weakness or viciousness in the administration of

a. In Genesis 39, Potiphar was an Egyptian officer of the Pharaoh who took Joseph in as overseer of his household. When Joseph refused the seductive advances of Potiphar's wife, she falsely accused him of attempted rape, and he was wrongfully imprisoned.

law, there must be a lack of justice, and where this is wanting nothing can make up the deficiency.

The strongest nation on earth cannot afford to deal unjustly towards its weakest and feeblest members. A man might just as well attempt to play with the thunderbolts of heaven and expect to escape unscathed, as for a nation to trample on justice and right and evade the divine penalty. The reason our nation snapped asunder in 1861 was because it lacked the cohesion of justice; men poured out their blood like water, scattered their wealth like chaff, summoned to the field the largest armies the nation had ever seen, but they did not get their final victories which closed the rebellion till they clasped hands with the negro, and marched with him abreast to freedom and to victory. I claim for the negro protection in every right with which the government has invested him. Whether it was wise or unwise, the government has exchanged the fetters on his wrist for the ballot in his right hand, and men cannot vitiate his vote by fraud, or intimidate the voter by violence, without being untrue to the genius and spirit of our government, and bringing demoralization into their own political life and ranks. Am I here met with the objection that the negro is poor and ignorant, and the greatest amount of land, capital, and intelligence is possessed by the white race, and that in a number of States negro suffrage means negro supremacy? But is it not a fact that both North and South power naturally gravitates into the strongest hands, and is there any danger that a race who were deemed so inferior as to be only fitted for slavery, and social and political ostracism, has in less than one generation become so powerful that, if not hindered from exercising the right of suffrage, it will dominate over a people who have behind them ages of dominion, education, freedom, and civilization, a people who have had poured into their veins the blood of some of the strongest races on earth? More than a year has passed since Mr. Grady[b] said, I believe, "We do not directly fear the political domination of the blacks, but that they are ignorant and easily deluded, impulsive and therefore easily led, strong of race instinct and therefore clannish, without information and therefore without political convictions, passionate and therefore easily excited, poor, irresponsible, and with no idea of the integrity of suffrage and

b. Henry Grady (1850–1889): Editor of the *Atlanta Constitution* and an avid promoter of what he called the "New South," which had put slavery and the Civil War behind it and merited Northern investment and favorable political treatment from the Federal government. His most famous speech was titled "The New South" and delivered in 1886. It is unclear which specific speech or article Harper is referencing here.

therefore easily bought. The fear is that this vast swarm, ignorant, purchasable, will be impacted and controlled by desperate and unscrupulous white men and made to hold the balance of power when white men are divided." Admit for one moment that every word here is true, and that the whole race should be judged by its worst, and not its best members, does any civilized country legislate to punish a man before he commits a crime?

It is said the negro is ignorant. But why is he ignorant? It comes with ill grace from a man who has put out my eyes to make a parade of my blindness,—to reproach me for my poverty when he has wronged me of my money. If the negro is ignorant, he has lived under the shadow of an institution which, at least in part of the country, made it a crime to teach him to read the name of the ever-blessed Christ. If he is poor, what has become of the money he has been earning for the last two hundred and fifty years? Years ago it was said cotton fights and cotton conquers for American slavery. The negro helped build up that great cotton power in the South, and in the North his sigh was in the whir of its machinery, and his blood and tears upon the warp and woof of its manufactures.

But there are some rights more precious than the rights of property or the claims of superior intelligence: they are the rights of life and liberty and to these the poorest and humblest man has just as much right as the richest and most influential man in the country. Ignorance and poverty are conditions which men outgrow. Since the sealed volume was opened by the crimson hand of war, in spite of entailed ignorance, poverty, opposition, and a heritage of scorn, schools have sprung up like wells in the desert dust. It has been estimated that about two millions have learned to read. Colored men and women have gone into journalism. Some of the first magazines in the country have received contributions from them. Learned professions have given them diplomas. Universities have granted them professorships. Colored women have combined to shelter orphaned children. Tens of thousands have been contributed by colored persons for the care of the aged and infirm. Instead of the old slave-pen of former days, imposing and commodious are edifices of prayer and praise. Millions of dollars have flowed into the pockets of the race, and freed people have not only been able to provide for themselves, but reach out their hands to impoverished owners.

Has the record of the slave been such as to warrant the belief that permitting him to share citizenship with others in the country is inimical to the welfare of the nation? Can it be said that he lacks patriotism, or a readiness to make common cause with the nation in the hour of peril? In the days of the American Revolution some of the first blood which was shed flowed from the veins of a colored man, and among the latest words that died upon his lips before they paled in death was, "Crush them underfoot," meaning the British guards.[c] To him Boston has given a monument. In or after 1812 they received from General Jackson the plaudit, "I knew you would endure hunger and thirst and all the hardships of war. I knew that you loved the land of your nativity, and that, like ourselves, you had to defend all that is most dear; but you have surpassed my hopes. I have found in you, united to all these qualities, that noble enthusiasm which impels to great deeds." And in our late civil conflict colored men threw their lives into the struggle, rallied around the old flag when others were trampling it underfoot and riddling it with bullets. Colored people learned to regard that flag as a harbinger of freedom and bring their most reliable information to the Union army, to share their humble fare with escaping prisoner; to be faithful when others were faithless and help turn the tide of battle in favor of the nation. While nearly two hundred thousand joined the Union army, others remained on the old plantations; widows, wives, aged men, and helpless children were left behind, when the master was at the front trying to put new rivets in their chains, and yet was there a single slave who took advantage of the master's absence to invade the privacy of his home, or wreak a summary vengeance on those whose "defenceless condition should have been their best defence?"

Instead of taking the ballot from his hands, teach him how to use it, and to add his quota to the progress, strength, and durability of the nation. Let the nation, which once consented to his abasement under a system which made it a crime to teach him to read his Bible, feel it a privilege as well as a duty to reverse the old processes of the past by supplanting his darkness with light, not simply by providing the negro, but the whole region in which he lives, with national education. No child can be blamed because he was born in the midst of squalor, poverty, and ignorance, but society is criminal if it permits him to grow up without proper efforts for ameliorating his condition.

Some months since, when I was in South Carolina, where I addressed a number of colored schools, I was informed that white children were in the factories, beginning from eight to ten years old, with working hours from six to seven o'clock; and one day, as a number of white children were

---

c. Harper is referencing Crispus Attucks (1723?–1770), an African American who was one of five Americans killed in 1770 as part of the "Boston Massacre." Most accounts report Attucks as the first of the Americans to be shot by the British in the incident, and thus shed the first blood of the American Revolution.

wending their way apparently from the factory, I heard a colored man say, "I pity these children." It was a strange turning of the tables to hear a colored man in South Carolina bestowing pity on white children because of neglect in their education. Surely the world does move. When parents are too poor or selfish to spare the labor of their children from the factories, and the State too indifferent or short-sighted to enforce their education by law, then let the Government save its future citizens from the results of cupidity in the parents or short-sightedness in the State. If to-day there is danger from a mass of ignorance voting, may there not be a danger even greater, and that is a mass of "ignorance that does not vote"? If there is danger that an ignorant mass might be compacted to hold the balance of power where white men are divided politically, might not that same mass, if kept ignorant and disfranchised, be used by wicked men, whose weapons may be bombs and dynamite, to dash themselves against the peace and order of society? To-day the hands of the negro are not dripping with dynamite. We do not read of his flaunting the red banners of anarchy in the face of the nation, nor plotting in beer-saloons to overthrow existing institutions, nor spitting on the American flag. Once that flag was to him an ensign of freedom. Let our Government resolve that as far as that flag extends every American-born child shall be able to read upon its folds liberty for all and chains for none.

And now permit me to make my final claim, and that is a claim upon our common Christianity. I believe in the Christianity of the Christ of Calvary, but I cannot believe in all its saddest and most terrible perversions. They are the shadow that has followed its sunshine and hindered its unfulfilled mission. I think of organized Christianity as a stream ploughing through different strata of earth, and partaking of the nature of the soil through which it percolates. It came to Latin races, but its shadow among them was the inquisition devising its tortures and the *auto-da-fe*[d] lighting its fires. It came to Slavic people, and we have the Greek Church with a background of Anti-Semitic persecutions and the horrors of Siberian prisons. Among English-speaking races we have weaker races victimized, a discontented Ireland, and a darkest England. In America we have had an emasculated Christianity,—a Protestantism shorn of protesting strength, which would sing—"Nothing in my hands I bring, / Simply to thy cross I cling."[e] When it should have brought in its hands the sacrifices of justice and mercy and

d. *Auto-da-fe*: During the Inquisition, the public announcement of the sentence for one found guilty of heresy; the term is also applied to the act of burning the heretic to death.
e. The opening lines of the third stanza of the hymn "Rock of Ages."

broken every yoke and let the oppressed go free. Degenerate Israel remaining amid the graves, with the host of abominable things in her vessels, said to those whom she rejected, "Stand by thyself. Come not near me; I am holier than thou."[f] A degenerate Christianity sitting by the dishonored tomb of American slavery and remaining amid the graves of the dead past still virtually says to millions of God's poor children, "Stand by thyself. Come not near me, for I am whiter than thou."

Underlying this racial question, if I understand it aright, is one controlling idea, not simply that the negro is ignorant; *that* he is outgrowing; not that he is incapable of valor in war or adaptation in peace. On fields all drenched with blood he made his record in war, abstained from lawless violence when left on the plantation, and received his freedom in peace with moderation. But he holds in this Republic the position of an alien race among a people impatient of a rival. And in the eyes of some it seems that no valor redeems him, no social advancement nor individual development wipes off the ban which clings to him. It is the pride of Caste which opposes the spirit of Christ, and the great work to which American Christianity is called is a work of Christly reconciliation. God has heaved up your mountains with grandeur, flooded your rivers with majesty, crowned your vales with fertility, and enriched your mines with wealth. Excluding Alaska, you have, I think, nearly three hundred millions of square miles. Be reconciled to God for making a man black, permitting him to become part of your body politic, and sharing one rood or acre of our goodly heritage. Be reconciled to the Christ of Calvary, who said, "And I, if I be lifted up will draw all men to me,"[g] and "It is better for a man that a millstone were hanged about his neck, and he were drowned in the depths of the sea, than that he should offend one of these little ones that believe in me."[h] Forgive the early adherents of Christianity who faced danger and difficulty and stood as victors by the side of Death, who would say, "I perceive that God is no respecter of persons."[i] "If ye have respect of persons ye commit sin."[j] "There is neither Greek nor Jew, circumcision nor uncircumcision, Scythian nor Barbarian, bond nor free, but Christ is all, and in all."[k]

f. Isaiah 65:5.
g. John 12:32.
h. Luke 17:2. A parallel passage may be found in Matthew 18:6, but Harper's quotation is from the King James Bible translation of Luke.
i. Acts 10:34.
j. James 2:9.
k. Colossians 3:11.

What I ask of American Christianity is not to show us more creeds, but more of Christ; not more rites and ceremonies, but more religion glowing with love and replete with life,—a religion which will be to all weaker races an uplifting power, and not a degrading influence. Jesus Christ has given us a platform of love and duty from which all oppression and selfishness is necessarily excluded. While politicians may stumble on the barren mountains of fretful controversy and ask in strange bewilderment, "What shall we do with weaker races?" I hold that Jesus Christ answered that question nearly two thousand years since. "Whatsoever ye would that men should do to you, do you even so to them."[1] When His religion fully permeates our civilization, and moulds our national life, the drink traffic will be abolished, the Indian question answered, and the negro problem solved.

1. Matthew 7:12.

Ida B. Wells-Barnett

Lynch Law in All Its Phases

Ida B. Wells-Barnett was unique among African American orators of the late nineteenth and early twentieth centuries. Although the African American community of the day could boast of many outstanding, strong-minded women orators—such as Mary Church Terrell, Charlotte Hawkins Brown, Frances Watkins Harper, and Anna Julia Cooper—none of Wells-Barnett's contemporaries embraced as confrontational and "masculine" a style as Wells. She was a passionate campaigner for her cause who delivered her message with a "dispassionate" objectivity, reserving her emotional appeals for select moments in her speeches. Although generally interested in all reforms that would advance her race and her gender, she most determinedly pursued the resolution of one particularly American problem: lynching. So strong an antilynching advocate was she that her reputation became inextricably linked with the cause. One cannot survey the history of the antilynching movement without featuring Ida B. Wells-Barnett's prominent role in it.

Ida B. Wells was born on July 16, 1862, in Holly Springs, Mississippi, the oldest child of James Wells and Elizabeth Warrenton, two slaves who would become legally married after emancipation in 1865. At the age of eighteen, James Wells, the son of the plantation owner, had been apprenticed by his father to a carpenter and had moved from the rural plantation to the town of Holly Springs. There he met "Lizzie" Warrenton, who worked as a cook to a contractor in town. After emancipation, James continued to work as a skilled tradesman for the carpenter he had served as an apprentice. Seeing education as the means to financial and legal security, the Wells family placed a heavy emphasis on the importance of schooling, and James Wells became a trustee of the newly formed Rust College (later, Shaw University), which Ida began attending when fifteen. In 1878, both of her parents and a brother passed away during a yellow fever epidemic. As the eldest child, Wells was suddenly the head of the household; she dropped out of college to become a teacher and, with the help of some relatives and friends, to assume responsibility for raising her siblings.[1]

Although teaching provided a stable income and an opportunity for Wells to work in a middle-class profession, it was not an occupation she enjoyed. Initially, she taught in county schools, first in Mississippi and then in Tennessee. In Tennessee, she moved the family to Memphis while she taught ten miles away and, on her weekend railroad commutes, actively began to confront the issues of segregation and civil rights. In 1881, Tennessee trains had become legally segregated under Jim Crow laws, but African Americans could still purchase first-class tickets to the "whites only" cars, and enforcement of the segregation codes was left to the conductors. In September 1883, when Wells refused to leave her seat in the first-class car and move to the "smoker" car, the conductor attempted to remove her by force. Wells resisted, even to the point of biting the conductor's hand, but fellow white passengers "aided" the conductor in evicting Wells. As had other African Americans, Wells sued the railroad. Wells won the initial verdict, but the railroad appealed. Meanwhile, Wells had again been evicted from a first-class railroad seat—although this time she did not physically resist—and she sued the railroad and again won the case in lower court. In the Tennessee State Supreme Court, however, the railroad prevailed. Despite overwhelming testimony to the contrary, the court agreed with the railroad's claim that the accommodations of the first-class car and the smoker car were "alike in every respect as to comfort, convenience and safety" and that Wells's resistance and subsequent lawsuit were the work of a troublemaker, designed to "harass" the railroad and the state.[2] From this experience, Wells seems to have drawn at least two lessons that affected her later oratory: that she needed overwhelming evidence in the face of prejudice and discrimination, and that any African American who directly demanded equality would be branded a "troublemaker."[3]

Out of her railroad lawsuits also grew her career change from teaching to journalism. Her first journalistic story chronicled her contest with the railroad and was published first in a Memphis African American–owned newspaper, then picked up as a national story by Thomas Fortune's *New York Freeman*. Encouraged by her success, she continued writing articles for local and national publications under the pen name "Iola," at first for no remuneration but then, beginning in 1886, for pay. Almost from the beginning, Wells's writing was typically confrontational and controversial. Unafraid to criticize publicly any perceived failings of African American leaders, it is not surprising that she made important friends as well as enemies in the African American community. In 1888, Wells began pursuing journalism as a career, although she did not leave teaching until 1891, when her teaching contract was not renewed after she had published a scathing article criticizing the lack of funding for African American schools in the city. Soon known as the "Princess of the Press," in June 1889, she purchased a one-third interest in the recently founded *Memphis Free Speech and Headlight.*[4] As chronicled in her speech, "Lynch Law in All Its Phases," as well as her autobiography, *Crusade for Justice*, it was a Memphis lynching and the *Free Speech*'s editorials on that affair that catapulted Ida B. Wells from political journalist to journalistic activist. After the March 1892 lynching of three African American grocers, Wells published a biting attack on the lynch mob and the city of Memphis in the *Free Speech.* In that article, she rebuffed the "thread-bare lie" that lynching occurred as an answer to the crime of rape, countering instead that it was being used as a weapon of intimidation to deprive African Americans of their rights, liberties, and property.[5] On May 27, 1892, the *Free Speech* building was ransacked and Wells's life threatened. She was fortunately away in New York at the time, and she remained up North, where in the fall of 1892 she published the pamphlet *Southern Horrors, Lynch Law in All Its Phases* and embarked upon a lecture tour devoted to her antilynching crusade.[6] "Lynch Law in All Its Phases," a lecture delivered in Boston as part of this tour, is the only complete text of the lecture that was published. As with many such public speaking tours, Wells recorded that she repeated substantially the same lecture at her various stops. It is clear from this text, however, that, like most such lecturers, Wells also modified the lecture as needed, updating it as new events occurred.[7] As with all of Wells's speeches and writings, "Lynch Law in All Its Phases" is most notable for the direct and vivid language of its claims, the detailed use of evidence, and the employment of language that was paradoxically dispassionate even as Wells expressed strong, emotional appeals.

From her experience with the railroad lawsuit, Wells understood that prejudice would lead many in her audience to dismiss her claims even when the evidence overwhelmingly disproved their prejudice. Rhetorically, she attempted to counter this problem in two ways: by consistently framing her claims simply and directly, and by combining those direct claims with detailed and voluminous evidence. Although an audience's biases could still lead them irrationally to an erroneous conclusion, Wells was determined to make complacency as difficult on the audience as possible. There would be no mistaking her claim nor the evidence that supported it.

The body of the speech is initiated with an extended narrative that was essentially the most recent chapter in the autobiography of Ida B. Wells, which serves to establish the reason that Wells has appeared to speak about lynching. The story does not begin with the Memphis lynching, but rather with Wells's evolution from teacher to journalist. The very first sentence of the speech justifies the narrative she is about to tell: "I am before the American people to day through no inclination of my own, but because of a deep seated conviction that the country at large does not know the extent to which lynch law prevails in parts of the Republic nor the conditions which force into exile those who speak the truth." Although the thesis of the speech will not directly involve the speaker herself—it will instead be about the extent to which lynch law prevails in parts of the Republic—Wells, as the speaker, figures prominently in establishing that case. The tumultuous events of her story lead her to speak "through no inclination of my own," and her "deep seated conviction" initially establishes the thesis; she is representative of those forced into exile because they spoke the truth. Wells interrupts this narrative in order to put forward the claims the speech will develop: that lynch law and mob rule exist in the South; that they constitute a "government by the mob" resulting in "lawlessness, murder and outrage"; that these are "repeated attacks on the life, liberty and happiness"; and that the justification for these lynchings—the outrage that African American men are raping white women and children—is "as false as it is foul."

After outlining these claims, Wells renews her autobiography: "Born and reared in the South, I had never expected to live elsewhere." What appears in this speech is, however, a severely truncated autobiography. She briefly relates that she had been a vocal advocate of race improvement, "preaching" in her columns "the doctrine of self-help, thrift and economy." When, however, she criticized the Memphis School Board for severely underfunding the African American schools—institutions that could abet the acquisition of self-help, thrift, and economy—she was summarily dismissed as a teacher despite having provided seven years of satisfactory service. Now turned full-time journalist, Wells was able to make the *Free Speech* a successful business because there was a sizeable middle-class population of African

Americans in Memphis. This portion of her autobiography accomplishes several purposes: it repeats her claim that she has reluctantly undertaken the role of antilynching advocate; her experience with the Memphis School Board foreshadows the burning of the *Free Speech* building and threats made upon Wells's life; and it establishes the fact that in Memphis, there were many middle-class African Americans who were capable of competing with the whites, African Americans whom whites would want to control through lynching.

In Wells's situation, the first purpose of this autobiography carried special importance beyond simply establishing her credibility as a reluctant witness—that is, one whose statement and revelation risks doing damage to one's own interests. From her experiences as a plaintiff and journalist, and even early in her antilynching lecture tour, Wells was acutely aware that, as a woman speaking as an agitator and speaking about the sexual issue of rape, she was stepping far beyond the traditional sphere allowed to women. Wells also knew that as an unmarried African American woman, criticism of her would be derogatory and spiteful. It was important that she do everything possible to suggest that she had accepted the role of advocate only reluctantly, forced by circumstances to speak the truth because there was no one else in a position to speak as effectively to the issue at this time.

The story of Calvin McDowell, Will Stewart, and Thomas Moss, the grocers lynched because they stood up to a white competitor, is representative of Wells's style. The story is amply detailed—the initial incident took place at the Curve, about a mile outside city limits; the young men consulted a lawyer about their rights to self-defense; Thomas Moss was "not allowed to eat the food his wife prepared for him"; the deputies "attacked" were wearing civilian clothing; a nearby locomotive "let off steam and blew the whistle to deaden the sound of the firing" (of the three men). The claims that the story supports are directly stated: "these men were murdered"; Barrett, the white competitor, "had indeed kept his word, and by aid of the authorities destroyed the People's Grocery Company root and branch"; and "the mob did what the law could not be made to do, as a lesson to the Afro-American that he must not shoot a white man, no matter what the provocation." As Wells then clearly summarizes the story's moral: "It was our first object lesson in the doctrine of white supremacy; an illustration of the South's cardinal principle that no matter what the attainments, character or standing of an Afro-American, the laws of the South will not protect him against a white man."

As with most of Wells's stories, this one is filled with irony. She juxtaposes the jury's finding that the lynching "was done by unknown men" with the detailed, "two column account" of the lynching that appeared the next day in the Memphis *Appeal-Avalanche.* "A real estate dealer" remarked to an African American that he did not know why the community was complaining, after all the white citizenry had "intended to kill every one of those thirty-one" African Americans who had been present at the confrontation "but concluded to let all go but the 'leaders.'" Wells's ironic conclusion of the story: "They did let all go to the penitentiary."

After specifically quoting at length from the Memphis papers, evidencing their agitation that caused the lynch mob to search for the *Free Speech*'s owners and the paper's building to be ransacked, Wells continues with other stories of Southern lynchings. She recounts the 1891 lynching of three Italian citizens in New Orleans, a crime for which the federal government apologized and paid reparations. No such apologies or reparations were made or offered when African Americans were lynched: for example, the Paris, Texas, lynching of Henry Smith, in which he was burned to death; the Indianola, Mississippi, lynching in which a man was accused of raping a twelve year old girl, but wherein the "victim" was in fact over eighteen and the liaison consensual; the murder of Will Lewis, lynched because he was "drunk and saucy to white folks"; or the African American woman hanged for poisoning the white woman for whom she cooked, although it was later discovered that the white woman's husband had been the murderer.

Wells's lectures and writings of this period are also marked by the detailed use of statistical evidence. She reports a table that describes the rise of lynchings over the previous ten year period, from 1882 to 1892. She notes that there have been "a dozen black men" lynched since the start of the new year, which was "not yet two months old." Of those lynched in the previous decade, the majority had not even been charged with the crime of rape, the widespread "rationale" for the rise of lynching. Wells's statistics are more specific than simply making a claim about a majority: "253 [were charged] with murder, 44 with robbery, 37 with incendiarism, 32 with reasons unstated . . . 27 with race prejudice, 13 with quarreling with white men, 10 with making threats, 7 with rioting, 5 with miscegenation, 4 with burglary." Rhetorically, the precision of Wells's statistical evidence stands in stark contrast to the apologists' sweeping and typical declarations that lynching is an "understandable" response to the crime of rape, which Wells also cites specifically in her speech so that the differences between her evidence and their claims cannot be overlooked.

As with her opening narrative, Wells regularly advances claims that are simple, direct, and categorical, claims that cannot be unintentionally misconstrued. Of course, the audience cannot appreciate the problem, because those living outside the South "cannot conceive how such a condition of affairs prevails so near them." The audience can, however, comprehend the new evil if they will recall that the Southern institution of slavery "was not only a monster but a tyrant": "That same tyrant is at work under a new name and guise. The lawlessness which has been here described is like unto that which prevailed under slavery. *The very same forces are at work now as then*" (emphasis hers). "The rule of the mob is absolute," she categorically and clearly declares to the audience, for "the South is as vindictive and bitter as ever." "Do you ask the remedy?" she inquires and then answers: "A public sentiment strong against lawlessness must be aroused."

Although her style is primarily plain and direct, Wells strategically employs vivid language to add an emotional appeal. "Not a week passes," she tells her audience, "but some poor soul is violently ushered into eternity on this trumped up charge [of rape]." "Men have literally been roasted to death," she observes, "to appease the fury of Southern mobs." She recounts stories of lynchings paradoxically, her journalistic objectivity combining with emotion-laden content to make the accounts even more evocative through vivid description: "The Texarkana man, Ed Coy, was charged with assaulting a white woman. A mob pronounced him guilty, strapped him to a tree, chipped the flesh from his body, poured coal oil over him and the woman in the case set fire to him. The country looked on and in many cases applauded, because it was published that this man had violated the honor of the white woman, although he protested his innocence to the last. Judge Tourjee in the Chicago *Inter Ocean* of recent date says investigation has shown that Ed Coy had financially supported this woman, (who was known to be of bad character,) and her drunken husband for over a year previous to the burning." Wells extended description of the burning of Henry Smith is even more detailed and graphic.

The story of Ed Coy, burned for "assaulting" a woman he had befriended and aided, typifies Wells's recurring use of irony. Bitter irony is present in her story of the Memphis lynchings, when the jury found that the prisoners had been lynched by "persons unknown," even while the next day's newspaper had carried a detailed account of the lynching. Although a New Orleans jury had acquitted the three Italians of murder, "the good, law abiding citizens of New Orleans" seized them from their jail cells and "lynched them at high noon." Wells is critical of the prevailing opinion in the North that, for the sake of restoring full union to the country, a blind eye needed to be turned towards lynching and other discriminatory practices on the rise in the South. "The South spares nobody else's feelings," Wells observes, "and it seems a queer logic that when it comes to a question of right, involving lives of citizens and the honor of the government, the South's feelings must be respected and spared." She does not hesitate to reveal the full irony of the situation: "And yet this Christian nation, the flower of the nineteenth century civilization, says it can do nothing to stop this inhuman slaughter."

Wells's Boston speech was well received by the African American community as well as by progressive whites. The Tremont Temple passed a resolution of strong support, applauding her "pathetic," that is, emotion-filled, "and unimpassioned recital of the horrible atrocities perpetuated in various parts of the South."[8] Reflecting on this lecture tour generally, the *American Citizen* wrote that "she is a heroine, would we had more with such zeal and nobility of womanhood."[9] The *Washington Bee* wrote about her opening lecture, delivered in New York, that is was "one of the finest testimonials ever rendered by an Afro-American."[10] Of *Southern Horrors: Lynch Law in All Its Phases*, the 1892 pamphlet based largely on Wells's lecture of this time, Frederick Douglass wrote: "There has been no word equal to it in convincing power. I have spoken, but my word is feeble in comparison. You give what you know and testify from actual knowledge. You have dealt with the facts with painstaking fidelity and left those naked and uncontradicted facts to speak for themselves."[11] Shortly after her 1892–93 lecture tour of the Northeast, Wells twice toured England, where British observers also noted her style of blending direct and simple claims with powerfully charged content and the occasionally vivid language that heightened the emotional effect of her discourse. The *Liverpool Daily Post* wrote that her delivery was "quiet and unimpassioned but earnest and forcible."[12] Richard Armstrong's letter to the *Christian Register* observed that she displayed "singular refinement, dignity and self-restraint, . . . nor have I ever met any 'agitator' so cautious and unimpassioned in speech. But by this marvelous self-restraint itself, she moves us more profoundly."[13] The *Manchester Guardian* judged that "her indictment is all the more telling from the absence of rhetoric."[14] Some in the Northern white press gave similar accounts. A reporter for the *New York Sun* wrote that she "spoke in the quiet undemonstrative style which is more eloquent than any of the tricks of oratory."[15] Not surprisingly, Wells was pilloried in the Southern press. Her gender and her unmarried status particularly attracted vicious attacks. The *Memphis Commercial* referred to "this Wells wench" and claimed that she was a "black harlot" who wanted a white husband for herself.[16] Reporting on her British tour, the *Memphis Appeal-Avalanche* railed that her audiences were composed of "credulous Englishmen under the ministrations of a negro adventuress of decidedly shady character."[17] The *Washington Post*, while not attacking her character, also called her veracity into question. Wells, the paper declared, focused only on the lynching of African Americans and ignored the lynchings of whites, and she "misrepresented" the strength of America's general opposition to the practice of lynching. Although Wells's "heart is evidently all right," she was "mistaken in judgment."[18] Undoubtedly, it would be attacks like these—on her character as well as the accuracy of her claims—criticisms that echoed the Tennessee Supreme Court's dismissal of her railroad lawsuit, that convinced her that a dispassionate style combined with voluminous evidence told in narratives and numbers, was her wisest rhetorical strategy.

Upon her return to the United States, Wells took up residence in Chicago, where she met and married Ferdinand Lee Barnett, editor of the *Chicago Conservator* and later an attorney and public official. In Chicago, Wells-Barnett was very active in the African American woman's club movement as well as in local civic reforms. She remained visible at the national level and served as a founding member of the National Association for the Advancement of Colored People (NAACP). Her direct and often confrontational style made her enemies as well as friends. She spoke her mind readily and truthfully in her private and public discourse. Although she spoke, wrote, and worked on behalf of many reforms to benefit the cause of civil rights, she remained always and especially committed to the antilynching cause. In spring of 1892, Wells had attended and spoken at an antilynching meeting in New York City. She was, however, barely noticed. After the Memphis events, however, Wells found her voice and her message, both in lectures and print. As biographer Linda McMurray wrote, "within two years . . . Ida B. Wells would be the best-known figure in the anti-lynching movement."[19] Although others lent their voices to oppose lynching, none matched Wells's, for none had Wells's remarkable ability to speak coolly and truthfully but also forcefully about a practice so unjust, inhuman, and contemptible.

Lynch Law in All Its Phases

February 13, 1893
Boston, Massachusetts

I am before the American people to day through no inclination of my own, but because of a deep seated conviction that the country at large does not know the extent to which lynch law prevails in parts of the Republic nor the conditions which force into exile those who speak the truth. I cannot believe that the apathy and indifference which so largely obtains regarding mob rule is other than the result of ignorance of the true situation. And yet, the observing and thoughtful must know that in one section, at least, of our common country, a government of the people, by the people, and for the people, means a government by the mob; where the land of the free and home of the brave means a land of lawlessness, murder and outrage; and where liberty of speech means the license of might to destroy the business and drive from home those who exercise this privilege contrary to the will of the mob.

Repeated attacks on the life, liberty and happiness of any citizen or class of citizens are attacks on distinctive American institutions; such attacks imperiling as they do the foundation of government, law and order, merit the thoughtful consideration of far sighted Americans; not from a standpoint of sentiment, not even so much from a standpoint of justice to a weak race, as from a desire to preserve our institutions. The race problem or negro question, as it has been called, has been omnipresent and all pervading since long before the Afro American was raised from the degradation of the slave to the dignity of the citizen. It has never been settled because the right methods have not been employed in the solution. It is the Banquo's ghost of politics, religion, and sociology which will not down at the bidding of those who are tormented with its ubiquitous appearance on every occasion. Times without number, since invested with citizenship, the race has been indicted for ignorance, immorality and general worthlessness declared guilty and executed by its self constituted judges.

The operations of law do not dispose of negroes fast enough, and lynching bees have become the favorite pastime of the South. As excuse for the same, a new cry, as false as it is foul, is raised in an effort to blast race character, a cry which has proclaimed to the world that virtue and innocence are violated by Afro-Americans who must be killed like wild beasts to protect womanhood and childhood. Born and reared in the South, I had never expected to live elsewhere. Until this past year I was one among those who believed the condition of masses gave large excuse for the humiliations and proscriptions under which we labored; that when wealth, education and character became more feral among us, the cause being removed the effect would cease, and justice being accorded to all alike. I shared the general belief that good newspapers entering regularly the homes of our people in every state could do more to bring about this result than any agency. Preaching the doctrine of self help, thrift and economy every week, they would be the teachers to those who had been deprived of school advantages, yet were making history every day and train to think for themselves our mental children of a larger growth.

And so, three years ago last June, I became editor and part owner of the Memphis *Free Speech*. As editor, I had occasion to criticize the city School Board's employment of inefficient teachers and poor school buildings for Afro-American children. I was in the employ of that board at the time, and at the close of that school term one year ago, was not re elected to a position I had held in the city schools for seven years. Accepting the decision of the Board of Education, I set out to make a race newspaper pay, a thing which older and wiser heads said could not be done. But there were enough of our people in Memphis and surrounding territory to support a paper, and I believed they would do so. With nine months hard work the circulation increased from 1,500 to 3,500; in twelve months it was on a good paying basis. Throughout the Mississippi Valley in Arkansas, Tennessee and Mississippi on plantations and in towns, the demand for and interest in the paper increased among the masses. The newsboys who would not sell it on the trains, voluntarily testified that they had never known colored people to demand a paper so eagerly.

To make the paper a paying business I became advertising agent, solicitor, as well as editor, and was continually on the go. Wherever I went among the people, I gave them in church, school, public gatherings, and home, the benefit of my honest conviction that maintenance of character, money getting and education would finally solve our problem and that it depended on us to say how soon this would be brought about. This sentiment bore good fruit in Memphis. We had nice homes, representatives in almost every branch of business and profession, and refined society. We had learned helping each other helped all, and every well conducted business by Afro-Americans prospered. With all our proscription in theatres, hotels and railroads, we had never had a lynching and did not believe we could have one. There had been lynchings and brutal outrages of all sorts in our state and those adjoining us, but we had confidence and pride in our city and the majesty of its laws. So far in advance of other Southern cities was ours, we were content to endure the evils we had, to labor and to wait.

But there was a rude awakening. On the morning of March 9, the bodies of three of our best young men were found in an old field horribly shot to pieces. These young men had owned and operated the "People's Grocery," situated at what was known as the Curve, a suburb made up almost entirely of colored people about a mile from city limits. Thomas Moss, one of the oldest letter carriers in the city, was president of the company, Cal McDowell was manager and Will Stewart was a clerk. There were about ten other stockholders, all colored men. The young men were well known and popular and their business flourished, and that of Barrett, a white grocer who kept store there before the "People's Grocery" was established, went down. One day an officer came to the "People's Grocery" and inquired for a colored man who lived in the neighborhood, and for whom the officer had a warrant. Barrett was with him and when McDowell said he knew nothing as to the whereabouts of the man for whom they were searching, Barrett, not the officer, then accused McDowell of harboring the man, and McDowell gave the lie. Barrett drew his pistol and struck McDowell with it; thereupon McDowell who was a tall, fine looking six footer, took Barrett's pistol from him, knocked him down and gave him a good thrashing, while Will Stewart, the clerk, kept the special officer at bay. Barrett went to town, swore out a warrant for their arrest on a charge of assault and battery. McDowell went before the Criminal Court, immediately gave bond and returned to his store. Barrett then threatened (to use his own words) that he was going to clean out the whole store. Knowing how anxious he was to destroy their business, these young men consulted a lawyer who told them they were justified in defending themselves if attacked, as they were a mile beyond city limits and police protection. They accordingly armed several of their friends not to assail, but to resist the threatened Saturday night attack. When they saw Barrett enter the front door and a half dozen men at the rear door at 11 o'clock that night, they supposed the attack was on and immediately fired into the crowd, wounding three men. These men, dressed in citizen's clothes, turned out to be deputies who claimed to be hunting for another man for whom they had a warrant, and whom any one of them could have arrested without trouble. When these men found they had fired upon officer of the law, they threw away their firearms and submitted to arrest, confident they should establish their innocence of intent to fire upon officers of the law.

The daily papers in flaming headlines roused the evil passions of whites, denounced these poor boys in unmeasured terms, nor permitted a word in their own defense. The neighborhood of the Curve was searched next day, and about thirty persons were thrown into jail, charged with conspiracy. No communication was to be had with friends any of the three days these men were in jail; bail was refused and Thomas Moss was not allowed to eat the food his wife prepared for him. The judge is reported to have said, "Any one can see them after three days." They were seen after three days, but they were no longer able to respond to the greetings of friends. On Tuesday following the shootings at the grocery, the papers which had made much of the sufferings of the wounded deputies, and promised it would go hard with those who did the shooting, if they died, announced that the officers were all out of danger, and would recover. The friends of the prisoners breathed more easily and relaxed their vigilance. They felt that as the officers would not die, there was no danger that in the heat of passion the prisoners would meet violent death at hands of the mob. Besides, we had such confidence in the law. But the law did not provide capital punishment for shooting which did not kill. So the mob did what the law could not be made to do, as a lesson to the Afro-American that he must not shoot a white man, no matter what the provocation.

The same night after the announcement was made in the papers that the officers would get well, the mob, in obedience to a plan known to every eminent white man in the city, went to the jail between two and three in the morning, dragged out these young men, hatless and shoeless, put them on the yard engine of the railroad which was in waiting just behind the jail, carried them a mile north of the city limits and horribly shot them to death while the locomotive at a given signal let off steam and blew the whistle to deaden the sound of the firing. "It was done by unknown men," said the jury, yet the *Appeal-Avalanche* which goes to press at 3 A.M., had a two column account of the lynching. The papers also told how McDowell got hold of the guns of the mob and as his grasp could not be loosened, his hand was shattered with a pistol ball and all the lower part of his face was torn away. There were four pools of blood found and only three bodies. It was whispered that he, McDowell killed one of the lynchers with his gun, and it is well known that a police man who was seen on the street a few days previous to the lynching, died very suddenly the next day after. "It was done by unknown parties," said the jury, yet the papers told how Tom Moss begged for his life, for the sake of his wife, his little daughter and his unborn infant. They also told us that his last words were, "If you will kill us, turn our faces to the West." All this we learn too late to save these men, even if the law had not been in the hands of their murderers.

When the colored people realized that the flower of our young manhood had been stolen away at night and murdered there was a rush for firearms to avenge the wrong, but no house would sell a colored man a gun; the armory of the Tennessee Rifles, our only colored military company, and of which McDowell was a member, was broken into by order of the Criminal Court judge, and its guns taken. One hundred men and irresponsible boys from fifteen years and up were armed by order of authorities and rushed out to the Curve, where it was reported that the colored people were massing, and at point of the bayonet dispersed these men who could do nothing but talk. The cigars, wines, etc., of the grocery stock were freely used by the mob, who possessed the place on pretence of dispersing the conspiracy. The money drawer was broken into and contents taken. The trunk of Calvin McDowell, who had a room in the store, was broken open, and his clothing, which was not good enough to take away, was throw out and trampled on the floor.

These men were murdered, their stock was attached by creditors and sold for less than one eighth of its cost to that same man Barrett, who is to day running his grocery in the same place. He had indeed kept his word, and by aid of the authorities destroyed the People's Grocery Company root and branch. The relatives of Will Stewart and Calvin McDowell are bereft of their protectors. The baby daughter of Tom Moss, too young to express how she misses her father, toddles to the wardrobe, seizes the legs of the trousers of his letter carrier uniform, hugs and kisses them with evident delight and stretches up her little hands to be taken up into the arms which will nevermore clasp his daughter's form. His wife holds Thomas Moss, Jr., in her arms, upon whose unconscious baby face the tears fall thick and fast when she is thinking of the sad fate of the father he will never see, and of the two helpless children who cling to her for the support she cannot give. Although these men were peaceable, law abiding citizens of this country, we are told there can be no punishment for their murderers nor indemnity for relatives. I have no power to describe the feeling of horror that possessed every member of the race in Memphis when the truth dawned upon us that the protection of the law which we had so long enjoyed was no longer ours; all had been destroyed in a night, and the barriers of the law had been down, and the guardians of the public peace and confidence scoffed into the shadows, and all authority given into the hands of the mob, and innocent men cut down as if they were brutes, the first feeling was one dismay, then intense indignation.

Vengeance was whispered from ear to ear, but sober reflection brought the conviction that it would be extreme folly to seek vengeance when such action meant certain death for the men, and horrible slaughter for the women and children, as one of the evening papers took care to remind us. The power of the State, country and city, and civil authorities and the strong arm of the military power were all on the side of the mob and of lawlessness. Few of our men possessed firearms, our only company's guns were confiscated, and the only white man who would sell a colored man a gun, was himself jailed, and his store closed. We were helpless in our great strength. It was our first object lesson in the doctrine of white supremacy; an illustration of the South's cardinal principle that no matter what the attainments, character or standing of an Afro-American, the laws of the South will not protect him against a white man. There was only one thing we could do, and a great determination seized the people to follow the advice of the martyred Moss, and "turn our faces to the West," whose laws protect all alike. The *Free Speech* supported ministers and leading business men advised the people to leave a community whose laws did not protect them. Hundreds left on foot to walk four hundred miles between Memphis and Oklahoma. A Baptist minister went to the territory, built a church, and took his entire congregation out in less than a month. Another minister sold his church and took his flock to California, and still another has settled in Kansas.

In two months, six thousand persons had left the city and every branch of business began to feel this silent resentment of the outrage, and failure of the authorities to punish lynchers. There were a number of business failures and blocks of houses for rent. The superintendent and treasurer of the street railway company called at the office of the *Free Speech*, to have us urge the colored people again on the street cars. A real estate dealer said to a colored man who returned some property he had been buying on the installment plan: "I don't see what you 'niggers' are cutting up about. You got off light. We first intended to kill every one of those thirty one niggers in jail, but concluded to let all go but the 'leaders.'" They did let all go to the penitentiary. These so-called rioters have since been tried in the Criminal Court for the conspiracy of defending their property, and are now serving terms of three, eight, and fifteen years each in the Tennessee State prison.

To restore the equilibrium and put a stop to the great financial loss, the next move was to get rid of the *Free Speech*, the disturbing element which kept the waters troubled; which would not let the people forget, and in obedience to whose advice nearly six thousand persons had left the city. In casting about for an excuse, the mob found it in the following editorial which appeared in the Memphis *Free Speech*, May 21, 1892: "Eight negroes lynched at Little Rock, Ark., where the citizens broke into the penitentiary and got their man; three near Anniston, Ala., and one in New Orleans, all on the same charge, the new alarm of assaulting white women and near Clarksville, Ga., for killing a white man. The same program of hanging then shooting bullets into the lifeless bodies was carried out to the letter. Nobody in this section of the country believes the old threadbare lie that negro men rape white women. If Southern white men are not careful they will overreach themselves, and public sentiment will have a reaction. A conclusion will then be reached which will be very damaging to the moral reputation of their women." Commenting on this, The *Daily Commercial* of Wednesday following said: "Those negroes who are attempting to make lynching of individuals of their race a means for arousing the worst passions of their kind, are playing with a dangerous sentiment. The negroes well understand that there is no mercy for the negro rapist, and little patience with his defenders. A negro organ printed in this city in a recent issue published the following atrocious paragraph: 'Nobody in this section believes the old threadbare lie that negro men rape white women. If Southern men are not careful they will overreach themselves and public will have a reaction. A conclusion will be reached which will be very damaging to the moral reputation of their women.' The fact that a black scoundrel is allowed to live and utter such loathsome and repulsive calumnies is a volume of evidence as to the wonderful patience of Southern whites. There are some things the Southern white man will not tolerate, and the intimidation of the foregoing has brought the writer to the very uttermost limit of public patience. We hope we have said enough."

The *Evening Scimitar* of the same day copied this leading editorial and added this comment: "Patience under such circumstances is not a virtue. If the negroes themselves do not apply the remedy without delay, it will be the duty of those he has attacked, to tie the wretch who utters these calumnies to a stake at the intersection of Main and Madison streets, and brand him in the forehead with a hot iron." Such open suggestions by the leading daily papers of the progressive city of Memphis were acted upon by the leading citizens and a meeting was held at the Cotton Exchange that evening. The *Commercial* two days later had the following account of it: "ATROCIOUS BLACKGUARDISM. There will be no Lynching and no Repetition of the Offense. In its issue of Wednesday The *Commercial* reproduced and commented upon an editorial which appeared a day or two before a negro organ known as the *Free Speech*. The article was so insufferably and indecently slanderous that the whole city awoke to a feeling of intense resentment which came within an ace of culminating in one of those occurrences whose details are so eagerly seized and so prominently published by Northern newspapers.

"Conservative counsels, however, prevailed, and no extreme measures were resorted to. On Wednesday afternoon a meeting of citizens was held. It was not an assemblage of hoodlums or irresponsible fire eaters, but solid, substantial business men who knew exactly what they were doing and who were far more indignant at the villainous insult to the women of the south than they would have been at any injury done themselves. This meeting appointed a committee to seek the author of the infamous editorial and warn him quietly that upon repetition of the offense, he would find some other part of the country a good deal safer and pleasanter place of residence than this. The committee called a negro named Nightingale, but he disclaimed responsibility and convinced the gentlemen that he had really sold out his paper to a woman named Wells. This woman is not in Memphis at present. It was finally learned that one Fleming, a negro who was driven out of Crittenden Co. during the trouble there a few years ago, wrote the paragraph. He had, however, heard of the meeting, and fled from a fate he feared was in store for him, and which he knew he deserved. His whereabouts could not be ascertained, and the committee so reported. Later on, a communication from Fleming to a prominent Republican politician, and that politician's reply were shown to one or two gentlemen. The former was an inquiry as to whether the writer might safely return to Memphis, the latter was an emphatic answer in negative, and Fleming is still in hiding. Nothing further will be done in the matter. There will be no lynching, and it is very certain that there will be no repetition of the outrage." The only reason there was no lynching of Mr. Fleming who was business manager and half owner of the Free Speech, and who did not write the editorials himself because this same white Republican told him the committee was coming and warned him not to trust them, but get out of the way.

The committee scoured the city hunting him, and had to be content with Mr. Nightingale, who was dragged to the meeting, shamefully abused (although it was known he had sold out his interest in the paper six months before). He was [hit] in the face and forced at the pistol's point to sign a letter which was written by them, in which he denied all knowledge of the editorial, denounced it and condemned it as slander on white women. I do not censure Mr. Nightingale for his action because, having never been at the pistol's point myself, I do not feel that I am competent to sit in judgment on him, or say What I would do under such circumstances. I had written that editorial with other matter for the week's paper before leaving home the Friday previous for the General Conference of the A.M.E. Church in Philadelphia. The conference adjourned Tuesday, and Thursday, May 25, at 3 P.M., I landed in New York City for a few days' stay before returning home, and there learned from the papers that my business manager had been driven away and the paper suspended. Telegraphing for news, I received telegrams and letters in return informing me that the trains were being watched, that I was to be dumped into the river and beaten, if not killed; it had been learned that I wrote the editorial and I was to be hanged in front of the court house and my face bled if I returned, and I was implored by my friends to remain away. The creditors attached the office in the meantime and the outfit was sold without more ado, thus destroying effectually that which it had taken years to build.

One prominent insurance agent publicly declares he will make it his business to shoot me down on sight if I return to Memphis in twenty years, while a leading white lady had remarked she was opposed to the lynching of those three men in March, but she wished there was some way by which I could be gotten back and lynched. I have been censured for writing that editorial, but when I think of five men who were lynched that week for assault on white women and that not a week passes but some poor soul is violently ushered into eternity on this trumped up charge, knowing the many things I do, and part of which tried to tell in the New York *Age* of June 25, (and in the pamphlets I have with me) seeing that the whole race in the South was injured in the estimation of the world because of these false reports, I could no longer hold my peace, and I feel, yes, I am sure, that if it had to be done over again (provided no one else was the loser save myself) I would do and say the very same again. The lawlessness here described is not confined to one locality. In the past ten years over a thousand colored men, women and children have been butchered, murdered and burnt in all parts of the South. The details of these terrible outrages seldom reach beyond the narrow world where they occur. Those who commit the murders write the reports, and hence these blots upon the honor of a nation cause but a faint ripple on the outside world. They arouse no great indignation and call forth no adequate demand for justice. The victims were black, and the reports are so written as to make it appear that the helpless creatures deserved the fate which overtook them. Not so with the Italian lynching of 1891. They were not black men, and three of them were not citizens of the Republic, but subjects of the King of Italy. The chief of police of New Orleans was shot and eleven Italians arrested and charged with the murder; they were tried and the jury disagreed; the good, law abiding citizens of New Orleans thereupon took them from the jail and lynched them at high noon. A feeling of horror ran through the nation at this outrage.

All Europe was amazed. The Italian government demanded thorough investigation and redress, and the Federal Government promised to give the matter the consideration which was its due. The diplomatic relations between the two countries became very much strained and for a while war talk was freely indulged. Here was a case where the power of the Federal Government to protect its own citizens and redeem its pledges to a friendly power was put to the test. When our State Department called upon the authorities of Louisiana for investigation of the crime and punishment of the criminals, the United States government was told that the crime was strictly within the authority of the State of Louisiana, and Louisiana would attend to it. After a farcical investigation, the usual verdict in such cases was rendered: "Death at the hand of parties unknown to the jury," the same verdict which had been pronounced over the bodies of over 1,000 colored persons!

Our federal government has thus admitted that it has no jurisdiction over the crimes committed at New Orleans upon citizens of the country, nor upon those citizens of a friendly power to whom the general government and not the State government has pledged protection. Not only has our general government made the confession that one of the states is greater than the Union, but the general government has paid $25,000 of the people's money to the King of Italy for the lynching of those three subjects, the evil doing of one State, over which it has no control, but for whose lawlessness the whole country must pay. The principle involved in the treaty power of the government has not yet been settled to the satisfaction of foreign powers; but the principle involved in the right of State jurisdiction in such matters, was settled long ago by the decision of the United States Supreme Court. I beg your patience while we look at another phase of the lynching mania. We have turned heretofore to the pages of ancient and medieval history, roman tyranny, the Jesuitical Inquisition of Spain for the spectacle of a human being burnt to death. In the past ten years three instances, at least, have been furnished where men have literally been roasted to death to appease the fury of Southern mobs.

The Texarkana instance of last year and Paris, Texas, case of this month are the most recent as they are the most shocking and repulsive. Both were charged with crimes from which the laws provide adequate punishment. The Texarkana man, Ed Coy, was charged with assaulting a white woman. A mob pronounced him guilty, strapped him to a tree, chipped the flesh from his body, poured coal oil over him and the woman in the case set fire to him. The country looked on and in many cases applauded, because it was published that this man had violated the honor of the white woman, although he protested his innocence to the last. Judge Tourjee in the Chicago *Inter Ocean* of recent date says investigation has shown that Ed Coy had supported this woman, (who was known to be a bad character,) and her drunken husband for over a year previous to the burning. The Paris, Texas, burning of Henry Smith, February 1st, has exceeded the others in its horrible details. The man was drawn through the streets on a float, as the Roman generals used to parade their trophies of war, while scaffold ten feet high, was being built, and irons were heated in the fire. He was bound on it, and red-hot irons began at his feet and slowly branded his body while the mob howled with delight at his shrieks. Red hot irons were run down his throat and cooked his tongue; his eyes were burned out, when he was at last unconscious, cotton seed hulls were placed under him, coal oil poured all over him, and a torch applied to the mass. When the flames burned away the ropes which bound Smith and scorched his flesh he was brought back to sensibility and burned and maimed and as he was, he rolled off the platform and away from the fire. His half-cooked body was seized and trampled and thrown back into the flames while a mob of twenty thousand persons who came from all over the country howled with delight, and gathered up some buttons and ashes after all was over to preserve for relics.

The man was charged with outraging and murdering a four year old white child, covering her body with brush, sleeping beside the body through the night, then making his escape. If true, it was the deed of a mad-man, and should have been clearly proven so. The fact that no time for verification of the newspaper reports was given, is suspicious, especially when I remember that a negro was lynched in Indianola, Sharkey Co., Miss. last summer. The dispatches said it was because he had assaulted the sheriff's eight year old daughter. The girl was more than eighteen years old and was found by her father in this man's room, who was a servant on the place. These incidents have been made the basis of this terrible story; they overshadow all others of a like nature in cruelty and represent the legal phases of the whole question. They could be multiplied without number and each outrival the other in the fiendish cruelty exercised, and the frequent awful lawlessness exhibited.

The following table shows the number of men lynched from January 1, 1882, to January 1, 1892: In 1882, 52; 1883, 39; 1884, 53; 1885, 77; 1886, 73; 1887, 70; 1888, 72; 1889, 95; 1890, 100; 1891, 169. Of these 728 black men who were murdered, 269 were charged with rape, 253 with murder, 44 with robbery, 37 with incendiarism, 32 with reasons unstated (it was not necessary to have a reason), 27 with race prejudice, 13 with quarreling with white men, 10 with making threats, 7 with rioting, 5 with miscegenation, 4 with burglary. One of the men lynched in 1891 was Will Lewis, who was lynched because "he was drunk and saucy to white folks." A woman who was one of the 73 victims in 1886, was hung in Jackson, Tenn., because the white woman for whom she cooked, died suddenly of poisoning. An examination showed arsenical poisoning. A search in the cook's room found rat poison. She was thrown into jail, and when the mob had worked itself up to the lynching pitch, she was dragged out, every stitch of clothing torn from her body, and was hung in the public court house square in sight of everybody. That white woman's husband has since died in the insane asylum, a raving maniac, and his ravings have led to the conclusion that he and not the cook, was the poisoner of his wife.

A fifteen year old colored girl was lynched last spring, at Rayville, La., on the same charge of poisoning. A woman was also lynched at Hollendale, Miss. last spring, charged with being an accomplice in the murder of her paramour who had abused her. These were only two of the 159 persons lynched in the South from January 1, 1892, to January 1, 1893. Over a dozen black men have been lynched already since this new year set in, not yet two months old. It will thus be seen that neither age, sex nor decency are spared. Although the impression has gone abroad that most of the lynchings take place because of assaults on white women only one third of the number lynched in the past ten years have been charged with that offense, to say nothing of those who were not guilty of the charge. And according to law none of them until proven so. But the unsupported word of any white person for any cause is sufficient to cause a lynching. So bold have the lynchers become masks are laid aside, the temples of justice and strongholds of law are invaded in broad daylight and prisoners taken out and lynched, while governors of states and officers of law stand by and see the work well done.

And yet this Christian nation, the flower of the nineteenth century civilization says it can do nothing to stop this inhuman slaughter. The general government is willingly powerless to send troops to protect the lives of its black citizens, but the state governments are free to use state troops to shoot them down like cattle, when in desperation the black men attempt to defend themselves, and then tell the world that it was necessary to put down a "race war." Persons unfamiliar with the condition of affairs in the Southern States do not credit the truth when it is told them. They cannot conceive how such a condition of affairs prevails so near them with steam power, telegraph wires, and printing presses in daily and hourly touch with the localities where such disorder reigns. In a former generation the ancestors of these same people refused to believe that slavery was the "league with death and the covenant with hell." Wm. Lloyd Garrison declared it to be, until he was thrown into a dungeon in Baltimore, until the signal lights of Nat Turners lit the dull skies of Northampton County, and until sturdy old John Brown made his attack on Harper's Ferry.

When freedom of speech was martyred in the person of Elijah Lovejoy at Alton, when the liberty of free discussion in Senate in the Nation's Congress was struck down in the person of the fearless Charles Sumner, the Nation was at last convinced that slavery was not only a monster but a tyrant. That same tyrant is at work under a new name and guise. The lawlessness which has been here described is like unto that which prevailed under slavery. The very same forces are at work now as then. The attempt is being made to subject to a condition of civil and industrial independence, those whom the Constitution declares to be free men. The events which have led up to the present wide spread lawlessness in the South can be traced to the very first year Lee's conquered veterans marched from Appomattox to their homes in the Southland. They were conquered in war, but not in spirit. They believed as firmly as ever that it was their right to rule black men and dictate to the National Government.

The Knights of White Liners, and the Ku Klux Klans were composed of veterans of the army who were determined to destroy the effect of all the slave had gained by the war. They finally accomplished their purpose in 1876. The right of the Afro American to vote and hold office remains in the Federal Constitution, but is destroyed in the constitution of the Southern states. Having destroyed the citizenship of the man, they are now trying to destroy the manhood of the citizen. All their laws are shaped to this end, —school laws, railroad car regulations, those governing labor liens on crops, every device is adopted to make slaves of free men and rob them of their wages. Whenever a malicious law is violated in any of its parts, any farmer, any railroad conductor, or merchant can call together a posse of his neighbors and punish even with death the black man who resists and the legal authorities sanction what is done by failing to prosecute and punish the murders. The Repeal of the Civil Rights Law removed their last barrier and the black man's last bulwark and refuge. The rule of the mob is absolute. Those who know this recital to be true, say there is nothing they can do. They cannot interfere and vainly hope by further concession to placate the imperious and dominating part of our country in which this lawlessness prevails.

Because this country has been almost rent in twain by internal dissension, the other sections seem virtually to have agreed that the best way to heal the breach is to permit the taking away of civil, political, and even human rights, to stand by in silence and utter indifference while the South continues to wreak fiendish vengeance on the irresponsible cause. They pretend to believe that with all the machinery of law and government in its hands; with the jails and penitentiaries and convict farms filled with pretty race criminals; with the well-known fact that no negro has ever been known to escape conviction and punishment for any crime in the South—still there are those who try to justify and condone the lynching of over a thousand black men in less than ten years an average of one hundred a year. The public sentiment of the country, by its silence in press, pulpit and in public meetings has encouraged this state of affairs, and public sentiment is stronger than law. With all this country's disposition to condone and temporize with the South and its methods; with its many instances of sacrificing principles to prejudice for the sake of making friends and healing the breach made by the late war; of going into the lawless country with capital to build up its waste places and remaining silent in the presence of outrage and wrong, the South is as vindictive and bitter as ever. She is willing to make friends as long as she is permitted to pursue unmolested and uncensored, her course of proscription, injustice, outrage and vituperation.

The malignant misrepresentation of General Butler, the uniformly indecent and abusive assault of this dead man whose only crime was a defence of his country, is a recent proof that the South has lost none of its bitterness. The Nashville American, one of the leading papers of one of the leading southern cities, gleefully announced editorially that "The Beast is dead." "Early yesterday morning, acting under the devil's orders, the angel of Death took Ben Butler and landed him in the lowest depths of hell, and we pity even the devil the possession has secured." The men who wrote these editorials are without exception young men who know nothing of slavery and scarcely anything of the war. The bitterness and hatred have been instilled in and taught them by their parents, and they are men who make and reflect the sentiment of their section. The South spares nobody else's feelings, and it seems a queer logic that when it comes to a question of right, involving lives of citizens and the honor of the government, the South's feelings must be respected and spared. Do you ask the remedy? A public sentiment strong against lawlessness must be aroused.

Every individual can contribute to this awakening. When a sentiment against lynch law as strong, deep and mighty as that roused by slavery prevails, I have no fear of the result. It should be already established as a fact and not as a theory, that every human being must have a fair trial for his life and liberty, no matter what the charge against him. When a demand goes up from fearless and persistent reformers from press and pulpit, from industrial and moral associations that this shall be so from Maine to Texas and from ocean to ocean, a way will be found to make it so. In deference to the few words of condemnation uttered at the M.E. General conference last year, and by other organizations, Governors Hogg of Texas, Northern of Georgia, and Tillman of South Carolina, have issued proclamations offering rewards for the apprehension of lynchers.

These rewards have never been claimed, and these governors knew they would not be when offered. In many cases they knew the ringleaders of the mobs. The prosecuting attorney of Shelby County, Tenn., wrote Governor Buchanan to offer a reward for the arrest of the lynchers of three young men murdered in Memphis. Everybody in that city and state knew well that the letter was written for the sake of effect and the governor did not even offer the reward. But the country at large deluded itself with the belief that the officials of the South and the leading citizens condemned lynching. The lynchings go on in spite of offered rewards, and in face of Governor Hogg's vigorous talk, the second man was burnt alive in his state with the utmost deliberation and publicity. Since he sent a message to the legislature the mob found and hung Henry Smith's stepson, because he refused to tell where Smith was when they were hunting for him. Public sentiment which shall denounce these crimes in season and out; public sentiment which turns capital and immigration from a section given over to lawlessness; public sentiment which insists on the punishment of criminals and lynchers by law must be aroused.

It is no wonder in my mind that the party which stood for their years as the champion of human liberty and human rights, the part of great moral ideas should suffer overwhelming defeat when it has proven recreant to its professions and abandoned a position it created; when although its followers were being outraged in every sense, it was afraid to stand for the right, and appeal to the American people to sustain them in it. It put aside the question of a free ballot and fair count of every citizen and give its voice and influence for the protection of the coat instead of the man who wore it, for the product of labor instead of the laborer; for the seal of citizenship rather than the citizen, and insisted upon the evils of free trade instead of the sacredness of speech. I am no politician but I believe if the Republican party had met issues squarely for human rights instead of the tariff it would have occupied a different position to day. The voice of the people is the voice of God, I long with all the intensity of my soul for the Garrison, Douglass, Sumner, Whittier, and Phillips who shall rouse this nation to a demand that from Greenland's icy mountains to the coral reefs of the Southern seas, mob rule shall be put down and equal and exact justice be accorded to every citizen of whatever race, who finds a home within the borders of the land of the free and the home of the brave. Then no longer will our national hymn be sounding brass and a tinkling cymbal, but every member of this great composite nation will be a living, harmonious illustration of the words, and all can honestly and gladly join in singing:

> My country! 'tis of thee,
> Sweet land of liberty
> Of thee I sing.
> Land where our fathers died,
> Land of the Pilgrim's pride,
> From every mountain side
> Freedom does ring.

Booker T. Washington

Atlanta Exposition Address
(Cotton States Exposition Address)

One of the most celebrated, and scorned, speeches in African American history is Booker T. Washington's "Atlanta Exposition Address," also often called the "Cotton States Exposition Address" and the "Atlanta Compromise Speech." Delivered on the opening day of the Exposition, the speech helped mark the exhibit building dedicated solely to African American economic achievements. Washington spoke on behalf of the industrial education of African Americans and the economic opportunities that awaited both races if the white South would cease its discriminatory ways and work in economic cooperation with African Americans in the South. Washington was eloquent and brief, and his use of story, metaphor, and language helped make his arguments memorable. Initially applauded by most observers of both races, the speech's eloquence and subsequent events have made it the object of sharp criticism in the years and even decades that have followed.

Born into slavery outside Roanoke, Virginia, in 1856, Washington was the son of the plantation's cook and a white man whose identity was never disclosed. At age 9, he moved to West Virginia to work in a salt mine. There he struck up a friendship with the wife of the mine's owner, who helped him attend the local one-room school. At school, when asked his last name, he decided to adopt that of the first president and named himself "Washington." In 1872, at the age of sixteen, the mine owner encouraged him to apply to Hampton Institute, a school founded by Samuel Armstrong and devoted to Armstrong's philosophy of "industrial education." Schools that followed the Hampton model provided African Americans with practical training in a trade and emphasized the "development" of thrift, industry, and other such virtues that, according to this philosophy, would allow these newly emancipated slaves with the means to accumulate wealth and eventually gain full equality of treatment in the United States.

At Hampton, Washington excelled in his studies, just as he had in the one room schoolhouse. He joined the institute's debating society and in 1875, delivered the commencement address at his graduation. He then took employment as a teacher back in West Virginia and continued his studies, first in the area of the law and then the ministry. In 1879, he returned to Hampton Institute as an instructor, and in 1881, he left to become head of Tuskegee Institute, a newly established school in Alabama founded in the tradition of Hampton's industrial education model. Washington proved himself an effective administrator and spokesman for Tuskegee, a leader with a remarkable ability to raise funds for Tuskegee from among Northern philanthropists such as Rockefeller and Carnegie. By 1895, he had established himself as a leader within the African American community, one to whom white politicians and businessmen often turned to "speak for" African Americans.

The period surrounding 1895 was a turbulent one for race relations and notable for the declining conditions under which African Americans were forced to live. The legal gains African Americans had made under Reconstruction had been steadily eroded since the last notable achievement (the Civil Rights Act of 1875) and the first reinstatement of Jim Crow laws (in Tennessee, also in 1875). The Supreme Court had overturned the Civil Rights Act of 1875, and in 1890, Mississippi became the first Southern state to rewrite the constitution it had adopted as part of Reconstruction. Like Mississippi's new document, the wave of revised Southern constitutions would include poll taxes, literacy tests, and other mechanisms designed to discourage African Americans from voting. In 1898, before rewriting its constitution, Louisiana had 130,344 registered African American voters. In 1900, under the rewritten state constitution, only 5,320 African Americans remained registered to vote. Throughout the 1880s, lynching became an increasingly employed weapon for increasing and enforcing white domination, and in the 1890s, the numbers of African Americans lynched reached a brutal crescendo. In 1896, the year following Washington's Atlanta Exposition address, the Supreme Court made its *Plessy v. Ferguson* ruling, which advanced the segregationist principle of "separate but equal."

Washington's "Atlanta Exposition Address" is at heart an economic treatise, celebrating what communication scholar Andrew King calls "heroic materialism," that is, the celebration of prosperity as an objective standard of virtue and the driving force of human nature.[1] Although the issues of political rights and legal equality play a role in the address, Washington invites the audience to view race relations exclusively through the lens of economics. Informally called the "Atlanta Compromise Address," Washington's proffered "compromise" was that Southern blacks would cease agitating for the "privileges of the law" and "social equality" in exchange for fully equal economic opportunity in the South. Fundamentally, this is a speech that represents the industrial education philosophy that Washington had studied under and then advocated for the previous two decades.

After beginning with some customary remarks of thanks to the organizers of the Exposition, Washington relates a story that is typical of the era. He recounts the tale of a ship lost at sea that has exhausted its store of water and, upon spying another vessel, signals the latter to ask for water. The rescue ship responds that the lost ship should "Cast down your bucket where you are." After a series of pleas for water and identical responses to cast down their bucket, the lost ship finally complies, only to find that they have sailed into the mouth of the Amazon River and the water surrounding them is fresh water fit for drinking. "Cast down your bucket where you are" becomes then the central message of the speech—that one will find economic prosperity in his or her own backyard using the resources that can be discovered there. That principle was the fundamental tenet of the industrial education movement, and was representative of the Gilded Age generally. Washington's story is reminiscent of Russell Conwell's "Acres of Diamonds," a story that Conwell would make famous several years later at the turn of the century. Like Washington, Conwell especially used the lecture to solicit support for an educational institution (Temple College in Philadelphia) that was founded especially to provide higher education to the laboring class.

Initially in the speech Washington uses the admonition "Cast down your bucket where you are" to identify why African Americans had not generally prospered after emancipation. Too many of his race, he says, had focused on starting "at the top." "Our greatest danger," he argues, "is, that in the great leap from slavery to freedom we may overlook the fact that the masses of us are to live by the productions of our hands, and fail to keep in mind that we shall prosper in proportion as we learn to dignify and glorify common labor." Washington's proposition is purely economic: "No race can prosper till it learns that there is as much dignity in tilling a field as in writing a poem. It is at the bottom of life we [African Americans] must begin, and not at the top." He thus arrives at the first half of the compromise: "Nor should we permit our grievances to overshadow our opportunities." African Americans, if they choose to cast down their bucket, will cease agitating for equal political treatment, and be content to focus on building their businesses and accumulating wealth. Southern whites, however, must also "cast down their bucket," a portion of the economic equation to which Washington next turns. "To those of the white race," he says, he would challenge them that they, too, should "Cast down your bucket where you are." Washington argues that in the South are eight million African Americans whose labor and habits are especially suited to building the economic prosperity of the "New South" that the Exposition was celebrating. Contrasting African Americans with the burgeoning immigrant population of the north, he holds that the former are people who "without strikes and labour wars" have "tilled your fields, cleared your forests, builded your railroads and cities, and brought forth treasures from the bowels of the earth, and helped make possible this magnificent representation of the progress of the South" (that is, the Exposition). After his recitation regarding all that the African American has to offer the southern white, and calling up a romantic, even maudlin, image of African Americans' faithfulness to their white counterparts during the Civil War, Washington summarizes the compromise with a vivid metaphor that has long been remembered and quoted: "In all things that are purely social we can be as separate as the fingers, yet one as the hand in all things essential to mutual progress."

It is important to note that, although Washington's allusion to "all things purely social" can be read broadly, white Americans of that era most often used the term "social equality" as a euphemism for the highly volatile perception that African American men were sexually rapacious, and that they particularly coveted white women. In an ironic move that turned history on its head—as Washington's own parentage attested—"social equality" was a sexually charged term used to arouse fear among white Americans and to justify a myriad of discriminatory actions against African Americans, particularly the use of lynching. Washington's message, then, was that African Americans were willing to forego those policies and laws that would place them on an equal social and political footing with white Americans—they were willing to keep to themselves within American society—as long as white America treated them equally in economic terms, that is, "in all things essential to mutual progress." In the areas of education, pay, interest rates, contract law, bank mortgages, business opportunities and the like, workers and entrepreneurs should all be treated equally regardless of race. Although in socio-political terms, Washington was willing to make many concessions as part of the compromise, it should be remembered that in economic terms he was calling for widespread and significant change from the business practices then current, despite his flattering statement at one point that "it is in the South that the Negro is given a man's chance in the commercial world." Had that statement been true literally, there would have been no need for Washington's compromise. It was true in a few instances—for example, Robert Church's acquisition of wealth in Memphis following his emancipation—but as Washington had argued in previous speeches, sharecropping laws and other economic practices in the South discriminated heavily against African American attempts to achieve prosperity.[2]

Washington's arguments on behalf of economic equality serve as a prelude to the most intriguing portion of the speech. "If anywhere there are efforts tending to curtail the fullest growth of the Negro," he urges, "let these efforts be turned into stimulating, encouraging, and making him the most useful and intelligent citizen." Such efforts, he says, will be "twice blessed" because, in theological language, those who aid the suffering are themselves blest, while those who oppress the oppressed are themselves spiritually oppressed. Employing parallel structure and antithesis, Washington issues a memorable and dire warning to the white members of his audience if the eight million African Americans continue to be treated unequally in economic matters: "Nearly sixteen millions of hands will aid you in pulling the load upward, or they will pull against you the load downward. We shall constitute one-third and more of the ignorance and crime of the South, or one-third [of] its intelligence and progress; we shall contribute one-third to the business and industrial prosperity of the South, or we shall prove a veritable body of death, stagnating, depressing, retarding every effort to advance the body politic." In retrospect, as the Southern states constructed a rigid caste system of segregation and sank into the poorest economic region of the United States, Washington's warning is prescient. He has offered the Southern whites in his audience, many of whom are influential leaders of their region, a compromise, but he has also told them in no uncertain terms what the results will be if the proffered compromise is spurned.[3]

Washington proceeds to reinforce his point, but now by accentuating the positive as he had done earlier. African Americans have made important strides, he tells his audience, as their Exhibit itself testified. Beginning with little but some quilts, pumpkins, and chickens, African Americans have constructed agricultural implements, created art, and managed banks and drug stores. He notes that the path has been difficult and makes a point of declaring that the exhibit also bears witness to the help that enlightened Southern whites and "especially" Northern white philanthropists have provided. Washington's narrative makes two points simultaneously. On the one hand, his description of African American accomplishments is an overture that flatters the white members of his audience—they have helped make the exhibit possible and African Americans are grateful. However, it also serves to demonstrate the point he had just made—African Americans are not a segregated portion of the Southern economy. They are, instead, an integral part of the Southern economy, and how they are treated by the other members of the economy will influence their ability to succeed (and pull the load upward) or fail (and pull the load downward).

As Washington concludes the body of his speech, he returns to the "Compromise," but here, unlike the preceding paragraphs, Washington is fully focused on the African Americans' side of the bargain. In a statement fraught with many layers of meaning, and open to the charge of pandering, Washington starts: "The wisest among my race understand that the agitation of questions of social equality is the extremest folly and that progress in the enjoyment of all the privileges that will come to us must be the result of severe and constant struggle rather than of artificial forcing." His word choices—"agitation," "social equality" and "extremest folly"—are emotionally charged. "Agitation," for example, was a term frequently associated with the labor organizers, socialists, and anarchists of the time but had also been an epithet applied to the abolitionists. Unlike the previous paragraph, this sentence places the burden squarely with the African American to achieve equality through "constant and severe struggle," rather than via the law, that is, through "artificial forcing." Washington reiterates his confidence in the inevitability of economic principles dictating laws and behaviors: "No race that has anything to contribute to the markets of the world is long in any degree ostracized." He concludes this section with a succinct summary of the principle tenet of the industrial education movement upon which Tuskegee Institute had been founded: "It is important and right that all privileges of the law be ours, but it is vastly more important that we be prepared for the exercise of these privileges. The opportunity to earn a dollar in a factory just now is worth infinitely more than the opportunity to spend a dollar in an opera-house."

The conclusion of the speech does not specifically repeat the compromise but is instead a hymn to the blessings of material prosperity. As does the opening story, the conclusion reminds the reader that Washington is a man of his times. As such, although his speech is marked with reference to God, spiritual and material prosperity are intimately related in the beliefs of the Gilded Age. Thus, Washington terms the exhibit an "altar"; and "the great and intricate problem which God has laid at the doors of the South" is in large part an economic one. How can the two races prosper together after having been so impoverished at the end of the Civil War? Now placing the responsibility for the "Compromise" in the hands of the Almighty, Washington asks the audience to "let us pray God, will come, in a blotting out of sectional differences and racial animosities and suspicions, in a determination to administer absolute justice, in a willing obedience among all classes to the mandates of law. This, coupled with our material prosperity, will bring into our beloved South a new heaven and a new earth."

Although later pilloried for its accommodationist stand—that is, the acceptance of legal segregation and unequal treatment until African Americans had "earned" their equality—Washington's Cotton States Exposition address was initially praised by almost everyone who heard and read it, Northerner and Southerner, African American and white. James Creelman, reporting for the *New York World*, wrote that the speech "marks a new epoch in the history of the South" and that "it electrified the audience."[4] "I have heard the great orators of many countries," Creelman claimed, "but not even Gladstone himself could have pleaded a cause with more consummate power."[5] Clark Howell, editor of the Atlanta *Constitution* concurred: "I do not exaggerate when I say that Prof. Booker T. Washington's address yesterday was one of the most notable speeches, both as to character and the warmth of its reception, ever delivered to a Southern audience." Like Creelman, Howell characterized the speech as "epoch-making." African Americans, too, praised the speech highly.[6] William Still, veteran of the Underground Railroad and the abolitionist movement, wrote to Washington that it was a "noble speech" and that "in my judgment our cause was absolutely advanced many degrees."[7] Echoing Washington's themes, the Rev. Burwell T. Harvey, from Antioch Baptist Church in Atlanta, congratulated Washington by writing that "leadership along the vital lines which you so earnestly and manly advocate will carry the race up the sure road to success in all walks of life."[8] W. E. B. Du Bois, then teaching at Wilberforce University, cabled simply that "it was a word fitly spoken," and many other contemporaries, black and white, wrote to Washington to congratulate him on his speech.[9]

Not all contemporary observers agreed, however. Some African American leaders and newspapers were critical of Washington's praise of Southern whites, his acceptance of segregation, and the blame he placed on those African Americans who placed "rights" above "economic advancement." Bishop Henry McNeal Turner, for example, wrote in the AME church newspaper that Washington "will have to live a long time to undo the harm he has done our race."[10] W. Calvin Chase, editor of the *Washington Bee*, wrote that "he said something that was death to the Afro-American and elevating to the white people."[11] The *Atlanta Advocate* called his attitude "sycophantic," writing that there "is no doubt in our minds that his race will suffer."[12] In 1903, W. E. B. Du Bois published *The Souls of Black Folks*, which included a chapter severely criticizing Washington for his accommodationist stand.[13] Modern historians and communication scholars have typically echoed the criticism of Turner, Chase, Du Bois, and the *Atlanta Advocate* editorialist. Andrew King provides an apt summary, writing that critics often see Washington as a "spokesman who made far too many concessions to his enemies, protested evil too mildly, and miscalculated the devotion of his allies."[14]

Washington was aware that he had been cautious that day. As he recalled the experience in his autobiography, *Up from Slavery*, "I was determined to say nothing that I did not feel from the bottom of my heart to be true and right. . . . [The board of directors of the exposition] knew that by one sentence I could have blasted, in a large degree, the success of the Exposition. I was also painfully conscious of the fact that, while I must be true to my own race in my utterances, I had it in my power to make such an ill-timed address as would result in preventing any similar invitation being extended to a black man again for years to come. I was equally determined to be true to the North, as well as to the best element of the white South, in what I had to say."[15] Nor does it seem that Washington's fears were unfounded. A scientist from the Smithsonian Institution, W. J. McGee, sitting in the white section of the audience that day, recorded the reaction of those around him. When Washington first walked out with the platform party, McGee observed that a number of whites in the audience asked each other "What's that n—— doing on stage?" and that at the beginning of his speech, the white section greeted him with "icy coldness."[16] Washington was aware, too, that after the "first burst of enthusiasm" from the African American people and newspapers, criticism had emerged because "they seemed to feel that I had been too liberal in my remarks toward the Southern whites, and that I had not spoken out strongly enough for what they term the 'rights' of the race."[17] By 1900, when writing his autobiography, Washington believed that those critics "seemed to have been won over to my way of believing and acting."[18] Du Bois's 1903 chapter harshly criticizing Washington and the 1905 Niagara movement's proclamation that demanded the granting of full and equal rights, contradicted Washington's conclusion that his critics had been "won over," however. Ironically, some black nationalists of the day, such as Edward Blyden, as well as later ones, such as Marcus Garvey, embraced Washington's compromise of social separatism and economic advancement.[19] Although the speech is commonly termed the "Atlanta Compromise," it is important to note that among the white press of the day, only one side of the "compromise" was typically reported. The *New York World*, for example, in covering Washington's exposition address, quoted his famous metaphor that in "all things that are purely social we can be as separate as the fingers."[20] It also quoted Washington's declarations that it was "in the South that the negro is given a man's chance" and that "no race can prosper" until it learns to begin at the bottom.[21] Similarly, the *New York Times* coverage of Washington's speech focused on the last half of the speech, particularly quoting the sections on African Americans' indebtedness to the generosity of Northern philanthropists, that the "wisest among my race understand that the agitation of questions of social equality is the extremist folly," and Washington's concluding pledge that African Americans would put forth their best efforts.[22] Except for two sentences in the *World*, both accounts omitted any mention of the portions of the speech in which Washington challenged Southern whites to work fairly and equitably with blacks, and neither newspaper repeated the vivid antithesis regarding the sixteen million hands. Thus, Washington's appeal for equal economic treatment was generally lost amid his praise for Southern opportunities and the need for African Americans to concentrate on their industrial education, and his dire warnings regarding the consequences for Southern whites if they did not accept the "compromise" were ignored completely.

As he recorded again in his autobiography, Washington espoused the belief that "say what we will, there is something in human nature which we cannot blot out, which makes one man, in the end, recognize and reward the merit in another, regardless of colour and race."[23] Washington's prediction that the South would suffer economically if it treated African Americans unequally was prescient. The wealthiest section of the country in the early nineteenth century had become the poorest by 1895 and would continue to be so under the policy of segregation. What Washington had failed to consider, however, was the influence of prejudice and short-term economic gain in people's calculations, and the role that those would play in preventing the "Compromise" from ever commencing.

Atlanta Exposition Address

(Cotton States Exposition Address)

September 18, 1895
Atlanta, Georgia

Mr. President[a] and gentlemen of the board of directors and citizens.

One-third of the population of the South is of the Negro race. No enterprise seeking the material, civil, or moral welfare of this section can disregard this element of our population and reach the highest success. I but convey to you, Mr. President and Directors, the sentiment of the masses of my race when I say that in no way have the value and manhood of the American Negro been more fittingly and generously recognized than by the managers of this magnificent Exposition at every stage of its progress. It is a recognition that will do more to cement the friendship of the two races than any occurrence since the dawn of our freedom.

Not only this, but the opportunity here afforded will awaken among us a new era of industrial progress. Ignorant and inexperienced, it is not strange that in the first years of our new life we began at the top instead of at the bottom; that a seat in Congress or the state legislature was more sought than real estate or industrial skill; that the political convention of stump speaking had more attractions than starting a dairy farm or truck garden.

A ship lost at sea for many days suddenly sighted a friendly vessel. From the mast of the unfortunate vessel was seen a signal, "Water, water; we die of thirst!" The answer from the friendly vessel at once came back, "Cast down your bucket where you are." A second time the signal, "Water, water; send us water!" ran up from the distressed vessel, and was answered, "Cast down your bucket where you are." And a third and fourth signal for water

a. Charles A. Collier (1848–1900): President of the Cotton States and International Exposition (Atlanta) and later mayor of Atlanta.

was answered, "Cast down your bucket where you are." The captain of the distressed vessel, at last heeding the injunction, cast down his bucket, and it came up full of fresh, sparkling water from the mouth of the Amazon River. To those of my race who depend on bettering their condition in a foreign land or who underestimate the importance of cultivating friendly relations with the Southern white man, who is their next-door neighbour, I would say: "Cast down your bucket where you are"—cast it down in making friends in every manly way of the people of all races by whom we are surrounded.

Cast it down in agriculture, mechanics, in commerce, in domestic service, and in the professions. And in this connection it is well to bear in mind that whatever other sins the South may be called to bear, when it comes to business, pure and simple, it is in the South that the Negro is given a man's chance in the commercial world, and in nothing is this Exposition more eloquent than in emphasizing this chance. Our greatest danger is that in the great leap from slavery to freedom we may overlook the fact that the masses of us are to live by the productions of our hands, and fail to keep in mind that we shall prosper in proportion as we learn to dignify and glorify common labour and put brains and skill into the common occupations of life; shall prosper in proportion as we learn to draw the line between the superficial and the substantial, the ornamental gewgaws of life and the useful. No race can prosper till it learns that there is as much dignity in tilling a field as in writing a poem. It is at the bottom of life we must begin, and not at the top. Nor should we permit our grievances to overshadow our opportunities.

To those of the white race who look to the incoming of those of foreign birth and strange tongue and habits for the prosperity of the South, were I permitted I would repeat what I say to my own race, "Cast down your bucket where you are." Cast it down among the eight millions of Negroes whose habits you know, whose fidelity and love you have tested in days when to have proved treacherous meant the ruin of your firesides. Cast down your bucket among these people who have, without strikes and labour wars, tilled your fields, cleared your forests, builded your railroads and cities, and brought forth treasures from the bowels of the earth, and helped make possible this magnificent representation of the progress of the South. Casting down your bucket among my people, helping and encouraging them as you are doing on these grounds, and to education of head, hand, and heart, you will find that they will buy your surplus land, make blossom the waste places in your fields, and run your factories. While doing this, you can be sure in the future, as in the past, that you and your families will be surrounded by the most patient, faithful, law-abiding, and unresentful people that the world has seen. As we have proved our loyalty to you in the past, in nursing your children, watching by the sick-bed of your mothers and fathers, and often following them with tear-dimmed eyes to their graves, so in the future, in our humble way, we shall stand by you with a devotion that no foreigner can approach, ready to lay down our lives, if need be, in defence of yours, interlacing our industrial, commercial, civil, and religious life with yours in a way that shall make the interests of both races one. In all things that are purely social we can be as separate as the fingers, yet one as the hand in all things essential to mutual progress.

There is no defence or security for any of us except in the highest intelligence and development of all. If anywhere there are efforts tending to curtail the fullest growth of the Negro, let these efforts be turned into stimulating, encouraging, and making him the most useful and intelligent citizen. Effort or means so invested will pay a thousand per cent. interest. These efforts will be twice blessed—"blessing him that gives and him that takes."

There is no escape through law of man or God from the inevitable:

The laws of changeless justice bind
Oppressor with oppressed;
And close as sin and suffering joined
We march to fate abreast.[b]

Nearly sixteen millions of hands will aid you in pulling the load upward, or they will pull against you the load downward. We shall constitute one-third and more of the ignorance and crime of the South, or one-third its intelligence and progress; we shall contribute one-third to the business and industrial prosperity of the South, or we shall prove a veritable body of death, stagnating, depressing, retarding every effort to advance the body politic.

Gentlemen of the Exposition, as we present to you our humble effort at an exhibition of our progress, you must not expect overmuch. Starting thirty years ago with ownership here and there in a few quilts and pumpkins and chickens (gathered from miscellaneous sources), remember the path that has led from these to the inventions and production of agricultural implements, buggies, steam-engines, newspapers, books, statuary, carving, paintings, the management of drug-stores and banks, has not been trodden without

b. Cecilia Devyr, "The Underground Railroad: Thoughts Suggested upon Hearing a Lecture by Edwin H. Coates in Mt. Lebanon, NY." Broadside (New York: N.p., n.d.). Copy held by the Historical Society of Pennsylvania.

contact with thorns and thistles. While we take pride in what we exhibit as a result of our independent efforts, we do not for a moment forget that our part in this exhibition would fall far short of your expectations but for the constant help that has come to our educational life, not only from the Southern states, but especially from Northern philanthropists, who have made their gifts a constant stream of blessing and encouragement.

The wisest among my race understand that the agitation of questions of social equality is the extremest folly, and that progress in the enjoyment of all the privileges that will come to us must be the result of severe and constant struggle rather than of artificial forcing. No race that has anything to contribute to the markets of the world is long in any degree ostracized. It is important and right that all privileges of the law be ours, but it is vastly more important that we be prepared for the exercises of these privileges. The opportunity to earn a dollar in a factory just now is worth infinitely more than the opportunity to spend a dollar in an opera-house.

In conclusion, may I repeat that nothing in thirty years has given us more hope and encouragement, and drawn us so near to you of the white race, as this opportunity offered by the Exposition; and here bending, as it were, over the altar that represents the results of the struggles of your race and mine, both starting practically empty-handed three decades ago, I pledge that in your effort to work out the great and intricate problem which God has laid at the doors of the South, you shall have at all times the patient, sympathetic help of my race; only let this be constantly in mind, that, while from representations in these buildings of the product of field, of forest, of mine, of factory, letters, and art, much good will come, yet far above and beyond material benefits will be that higher good, that, let us pray God, will come, in a blotting out of sectional differences and racial animosities and suspicions, in a determination to administer absolute justice, in a willing obedience among all classes to the mandates of law. This, this, coupled with our material prosperity, will bring into our beloved South a new heaven and a new earth.

Mary Church Terrell

What It Means to Be Colored in the Capital of the United States

In the late nineteenth and early twentieth centuries, African American women had an especially pronounced effect on their communities. Through their work as educators, as members of women's clubs, or as social activists—and frequently as all three—women such as Anna Julia Cooper, Charlotte Hawkins Brown, Fannie Barrier Williams, and Mary McLeod Bethune established schools, lobbied for reforms, and helped found landmark organizations such as the National Association for the Advancement of Colored People (NAACP). Mary Church Terrell was one of these active and influential women.

Mary Church was born on September 23, 1863, in Memphis, Tennessee, to two newly emancipated slaves, Robert Reed Church and Louisa Ayres Church. Church's parents had enjoyed more privileges and opportunities than most slaves, including receiving an education, and upon emancipation, they were able to prosper. Louisa opened shop as a hairdresser, and her husband used the cash she accumulated from her work to invest in Memphis real estate during a yellow fever epidemic shortly after the Civil War. When Memphis came back economically after the epidemic, the Churches became the first African American millionaires in the South.[1]

Although Mary Church grew up in material prosperity, which shielded her from many of the day-to-day brutalities of prejudice and discrimination, there were several vivid episodes that made her aware that her skin color counted more than her family's wealth, education, or social standing. Her maternal grandmother, for example, "Aunt Liza," recounted horrific and tragic stories of her own slavery experiences.[2] When Mary was nine, her parents divorced, and she moved with her mother to New York City. She was, however, sent away to progressive, integrated boarding schools in Ohio, but even there she encountered everyday prejudice at the hands of her fellow students and teachers. In 1884, she became one of only three African American women to graduate from Oberlin College, and the first to graduate with the AB degree in the classics, a course of study normally reserved for men.[3]

After graduation, Mary Church took a teaching position at Wilberforce College in Wilberforce, Ohio, the leading institution of higher learning for African American students. In 1887, she moved to Washington, DC, where she taught the classics at M Street Colored High School, a highly respected school for African American children. Acceding to her father's wishes, Church took two years away from teaching to tour Europe, where she particularly polished her language skills in French, German, and Italian. She returned to Washington, DC, and M Street Colored High School, and in 1891, she married Robert H. Terrell, a graduate of Harvard who had been chair of the Latin department in which she taught. In 1910, he was appointed a judge in the District of Columbia municipal court.[4]

Following the custom of the time, Mary Church Terrell resigned her teaching post upon her marriage to Robert. Although "retired" from teaching, Terrell was actively employed in civic and political affairs. In 1895, she became one of two women appointed to the District of Columbia Board of Education, assuming responsibility for supervising the "colored" schools. In that position, she strongly advocated for equal educational opportunities and for increased control of the schools by African American administrators. That year, she was also elected president of the National Association of Colored Women (NACW). Terrell was active in the woman's suffrage movement and a frequent contributor to reform-minded magazines and newspapers such as the *Independent*.

When Mary Church Terrell delivered her 1906 lecture "What It Means to be Colored in the Capital of the United States," the District of Columbia had earned the reputation of being "The Colored Man's Paradise." Governed by federal statute, enlightened laws such as the Thirteenth, Fourteenth, and Fifteenth Amendments and the Civil Rights Act of 1875 provided legal freedoms that African Americans governed by state and local laws did not have. Because of such federal "protection," many emancipated slaves moved to DC after the Civil War.[5] By 1900, over eighty thousand African Americans lived in Washington, comprising 31 percent of the district's total population.[6] Despite constituting such a large proportion of the population and the federal government's ostensible commitment to racial equality, segregation and discriminatory practices persisted. The district's school system was segregated, as were its theaters, restaurants, and other public accommodations, and the apparent intent of Terrell's speech was to enlighten her audience about the African American experience of living in Washington. The speech was delivered to the United Women's Club, although who comprised this assemblage—whether white or African American, male or female—is unknown. Traditionally, scholars have analyzed the speech assuming, through textual clues, that the audience was composed of white club women.[7] Rhetorical critic Cynthia King has argued that the lack of records about the club supports the conclusion that it was an African American women's club.[8] The adjective "United" in the club's title suggests that it was perhaps an integrated organization. The speech itself seems intended to enlighten a white audience about the realities of living as an African American in the supposed "Colored Man's Paradise," rather than simply to confirm for African American women what they already knew. Subsequently, the speech was published in the *Independent*, a reform magazine with a broad readership.

In "What It Means to Be Colored in the Capital of the United States," Mary Church Terrell reveals herself to be a storyteller of the first order, with a meticulous eye for detail and a refined sense of irony. Indeed, the organization of the speech itself is one that underscores her emphasis on storytelling, as it mimics conversation by telling story after story, often turning back upon itself as it retraces topics already covered. Most speeches are organized deductively, with larger topics broken into subtopics and subtopics then further divided. Henry Highland Garnet's, Frederick Douglass's and Frances Harper's speeches are all examples of deductively organized speeches. Terrell was certainly aware of and capable of organizing her speeches and magazine articles in a deductive fashion. Her first presidential speech delivered to the NACW in 1897, or her 1905 essay "Service Which Should be Rendered the South," published in the *Voice of the Negro*, demonstrate her ability and even proclivity to use that more traditional structure built on deductive logic.[9] For this speech, however, Terrell selected an inductive structure, one in which she recounts story after story until the larger, overarching story emerges: that the prejudice and discrimination rampant in the capital city make it an oppressive place for African Americans to reside.

The speech is introduced with a series of generalized examples of discrimination. Terrell begins with public accommodations—boarding houses and restaurants—that even an African American of means such as herself cannot use. She continues with similar examples of attending church, seeking employment, attending the theater (yet a different public accommodation), and seeking advanced schooling. In the course of this litany of generalized examples, however, Terrell begins, while discussing discrimination and the theater, to use examples that had actually occurred. The transition from generalized story to actual story, though, is subtly accomplished. Terrell's initial examples are told in the first person—"As a colored woman I might enter Washington any night," "As a colored woman I may walk from the Capitol to the White House," "As a colored woman I may enter more than one white church in Washington." Her first example grounded in a specific instance is also a first person story, one in which she tells how she telephoned a ticket seller to see if an African American taking care of a white child would be allowed to accompany the child into the main seating section of the theater.

From there, however, her stories move from first person to third person stories—"a colored woman who possessed great (artistic) talent," "a young woman who had already attracted some attention in the literary world," "another young friend," "a colored school teacher," "a colored clerk," or "one of the most skilful laborers in the hardware business." Again, though, the presentation of the stories is seemingly without order. The first two stories concern discriminatory admissions practices for schools. Terrell then moves to telling stories about discriminatory practices in employment, where African Americans are either not hired or dismissed from their job once their race has been discovered. She then returns to the issue of public accommodations in restaurants and theaters. After several stories on that theme, she renews her discussion of discriminatory employment practices in the district's schools, then narrates the inability of African American teachers to attend a professional development lecture, returns again to the issue of public accommodations (streetcars), and finally relates one more employment example. Rhetorically, Terrell uses what is called *enumeration*, a persuasive technique whereby one recounts a telling series of examples that illustrate the point being made. Although enumeration can be employed through a variety of methods, Terrell's inductive approach of "haphazardly" arranging the stories imitates everyday conversation, in which the speaker relates stories extemporaneously, as they come to mind.[10] As a result, Terrell gives the impression that these are unplanned examples—stories called to mind as she discusses the problem—and that, in common parlance, she has plenty more where these came from.

Although the organization of her speech suggests that these are stories spontaneously recollected, Terrell relates the stories with keen attention to details that enhance the rhetorical power of the stories. The art student denied admission to the Corcoran Arts School of Washington is in contrast accepted for study at the Woman's Art School of Cooper Union in New York, and after graduation has continued to study in Paris. After the African American teachers are not permitted to attend some lectures by a famous kindergarten educator, a white teacher in attendance offers to "repeat them as best she could . . . for half the price she herself paid." The senior proprietor of the largest department store in Washington, who practices discrimination, "originally hailed from Boston, once the home of William Lloyd Garrison, Wendell Phillips and Charles Sumner, if my memory serves me right." Six girls were taken by an African American gentleman to the theater. Five were allowed to "pass," but the sixth—sister to two of the girls already allowed entrance—was not.

Each detail of the story Terrell recounts adds rhetorical power. The Corcoran was a prestigious art school, but it lost a very talented artist to a lesser school because of its mindless policy of discrimination. The white teacher profits solely because of the color of her skin when she charges an admission fee to the African American teachers, committed to improving themselves professionally, so that she can repeat another individual's lecture "as best she could." The proprietor from Boston, geographical center of the American Anti-Slavery Society, is as discriminatory as a white American born anywhere else in the United States. A young girl is refused entrance to a play, while two of her lighter skinned blood relatives, sharing the same gene pool as herself, are allowed in. These are not simply details that Terrell recollects extemporaneously; these have been mindfully selected to enhance the persuasiveness of each story.

Throughout Terrell's stories runs a strong thread of irony. She notes in her opening sentences that the title "The Colored Man's Paradise" had perhaps been bestowed upon the nation's capital "in bitter irony," and irony is woven into the fabric of almost every story she tells. "As a colored woman," she says, "I may walk from the Capitol to the White House ravenously hungry and abundantly supplied with money with which to purchase a meal, without finding a single restaurant in which I would be permitted to take a morsel of food." Certainly the audience would perceive the irony. Terrell, daughter of a millionaire, wife of a Harvard graduate and lawyer, and herself a college graduate, would not *perhaps* be "abundantly supplied with money," she *was* abundantly supplied with money. Yet even she, with all her wealth and social standing, would be unable to purchase "a morsel" to eat due to the color of her skin.

Her description of an African American attempting to attend a white church similarly drips with irony. Instead of literally discussing willful discrimination by whites, Terrell employs a figurative physical ailment. The usher seems to suffer from "color blindness," a disability that prevents African Americans from "making any impression whatsoever upon his retina, so that it is impossible for him to see colored people at all." The impossibility of one actually suffering from such a physical disability serves to heighten the illogic and injustice of discriminating on the basis of appearance. Terrell's ironic tone continues, as she mockingly chides the "dusky Christians" who have the "temerity to thrust themselves into a temple where only the fair of face are expected to worship God." Such perspective by incongruity continues as a theater ticket seller earnestly tells Terrell over the telephone that "in Washington it was very poor policy to employ colored nurses," obviously unaware that the woman to whom he was speaking was herself African American. A young woman with the literary ability to write and publish short stories cannot obtain employment as a stenographer, and the man who sued a theater for wrongful ejection won the case in court, but was awarded damages that "amounted to the munificent sum of one cent." The department store owner who dismisses the saleswoman because of her ethnicity is himself Jewish, and by inference has himself been the victim of discrimination. In story after story, the audience is invited to contemplate the irony—that things should be the opposite of how they are described, which is, of course, the point of Terrell's speech. African Americans' quality of life in the nation's capital should be exactly the opposite of what she describes.

One story particularly tinged with irony is that of the African American gentleman who attempts to treat six little girls from the neighborhood to a matinee performance at the theater. One girl is refused admission although her two sisters have already been "passed" in. Terrell recounts that the gentleman was quite equal to the "emergency"—highlighting again the capriciousness of prejudice that it should ever cause an episode that is an "emergency." The unanticipated climax of the story, however, is that the gentleman claims the African American child is Filipino, to which the ticket taker responds, "Beg your pardon. . . . Of course she can go in." The gentleman's claim as to the child's heritage is ironic in two regards. First, it reiterates the point often made by African Americans that white Americans treat foreign-born people of color who have just arrived on US shores better than African Americans whose ancestors have been American for centuries. As an African American, the girl cannot attend the theater. As a newly arrived Filipino, she is not only welcome to attend, but the ticket taker is "begging" their "pardon." The second layer of irony in the claim is that the Philippines had only recently come under US control as a result of the 1898 Spanish-American War. In the popular American conception, the United States' involvement in the Philippines was to "save" the "uncivilized" Filipino natives from the "barbarism" of the Spanish. This explains the ticket taker's particular haste to apologize. White Americans were performing their "Christian" duty of "manifest destiny" by caring for Filipinos such as this alleged Filipino child. Although vocal in their concern about the "barbarism" the Spanish displayed for those native peoples, white Americans were blind to their uncivilized behavior towards their own citizens of African descent.

An ironic detail that recurs in Terrell's stories is her reference to the protagonist as "fair." The African American short story writer who applied for the position of stenographer was "very fair." The sales clerk was dismissed after "it had been discovered that she was colored." Another dismissed sales clerk is described as being "fair as a lily," but dismissed when "the proprietor accidentally discovered that a fatal drop of African blood was percolating somewhere thru her veins." Five of the little girls are fair enough to "pass" as white and be admitted entrance to the theater. The colored clerk who sued the theater "looks more like his paternal ancestors"—that is, white male slave owners—"than his grandmothers"—that is, the female slaves. Terrell's own father appeared so Caucasian that he could frequently pass as white, although, like Terrell herself, he appears to have chosen not to do so.[11] Terrell's repeated reference to complexion is intended to heighten the irrational nature of the country's prejudice. Whites discriminated on the basis of skin color, but often they could not tell African American from Caucasian because the races had been so intermingled. Only the figuratively blind, like the "color-blind" usher at the church, would fail to see that they literally could *not* see the difference between many of the individuals of each race.

Terrell's stories, replete with ironic twists, were intended to help her white audience understand the world from the perspective of the African American. Indeed, at the end of her speech, she finally announces the ironic conclusion the audience should have arrived at inductively: "And so I might go on citing instance after instance," she tells her listeners. The kinds of stories she has told here, as they have "come to mind," she could continue recounting for hours. Although she has tried to help her audience to see what African Americans' lives are like, "it is impossible for any white person in the United States, no matter how sympathetic and broad," to empathize fully with the harsh conditions that racial prejudice and discrimination impose. Terrell concludes, "And surely nowhere in the world do oppression and persecution based solely on the color of the skin appear more hateful and hideous than in the capital of the United States, because the chasm between the principles upon which this Government was founded, in which it still professes to believe, and those which are daily practiced under the protection of the flag, yawns so wide and deep." Terrell's final sentence summarizes the irony that African Americans, living in "The Colored Man's Paradise" and the national capital of a country devoted to the ideals of freedom and liberty, suffer from freedoms denied in a city that is hardly idyllic.

There is no record of how this particular speech was received, but Mary Church Terrell remained very active and well regarded in many activist and reform-minded circles. As did many African Americans, such as W. E. B. Du Bois, around the time of this speech, Terrell broke with Booker T. Washington. In 1909, she was deeply involved in helping establish the National Association for the Advancement of Colored People (NAACP). In politics, she served on the Republican National Committee and participated in the presidential campaigns of Harding and Coolidge and the 1930 senatorial campaign of Ruth Hanna McCormick in Illinois. She continued to write articles for reform magazines and newspapers and in 1940, published her autobiography. In her later years, Terrell lent her support to a variety of causes, such as the campaign to save the accused Communist spies Ethel and Julius Rosenberg from execution and the early 1950s movement in Washington, DC, to eliminate de facto segregation from public accommodations such as restaurants. In 1954, Mary Church Terrell passed away at the age of ninety-one.[12]

What It Means to Be Colored in the Capital of the United States

October 10, 1906
Washington, DC

Thank you very much.

Washington, D.C., has been called "The Colored Man's Paradise." Whether this sobriquet was given to the national capital in bitter irony by a member of the handicapped race, as he reviewed some of his own persecutions and rebuffs, or whether it was given immediately after the war by an ex-slave-holder who for the first time in his life saw colored people walking about like free men, minus the overseer and his whip, history saith not. It is certain that it would be difficult to find a worse misnomer for Washington than "The Colored Man's Paradise" if so prosaic a consideration as veracity is to determine the appropriateness of a name.

For fifteen years I have resided in Washington, and while it was far from being a paradise for colored people when I first touched these shores it has been doing its level best ever since to make conditions for us intolerable. As a colored woman I might enter Washington any night, a stranger in a strange land, and walk miles without finding a place to lay my head. Unless I happened to know colored people who live here or ran across a chance acquaintance who could recommend a colored boarding-house to me, I should be obliged to spend the entire night wandering about. Indians, Chinamen, Filipinos, Japanese and representatives of any other dark race can find hotel accommodations, if they can pay for them. The colored man alone is thrust out of the hotels of the national capital like a leper.

As a colored woman I may walk from the Capitol to the White House, ravenously hungry and abundantly supplied with money with which to purchase a meal, without finding a single restaurant in which I would be permitted to take a morsel of food, if it was patronized by white people, unless I were willing to sit behind a screen. As a colored woman I cannot visit the tomb of the Father of this country, which owes its very existence to the love of freedom in the human heart and which stands for equal opportunity to all, without being forced to sit in the Jim Crow section of an electric car[a] which starts form the very heart of the city—midway between the Capitol and the White House. If I refuse thus to be humiliated, I am cast into jail and forced to pay a fine for violating the Virginia laws. Every hour in the day Jim Crow cars filled with colored people, many of whom are intelligent and well to do, enter and leave the national capital.

As a colored woman I may enter more than one white church in Washington without receiving that welcome which as a human being I have the right to expect in the sanctuary of God. Sometimes the color blindness of the usher takes on that peculiar form which prevents a dark face from making any impression whatsoever upon his retina, so that it is impossible for him to see colored people at all. If he is not so afflicted, after keeping a colored man or woman waiting a long time, he will ungraciously show these dusky Christians who have had the temerity to thrust themselves in a temple where only the fair of face are expected to worship God to a seat in the rear, which is named in honor of a certain personage, well known in this country, and commonly called Jim Crow.

Unless I am willing to engage in a few menial occupations, in which the pay for my services would be very poor, there is no way for me to earn an honest living, if I am not a trained nurse or a dressmaker or can secure a position as teacher in the public schools, which is exceedingly difficult to do. It matters not what my intellectual attainments may be or how great is the need of the services of a competent person, if I try to enter many of the numerous vocations in which my white sisters are allowed to engage, the door is shut in my face.

From one Washington theater I am excluded altogether. In the remainder certain seats are set aside for colored people, and it is almost impossible to secure others. I once telephoned a ticket seller just before a matinee and asked if a neat-appearing colored nurse would be allowed to sit in the parquet[b] with her little white charge, and the answer rushed quickly and positively thru the receiver—NO. When I remonstrated a bit and told him that in some of

a. Streetcar, or trolley.

b. The parquet was the main floor of the theater, located between the orchestra seats and the balcony.

the theatres colored nurses were allowed to sit with the white children for whom they cared, the ticket seller told me that in Washington it was very poor policy to employ colored nurses, for they were excluded from many places where white girls would be allowed to take children for pleasure.

If I possess artistic talent, there is not a single art school of repute which will admit me. A few years ago a colored woman who possessed great talent submitted some drawings to the Corcoran Arts School, of Washington, which were accepted by the committee of awards, who sent her a ticket entitling her to a course in this school. But when the committee discovered that the young woman was colored they declined to admit her, and told her that if they had suspected that her drawings had been made by a colored woman they would not have examined them at all. The efforts of Frederick Douglass and a lawyer of great repute who took a keen interest in the affair were unavailing. In order to cultivate her talent this young woman was forced to leave her comfortable home in Washington and incur the expense of going to New York. Having entered the Woman's Art School of Cooper Union, she graduated with honor, and then went to Paris to continue her studies, where she achieved signal success and was complimented by some of the greatest living artists in France.

With the exception of the Catholic University, there is not a single white college in the national capital to which colored people are admitted, no matter how great their ability, how lofty their ambition, how unexceptionable their character or how great their thirst for knowledge may be.

A few years ago the Columbian Law School admitted colored students, but in deference to the Southern white students the authorities have decided to exclude them altogether.

Some time ago a young woman who had already attracted some attention in the literary world by her volume of short stories answered an advertisement which appeared in a Washington newspaper, which called for the services of a skilled stenographer and expert typewriter. It is unnecessary to state the reasons why a young woman whose literary ability was so great as that possessed by the one referred to should decide to earn money in this way. The applicants were requested to send specimens of their work and answer certain questions concerning their experience and their speed before they called in person. In reply to her application the young colored woman, who, by the way, is very fair and attractive indeed, received a letter from the firm stating that her references and experience were the most satisfactory that had been sent and requesting her to call. When she presented herself there was some doubt in the mind of the man to whom she was directed concerning her racial pedigree, so he asked her point-blank whether she was colored or white. When she confessed the truth the merchant expressed great sorrow and deep regret that he could not avail himself of the services of so competent a person, but frankly admitted that employing a colored woman in his establishment in any except a menial position was simply out of the question.

Another young friend had an experience which, for some reasons, was still more disheartening and bitter than the one just mentioned. In order to secure lucrative employment she left Washington and went to New York. There she worked her way up in one of the largest dry goods stores[c] till she was placed as saleswoman in the cloak department. Tired of being separated from her family she decided to return to Washington, feeling sure that, with her experience and her fine recommendations from the New York firm, she could easily secure employment. Nor was she overconfident, for the proprietor of one of the largest dry goods stores in her native city was glad to secure the services of a young woman who brought such hearty credentials from New York. She had not been in this store very long, however, before she called upon me one day and asked me to intercede with the proprietor in her behalf, saying that she had been discharged that afternoon because it had been discovered that she was colored. When I called upon my young friend's employer he made no effort to avoid the issue, as I feared he would. He did not say he had discharged the young saleswoman because she had not given satisfaction, as he might easily have done. On the contrary, he admitted without the slightest hesitation that the young woman he had just discharged was one of the best clerks he had ever had. In the cloak department, where she had been assigned, she had been a brilliant success, he said. "But I cannot keep Miss Smith in my employ," he concluded. "Are you not master of your own store?" I ventured to inquire. The proprietor of this store was a Jew, and I felt that it was particularly cruel, unnatural and cold-blooded for the representative of one oppressed and persecuted race to deal so harshly and unjustly with a member of another. I had intended to intercede for my young friend, but when I thought how a reference to the persecution of his own race would wound his feelings, the words froze on my lips. "When I first heard your friend was colored," he explained, "I did not believe it and said so to the clerks who made the statement. Finally,

c. Dry goods were typically clothing and other textiles. Dry goods stores were the forerunner of the modern department store.

the girls who had been most pronounced in their opposition to working in a store with a colored girl came to me in a body and threatened to strike. 'Strike away,' said I, 'your places will be easily filled.' Then they started on another tack. Delegation after delegation began to file down to my office, some of the women my very best customers, to protest against my employing a colored girl. Moreover, they threatened to boycott my store if I did not discharge her at once. Then it became a question of bread and butter and I yielded to the inevitable—that's all. Now," said he, concluding, "if I lived in a great, cosmopolitan city like New York, I should do as I pleased, and refuse to discharge a girl simply because she was colored." But I thought of a new similar incident that happened in New York. I remembered that a colored woman, as fair as a lily and as beautiful as a Madonna, who was the head saleswoman in a large department store in New York, had been discharged, after she had held this position for years, when the proprietor accidentally discovered that a fatal drop of African blood was percolating somewhere thru her veins.

Not only can colored women secure no employment in the Washington stores, department and otherwise, except as menials, and such positions, of course, are few, but even as customers they are not infrequently treated with discourtesy both by the clerks and the proprietor himself. Following the trend of the times, the senior partner of the largest and best department store in Washington, who originally hailed from Boston, once the home of Wm. Lloyd Garrison,[d] Wendell Phillips[e] and Charles Sumner,[f] if my memory serves me right, decided to open a restaurant in his store. Tired and hungry after her morning's shopping a colored school teacher, whose relation to her African progenitors is so remote as scarcely to be discernible to the naked eye, took one seat at one of the tables in the restaurant of this Boston store. After sitting unnoticed a long time the colored teacher asked a waiter who passed her by if she would not take her order. She was quickly informed that colored people could not be served in that restaurant and was obliged to leave in confusion and shame, much to the amusement of the waiters and

d. William Lloyd Garrison (1805–1879): Noted abolitionist, editor of the *Liberator* and one of the founders of the American Anti-Slavery Society.

e. Wendell Phillips (1811–1884): Harvard educated lawyer and famous abolitionist orator. Also a member of the American Anti-Slavery Society.

f. Charles Sumner (1811–1874): US senator from Massachusetts, in 1856 caned in the US Senate by Preston Brooks of South Carolina for having delivered a vehement speech in opposition to the Kansas-Nebraska Act. Also the Senate leader of the Radical Republicans in the Reconstruction era.

guests who had noticed the incident. Shortly after that a teacher in Howard University, one of the best schools for colored youth in the country, was similarly insulted in the restaurant of the same store.

In one of the Washington theaters from which colored people are excluded altogether, members of the race have been viciously assaulted several times, for the proprietor well knows that colored people have no redress for such discriminations against them in the District courts. Not long ago a colored clerk in one of the departments who looks more like his paternal ancestors who fought for the lost cause[g] than his grandmothers who were victims of the peculiar institution,[h] bought a ticket for the parquet of this theater in which colored people are nowhere welcome, for himself and mother, whose complexion is a bit swarthy. The usher refused to allow the young man to take the seats for which his tickets called and tried to snatch from him the coupons. A scuffle ensured and both mother and son were ejected by force. A suit was brought against the proprietor and the damages awarded the injured man and his mother amounted to the munificent sum of one cent. One of the teachers in the Colored High School received similar treatment in the same theater.

Not long ago one of my little daughter's bosom friends figured in one of the most pathetic instances of which I have ever heard. A gentleman who is very fond of children promised to take six little girls in his neighborhood to a matinee. It happened that he himself and five of his little friends were so fair that they easily passed muster, as they stood in judgment before the ticket-seller and the ticket taker. Three of the little girls were sisters, two of whom were very fair and the other a bit brown. Just as the little girl, who happened to be last in the procession, went by the ticket taker, that argus-eyed sophisticated gentleman detected something which caused a deep, dark frown to mantle his brow and he did not allow her to pass. "I guess you have made a mistake," he called to the host of this theatre party. "Those little girls," pointing to the fair ones, "may be admitted, but this one," designating the brown one, "Can't." But the colored man was quite equal to the emergency. Fairly frothing at the mouth with anger he asked the ticket taker what he meant, what he was trying to insinuate about that particular little girl. "Do you mean to tell me," he shouted in rage, "that I must go clear to the Philippine Islands to bring this child to the United States and then I can't take her to the theatre in the National Capital?" The little ruse succeeded brilliantly,

g. "The Lost Cause" is a common epithet for the Confederacy.
h. "The Peculiar Institution" was a common term for slavery.

as he knew it would. "Beg your pardon," said the ticket taker, "don't know what I was thinking about. Of course she can go in."

"What was the matter with me this afternoon? Mother," asked the little brown girl innocently, when she mentioned the affair at home. "Why did the man at the theatre let my two sisters and the other girls in and try to keep me out?" In relating this incident, the child's mother told me her little girl's question, which showed such blissful ignorance of the depressing, cruel conditions which confronted her, completely unnerved her for a time.

Altho white and colored teachers are under the same Board of Education and the system for the children of both races is said to be uniform, prejudice against the colored teachers in the public schools is manifested in a variety of ways. From 1870 to 1900 there was a colored superintendent at the head of the colored schools. During all that time the directors of the cooking, sewing, physical culture, manual training, music and art departments were colored people. Six years ago a change was inaugurated. The colored superintendent was legislated out of office and the directorships, without a single exception, were taken from colored teachers and given to the whites. There was no complaint about the work done by the colored directors no more than is heard about every officer in every school. The directors of the art and physical culture departments were particularly fine. Now, no matter how competent or superior the colored teachers in our public schools may be, they know that they can never rise to the height of a directorship, can never hope to be more than an assistant and receive the meager salary therefore, unless the present regime is radically changed.

Not long ago one of the most distinguished kindergartners in the country came to deliver a course of lectures in Washington. The colored teachers were eager to attend, but they could not buy the coveted privilege for love or money. When they appealed to the director of kindergartens, they were told that the expert kindergartner had come to Washington under the auspices of private individuals, so that she could not possibly have them admitted. Realizing what a loss colored teachers had sustained in being deprived of the information and inspiration which theses lectures afforded, one of the white teachers volunteered to repeat them as best she could for the benefit of her colored co-laborers for half the price she herself had paid, and the proposition was eagerly accepted by some.

Strenuous efforts are being made to run Jim Crow cars in the national capital. "Resolved, that a Jim Crow law should be adopted and enforced in the District of Columbia," was the subject of a discussion engaged in last

January by the Columbian Debating Society of the George Washington University in our national capital, and the decision was rendered in favor of the affirmative. Representative Heflin, of Alabama, who introduced a bill providing for Jim Crow street cars in the District of Columbia last winter, has just received a letter from the president of the East Brookland Citizens' Association "indorsing the movement for separate street cars and sincerely hoping that you will be successful in getting this enacted into a law as soon as possible." Brookland is a suburb of Washington.[i]

The colored laborer's path to a decent livelihood is by no means smooth. Into some of the trades unions here he is admitted, while from others he is excluded altogether. By the union men this is denied, altho I am personally acquainted with skilled workmen who tell me they are not admitted into the unions because they are colored. But even when they are allowed to join the unions they frequently derive little benefit, owing to certain tricks of the trade. When the word passes round that help is needed and colored laborers apply, they are often told by the union officials that they have secured all the men they needed, because the places are reserved for white men, until they have been provided with jobs, and colored men must remain idle, unless the supply of white men is too small.

I am personally acquainted with one of the most skilful laborers in the hardware business in Washington. For thirty years he has been working for the same firm. He told me he could not join the union, and that his employer had been almost forced to discharge him, because the union men threatened to boycott his store if he did not. If another man could have been found at the time to take his place he would have lost his job, he said. When no other human being can bring a refractory chimney or stove to its senses, this colored man is called upon as the court of last appeal. If he fails to subdue it, it is pronounced a hopeless case at once. And yet this expert workman received much less for his services than do white men who cannot compare with him in skill.

And so I might go on citing instance after instance to show the variety of ways in which our people are sacrificed on the altar of prejudice in the Capital of the United States and how almost insurmountable are the obstacles which

i. Brookland is a section of the District of Columbia that lies close to its northeast border. Catholic University is located in the Brookland area. The last sentence may well have been inserted specifically for the *Independent* article, since residents of the district would not likely have needed the location of the neighborhood identified. As is evident from the 1940 version of this speech, Terrell edited her essays for the audience who would be reading or hearing them.

block his path to success. Early in life many a colored youth is so appalled by the helplessness and hopelessness of his situation in this country that in a sort of stoical despair he resigns himself to his fate. "What is the good of our trying to acquire an education? We can't all be preachers, teachers, doctors and lawyers. Besides those professions there is almost nothing for colored people to do but engage in the most menial occupations, and we do not need an education for that." More than once such remarks, uttered by young men and women in our public schools who possess brilliant intellects, have wrung my heart.It is impossible for any white person in the United States, no matter how sympathetic and broad, to realize what life would mean to him if his incentive to effort were suddenly snatched away. To the lack of incentive to effort, which is the awful shadow under which we live, may be traced the wreck and ruin of scores of colored youth. And surely nowhere in the world do oppression and persecution based solely on the color of the skin appear more hateful and hideous than in the capital of the United States, because the chasm between the principles upon which this Government was founded, in which it still professes to believe, and those which are daily practiced under the protection of the flag, yawns so wide and deep.

William Edward Burghardt Du Bois

Disfranchisement

W. E. B. Du Bois was a brilliant scholar who emerged as one of, if not the, most important civil rights leaders of the first half of the twentieth century. Although his accomplishments were many, Du Bois is most remembered as the driving force of the National Association for the Advancement of Colored People (NAACP) during its early years and as a vocal opponent of Booker T. Washington's accommodationist stand. Du Bois was a writer first; he authored several books and many articles and conference papers and for many years edited the *Crisis*, the NAACP's newsletter, and for that organ, authored its editorials. His public speaking mirrored his writing. His speaking voice sounded very much like his written voice, and in speeches he addressed the same issues about which he was writing. This is not to devalue the importance of his oratory. Speaking face-to-face with audiences was often critical to his work, as when he led the Niagara movement conference in 1905 or struggled for leadership at the 1909 National Negro Conference, which founded the NAACP. Rhetorically, however, Du Bois seems to have expected his audiences to rise to his level of reasoning and vocabulary. Neither his written nor oral discourse demonstrated any inclination to "talk down" to his audiences. His speeches, like his written works, are scholarly: analytically reasoned, carefully worded, and sharply attentive to the workings of human society.

William Edward Burghardt Du Bois was born in Great Barrington, Massachusetts, on February 23, 1868. Light-skinned, Du Bois was multiracial, of African, French Huguenot, Dutch, and Haitian descent. His mother was Mary Burghardt, whose grandfather had earned his freedom from slavery by having fought in the American Revolution, and whose family had farmed in the Great Barrington community ever since. His father, Alfred Du Bois, the son of a ship's steward, had been born in Santo Domingo, Cuba, and after many travels, came to Great Barrington as a barber. Alfred left the family while Du Bois was still very young, and his mother reared him by herself. Strongly committed to the idea that education would be the path to her son's success, as soon as he was of school age, she moved to town from the family farm so that he could attend public school.[1]

In the latter half of the nineteenth century, Great Barrington's African American community was small and well integrated into the social life of the town; the more recent Irish and Czech immigrant millworkers were the "outsiders." Du Bois's recollections are that he did not experience discrimination on the basis of race until he enrolled at Fisk University, a college for freedmen in Nashville, Tennessee. Upon graduation from Fisk, he enrolled in Harvard University with a financial grant to support his further study. After he had now departed the segregated South and returned to his native New England, Du Bois continued to be confronted with the daily experiences of racial prejudice, even at Harvard. He persevered, however, studying philosophy and the then-youthful discipline of sociology. He graduated with a baccalaureate degree in 1890 and was voted one of the six class-day speakers by his fellow students, only the second African American to be so honored. He then traveled abroad, studying at the University of Berlin. He was awarded a doctorate from Harvard University in 1895, although most of his graduate education had been acquired in Berlin.

In 1894, while completing his PhD, he accepted a teaching position at Wilberforce University. His time at Wilberforce was not a happy one, as he clashed with the university's religious and conservative culture. Booker T. Washington also offered him a teaching position, at Tuskegee Institute, in 1894, but Du Bois had already accepted the position at Wilberforce. Later there would be some personal controversy as to whether Washington's offer had been open-ended when he later dismissed a job inquiry from Du Bois. After two years at Wilberforce, Du Bois accepted a research position at the University of Pennsylvania to study the African American community. The result was *The Philadelphia Negro*, an exceptional, rigorous sociological study that quantitatively established the environmental causes of poverty in that community. Du Bois's rigorous academic study stood in stark contrast to the pseudo-scientific social Darwinist essays of the day that argued from effect back to cause—that African Americans' poverty was "proof" of their hereditary inferiority. In 1897, he accepted a teaching position at Atlanta University as a professor of sociology.

Although Du Bois's scholarly work was categorical in its support of African Americans and its condemnation of white racism, his politics in the 1890s were more pragmatic. He believed that the policy of promoting industrial education for African Americans was useful, as was providing opportunities for the pursuit of traditional, classical studies. He accepted the idea of literacy and education requirements for voting, although he argued vigorously for their equal application. By the turn of the century, however, his thinking was evolving, and in 1903, he published one of his best-known works, *The Souls of Black Folk*, which was a strong indictment of Booker T. Washington's policy of accommodation.[2] In 1905, he helped convene a conference that met in Niagara, New York, which subsequently became known as the Niagara movement. In many regards a precursor of the NAACP, the Niagara movement espoused political and social agitation, arguing that only full political equality would yield the economic changes that the African American community needed and deserved.[3]

The 1906 Atlanta race riot seems to have been a turning point in Du Bois's activism. While it is clear that his reform perspective had been evolving since his arrival at Atlanta University, the 1906 riot was a particularly bloody and violent affair in which some ten thousand whites invaded the African American community for the purpose of terrorizing and intimidating them out of the ballot.[4] Du Bois himself saw his Atlanta years as being particularly formative—hardening his determination that African Americans achieve full and equal rights—and of the 1906 violence he wrote simply: "I saw the Atlanta riot."[5] In 1909, a group of African Americans and activist white liberals met at the National Negro Conference in New York, a meeting called at least partly in response to the Springfield, Illinois, 1908 race riot.[6] From that conference evolved the National Association for the Advancement of Colored People, and at the 1910 conference, Du Bois was named the director of research and publicity. That summer, he resigned from Atlanta University and moved to New York City to assume that position, and in November of that year, the first issue of the *Crisis* appeared, the NAACP magazine that Du Bois would edit until 1943.[7]

As director of research and publicity, Du Bois accepted many speaking engagements. Frequently, his speaking was coordinated with the editorial content of the *Crisis*. Du Bois's campaign in relation to the National American Association of Woman's Suffrage was representative. Prior to and immediately following the Civil War, abolitionists and woman suffragists shared common cause. Most of the reformers engaged in one cause actively supported the other and were united in the American Equal Rights Association. Within the language of the Fourteenth Amendment that guaranteed equal rights to all citizens, many suffragists discerned the rationale for giving women the ballot.[8] As the country debated adoption of the Fifteenth Amendment, which guaranteed African American men the right to vote, a fissure between the two movements emerged. Abolitionists such as Frederick Douglass, who had been ardent supporters of women's rights, argued that it was politically infeasible to expand the equal rights amendments to include women. They argued that it was imperative to solidify the abolition of slavery by ensuring African American men the protection of the ballot, and once passed, seek a separate amendment for woman suffrage. In 1869, two woman suffrage organizations emerged: the American Woman Suffrage Association (AWSA), which supported the two-amendment strategy, and the National Woman Suffrage Association (NWSA), under the leadership of Elizabeth Cady Stanton and Susan B. Anthony, which spurned that strategy.[9] In 1890, the two organizations reunited to become the National American Woman Suffrage Association (NAWSA), but the schism between NAWSA and African Americans remained.[10] For example, although the National Association of Colored Women was one of only two major women's organizations that officially endorsed woman suffrage, African American women were not permitted to join whites-only chapters, nor were African American suffrage organizations allowed to affiliate with NAWSA.[11]

By fall of 1911, Du Bois decided to address the issue of this continuing split between the two major rights movements. He decried the woman suffrage calculus of distancing their cause from that of the African American. In the *Crisis*, he criticized the president of the NAWSA, Anna Howard Shaw, for having recommended to suffragists, "Do not touch the Negro problem. It will offend the South."[12] Du Bois similarly challenged his male readers to support woman suffrage: "Every argument for Negro suffrage is an argument for women's suffrage; every argument for woman suffrage is an argument for Negro suffrage; both are great moments in democracy. There should be on the part of Negroes absolutely no hesitation whenever and wherever responsible human beings are without voice in their government. The man of Negro blood who hesitates to do them justice is false to his race, his ideals and his country."[13] In the middle of this coordinated campaign to heal the rift, on November 24, 1912, Du Bois addressed the NAWSA annual convention with a speech entitled "Disfranchisement."

Dr. Du Bois's public speeches are remarkably consistent and are themselves emblematic of the man—academic in style, intellectually engaged, and socially concerned. "Disfranchisement" is no exception. The speech is analytically constructed, presenting the issue of suffrage from the perspective of first premises and sociological implications. Du Bois's analysis also presents itself as exhaustive, repeatedly analyzing an issue from all possible angles. As with most of Du Bois's speeches, "Disfranchisement" is one that could be presented at an academic conference rather than a gathering of political activists and reformers. His language is neither emotional nor vehement, and he does not relate any horrific anecdotes illustrating prejudice. Those kinds of rhetorical appeals seem foreign to his nature. Yet, Du Bois is certainly aware of the rhetorical nature of the situation, and "Disfranchisement" is designed both to edify and to persuade. In this speech, he most commonly yokes his appeal for African American suffrage to the audience's expressed goal of gaining woman's suffrage.

Du Bois is ever the sociologist as he approaches the subject of voting rights. He scrutinizes the topic analytically to determine what the true sociological causes and effects are. Each issue is viewed from every possible angle, distilling the issues down to their first principles, essential principles that address how society operates and in what manner it should operate. The opening of his speech is representative. At the very outset, he tells his audience that nations typically exclude certain populations from voting for one of five reasons: the group is too ignorant, is too inexperienced, would misuse the ballot, does not need the ballot, or does not want the ballot. These are, however, sham arguments, he says; instead they "are in reality arguments addressed to the self-interest of the present rulers." Further, he posits that, to support suffrage rights with a counterargument of expediency—that is, because the excluded populations will become rebellious—is a dangerous argument because then the dispute can devolve into whether or not the excluded group *ought* to be controlled. Better, Du Bois holds, for the suffragists' response to remain based upon first principles: "The real underlying and eternally valid arguments for extending as far as possible the participation of human beings in their own government must lie deeper than these phrases and be more carefully framed. If this is done then the advance of democracy will be made easier and more effective, since we can scrutinize the essential facts and not be distracted by immaterial suggestions." In typically analytical fashion, Du Bois then proposes to examine the five fallacious arguments for excluding certain groups from voting, and in that way discover "the essential argument for extending the right to vote."

Regarding the argument that some groups are "too ignorant" to be entitled to vote, he observes that "we say easily, 'The ignorant ought not to vote.'" It is important to Du Bois that we discern the reality: "We *mean* to say, 'There should be in the state, no grown person of sound mind who is not intelligent enough to vote'" (emphasis ours). Once that reality emerges from the discussion, the burden shifts from the excluded group being forced to prove that they are not "ignorant," and onto the state to ensure that no grown person is uneducated and thus too ignorant to vote. The remedy to ignorance is not exclusion, but education. Du Bois thus proceeds deliberately through each of the five fallacious arguments, logically dispelling each in turn.

In similar fashion, Du Bois approaches the principle of democracy. He posits that there are three "methods" of government: the benevolent tyrant, the select few, and the excluded groups. The methods are evolutionary; that is, as societies recognize the hazards of entrusting the decisions of government to one or a few, the method of government inexorably expands to include more and more "decision-makers." It thus progresses towards greater and greater democracy. "So soon as a nation discovers that it holds in the heads and hearts of its individual citizens the vast mine of knowledge out of which it may build a just government," he observes, "then more and more it calls those citizens to select their rulers and judge the justice of their acts." The "first principle" of government is that "the *real* argument for democracy is then that in the people we have the *real* source of that endless life and unbounded wisdom which the *real* ruler of men must have" (emphases ours). From this philosophy of democracy, Du Bois draws his arguments in support of suffrage rights for both women and African Americans: "Democracy alone is the method of storing the whole experience of the race for the benefit of the future, and if democracy tries to exclude women or Negroes or the poor or any class because of the innate characteristics which do not interfere with intelligence then that democracy cripples itself and belies its name." A society that is both wise and just will do everything in its power not only to provide its citizens with every possible opportunity to participate in government, but it will do all it can to educate them and empower them to do so capably.

Du Bois seems ever mindful of his audience. He consistently applies his arguments for democracy first to woman suffrage and applies the same argument to African American voting rights. For example, some groups have been excluded because it has been claimed that they "do not need the ballot." Du Bois notes that "This is often said of women. It is argued that everything that women might do for themselves with the ballot can be done for them; that they have influence and friends "at court," and that their enfranchisement would simply double the number of ballots." He then compares women's case with African Americans': "So, too, we are told that Negroes can have done for them by others all that they could possibly do for themselves with the ballot, and much more because the whites are more intelligent." He reports that similar arguments are made that neither group "wants" the ballot. Such arguments, as applied to either women or African Americans, are irrelevant when considered in the context of the philosophy of democracy: "We must remember that if the theory of democracy is correct, the right to vote is not merely a privilege, not simply a method of meeting the needs of a particular group, and least of all a matter of recognized want or desire. Democracy is a method of realizing the broadest measure of justice to all human beings."

Du Bois returns to this analogy three more times in the speech, and as the speech progresses, he makes the analogy ever more explicit. "When women ask for the ballot they are asking not a privilege but a necessity," he tells his audience; "so too with American Negroes." When a group is excluded from the franchise, then it "excludes from its expressed wisdom," the experience and knowledge possessed by that group, as, for example, in the case of "the knowledge possessed by mothers, wives and daughters." "The same argument," he tells his audience directly, "applies to other excluded groups" such as African Americans. Du Bois argues that "the feeling and experience of that race," as expressed by their votes, "is absolutely necessary to the realization of the broadest justice for all citizens."

Du Bois's rhetorical overture to his audience of woman suffragists includes one particularly interesting passage. As he discusses the evolution of government from the method of the benevolent tyrant to the democratic participation of citizens, Du Bois argues that democracy's collective wisdom and greater concern for justice derives from the fact that no surrogate can know another individual's perspective: "In the last analysis, the man himself, however humble, knows his own condition. He may not know how to remedy it, he may not realize just what is the matter, but he knows when something hurts, and he alone knows how that hurt feels. Or if, sunk below feeling or comprehension or complaint, he does not even know that he is hurt, God help his country, for it not only lacks knowledge, but has destroyed some of the sources of knowledge!" Du Bois's argument and language here closely mirror one of the most famous speeches delivered by Elizabeth Cady Stanton, the former president of the NAWSA. Cady Stanton gave the speech, entitled "Solitude of Self," three times in January 1892. The speech was delivered in written form to the House Committee on the Judiciary, presented at a hearing of the Senate Committee on Woman Suffrage, and delivered to a convention of NAWSA.[14] The thesis of Stanton's speech iterates the central argument of Du Bois's "Disfranchisement." As Stanton summarizes it: "The point I wish plainly to bring before you on this occasion is the individuality of each human soul—our Protestant idea, the right of individual conscience and judgment—our republican idea, individual citizenship."[15] Stanton develops several narratives that illustrate her point, and one of those, like Du Bois's, focuses on the individual nature of suffering. No one can know the suffering that another person experiences: "Alone we sit in the shadows of our affliction. . . . In hours like these we realize the awful solitude of individual life, its pains, its penalties, its responsibilities; . . . Seeing that life must ever be a march and a battle, that each soldier must be equipped for his own protection, it is the height of cruelty to rob the individual of a single natural right. . . . No one can share her fears, no one can mitigate her pangs; and if her sorrow is greater than she can bear, alone she passes beyond the gates into the vast unknown."[16] Du Bois employs remarkably similar language to make the same argument: "Only the sufferer knows his sufferings, and . . . no state can be strong which excludes from its expressed wisdom, the knowledge possessed by mothers, wives and daughters." Du Bois's rhetoric is sophisticated here. On one level, he implicitly evokes one of the leading figures of the woman's suffrage movement; on the other his focus on "suffering" reminds his audience of the travails that inspire his immediate plea: for equal rights for African Americans.

Although the language, organization, and analytical nature of his arguments convey a general sense that the speech is a dispassionate scholarly treatise, at key junctures of the speech Du Bois strategically employs evocative rhetorical language. He is, for example, categorically dismissive of the opposition's arguments. "The second argument that experience is a necessary prerequisite to voting," he declares unequivocally, "is absurd." Similarly, when a democracy excludes groups of otherwise capable citizens, it "cripples itself and belies its name." Or, as he characterizes the situation regarding the proposal that African Americans secure equal and voting rights for themselves: "Every white southerner who wants peons beneath him, who believes in hereditary menials and a privileged aristocracy, or who hates certain races because of their characteristics, would resent this." Du Bois also employs evaluative verbs, adverbs, and adjectives to convey an indisputably rhetorical message. We have only to look at the problems of the world that involve women and children, he says, in order "to realize how *desperately* we need this excluded wisdom" that would be supplied by woman suffrage (emphasis ours). Similarly, he summarizes his argument that a just society requires woman's participation through the ballot: "They need it to right the balance of a world *sadly* awry because of its *brutal* neglect of the rights of women and children. With the best will and knowledge no man can know women's wants as well as women themselves. To disfranchise them is *deliberately* to turn from knowledge and *grope* in ignorance" (emphases ours). As Du Bois aptly and rhetorically summarizes the heart of his speech, "The cure for the ills of democracy is seen to be more democracy. We are rapidly changing from a form of social control dictated by the interests of a few to one dictated by the interests of a large and larger majority."

Measured by NAWSA's continuing exclusion of African Americans from its organization, Du Bois's speech was not successful.[17] Although the NAACP was able to regain some legal rights for African Americans, those gains were painfully slow and primarily earned through court battles rather than by persuading the general American population. Increasingly, Du Bois turned to more wide-reaching methods and philosophies, ultimately embracing both pan-Africanism and socialism. In 1943, he lost the editorship of his beloved *Crisis* and in 1961 emigrated from the United States to Ghana. Most observers agree that his emigration resulted from his inability to bring about the change he desired. There is no dispute however, that his scholarly works, his *Crisis* editorials, and his speeches have influenced the thinking of several generations of Americans. Few today would argue against the philosophy of government he espoused in "Disfranchisement," for example. America simply needed to catch up to where W. E. B. Du Bois already was.

Disfranchisement

November 24, 1912
Philadelphia, Pennsylvania

The mere fact that democratic government has spread in the past and is still spreading does not prove that those concerned in its spread always realize the broader foundations of the argument that supports it. Usually nations are dealing with concrete groups whose enfranchisement is advocated and the arguments against the steep fall under these categories:

a. The persons in the group are too ignorant to vote intelligently.
b. The persons are too inexperienced to be trusted with so great responsibility.
c. The persons would misuse the privilege.
d. They do not need the ballot.
e. They do not want the right to vote.

The obvious assumptions behind these objections are that only the intelligent should have the right to vote; that voters should possess some technical knowledge of the government; that only those should have the franchise who do not misuse it for selfish or other ends, and who need the ballot for their good and are anxious to have it.

No sooner, however, do we express these qualifications than it is manifest that these are not such qualifications as one could reasonably require. They are in reality arguments addressed to the self-interest of the present rulers and calculated to show that sharing their prerogative with another group will not disturb or prejudice their present power or perquisites.

While it is manifestly the part of practical political wisdom thus to cajole the present ruler, the weapon used is dangerous and the argument is only partially valid. The real underlying and eternally valid arguments for extending as far as possible the participation of human beings in their own government must lie deeper than these phrases and be more carefully framed. If this is done then the advance of democracy will be made easier and more effective, since we can scrutinize the essential facts and not be distracted by immaterial suggestions.

What is then the essential argument for extending the right to vote? We may possibly reach it by clearing away the misapprehensions that lurk in the arguments mentioned above

For instance, we say easily, "The ignorant ought not to vote." We mean to say, "There should be in the state, no grown person of sound mind who is not intelligent enough to vote." These two statements may seem to be essentially the same, but they have vastly different implications. In the one case we cast the ignorant aside. They ought not to vote and the implication is that it is their fault. Their interests, we assume will be looked after by others and if they are not, we acknowledge no responsibility. On the other hand, if we stress the responsibility of the state for the education of its citizens as prior to political rights, then the conclusion is that if a state allows its citizens to grow up in ignorance it ought to suffer from an ignorant ballot: that it is the threat of ignorant votes that makes good schools.

The second argument that experience is a necessary prerequisite to voting is absurd. According to this we should have no new voters, unless we assume that the capacity to rule is hereditary. Such assumptions have been made in the past with regard to certain races and one sex. It can scarcely be said, however, that any adequate proof exists which proves that only Englishmen or only persons of the male sex are capable of learning to take part in democratic government. When we consider that the civilized world today is being ruled by classes who were pronounced utterly incapable of self-rule or of being trained for self-rule a century ago, we must conclude that the ability to rule is, on the whole, a matter of individual social training and that consequently there must always be a part of the body politic without experience who must be trained by the others. In voting as in other matters we learn by doing. It is to be expected that every new voting class and every new democracy will make its costly and ridiculous mistakes—will pass through demagoguery, extravagance, "boss" rule, bribery and the like; but it is through such experience that voters learn to rule and the cost although vast is not excessive if the end is finally gained.

Thus we see that ignorance is a warning and a public responsibility rather than a permanent excuse for disfranchisement, save in the case of the small number who cannot be educated; that inexperience can only be cured by experience and is consequently no reason for disfranchisement; and that misuse of the ballot is perhaps the most effective way of teaching its right use.

There are, however, people who insist on regarding the franchise not as a necessity for the many but as the privilege of the few. They say of persons and classes, "They do not need the ballot." This is often said of women. It is argued that everything that women might do for themselves with the ballot can be done for them; that they have influence and friends "at court," and that their enfranchisement would simply double the number of ballots. So, too, we are told that Negroes can have done for them by others all that they could possibly do for themselves with the ballot, and much more because the whites are more intelligent.

Further than this it is argued that many of the disfranchised recognize this. "Women do not want the ballot," has been a very effective counter war cry; so much so that many a man has taken refuge in the declaration, "When they want to vote, why then—."

Such phrases show so curious a misapprehension of the foundations of the argument for democracy that this argument must be continually restated and emphasized. We must remember that if the theory of democracy is correct, the right to vote is not merely a privilege, not simply a method of meeting the needs of a particular group, and least of all a matter of recognized want or desire. Democracy is a method of realizing the broadest measure of justice to all human beings. The world has in the past attempted various methods of attaining this end, most of which can be summed up in three categories:

The method of the benevolent tyrant
The method of the select few
The method of the excluded groups.

The method of entrusting the government of a people to a strong ruler has great advantages when the ruler combines strength with ability, unselfish devotion to the public good and knowledge of what that good calls for. Such a combination is, however, rare and the selection of the right ruler is very difficult. To leave the selection to force is to put a premium on physical strength, chance and intrigue. To make the selection a matter of birth simply transfers the real power from sovereign to selected minister. Inevitably the choice of real rulers must fall on electors.

Then comes the problem. Who shall elect? The earlier answer was: a select few, such as the wise, the best born, the able. Many people assume that it was corruption that made such aristocracies fail. By no means. The best and most effective aristocracy, like the best monarchy, suffered from lack of knowledge; they did not know or understand the needs of the people, and they could not find out, for in the last analysis only the man himself, however humble, knows his own condition. He may not know how to remedy it, he may not realize just what is the matter, but he knows when something hurts, and he alone knows how that hurt feels. Or if, sunk below feeling or comprehension or complaint, he does not even know that he is hurt, God help his country, for it not only lacks knowledge, but has destroyed some of the sources of knowledge!

So soon as a nation discovers that it holds in the heads and hearts of its individual citizens the vast mine of knowledge out of which it may build a just government, then more and more it calls those citizens to select their rulers and judge the justice of their acts.

Even here, however, the temptation is to ask only for the wisdom of citizens of a certain grade, or those of recognized worth. Continually some classes are tacitly or expressly excluded. Thus women have been regularly excluded from modern democracy, because of custom, because of the persistent theory of female subjection, and because it was argued that their husbands or other male folk would look to their interests. Now manifestly most husbands, fathers and brothers will so far as they know how, or so far as they realize women's needs, look after them. But remember that the foundation of the argument is that in the last analysis only the sufferer knows his sufferings, and that no state can be strong which excludes from its expressed wisdom, the knowledge possessed by mothers, wives and daughters. Certainly we have but to view the unsatisfactory relations of the sexes the world over and the problem of children, to realize how desperately we need this excluded wisdom.

The same argument applies to other excluded groups: if a race like the Negro race is excluded from the ballot, then so far as that race is a part of the economic and social organization of the land, the feeling and experience of that race is absolutely necessary to the realization of the broadest justice for all citizens. Or if the "submerged tenth" be excluded, then again there is lost experience of untold value, and the submerged must be raised rapidly to a plane where they can speak for themselves.[a]

In the same way and for the same reason children must be educated, insanity prevented and only those put under guardianship of others who can in no way be trained to speak for themselves.

The real argument for democracy is then that in the people we have the real source of that endless life and unbounded wisdom which the real ruler of men must have. A given people today may not be intelligent, but through a democratic government that recognizes not only the worth of the individual to himself but the worth of his feelings and experiences to all, they can educate not only the individual unit, but generation after generation until they accumulate vast stores of wisdom. Democracy alone is the method of storing the whole experience of the race for the benefit of the future, and if democracy tries to exclude women or Negroes or the poor or any class because of the innate characteristics which do not interfere with intelligence then that democracy cripples itself and belies its name.

From this point of view we can easily see the weakness and the strength of current criticism of extensions of the ballot. It is the business of modern government to see to it, *first*, that the number of the ignorant within its bounds is reduced to the very smallest number. *Secondly*, it is the duty of every such government to extend as quickly as possible the number of grown persons of mature age who can vote. Such possible voters must be regarded not as sharers of a limited treasure, but as sources of new national wisdom and strength.

The addition of the new wisdom, the new points of view and new interests must of course be, from time to time, bewildering and confusing. Today those who have a voice in the body politic have expressed their wishes and sufferings. The result has been a more or less effective balancing of their conflicting interests. The appearance of new interests and complaints means disarrangement and confusion to the older equilibrium. But this is not in itself evil—it is the inevitable preliminary step to that larger equilibrium in which the interests of no human soul will be neglected. These interests will not, surely, be all fully realized but they will be recognized and given as full weight as the conflicting interests of others will allow. The problem

a. The submerged tenth refers to those in society so desperately impoverished that they largely live "outside" society. It was a term used by Du Bois in his landmark study of socioeconomic classes in Philadelphia as well as by William Booth, founder of the Salvation Army.

of government thereafter will be to reduce the necessary conflict of human interests to the minimum.

From such a point of view one easily sees the strength of the demand for the ballot on the part of certain disfranchised classes. When women ask for the ballot they are asking not a privilege but a necessity. You may not see the necessity; you may easily argue that women do not need to vote. Indeed the women themselves in considerable number may feel the same. Nevertheless they do need the ballot. They need it to right the balance of a world sadly awry because of its brutal neglect of the rights of women and children. With the best will and knowledge no man can know women's wants as well as women themselves. To disfranchise them is deliberately to turn from knowledge and grope in ignorance.

So too with American Negroes: the South continually insists that a benevolent guardianship of whites over blacks is the ideal thing. They assume that white people not only know better what Negroes need than Negroes themselves, but are anxious to supply those needs. As a result, instead of knowledge they grope in ignorance and helplessness. They cannot "understand" the Negro, they cannot protect him from cheating and lynching and in general instead of loving guardianship, we see anarchy and exploitation. If the Negro could speak for himself in the South instead of having to depend on the chance sympathy of white citizens, how much healthier growth of democracy the South would have.

It is not for a moment to be assumed that enfranchising women would not cost something. It would for many years confuse our politics. It would change the composition of family and social life. It would admit to the ballot thousands of inexperienced persons unable to vote intelligently. Above all it would interfere with some of the present prerogatives of men and probably for some time to come to annoy them considerably.

So, too, Negro enfranchisement meant Reconstruction with its theft, bribery and incompetency. It would mean today that black men in the South would have to be treated with consideration, have their wishes more respected and their manhood recognized. Every white southerner who wants peons beneath him, who believes in hereditary menials and a privileged aristocracy, or who hates certain races because of their characteristics, would resent this.

Notwithstanding this, if America is ever to become a government built on the broadest justice to every citizen, then every citizen must be enfranchised. There may be temporary exclusions until the ignorant or their children are taught, or to avoid too sudden an influx of inexperienced voters. But such exclusions can be but temporary if justice is to prevail.

While many of those seeking enfranchisement recognize the broad demand of justice for all human beings which underlies their argument, they are often tempted by the exigencies of the situation to ignore the application of those underlying principles to any but themselves, or even to deny and attack the justice of equally just demands for the ballot. The advocates of woman suffrage have continually been in great danger of asking the ballot not because they are citizens, but because they occupy a certain social position, are of a certain grade of intelligences, or are "white." Continually it has been said in America, "If paupers and Negroes vote why not college-bred women of wealth and position?" The assumption is that such a woman has superior right to have her interests represented in the nation and that Negroes and paupers have few rights which society leaders are bound to respect. So, too, many colored people, in arguing their own enfranchisement, are willing to be counted against the enfranchisement of women or foreigners or the unfortunate. Such argument or neglect is both false and dangerous, and while its phrasing may be effective at times it represents a climbing of one class on the misery of another.

The insistent call of democracy is ringing in the ears of all people today as never before in spite of the hard experiences of the past. The cure for the ills of democracy is seen to be more democracy. We are rapidly changing from a form of social control dictated by the interests of a few to one dictated by the interests of a large and larger majority. Not only is this true in what is usually called politics but also in industry. In fact our political interests are becoming more and more industrial and our industry is assuming larger and larger political aspects. In the industrial world we are still under the rule of the strong monarch, with at most the mitigation of the power of the selected few. We feel the consequent confusion. We lack knowledge of industrial conditions. We have no standard of industrial justice. Whence shall knowledge and standards come? Through democracy. Through having the rights and wishes of every worker represented in the power that controls industry. This will be hard to attain. The passing of the strong monarch in industry as in politics will spell anarchy in many places, but social justice will eventually come. How necessary then to build a state of the broadest democracy to cope with the industrial problem within nations and between nations and races.

Marcus Mosiah Garvey

The Principles of the Universal Negro Improvement Association

Even during his lifetime, Marcus Garvey appeared to his followers, and even his detractors, to be a historic figure whose ambitions for himself and his race made him larger than life. He was the first black nationalist to assemble a mass following, but he also attracted numerous powerful enemies representing very diverse aims and ideologies. He was a flamboyant writer and orator, one whose penchant for pomp and exaggeration provided fuel for his critics. Yet the philosophy to which he gave voice was sophisticated and well developed, and many subsequent leaders such as Malcolm X, Louis Lomax, and Stokely Carmichael were his intellectual heirs. He spoke simultaneously to the frustrations and the hopes of people of African descent around the world. He spoke assertively of black pride and racial purpose to an audience who had heard so often that their skin color proved their lack of worth. Although Marcus Garvey was often dismissed as a "showman," there was considerable and important substance to the show.

Marcus Garvey was born on August 17, 1887, in St. Ann's Bay, Jamaica, the son of Marcus and Sarah Garvey. Marcus Garvey Sr. was a stonemason and small farmer, said to be descended from the Maroons, the escaped Jamaican slaves who had fought and won their independence in the eighteenth century. Although such lineage was on one hand a point of pride, Jamaica's culture at the time remained stratified by color, with its disenfranchised African descendants comprising the lowest tier, white descendents of British colonists the highest, and mulattoes filling in the middle. Garvey received his education from a variety of sources, including elementary school, private tutors, Sunday school, and his father, who was himself well-read and often served locally as a kind of legal advisor in St. Ann's Bay. At the age of fourteen, Garvey was apprenticed to a printer and there continued his informal education, through both his own reading and his participation in literary and political societies. At sixteen, he moved to Kingston, Jamaica's capital, and by the age of eighteen, he had already been appointed the manager of a printing house. This was a signal accomplishment in two regards—both his age and his color worked against his receiving this promotion. Most printing foremen in Jamaica were older, white emigrants from elsewhere in the British Commonwealth. In 1907, Garvey lost his position when he helped lead a printers' strike, siding with the workers rather than management. Throughout his life, Garvey would incur personal costs for political positions he took on behalf of those who were less well-off than himself.[1]

Although fired and blacklisted from private printing firms, Garvey quickly found new employment with the government printing agency, about the same time that he also became involved in the first of his organized political activities, including the launch of an unsuccessful publication, *Garvey's Watchman*. In 1910, in need of a better financial foundation from which to engage in politics, he left Jamaica to seek more lucrative work in Central America. There he undertook a variety of jobs, first in Costa Rica and later in Panama and Ecuador; in Costa Rica he also edited *La Nacion*, and in all three countries, he found himself drawn into local politics. Wherever he traveled, Garvey was struck by the poor working and social conditions endured by those of African descent. From Latin America, Garvey traveled back to Jamaica and then on to England, where he worked for a time for the *Africa Times and Orient Review*, delivered speeches at the famed Hyde Park's Speaker's Corner, attended law lectures at Birkbeck College of the University of London, and traveled to a variety of European countries. In England, he witnessed for himself the disparity between the workings of democracy in that country as compared to the colonial system in Jamaica. His political philosophy was further shaped by his involvement with the *Africa Times and Orient Review*, which regularly published articles written by prominent African Americans such as Booker T. Washington and W. E. B. Du Bois. In 1914, he returned to Jamaica, where he founded the Universal Negro Improvement and Conservation Association and African Communities League, later shortened to the Universal Negro Improvement Association (UNIA). The UNIA was part of the larger pan-African movement, committed to the betterment of living conditions for black persons around the world and to the establishment of a central African nation that blacks could govern and in which they could grow and prosper.[2]

In 1915, with the proffered support of Booker T. Washington, whose message of self-help and industry he admired, Garvey planned a fundraising tour of the United States.[3] Washington's death delayed Garvey's arrival until 1916, at which time he embarked on a year-long tour that included visits to thirty-eight states and countless meetings with African American leaders and intelligentsia. In 1917, Garvey established his base in Harlem, the center of the African American intellectual "renaissance," and on June 12 of that year, he delivered his famed Liberty League address, a speech that catapulted him to the attention of African Americans. Building on that foundation of attention, the UNIA rapidly grew to a membership of hundreds of thousands, Garvey launched the successful and influential *Negro World*, and his speeches at UNIA functions drew widespread attention.[4]

Committed to a platform of black self-help and separatism, the UNIA was part business operation, part social organization, and part political agitator. Among other enterprises, it operated "laundries, restaurants, a doll factory, [and] tailoring and millinery establishments," but its most famous operation was its cargo and passenger steamship corporation, the Black Star Line.[5] Growing quickly to three steamships, the Black Star Line was promoted among those of African descent, in America and abroad, as a major business undertaking that would be solely owned and operated by blacks. The steamship line was envisioned as a highly visible business that would connect blacks around the world and demonstrate their economic acumen and purchasing power. The line was highly popular, drawing stock purchasers from around the world, and helped fuel interest in the UNIA.[6]

The *Negro World*, Garvey's newspaper at the time, also played a significant role in the rapid growth of the UNIA. Published in New York but, like many African American newspapers, distributed worldwide, the weekly *Negro World* boasted a circulation of fifty thousand by 1920.[7] Passed from person to person and often read communally, scholars estimate that, in this era, African American newspapers typically reached more than six readers for each paper printed, and that communal "readings" of the paper undoubtedly produced an even larger audience.[8] Each week, the *Negro World* probably enjoyed an audience of over a half million readers. In contrast to the cultural drumbeat from the white media that the African continent was "backward" and "uncivilized," the readers of the *Negro World* were provided with articles that described Africa's storied past and great accomplishments, histories that explicitly promoted racial pride. They were also treated to stories that excoriated European colonization of Africa and attacked those of African descent who cooperated with whites or who promoted integration. Each week, a column written by Garvey appeared on the front page. Through this forum, Garvey advanced his ideas concerning "race pride," the economic uplift of the black community, and the necessity of reclaiming the African continent for the Africans and those of African descent. It was also a platform from which he could attack his critics.[9] In many regards, Marcus Garvey's public address was a communal expression of the ideas and arguments that his audience had already read in the *Negro World*. His speeches were opportunities for his followers and himself to come together and give voice to that which they already believed.

Although estimates of its membership vary greatly, the UNIA's ability to draw hundreds of thousands of enthusiastic supporters brought it into direct competition with other socio-economic groups who pursued the same audience, organizations such as black churches, the National Association for the Advancement of Colored People (NAACP), the Communist Party, and black labor unions. In his speeches and the pages of the *Negro World*, Garvey was often highly critical of any blacks who accepted compromise or who thought that blacks could work cooperatively with whites. He was also highly critical of European colonial policies, especially those of Great Britain. By 1921, Garvey's political enemies included W. E. B. Du Bois, labor leader A. Philip Randolph, and the British and United States governments.[10] Harassed continually on many fronts, in 1923, Garvey was convicted by the United States government on charges of mail fraud in connection with solicitation of stock purchases of the Black Star Line. After months of appeals, he was imprisoned in 1925, but after many protests on his behalf, the US government freed Garvey in 1927, upon condition of his deportation from America.[11]

"The Principles of the Universal Negro Improvement Association," delivered in 1922 after the decline of the Black Star Line but before the UNIA became highly fractured, is representative of Garvey's oratory, particularly during the time of his residence in the United States. His speeches do not contain the artistry of those by Douglass, King, or Malcolm X, nor are they highly organized like those delivered by Du Bois, Jordan, or Jackson. On the printed page, even his climactic perorations, such as in this speech—"hold the fort, for we are coming, 400,000,000 strong"—lack the rhetorical power that numerous observers credit to Garvey's public speaking. Contemporary accounts of the audiences' emotional responses to Garvey's speeches suggest that the potency of his public speaking lay in part in his energetic delivery as well as in the powerful spectacle and excitement that regularly accompanied his orations. His rhetorical acumen should also be partly understood in light of the columns and stories of the *Negro World* that prepared Garvey's audiences to be moved emotionally. Finally, it is important to understand the strong emotional appeal of the arguments Garvey was making. Garvey spoke candidly and strongly to the frustrations that many of African descent felt, but especially African Americans. Half a century had elapsed since the Civil War, and the promised fruit of the Emancipation Proclamation and Reconstruction amendments had withered on the vine. For forty years, African Americans, in the South especially, had been the targets of legally sanctioned violence, mayhem designed to keep the race in check. In the early twentieth century, the Great Migration North had brought millions of African Americans to the Northern cities. By 1920, the promise of better treatment up North had been fundamentally broken. African Americans had fought with distinction in World War I for the liberation and democratization of eastern Europe, only to return home to find that systematic and often violent discrimination against blacks remained intact, North and South. Marcus Garvey's speeches gave voice to his audiences' frustration, renewed their pride in self and race, and provided them with hope for a far better, more opportunity-laden future.

The early twentieth century notion of "self-determination" served as the intellectual keystone of Garvey's speech "The Principles of the Universal Negro Improvement Association," an address delivered to a meeting of the UNIA. Articulated by many and codified in Woodrow Wilson's Fourteen Points, self-determination was the idea that each race or ethnic group had a unique cultural identity and that each was entitled to their "homeland." In Wilson's language, each "peoples and nationality" were entitled to "autonomous development."[12] In practice, this political philosophy was particularly relevant to the creation of the eastern European countries after World War I as the Austro-Hungarian Empire and parts of the Russian Empire were carved up into Poland, Czechoslovakia, Romania, Bulgaria, Serbia, and other countries. Self-determination provided the philosophical underpinnings for political movements such as Zionism, the campaign to create a Jewish state in Palestine, and the Irish Republican movement, which sought an Ireland independent of British rule.

Self-determination was grounded in the belief that the bonds of *ethnicity* or *race*—two terms that are typically blurred in this discussion—are stronger than those based on national boundaries or political philosophy. Thus, Garvey asserted, this "question of nationality among Negroes . . . counts for nought [*sic*] when that nationality comes in conflict with the racial idealism of the group that rules." He continued: "When our [blacks'] interests clash with those of the ruling faction [whichever race is in control of a nation] then we find that we have absolutely no rights." Each race will favor its own, and so in all those countries in which those of African descent are the minority, their rights and liberties will not be respected. Prejudice, he was arguing, can *never* be legislated out of existence. Laws cannot trump the bonds of race and ethnicity. Those hoping for a change in the natural order of the world, hope in vain: "You and I can live in the United States of America for a hundred more years, and our generations may live for two hundred years or for five thousand more years, and so long as there is a black and white population, when the majority is on the side of the white race, you and I will never get political justice or get political equality in this country." In Garvey's peroration, he argued again that the bonds of race and ethnicity are stronger than those of laws or nationality, for blacks will "march out" on behalf of Africa with a "greater loyalty" than they had marched for America, Britain, or France. Although their loyalty for those countries had been strong—as they had demonstrated during World War I—their "loyalty" would be greater still when it was "the loyalty of race." Thus the UNIA's primary goal of creating a nation for those of African descent: "We are not engaged in domestic politics, in church building or in social-uplift work, but we are engaged in nation building." Repeatedly in this speech as in others, Garvey contrasts the UNIA with all other organizations working among African Americans, because those groups seek to improve the African American's life in America. Because race and ethnicity are *inherently* a defining characteristic of being human, Garvey argued that race should be placed as the first consideration: "We differ from the organizations in America because they seek to subordinate the Negro as a secondary consideration in a great civilization, [despite] knowing that in America the Negro will never reach his highest ambition, knowing that the Negro in America will never get his Constitutional rights."

If a nation built upon the foundation of race could be established, however, then blacks could in fact reach their "highest ambition." History demonstrated that they were certainly capable, and here Garvey wove the themes of black pride and memory of past achievements. "[T]he black man of Africa has contributed as much to the world as the white man of Europe and the brown man and yellow man of Asia" and was thus entitled to a nation dedicated to those of African descent. Although Garvey asserted this point without formal support, his audience of loyal followers would certainly recall the myriad stories of historic and modern black achievements that were regularly published in Garvey's *Negro World.* At other points of the speech, he reminded his audience of blacks' military contributions to American wars, especially the work of the "black hell fighters" in Europe's recent war, which, in the popular mind at least, had been fought specifically on behalf of the principle of self-determination. "We have saved many nations in this manner," Garvey told his audience; now it was time to save their own nation—Africa. In the latter part of the speech, he also reminded his audience of the biblical story of Simon the Cyrenian—a man of African descent—who "took up the cross" of Jesus. Rhetorically, however, these two features were the proverbial tips of the iceberg; the preponderance of evidence for Garvey's appeals to racial pride had been provided in other venues prior to the delivery of this particular speech.

Garvey also invoked pride in race through an appeal to the strength of the race. Some of the strength lay in the continent of Africa itself, a continent that "looms as the greatest commercial, industrial and political prize in the world." Black strength also resided in its numbers. Repeatedly, in this speech as well as his other speeches and newspaper columns, Garvey reminded his audience that they were "400,000,000 Negroes." His concluding call echoed Garnet's 1843 appeal to the "four million" African Americans, asking his audience that "we should say to the millions who are in Africa to hold the fort, for we are coming, 400,000,000 strong."

The strongest appeals to racial pride, however, were Garvey's militant declarations that the time had come for the black race to assert itself. "The question often asked is, what does it require to redeem a race and free a country?" His reply: "If it takes man power, if it takes scientific intelligence, if it takes education of any kind, or if it takes blood, then the 400,000,000 Negroes of the world have it." In pursuing this goal of full rights in the citizenship of the world, the UNIA was the vanguard: "We of the Universal Negro Improvement Association demand that the white, yellow and brown races give to the black man his place in the civilization of the world. We ask for nothing more than the rights of 400,000,000 Negroes." Although Garvey initially demanded that the other races "give to the black man" those rights of citizenship, it became evident as the speech progressed that blacks would assertively fight for and take possession of those rights, regardless of what the other races may voluntarily "give": "[U]nder the leadership of the U.N.I.A., we are marshaling the 400,000,000 Negroes of the world to fight for the emancipation of the race and for the redemption of the country of our fathers (Africa)." In addition to the martial tone of the language, part of the speech's militancy lay in Garvey's refusal to accept second-class treatment. "Why should [the white man], because of some racial prejudice, keep me down and why should I concede to him the right to rise above me and to establish himself as my permanent master? . . . I refuse to stultify my ambition, and every true Negro refuses to stultify his ambition to suit any one." Garvey's charge to Africa to "hold the fort, for we are coming" must be understood within the context of his assertively expressed demand for the restoration of the rights of his race and the "redemption of our own country, our motherland, Africa." Rights that African Americans had sought as they migrated northward and served in World War I had been denied to them even as European colonization of Africa had been renewed with increased vigor. In his speech, Garvey spoke persuasively for the reclamation of those rights, and the ability of his race to succeed in this reclamation. His was a popular message to many who looked for renewed hope in the future.

Along with this positive call for rights, however, Garvey wove a lesser, critical theme that challenges blacks to do better. This theme—the call for blacks to engage in self-help and self-improvement—was the portion of his rhetoric that echoed the work of Booker T. Washington. "We have been satisfied to allow ourselves to be led, educated, to be directed by the other fellow," Garvey declared, and "allowed ourselves for the last five hundred years to be a race of followers." Although in this speech he did not elaborate on the need for blacks to develop wealth, he did assert that "The U.N.I.A. is reversing the old-time order of things. We refuse to be followers any more. We are leading ourselves." Although on the surface the speech finds its theme in criticism and rebuke, it also appeals to nascent pride in declaring that the race could and would become better.

Locating his call for the restoration of rights within the principle of self-determination allowed Garvey also to ground his demand for radical change in a mainstream and widely held philosophy of government. He could thus balance his militancy with a tone of reasonableness. Because the principle of self-determination crossed racial boundaries, the UNIA could stand for "human rights, not only for Negroes, but for all races." Just as Africa should be restored to the Africans, Palestine should be restored to the Jews and Ireland to the Irish. Rhetorically, the reverse was also true. The establishment of a Poland for the Poles and Hungary for the Hungarians justified the call of Africa for the Africans. "We are not preaching a propaganda of hate against anybody," Garvey pointed out, implicitly responding to those who heard in his militant calls to fight for freedom a threat to themselves. "We love the white man," Garvey continued, "we love all humanity, because we feel we cannot live without the other." However, what was good for whites—self-government—was also good for blacks. Using the language of Teddy Roosevelt, Garvey simply requested—or demanded—a "square deal." "We are not seeking," he reiterated, "to destroy or disrupt the society or the government of other races, but we are determined that 400,000,000 of us shall unite ourselves to free our motherland from the grasp of the invader."

In "The Principles of the Universal Negro Improvement Association" can be discerned all the common rhetorical themes that Garvey sounded in his speeches. The black race could and would reassert itself, ultimately by liberating Africa from European colonization and establishing on the continent a nation that would be governed by Africans. To that nation of Africa those in the diaspora could return, and there they would establish African civilization, wealth and glory. Those of African descent were demanding nothing less than what was being granted to other races and ethnic groups around the globe, but especially in Europe. Not all the elements of Garvey's rhetoric are as well developed in this speech as they are in other speeches or the *Negro World*, especially his twin messages of historic and modern black achievements and the need for black self-help. Nor is the full power of Garvey's rhetoric apparent from the printed page. All contemporary reports, however, indicate that his audiences were enthusiastic and his speeches well received. "Cheering Negroes Hail Black Nation" wrote the *New York Times* in 1920. Writing about that day in Madison Square Garden, the reporter observed that the crowd answered Marcus Garvey's speech with "applause that shook the building."[13] Historian Tony Martin quotes the report of a British colonial police officer in Honduras who had been dispatched to keep an eye on the UNIA rally. Although patently critical of Garvey, the officer's account of Garvey's energetic delivery and the audience's enthusiastic response corresponds with other contemporary descriptions of his public speaking: "He nevertheless knew how to get his hearers and was cheered heartily time and again. Garvey in his serious moments did not lack humour which was appreciated. . . . There were moments of enthusiastic madness into which he worked himself while speaking when I thought the aid of a medical man would be absolutely necessary but, such was not to be."[14] Robert Minor, writing in 1924 for the Workers Party USA, observed that Garvey was "one of the most powerful personalities that I have ever seen on the platform."[15]

Although Garvey remained active in the UNIA for the remainder of his life, political infighting, particularly in the US branches, served to reduce both the popularity of the organization and his influence on it. He frequently traveled between Jamaica and England, attending international conferences, establishing new publications, and speaking to audiences on behalf of those causes he continued to support most fervently: pan-Africanism, black pride, and black self-help. Even after his death in 1940, Garvey continued to attract the allegiance of thousands of followers, typically termed "Garveyites."[16] Biographer Edmund David Cronon writes that Garvey's major contribution was inherently rhetorical, that is, "more than any other single leader he helped to give [blacks] everywhere a reborn feeling of collective pride and a new awareness of individual worth."[17] Historian Judith Stein points more specifically to Garvey's particular, and popular, articulation of black nationalism as the source of his immediate and historical impact.[18] Marcus Garvey was highly controversial during his lifetime, and, unsurprisingly, remains so in regard to his historical legacy. What is clear, however, is that he was a popular and persuasive platform speaker, one whose ideas continue to reverberate almost one hundred years later.

The Principles of the Universal Negro Improvement Association

November 25, 1922
New York, New York

Over five years ago the Universal Negro Improvement Association placed itself before the world as the movement through which the new and rising Negro would give expression of his feelings. This Association adopts an attitude not of hostility to other races and peoples of world, but an attitude of self-respect, of manhood rights on behalf of 400,000,000 Negroes of the world.

We represent peace, harmony, love, human sympathy, human rights and human justice, and that is why we fight so much. Wheresoever human rights are denied to any group, wheresoever justice is denied to any group, there the U.N.I.A. finds a cause. And at this time among all the peoples of world, the group that suffers most from injustice, the group that is denied most of those rights that belong to humanity, is the black group of 400,000,000. Because of that injustice, because of that denial our rights, we go forth under the leadership of the One who is always on side of right to fight the common cause of humanity; to fight as we fought in the Revolutionary War, as we fought in Civil War, as we fought in the Spanish-American War, and as we fought in the war between 1914–18 on the battle plains of France and Flanders. As we fought up the heights of Mesopotamia[a]; even so under the leadership of the U.N.I.A., we are marshaling the Negroes of the world to fight for the emancipation of the race and the redemption of the country of our fathers.

a. Probably refers to the 1917 Mesopotamia campaign in which the British Egyptian Expeditionary Force defeated the Ottoman Turks in modern-day Iraq. The Egyptian Expeditionary Force was comprised of a combination of British and Egyptian troops.

We represent a new line of thought among Negroes. Whether you call it advanced thought or reactionary thought, I do not care. If it is reactionary for people to seek independence in government, then we are reactionary. If it is advanced thought for people to seek liberty and freedom, then we represent the advanced school of thought among the Negroes of this country. We of the U.N.I.A. believe that what is good for the other fellow is good for us. If government is something that is worth while; if government is something that is appreciable and helpful and protective to others, then we also want to experiment in government. We do not mean a government that will make us citizens without rights or subjects without consideration. We mean the kind of government that will place our race in control, even as other races are in control of their own governments.

That does not suggest anything that is unreasonable. It was not unreasonable for George Washington, the great hero and father of the country, to have fought for the freedom of America giving to us this great republic and this great democracy; it was not unreasonable for Liberals of France to have fought against the Monarchy to give to the world French Democracy and French Republicanism; it was no unrighteous cause that led Tolstoi[b] to sound the call of liberty in Russia, which has ended in giving to the world the social democracy of Russia, an experiment that will probably prove to be a boon and a blessing to mankind. If it was not an unrighteous cause that led Washington to fight for the independence of this country, and led the Liberals of France to establish the Republic, it is therefore not an unrighteous cause for the U.N.I.A. to lead 400,000,000 Negroes all over the world to fight for the liberation of our country.

Therefore the U.N.I.A. is not advocating the cause of church building because we have a sufficiently large of number churches among us to minister to the spiritual needs of the people, and we are not going to compete with those who are engaged in so splendid a work; we are not engaged in building any new social institutions, and the Y.M.C.A.'s or Y.W.C.A.'s, because there are enough social workers engaged in those praise-worthy efforts. We are not engaged in politics because we have enough local politicians, Democrats, Socialists, Soviets, etc., and the political situation is well taken care of. We are not engaged in domestic politics, in church building or in social uplift work, but we are engaged in nation building.

---

b. Leo (Lev) Nikolayevich Tolstoy (1828–1910): Russian author of *War and Peace* and *Anna Karenina*, also an advocate of educational and government reform.

In advocating the principles of this Association we find we have been very much misunderstood and very much misrepresented by men from within our own race, as well as others from without. Any reform movement that seeks to bring about changes for the benefit of humanity is bound to be misrepresented by those who have always taken it upon themselves to administer to, and lead the unfortunate, and to direct those who may be placed under temporary disadvantages. It has been so in all other movements whether social or political; hence those of us in the Universal Negro Improvement Association who lead, do not feel in any way embarrassed about this misrepresentation, about this misunderstanding as far as the Aims and Objects of the Universal Negro Improvement Association go. But those who probably would have taken kindly notice of this great movement, have been led to believe that this movement seeks, not to develop the good within the race, but to give expression to that which is most destructive and most harmful to society and to government.

I desire to remove the misunderstanding that has been created in the minds of millions of peoples throughout the world in their relationship to the organization. The Universal Negro Improvement Association stands for the Bigger Brotherhood; the Universal Negro Improvement Association stands for human rights, not only for Negroes, but for all races. The Universal Negro Improvement Association believes in the rights of not only the black race, but the white race, the yellow race and the brown race. The Universal Negro Improvement Association believes that the white man has as much right to be considered, the yellow man has as much right to be considered, the brown man has as much right to be considered as well as the black man of Africa. In view of the fact that the black man of Africa has contributed as much to the world as the white man of Europe, and the brown man and yellow man of Asia, we of the Universal Negro Improvement Association demand that the white, yellow and brown races give to the black man his place in the civilization of the world. We ask for nothing more than the rights of 400,000,000 Negroes. We are not seeking, as I said before, to destroy or disrupt the society or the government of other races, but we are determined that 400,000,000 of us shall unite ourselves to free our motherland from the grasp of the invader. We of the Universal Negro Improvement Association are determined to unite 400,000,000 Negroes for their own industrial, political, social and religious emancipation.

We of the Universal Negro Association are determined to unite the 400,000,000 Negroes of the world to give expression to their own feeling;

we are determined to unite the 400,000,000 Negroes of the world for the purpose of building a civilization of their own. And in that effort we desire to bring together the 15,000,000 of the United States, the 180,000,000 in Asia, the West Indies and Central and South America, and in the 200,000,000 in Africa. We are looking toward political freedom on the continent of Africa, the land of our fathers.

Not Seeking a Government within a Government

The Universal Negro Improvement Association is not seeking to build up another government within bounds or borders of the United States of America. The Universal Negro Improvement Association is not seeking to disrupt any organized system of government, but the Association is determined to bring Negroes together for the building up of a nation of their own. And why? Because we have been forced to it. We have been forced to it throughout the world; not only in America, not only in Europe, not only in the British Empire, but wheresoever the black man happens to find himself, he has been forced to do for himself.

To talk about Government is a little more than some of our people can appreciate just at this time. The average man does not think that way, just because he finds himself a citizen or a subject of some country. He seems to say, "Why should there be need for any other government?" We are French, English or American. But we of the U.N.I.A. have studied seriously the question of nationality among Negroes—this American nationality, this British nationality, this French, Italian, or Spanish nationality, and have discovered that it counts for nought [*sic*]when that nationality comes in conflict with the racial idealism of the group that rules. When our interests clash with those of the ruling faction, then we find that we have absolutely no rights. In times of peace, when everything is all right, Negroes have a hard time, wherever we go, wheresoever we find ourselves, those rights that belong to us, in common with others whom we claim as fellow citizens; getting that consideration that should be ours by right of the constitution, by right of the law; but in the time of trouble they make us all partners in the cause, as happened in the last war, when we were partners, whether British, French or American Negroes. And we were told that we must forget everything in an effort to save the nation.

We have saved many nations in this manner, and we have lost our lives doing that before. Hundreds of thousands—nay, millions of black men, lie buried under the ground due to that old-time camouflage of saving the nation. We saved the British empire; we saved the French empire; we saved this glorious country more than once; and all that we have received for our sacrifices, all that we have received for what we have done, even in giving up our lives, is just what you are receiving now, just what I am receiving now.

You and I fare no better in America, in the British empire, or in any other part of the white world; we fare no better than any black man wheresoever he shows his head. And why? Because we have been satisfied to allow ourselves to be led, educated, to be directed by the other fellow, who has always sought to lead the world in that direction that would satisfy him and strengthen his position. We have allowed ourselves for the last 500 years to be a race of followers, following every race that has led, in the direction that would make them more secure.

The U.N.I.A. is reversing the old-time order of things. We refuse to be followers any more. We are leading ourselves. That means, if any saving is to be done, later on, whether it is saving this one nation or that one government, we are going to seek a method of saving Africa first. Why? And why Africa? Because Africa has become the grand prize of the nations. Africa has become the big game of the nation hunters. To-day Africa looms as the greatest commercial, industrial and political prize in the world.

The Difference between the U.N.I.A. and Other Organizations

The difference between the Universal Negro Improvement Association and the other movements of this country, and probably the world, is that the Universal Negro Improvement Association seeks independence of government, while the other organizations seek to make the Negro a secondary part of existing governments. We differ from the organizations in America because they seek to subordinate the Negro as a secondary consideration in a great civilization, knowing that in America the Negro will never reach his highest ambition, knowing that the Negro in America will never get his constitutional rights. All those organizations which are fostering the improvement of Negroes in the British Empire know that the Negro in the British Empire will never reach height of his constitutional rights. What do I mean by constitutional rights in America? If the black man is to reach the height of his ambition in this country—if the black man is to get of his constitutional rights in America—then the black man should have the same chance in the nation as any other to become president of the nation, or a street cleaner in New York. If the black man in the British Empire is to have his constitutional rights it means that the Negro in the British Empire should have at least the same right to become premier of Britain as he has to become street cleaner in city of London. Are they prepared to give us such political equality? You and I can live in the United States of America for 100 more years, and our generations may live for 200 years or for 5,000 more years, and so long as there is a black and white population, when the majority is on the side of the white race, you and I will never get political justice or get political equality in this country. Then why should a black man with rising ambition, after preparing himself in every possible way to give expression to that highest ambition, allow himself to be kept down by racial prejudice within a country? If I am as educated as the next man; if I am as prepared as the next man, if I have passed through the best schools and colleges and universities as the other fellow, why should I not have a fair chance to compete with the other fellow for the biggest position in the nation? I have feelings, I have blood, I have senses like the other fellow; I have ambition, I have hope. Why should he, because of some racial prejudice, keep me down and why should I concede to him the right to rise above me, and to establish himself as my permanent master? That is where the U.N.I.A. differs from other organizations. I refuse to stultify my ambition, and every true Negro refuses to stultify his ambition to suit any one, and therefore U.N.I.A. decides if America is not big enough for two presidents, if England is not big enough for two kings, then we are not going to quarrel over the matter; we will leave one president in America, we will leave one king in England, we will leave one president in France and we will have one president in Africa. Hence, the Universal Negro Improvement Association does not seek to interfere with the social and political systems of France, but by the arrangement of things to-day the U.N.I.A. refuses to recognize any political or social system in Africa except that which we are about to establish for ourselves.

Not Preaching Hate

We are not preaching a propaganda of hate against anybody. We love the white man; we love all humanity, because we feel we cannot live without the other. The white man is as necessary to the existence of the Negro as the Negro is necessary to his existence. There is a common relationship that we cannot escape. Africa has certain things that Europe wants, and Europe has certain things that Africa wants, and if a fair and square deal must bring white and black with each other, it is impossible for us to escape it. Africa has oil, diamonds, copper, gold and rubber and the minerals that Europe wants, and there must be some kind of relationship between Africa and Europe for a fair exchange, so we cannot afford to hate anybody.

Negroes Ever Ready to Assist Humanity's Cause

The question often asked is what does it require to redeem a race and free a country. If it takes man power, if it takes scientific intelligence, if takes education of any kind, or if it takes blood, then the 400,000,000 Negroes of the world have it.

It took the combined manpower of the Allies to put down the mad determination of the Kaiser[c] to impose German will upon the world and upon humanity. Among those who suppressed his mad ambition were two million Negroes who have not yet forgotten how to drive men across the firing line. Surely those of us who faced German shot and shell at the Marne,[d] at Verdun,[e] have not forgotten the order of our Commander-in-Chief. The cry that caused us to leave America in such mad haste, when white fellow citizens of America refused to fight and said, "We do not believe in war and therefore, even though we are American citizens, and even though the nation is in danger, we will not go to war." When many of them cried out and said, "We are German-Americans and we cannot fight," when so many white men refused to answer the call and dodged behind all kinds of excuses, 400,000 black men were ready without a question. It was because we were told it was a war of democracy; it was a war for the liberation of the weaker peoples of the world. We heard the cry of Woodrow Wilson,[f] not because we liked him so, but because the things he said were of such a nature that they appealed to us as men. Wheresoever the cause of humanity stands in need of assistance, there you will find the Negro ever ready to serve.

He has done it from the time of Christ to now. When the whole world turned its back upon the Christ, the man who was said to be the Son of God; when the world cried out, "Crucify Him," when the world spurned Him and spat upon Him, it was a black man, Simon, the Cyrenian, who

c. Kaiser Wilhelm II (1849–1941): Emperor of Germany during World War I, abdicated his throne in 1918 at the conclusion of the war.

d. Probably refers to the second battle of the Marne in World War I (15 July–6 Aug. 1918). This was the last major German offensive of the war and involved eight divisions of the US Army.

e. The battle of Verdun (21 Feb.–15 Dec. 1916) was one of the longest and bloodiest battles in World War I.

f. Thomas Woodrow Wilson (1856–1924): Twenty-fourth president of the United States, from 1913 to1921. He asked Congress for a declaration of war on Germany, arguing that the world "be made safe for democracy" (12 Apr. 1917).

took up the cross.[g] Why? Because the cause of humanity appealed to him. When the black man saw the suffering Jew, struggling under the heavy cross, he was willing to go to His assistance, and he bore that cross up to the heights of Calvary. In the spirit of Simon, the Cyrenian, 1,900 years ago, we answered the call of Woodrow Wilson, the call of a larger humanity, and it was for that that we willingly rushed into the war from America, from the West Indies, over 100,000; it was for that that we rushed into the war from Africa, 2,000,000 of us. We met in France, Flanders[h] and in Mesopotamia.[i] We fought unfalteringly. When the white men faltered and fell back on their battle lines, at the Marne and at Verdun, when they ran away from the charge of the German hordes, the black hell fighters stood before the cannonade, stood before the charge, and again they shouted, "There will be a hot time in the old town to-night."[j]

We made it so hot a few months after our appearance in France and on the various battle fronts, we succeeded in driving German hordes across the Rhine,[k] and driving the Kaiser out of Germany, and out of Potsdam[l] into Holland.[m] We have not forgotten the prowess of war. If we have been liberal minded enough to give our life's blood in France, in Mesopotamia and elsewhere, fighting for the white man, whom we have always assisted, surely we have not forgotten to fight for ourselves, and when time comes that the world will again give Africa an opportunity for freedom, surely 400,000,000 black men will march out on the battle plains of Africa, under the colors of the black and the green.

We shall march out, yes, as black American citizens, as black British subjects, as black French citizens, as black Italians or as black Spaniards, but we shall march out with a greater loyalty, the loyalty of race. We shall march out in answer to the cry of our fathers, who cry out to us for the redemption of our own country, our motherland, Africa.

g. Matthew 27:32; Mark 15:21; Luke 23:26. Cyrene was a town in modern-day Libya.

h. Belgium, or northern Belgium.

i. Refers to the British campaign against the Turkish Empire in modern Iraq, summer 1916–winter 1917.

j. Lyrics from an 1896 ragtime song of the same name. It was a popular song with American soldiers because its lyrics could be applied to military fighting as well as the literal meaning of going out to dance.

k. German river, which, in places, serves as the boundary between France and Germany.

l. German city twenty-five miles southwest of Berlin. Until 1918, it served as the residence of the Prussian kings, such as Kaiser Wilhelm II.

m. Upon abdicating the throne, Kaiser Wilhelm II went into exile in the Netherlands.

We shall march out, not forgetting the blessings of America. We shall march out, not forgetting the blessings of civilization. We shall march out with a history of peace before and behind us, and surely that history shall be our breastplate, for how can man fight better than knowing that the cause for which he fights is righteous? How can man fight more gloriously than by knowing that behind him is a history of slavery, a history of bloody carnage and massacre inflicted upon a race because of its inability to protect itself and fight? Shall we not fight for the glorious opportunity of protecting and forever more establishing ourselves as a mighty race and nation, never more to be disrespected by men[?] Glorious shall be the battle when the time comes to fight for our people and our race.

We should say to the millions who are in Africa to hold the fort, for we are coming 400,000,000 strong.

Vernon Johns

Rock Foundations

By all accounts, the Reverend Vernon Johns was a brilliant, iconoclastic preacher who regularly spoke to church and college audiences with great eloquence. Frequently an itinerant preacher and scholar, many of Johns's lectures and sermons were never recorded and many of those that were written down were destroyed in a house fire, although a collection of undated sermons has been reprinted in Samuel Gandy's *Human Possibilities*.[1] Johns's 1926 sermon "Transfigured Moments" was the first by an African American to be included in the highly regarded Best Sermons collection, an annual volume that published sermons by influential theologians such as Reinhold Niebuhr and noted ministers such Harry Emerson Fosdick. Like many African American intellectuals in the first half of the twentieth century—such as Mordecai Johnson or the Grimke brothers—Vernon Johns was well known throughout the African American community but largely ignored and then forgotten by white Americans. His public speeches and sermons, although individually styled to reflect his particular messages, resembled those of many African American leaders of the first half of the twentieth century. Grounded in the Social Gospel, his oratorical canon was staunchly supportive of civil rights but also distinctively demanded that African Americans work diligently to improve their circumstances in America.

Vernon Johns was born in 1892 in Farmville, Virginia, to Willie and Sallie Price Johns. His paternal grandfather was famous in that part of Virginia for having reputedly cut his white master in two with a scythe, an act for which he had been promptly hanged. His maternal grandfather, David Price, was a white man who maintained two families—one with his white wife and one with his African American mistress. In *Parting the Waters*, Taylor Branch concludes that Price was a "mean, violent complicated man."[2] Price served time in prison for killing a white man who tried to rape Sallie Price's mother, and when Sallie's mother passed away, Price moved his African American children into his home to be reared by his childless white wife. Following the customs of the time, the Prices pretended that it was an act of charity and that they were simply caring for orphaned African American children. The matter of being biologically related to each other was never spoken of, publicly or privately. Vernon, the oldest child of Willie and Sallie, grew up on the family farm, where he educated himself. His father, Willie, was a full-time farmer and part-time preacher, a formula that Vernon would reverse in his life.[3]

Early on, Vernon Johns displayed a prodigious intellect. He recited long biblical passages and poetry, and as a teenager talked his way into several schools in Virginia, including Virginia Seminary in Lynchburg. Due either to rebelliousness or just his contrary nature, he was either dismissed or voluntarily left them all. He applied to Oberlin College in Ohio and, when he was turned down, went to argue his case in person. As the story goes, when the associate dean pointed out that Johns had been denied admission due to invalid educational credits, the erstwhile student replied "I got your letter, Dean Fiske, but I want to know whether you want students with credits or students with brains."[4] Dean Fiske then set him to the task of translating a book written in German. When he did so immediately, Fiske sent him along to Edward Increase Bosworth, the dean of Oberlin Seminary. Bosworth also asked Johns to translate a text, but this time in Greek. When Johns promptly completed this second task, Bosworth took him on as a "provisional" student, and in 1918, Vernon Johns graduated from Oberlin Seminary first in his class. When Robert Maynard Hutchins, the student who had previously occupied the top rank and later became president of University of Chicago, heard Johns had replaced him in academic standing, he remarked that the "country Negro" could only have done so by cheating. Characteristically, Johns confronted Hutchins, punching him in the mouth and demanding an apology. Subsequently, the two became lifelong friends.[5]

After graduation, Vernon attended the University of Chicago graduate school of theology, the intellectual home of the Social Gospel movement. This group of theologians argued that the teachings of Christ required his followers to work vigorously for the care and well-being of everyone, particularly at the societal level. From the University of Chicago, Johns accepted a teaching position at Virginia Theological Seminary. Shortly after, he assumed the position of pastor for the Court Street Church in Lynchburg.

In 1926, Johns published "Transfigured Moments" in the highly respected Best Sermons series. These volumes were published by liberal theologians and preachers who were, at that time, contesting with their fundamentalist brethren for the philosophical leadership of the Christian church. Although the headnotes in *Best Sermons of 1926* suggest that it was a sermon delivered at "Court Street Baptist Church (Colored), Lynchburg, VA," it is not clear that it was ever delivered as a sermon at all. Taylor Branch reports that Johns wrote the sermon specifically for inclusion in the volume. Several times, Johns had submitted to the editors copies of sermons that had been delivered by the better known Mordecai Johnson, president of Howard University, and Howard Thurman, a rising star among African American theologians. Frustrated by the rejection of those sermons by the editors, Johns penned one of his own, "Transfigured Moments," which became the first sermon by an African American to be included in the series.

Highly respected for such intellectual prowess, Johns's pugnacious, combative nature and personal idiosyncracies often caused him to wear out his welcome. He had already left Court Street Church when, in 1927, he married Altona Trent, daughter of William Trent, the president of Livingstone College in Salisbury, North Carolina. Johns was now pastor of First Baptist Church in Charleston, West Virginia, a position he held for eleven months. He returned to Lynchburg in 1929, where he served as president of Virginia Theological Seminary until 1933. There he was credited with saving the college from financial bankruptcy during the difficult early days of the Depression. After his presidency, he returned to holding a series of pastorates, intermixed with itinerant lecturing and preaching as well as farming. Branch writes that Johns seemed happiest when touring, traveling from college to college, church to church, delivering guest lectures for which he received sufficient remuneration to support himself and his family.[6]

From 1948 to 1952, Johns held the job for which he is most famous today—as the pastor of the Dexter Avenue Baptist Church in Montgomery, Alabama, immediately preceding Martin Luther King Jr.'s assumption of that pastorate. His intellectualism was prized by the Dexter congregation, but his espousal of manual labor—in sermons such as "Mud Is Basic" and through practices such as selling watermelons outside church after Sunday worship—proved a source of friction. Johns was also an outspoken critic of segregation and the racist practices common in Montgomery. As with all his formal positions, the Dexter pastorship did not last. He returned to his itinerant preaching and lecturing and continued to do both in conjunction with his family farming until his death in 1965.[7]

"Rock Foundations" is a sermon probably delivered at Johns's Court Street Baptist Church sometime late in 1926, before he left that pastorate. Although neither the time nor place of the sermon is noted, in it Johns references lynchings that had occurred at Wytheville, Virginia, on August 25, 1926, and Aiken, South Carolina, on October 23, 1926. He does not detail the events of either lynching but, rather, references them in a way that suggests that these were recent events of which everyone was aware.

One of the most distinguishing features of "Rock Foundations" is Johns's involvement of the audience. Despite his reputation as an intellectual, Johns does not talk down to his audience; instead, he treats them as equals. The speech is replete with enthymemes, rhetorical questions, and ironic comments, the content of which invite the audience to participate in "thinking through" the central theme of the sermon—that following Jesus's practical teaching is more important than discerning "correct" Christian theology.

Johns opens the sermon with a series of enthymemes—in this instance, predicated upon maxims (aphorisms or proverbs)—that invite the audience to a broader contemplation of the transitory nature of life. He begins with the sweeping observation that "Time works havoc with our most treasured possessions." He follows that maxim with additional maxims that apply this broad principle to particular areas of our lives, for example, physical beauty, kingdoms, and even geographic elements such as oceans: "seashells are left stranded on mountain tops." These opening maxims ask the audience to consider how these truths touch their lives—how their health, wealth, communities, government, and all manner of other elements of their lives have been changed over time. Johns then reverses course with a major premise drawn from the preaching of Jesus: "But whosever hears these words of mine, and doeth them, shall be likened unto a wise man who built his house upon a rock, and the rains descended and the floods came, and the winds blew and beat upon that house, but it fell not; for it was founded upon a rock." In these few short lines, Johns not only invites the audience to participate psychologically in the construction of his message, but he sets forth the central, ironic thesis of the sermon. He has asserted, through a biblical text with which all would be familiar, that Jesus's preaching is the one constant that does not change over time. While time "works havoc" on most things, Jesus's message is unchanging. The audience is thus faced with reconciling two competing sets of maxims: that time changes all things and that Jesus's teachings do not change with time. After briefly intertwining the conflicting maxims once more, Johns poses a rhetorical question, asking his audience how they would resolve the dilemma: "Is it worthwhile to listen to Him?"

Maxims and sweeping generalizations are numerous in this sermon. Some of the maxims make observations on the world as it is, underscoring the temporary nature of human acts and the foolishness of yielding to pragmatism as an ethical standard. "Civilizations practice the latter" (the principle of self-defense), Johns tells the audience, "and destroy themselves." Or, later, he observes that "the nastiest and deadliest problem before the world today is the insane hatred between races," and that "when we lose the sense of justice or the capacity to act on it the best is already consumed." Other maxims repeat or develop the message of Jesus, for example, "Life is bearable because of the variety it offers." Throughout the body of the sermon, and in the introduction and conclusion as well, Johns places these broad generalizations in juxtaposition with each other, inviting the audience to consider which set of principles they will follow in their own lives.

In his conclusion, Johns continues to use maxims to the same purpose. People's ways are temporary: "Any structure built on foundations less broad [than God's principles] is foredoomed to failure by nature and nature's God." Only God's principles are permanent: "An enduring civilization must be one that exists for the good of all." Even Johns's final call to action, like his very first sentence, is a broad, sweeping maxim: "Let every one take heed how he builds!" Filled with such principles expressed as maxims, Johns's sermon conveys the impression that it, like Jesus's teachings, is immutable. The form of the sermon thus underscores its content. Maxims thus used also serve the further rhetorical purposes of speaking with the audience, for it is they who are asked to reason through the application and contradictions of the various maxims, even as those wise adages also serve to enhance Johns's credibility. As Aristotle observed, the effective use of maxims in a speech creates an impression of wisdom and, to the extent that a speaker can employ them effectively, they confer that association upon the speaker's ethos.

Johns's maxims frequently delineate the irony of Jesus's teachings and the actions of his "followers," and irony is indeed the hallmark of "Rock Foundations." Throughout the sermon, Johns contrasts the "pragmatic" way with the "idealistic" path that Jesus has preached, inevitably noting how, ironically, "pragmatism" does not work. The "practical temperament" judges Jesus's Sermon on the Mount as "lofty idealism," but, Johns asks, "has its opposite worked?" Before World War I, he observes, Germans had preached preparedness. That pragmatic philosophy brought to Germany "retrenchment and not expansions." Johns recounts the ironic Gospel story of the "certain man" who had two sons, one who said he would obey but did not and one who said he would not obey but who did. Johns points out the irony of holding fast to theological dogma that will have no practical effect on society, credos such as "born of a virgin" or that the "world was made in six days." Will carefully reciting these dicta "muzzle our deadly guns" or "kindle in humanity that redeeming spirit of brotherhood"? As Johns twice opines in biting irony: "The phraseology would be mighty magic if it did."

Turning to the issue of lynching, Johns focuses directly on the irony inherent in the situation. Lynching occurs, he notes, in the "very section" of the country which "is unquestionably the chief seat of orthodoxy" even as it is "at the same time the dependable theatre of our most heartless inhumanities." Even the employment of the term "theatre" carries rich irony. Lynchings were very often dramatic spectacles of the most horrific kind. They regularly attracted mobs who would watch and cheer and sometimes participate. Ironically, the term "theatre" carries with it a sense of playacting, yet Johns's point was that the theatre of lynching was very real; society's religious orthodoxy was the true charade. In the eyes of the white, orthodox Southern Christians, a science textbook that included evolution was "a tragedy" like the sacking "of Troy," while lynchings ironically recurred "as regularly as Holy Communion." Even Johns's concluding sentence in this portion of the sermon addressing lynching is tinged with irony: "If one opens his mind on the subject of religion, he may have to keep it open on questions of justice." In our usual calculus, religion and justice are considered to be synonymous, but Johns divides the two, underscoring the irony of those who maintain religious orthodoxy even as they perpetuate the most terrible of injustices. Like his use of maxims, Johns's irony in "Rock Foundations" creates a bond between the speaker and his audience. Irony is only effective when both sides understand the hidden implication; the shared meaning here underscored the connection between Johns and his congregation. He thus succeeds at talking with them, not at them, as he and the audience create ironic meanings together.

As with his use of maxims, Johns's frequent use of rhetorical questions generally serves dual purposes—to highlight the situation's irony and to involve the audience in the persuasive message of the sermon. His questions are usually pointed, emphasizing the absurdity that lay within the ironic contradiction between our theology and our deeds: "Well, has its opposite worked?" "Will this [pious dogma] hold back the gathering storm, or quench the smoldering inferno?" "Might it not, then, become impossible to comprehend the genius and resources of civilization in the low work of murder?" So integral are rhetorical questions to the composition of the sermon that they are featured elements of both his introduction and conclusion. He summarizes his introduction with two questions. The first question is short and direct: "Is it worthwhile to listen to Him?" The second asks the same question, but the question itself constitutes the entire paragraph. Johns recounts all the great and mighty things that have proven transient over time, finishing the question with the inquiry "may it not be wise to listen when Jesus offers to show us a better way?" While the introductory questions broadly pose the ironic contradiction, Johns's questions that begin his conclusion present the issue more specifically: "When will the Christian ministry point them to the rock? When will we put a red lantern on the sand pile? When will Christian preachers either preach Jesus or save the public from further deception by unfrocking themselves of His name?"

His questions do more than make pointed arguments, however. Invariably, Johns poses questions that ask his audience to contemplate the answer and thus involve themselves directly in the communicative act. "If we say the world was made in six days," he queries, "will the statement guarantee to all men 'life, liberty, and the pursuit of happiness?' If we say Jesus was born of a virgin, will the dictum cause every valley to be exalted, every mountain and hill to be brought low?" Like his maxims, his questions are in part easily answered—everyone knows the correct response. Still, the questions invite the audience to consider the answers and the ramifications of those answers. Does belief in the peculiarities of dogma make a difference? Which religious beliefs *could* guarantee life, liberty, and the pursuit of happiness, or bring the promised day of Amos? How do those questions and answers apply to each audience member's life specifically? Johns's questions are narrow enough that the implied answer is clear, but broad enough to allow diverse applications of the answers to a variety of lives.

Johns's sermon is drawn from the passage in the book of Matthew in which Jesus instructs his followers to build their houses on foundations of rock, and he weaves the imagery of rock and sand throughout his sermon. In the middle of the sermon, however, he turns to a biblical question to summarize the heart of the matter: "Why call ye me Lord, 'Divine,' and do not the things which I say?" It was the religious deeds, founded upon the rock of the Golden Rule, that Johns desired, not the "sand" of "ecclesiastical dogmas." Rhetorical questions helped convey that message unmistakably, even as they allowed the audience the rhetorical space to apply those questions and answers to their own situations.

In the *Rhetoric*, Aristotle discusses the enthymeme, the unit of rhetorical deduction that often invites the audience to be coparticipants in creating the argument by filling in any unstated propositions. In "Rock Foundations," Johns demonstrates himself to be a master of the enthymeme. Time and again, he draws his audience in through his maxims, his irony, and his rhetorical questions, all of which constitute enthymemes that the audience must complete by adding a suppressed premise. Although clearly an erudite man, the minister in this sermon is talking *with* his audience, in order for all to understand better the deep irony at work in the world around them. It is a world that believes it is building upon rock, but whose foundations are set in sand. It is a pragmatic world that does not understand that the ultimate pragmatism is found in the Gospel's idealism. It is a world that is orthodox in its dogma, but abandons the ethics of its religion. As Johns succinctly puts it, "there is a world of disparity between the idealism of Jesus and the practices of men." "But," he observes, "Jesus is not crazy. We are crazy."

Rock Foundations

circa 1926
Lynchburg, Virginia

> Whosoever hears these words of mine, and doeth them, shall be likened unto a wise man who built his house upon a rock; and the rains descended and the floods came and the winds blew and beat upon that house, but it fell not: for it was founded upon a rock.
>
> —Matthew 7:24–25

Time works havoc with our most treasured possessions. Beauty turns to ashes beneath its touch. The channels of rivers and the course of history change. Debris piles on the faces of queens and kings, and seashells are left stranded on mountain tops. Our health, our wealth, our friends, our ascendancy, go whirling away in the current of the years. When the sands have run sufficiently, they leave Nineveh[a] but a name and the Parthenon[b] a heap of rubbish. "But whosoever hears these words of mine," says Jesus, "and doeth them, shall be likened unto a wise man who built his house upon a rock, and the rains descended and the floods came, and the winds blew and beat upon that house, but it fell not; for it was founded upon a rock." In a world of wreck on wreck, and while the stones under Jerusalem and Rome were swiftly sliding to bring a debacle more ruinous still, Jesus asserted His faith in a wisdom that can build securely. Is it worth while to listen to Him?

a. Ninevah was the capital of Assyria in the seventh century B.C., widely renowned for its wealth and status. It is frequently mentioned in the Bible.
b. The Parthenon is the great Greek temple in Athens built in honor of Athena, the patron goddess of the city.

If all around us, and over and over again, our heavy, costly structures keep falling and catching us in the ruins, if the industrial revolution, which once seemed so promising, threatens to result in the extermination of the human race and its disappearance from the planet; if we expected great things of liberty and education, and have found them broken reeds; if armies and navies built and maintained at infinite cost, for our protection, stare in our faces and roar in our ears as unmistakably our mightiest perils, may it not be wise to listen when Jesus offers to show us a better way?

The practical temperament regards the Sermon on the Mount as lofty idealism which will not work. Well, has its opposite worked? Alas! We have no mind to review the colossal achievements! I have an acquaintance, a practical man, who is alarmed that I travel so much and without a pistol. I need one he thinks to fight off robbers. Thus far, I have not encountered any robbers. When I do, and the robbers go off with my money, I want them to leave me intact. Staging a pistol duel with a gunman, with my pocket change as the stake, strikes me as nonsense. My honor? I can find better ways to be honorable. My courage? Courage is not properly measured by the notches on the butt of a gun. Not the injuries we inflict on others in alleged defense of ourselves, but what we suffer ourselves to make a fairer world with a finer humanity; that is the courage from which redemption comes. Jesus enjoins the principal of sacrifice in substitution of the old principle of defense. Civilizations practice the latter and destroy themselves.

An apostle of pacifism in the Europe of 1910 would have found Germany his slowest disciple. For a long time the highest wisdom in Germany had been preparedness. Preparedness it was, but it brought retrenchment and not expansions. "Oh, that thou knewest, in this thy day, the things upon which our peace depends. But it is hidden from thee!"[c] There is a world of disparity between the idealism of Jesus and the practices of men. But, Jesus is not crazy. We are crazy.

The church has not formally denounced the Sermon on the Mount. It has merely let it slide. The church has formally proclaimed the sovereignty of

c. Jesus's lamentation regarding Jerusalem, just before entering the city on Palm Sunday. Luke 19: 41–44: "As he came near and saw the city, he wept over it, saying, 'If you, even you, had only recognized on this day the things that make for peace! But now they are hidden from your eyes. Indeed, the days will come upon you, when your enemies will set up ramparts around you and surround you, and hem you in on every side. They will crush you to the ground, you and your children within you, and they will not leave within you one stone upon another; because you did not recognize the time of your visitation from God.'"

Jesus; but it persistently inflicts the movement of Jesus with a disastrously mistaken emphasis. It has shown builders *sand instead of rock*. Jesus plainly tells the disciples what their foundation must be: "Whosoever hears these sayings of mine and doeth them." Not what we say about Jesus, of Genesis, or inspiration, but what we do concerning that which Jesus says to us! The basis of an enduring civilization will not be "Sound Doctrine" but a certain kind of practice. The Master's difficulty now with religious leaders can be stated as He stated it two thousand years ago: "They say, and do not." Jesus once discussed the relative merit of correct statement and obedient action. "A certain man had two sons, and he said unto one, 'Go do thus and so;' and his son replied, 'I go, sir,' but went not. The father said to the second son, 'Go do thus and so,' and this son answered, 'I go not, sir,' but he went. Which, think you," asks Jesus, "did the will of his father?" The Pharisees guessed the proper answer, and so can we. "What you do talks so loud that I cannot hear what you say." "Not every one that says, 'Lord, Lord,' shall enter the Kingdom of Heaven: but he that doeth the will of my Father who is in Heaven." "Why call ye me Lord, 'Divine,' and do not the things which I say?"

The Christian civilization, and a decent and sane and happy world, are not hindered in their advent for want of orthodox statements concerning the mystery of the Person of Jesus: they are hindered for lack of a heroic and kindly practice of the simple teaching of Jesus. We are trying to substitute magic for ethics; theological catch words for Christian character. It is a base and foolish practice. We are building houses on the sand. The ethical ideal embodied in the Master's words and realized in His conduct is humanity's only dependable standing ground.

What are the possibilities of the doctrines of the church and the ethics of Jesus in their respective bearing on the present needs of men? For instance, we need security from the damnation and hell of war. Suppose that a dozen mighty nations are getting ready to gouge the eyes and slit throats by the millions, selecting the physically and mentally and morally fit as the first victims of this brutality. What doctrine can we proclaim to avert the approaching holocaust. In our desperation let us turn to all the creeds. Let us repeat piously, "Born of a Virgin." Let us call Jesus "Very God of very God." Let us assert the infallibility of Scripture. Will this hold back the gathering storm, or quench the smoldering inferno? I do not ask whether these confessions be true; I ask whether they can put an end to the goose-stepping of Japanese or Englishmen, or muzzle our deadly guns? The phraseology would be mighty magic if it did.

But another way stands out before us, a way that has never been tried. Let a hundred million Christians, scattered throughout the world, passionately reassert the hopelessness of violence which Jesus so emphatically proclaimed; let them meet the prospect of wholesale and promiscuous slaughter with Jesus' insistence upon the sovereign requirement of love for all men. Might it not, then, become impossible to comprehend the genius and resources of civilization in the low work of murder? Placing the words and spirit of Jesus on the throne where Doctrine sits would save Christianity from periodic transformation into camps of knaves and fools, and rid us also of the spirit of war in the walks of peace; a war, "the viler as underhand, not openly bearing the sword."[d]

The nastiest and deadliest problem before the world today is the insane hatred between races. Life is bearable because of the variety it offers; yet here are men hating other men to the murder point, legislating against children before they are born, because their skins, their circumstance, their backgrounds are different. Men as white as Madison Grant[e] and Lothrop Stoddard,[f] men as black as William Pickens[g] and Marcus Garvey, and men ranged all the way between, know that this vile and foolish hatred threatens to devour civilization like a moth caught in hellfire. Mr. Wells tells us that any public policy which does not aim at the union of mankind in the Kingdom of Heaven under the fatherhood of God, is ultimately, foolishness, and a way to death.[h] But we need not wait for this conflagration to flare up the world over in actual flames; when we lose the sense of justice or the capacity to act on it the best is already consumed. Now, will rigid adherence to ecclesiastical dogmas kindle in humanity that redeeming spirit of brotherhood, that good-will for all, which is our only hope? If we say the

d. Alfred Lord Tennyson, "Maud."

e. Madison Grant (1865–1937): Lawyer and author of *The Passing of the Great Race* (1916); argued for the superiority of the "Nordic" race and campaigned for racial purity.

f. Lothrop Stoddard (1883–1950): Author of *the Rising Tide of Color against White World-Supremacy* (1920); espoused racial philosophies similar to those of Madison Grant.

g. William Pickens (1881–1954): Graduate of Yale University, dean of academics at Morgan State University, and officer of the NAACP. Author of *Bursting Bonds* (1923), an autobiography that attacked the racist arguments used to justify lynching. He was also one of the eight signatories to the "Garvey Must Go" letter (1923) sent to the US attorney general.

h. Probably referring to H. G. Wells, *A Short History of the World* (London: Cassell and Co., 1922), chapter 37, "The Teaching of Jesus."

world was made in six days, will the statement guarantee to all men "life, liberty and the pursuit of happiness?" If we say Jesus was born of a virgin, will the dictum cause every valley to be exalted, every mountain and hill to be brought low? Will it make the crooked way straight and the rough way smooth so that the glory of the Lord shall be revealed, and all flesh shall see it together? The phraseology would be wonderful magic if it did.

It so happens in our country that the very section of it which is unquestionably the chief seat of orthodoxy is at the same time the dependable theatre of our most heartless inhumanities. "This people honor me with their mouth, but their heart is far from my reins."[i] The appearance of an up-to-date text-book on science is a tragedy of Troy, but crimes like those at Aiken and Wytheville[j] recur as regularly as Holy Communion, and the perpetrators and abettors are at peace with their ritual-loving God. If one opens his mind on the subject of religion, he may have to keep it open on questions of justice.

In the Sermon on the Mount there is not one word of dogma. But these great words are there: "All things therefore, whatsoever ye would that men should do to you, do ye ever so to them."

For a long time men have been looking for a civilization which hath foundations. When will the Christian ministry point them to the rock? When will we put a red lantern on the sand pile? When will Christian preachers either preach Jesus or save the public from further deception by unfrocking themselves of His name? Again and again, obeying architectural instincts that are not a God, we have sent structure after structure towering in the air, but scarcely had the noise of the builders ceased when, above glistening spires and minarets, a voice, indifferent to the sanction of mighty men, was heard: "Except the Lord build the house they labor in vain that build it."[k] Then the God of Amos appeared, standing beside a crooked wall, with a plumbline in His hand, and the achievement of 1,000 years went down with a mighty crash! God is the Father of all His children; willing the highest good of all. Any structure built on foundations less broad is foredoomed to failure by nature and nature's God.

An enduring civilization must be one that exists for the good of all. Such a civilization none will wish to overthrow, for none will profit by its

i. Jeremiah 12:2; Matthew 15:8.
j.Both Wytheville, Virginia (25 Aug. 1926), and Aiken, South Carolina (23 Oct. 1926), had been sites of horrific lynchings that year.
k. Psalm 127:1.

downfall. Build however else we will, but there are winds in the cave of Aeolus which will blow our building down![l] The engineers of the stable civilization will measure their foundations by the Golden Rule; the practice of the principles of Jesus will be the chief cornerstone. "Let every one take heed how he builds!"[m]

---

l. In Homer's *Odyssey*, Aeolus is the "keeper of the four winds," who provides Odysseus with a west wind to propel the ship home and with a bag containing the four winds for when they arrive there. Odysseus's crew open the bag before reaching home, however, and are driven back to the island of Aeolia.

m. 1 Corinthians 3:10.

Martin Luther King Jr.

I Have a Dream

Martin Luther King's historic speech on the steps of the Lincoln Memorial in 1963 is among the most memorable and inspirational in American history. Many historians of American public address rate it as the best speech of the twentieth century. Few people who saw King deliver the speech failed to be profoundly moved by its appeal, by King's charisma, and by the turbulent moment in American history the speech symbolized. The electrifying conclusion of the speech asks all Americans to rally around a prophetic vision of a just society. King foresees the day when "all of God's children, black men and white men, Jews and Gentiles, Protestants and Catholics, will be able to join hands and sing in the words of the old Negro spiritual: 'Free at last, free at last, thank God almighty, we are free at last.'" King's eloquent words and courageous deeds throughout the civil rights movement inspired victims of discrimination to demand equality, encouraged national politicians to dismantle pernicious Jim Crow laws, and goaded the federal government to pass legislation protecting the freedoms of all citizens. The effectiveness of King's oratory resulted as much from his perceived authority and leadership as his eloquence and wisdom. His voice rang out in a song of justice for black Americans. No other American in the twentieth century was as effective in touching the chords of the despair and longing of blacks or the conscience and idealism of whites.

Martin Luther King was born Michael King on January 15, 1929, in Atlanta, Georgia; King's father later changed both their names to "Martin

Marilyn DeLaure cowrote this introduction.

Luther." His father and maternal grandfather were both pastors of Baptist congregations, and King grew up listening to the themes and cadences of black preaching. The middle of three children, King was a precocious and sensitive youth who skipped several grades in school. He enrolled at Atlanta's historically black Morehouse College at age 15, where he majored in sociology and minored in English. Morehouse faculty, including Gladstone Lewis Chandler—a notably eloquent English professor who emphasized clarity of style and a rich, expansive vocabulary—and Benjamin Mays, the college president, influenced King deeply. In Mays, King saw a ministerial model, a moral leader engaged in social activism.[1] At age 17, he decided to become a preacher; he was ordained in 1947 and became assistant pastor of his father's church, Ebenezer Baptist.

After graduating college, King entered Crozer Seminary in Chester, Pennsylvania. During his time at Crozer, King attended a lecture on the life and teachings of Gandhi; he was deeply moved and inspired by Gandhi's method of nonviolent resistance, derived from Thoreau's essay on civil disobedience. Gandhi challenged British rule over India not with violence or hatred, but with *Satyagraha*, the force of love and divine justice. Here King found a model for uniting religious faith and social activism: *Satyagraha* was much like agape, the redemptive Christian love for all humankind that leads to the "beloved community."[2]

King finished Crozer at the top of his class, won a $1,300 scholarship for graduate study, and decided to pursue a doctorate in theology at Boston University. Upon completing his PhD coursework, King accepted a post at Dexter Avenue Baptist Church in Montgomery, Alabama. He gave his first sermon to Dexter's largely middle-class black congregation in May 1954; less than a month later, the US Supreme Court handed down the *Brown v. Board of Education* decision, outlawing segregation in public schools. The following year, Rosa Parks, a respected young tailor's assistant, became an icon of the civil rights movement by refusing to relinquish her seat on the bus to a white man. Negro passengers in Montgomery had long endured segregated public transportation and mistreatment by white drivers. Parks's arrest by local authorities outraged the Montgomery black community, but also excited its leaders. Here was a viable test case of a Negro being charged for violating the city's Jim Crow laws, which could be proved unconstitutional in the wake of the *Brown* decision. The next evening, nearly fifty ministers and civic leaders gathered at King's church to plan a bus boycott, to begin the following Monday. Organizers printed leaflets, pastors alerted their congregations, and on the next day, the boycott began with nearly one hundred percent participation.[3]

The Montgomery Improvement Association (MIA), a group newly formed to direct the bus boycotts, elected the unassuming but charismatic King their president. King's leadership and advocacy for the MIA thrust him into the public spotlight, and he now spoke as a civil rights organizer and social reformer. He preached the philosophy of nonviolent resistance he had explored intellectually as a divinity student and confronted the practical rhetorical challenge of arousing an audience to action while simultaneously urging prudent moderation and pacifism. Even when his home was bombed and his life threatened, King countered aggression with high-minded pacifism and instructed his people to respond with equal restraint. After more than a year of protest, segregationist backlash, and litigation, the US Supreme Court declared Alabama's laws requiring segregation on buses unconstitutional. Following the Montgomery victory, King and other leaders formed the Southern Christian Leadership Conference (SCLC) in order to coordinate nonviolent protest and activism throughout the South.

Nineteen sixty-three was a pivotal year for King. Beginning in February, the SCLC led "Project C" (for "confrontation") in Birmingham, Alabama, to force desegregation of all public facilities, including private businesses. King was jailed in April, when his fourth child, Bernice, was just weeks old. During his confinement, he wrote "Letter from a Birmingham Jail" in response to criticism by a group of eight white clergymen.[4] In early May, Project C drew international attention as thousands of children joined the march for freedom, thousands of demonstrators were jailed, and many were injured when Police Commissioner Eugene "Bull" Connor turned fire hoses and unleashed attack dogs on the demonstrators. The photographs and film footage of these events, combined with the powerful rhetoric of civil rights leaders such as King, turned the tide in a state whose governor, George Wallace, had vowed in his 1963 inaugural address, "segregation today . . . segregation tomorrow . . . segregation forever." On May 10 of the same year, an agreement to desegregate Birmingham was reached.

That summer, President John F. Kennedy addressed the nation in a televised speech on civil rights and submitted a bill to Congress that would outlaw segregation in interstate public facilities and allow federal enforcement of school integration. In hundreds of cities, demonstrators engaged in nonviolent, direct action campaigns to spark desegregation. On August 28,

King helped lead the largest march to date on Washington, DC, culminating in the rally at the Lincoln Memorial and his most famous speech, "I Have a Dream." Later that year, King was named *Time* magazine's Man of the Year. In November, JFK was assassinated.

Prior to the August March on Washington, King had spent much of the summer speaking coast to coast, riding the victory in Birmingham and pressing forth the cause. In a speech delivered at the close of a Freedom Walk in Detroit in June of 1963, King anticipated the more momentous March on Washington and also rehearsed many of the most potent passages of "I Have a Dream." He spoke emphatically about the importance of continued "determined pressure" to achieve the passage of Kennedy's civil rights bill: "In order to put this bill through, we've got to arouse the conscience of the nation, and we ought to march to Washington more than 100,000 . . . to engage in a nonviolent protest." In Detroit, King declared that one hundred years after the Emancipation Proclamation, "the Negro in the United States still isn't free." As in Washington, he expressed his apprehension that the movement would lose its momentum. Sensitive to the dynamics of social movements, he cautioned against heeding those who would cry "Slow up and cool off." "There is," he joked, "always the danger if you cool off too much that you will end up in a deep freeze." The famous "dream" section, which had first appeared in a 1961 speech to the AFL-CIO,[5] found even more concrete and poetic form in the Detroit address.

King's speech on the steps of the Lincoln Memorial represented the apotheosis of his oratory. He addressed a throng of more than two hundred thousand people who had gathered to press the passage of the historic legislation that would transform a nation rent by racial tensions and embarrassed by the bigotry and paternalism that had been institutionalized in much of the South but existed de facto in every corner of the country. Public memory of King is fixed by this important, though often uncritically mythologized, speech.[6]

The speech inspired Americans already committed to racial justice and encouraged many others to support blacks in their quest for legal, economic, and social equality. The substance of King's speech invited comparison with Lincoln's own rhetoric on behalf of the rights of blacks. In his Second Inaugural Address, Lincoln argued that slavery had caused the Civil War and that blacks deserved the "sweat from their own brows." Reflecting upon the Emancipation Proclamation, signed on January 1, 1863, King reminded his audiences, in the first of many anaphoras (repetition of word or phrase for rhetorical effect), that: "One hundred years later, the Negro still is not free. . . . One hundred years later, the Negro lives on a lonely island of poverty in the midst of a vast ocean of material prosperity."

King expressed the dream of black Americans in distinctly economic terms. His dream, he declared, was "deeply rooted in the American dream," and King's metaphors reminded his audience of the economic consequences of racial discrimination. He asserted unabashedly that: "We've come to our nation's capital to cash a check," promising "the unalienable rights of life, liberty, and the pursuit of happiness" articulated in the Declaration of Independence. Historian Gary Wills has noted that, in his Gettysburg Address, Lincoln gave the nation a new political creed of racial equality by cannily using the authority of the Declaration of Independence, an antimonarchist document, to claim for emancipated slaves the economic rights of all men.

The signers of the Declaration understood the "pursuit of happiness" as a God-given natural right to prosper materially. They did not foresee that such a doctrine would be used as a basis for racial equality. In quoting the Declaration of Independence and speaking of a "promissory note to which every American was to fall heir," King appropriated Lincoln's radical reinterpretation of Jefferson's eloquent claim to human freedom and equality. Through his economic metaphor, King persuasively fused the philosophical and legal concepts of justice with the financial metaphor of the check or promissory note. Although he used the metaphor to "demand the riches of freedom and the security of justice," the transcendental dream serves also to remind his audience of the "shameful condition" it would replace. King insisted that it would be "fatal for the nation to overlook the urgency of the moment." He realized how easily social movements can be thwarted by partial and Pyrrhic victories. He warned against taking "the tranquilizing drug of gradualism," although Lincoln, whose authority King invoked, had advocated precisely such a policy concerning black civil rights.

Many citizens, including those who supported civil rights for black Americans, feared that the movement would grow more violent. King's persuasiveness among white Americans was predicated upon his support for nonviolent solutions, even in the face of the taunts and the brutality that civil rights protestors had experienced. King admonished his audience that: "The whirlwinds of revolt will continue to shake the foundations of our nation until the bright day of justice emerges" but quickly added that blacks must not commit "wrongful deeds." Many, including Malcolm X, did not agree with his Gandhian approach to protest, and King inclusively acknowledged this difference in outlook by noting the "marvelous new militancy which has engulfed the Negro community," while counseling blacks to meet "physical force with soul force."

The effectiveness of King's message depended upon his audience's acceptance of him as the presumptive leader of the civil rights movement. The paragraph in which King acknowledged the divergence of viewpoints in the movement tellingly began with the pastoral declaration that King had something to say to "my people." Here King asserted authority as the leader of black Americans, but the greater effect of the speech as a whole was to cast King as a prophet not only for blacks but for whites in America, "[who] have come to realize that their destiny is tied up with our destiny, and that their freedom is inextricably bound to our freedom." This unifying sentiment, which appears in many of King's addresses, reflected the influence of Morehouse president Benjamin Mays, who had imparted the idea to him: "The destiny of each individual . . . is tied up with the destiny of all men that inhabit the globe," Mays had said.[7] King's speech is sometimes addressed specifically to African Americans ("But there is something I must say to my people, who stand on the warm threshold that leads into the palace of justice," or "I am not unmindful that some of you . . . have come fresh from narrow jail cells"), but these moments are also intended to involve the larger audience. King's prophecy was not simply of justice for blacks but of reconciliation and unification with whites, exemplified by the following powerful passage: "I have a dream that one day on the red hills of Georgia, the sons of former slaves and the sons of former slave owners will be able to sit down together at the table of brotherhood."

Other metaphors and references in the speech reflect King's consciousness of time and space. The speech is organized temporally, beginning with the social and political declarations of the nation's founders, proceeding to insist on the "fierce urgency of the moment," and concluding with King's expression of an as yet unrealized dream.[8] The place from which he delivered the speech and the places from which his audience and fellow activists have come also figure prominently. King transformed the steps of the Lincoln Memorial into a place of revelation, presenting his inspired moral and civic prophecy. He brought a movement, whose roots are mainly in the Deep South, to the Washington Mall, the symbolic center of the nation. He referenced disparate parts of the nation by claiming, for example, that "a Negro in Mississippi cannot vote and a Negro in New York believes he has nothing for which to vote." In a spirit of benediction, he told his brethren to "go back" with renewed hope, not only to the Southern states that were the fiercest battleground of the civil rights movement, but also to "the slums and ghettos of our northern cities." In the conclusion, he rhetorically and geographically unified the movement by proposing that the new freedom should ring from landmark promontories throughout the nation—"from the heightening Alleghenies of Pennsylvania . . . [to] every hill and every molehill of Mississippi." The metaphors of unity that King used are distinctly musical. Not only did he describe freedom as a peal of bells, he spoke of transforming "the jangling discords of our nation into a beautiful symphony of brotherhood." He drew his audience into a dream that is as much aural as visual.

King delivered his rhapsodic paean of economic freedom, social justice, and racial brotherhood as if from a musical score. His prologue was delivered deliberately, sometimes almost haltingly, though not without passion and force, whereas the prophetic dream was expressed in an entirely different key, ascending in emotional and auditory leaps. King was tied to his manuscript in roughly the opening two-thirds of his speech but spoke with little reference to his text during the last third, when he articulated his dream. Prophecy, if truly inspired, should not require a rehearsed text. In fact, King reported that he included the scintillating "I have a dream" section of the speech on an impulse: "I just felt I wanted to use it here. I don't know why. I hadn't thought about it before the speech."[9] King had departed from his text directly after reading: "We will not be satisfied until justice runs down like waters and righteousness like a mighty stream." The voluble affirmation from the audience made King reluctant to continue reading from his manuscript. At this crucial turn, King recast the subdued request that the attendees should "go back to our communities" with a dynamic series of imperatives: "Go back to Mississippi, go back to Alabama, go back to South Carolina, go back to Georgia, go back to Louisiana, go back to the slums and ghettos of our northern cities, knowing that somehow this situation can and will be changed. Let us not wallow in the valley of despair." Mahalia Jackson, who had earlier sung a black spiritual, shouted from behind King: "Tell 'em about the dream, Martin." Whether through the singer's prompting or by his own initiative, King launched nearly seamlessly into the now famous sentences that expressed his dream.[10] The difference in delivery between the planned and improvisational sections of the speech provides a casebook example of the relative virtues of extemporaneity.

King's delivery is a study in climax, wherein successive paragraphs build slowly to intermediary climaxes or crescendos, often achieved with quotations from or paraphrases of the Bible delivered in King's thundering, sonorous voice. At the conclusion of each of these intermediary climaxes, King reduced his volume and often his rate of utterance, and then built again to yet another climax. Many times throughout the speech, including those sections where crescendos are built, King made use of anaphora to help create climaxes in delivery and emotional evocation. Examples of anaphora include the eight-times repeated "I have a dream," and the six-times repeated "Let freedom ring from . . . "

King rode the wave of audience response to the various climaxes in his speech. When the audience was at a pitch of emotion after the "I have a dream" sequence, he paused only briefly and then continued to make another ascent to the final emotional peak of the speech. The growing intensity of his delivery, exemplified in a series of emphatic declarations—"This is our hope," "This will be the day"—and the passionate timbre of his voice demonstrate that, while a master of shaping audience response, King, the consummate performer, was also always an audience for his own potent message.

Some passages of King's oratory, particularly in the section that begins with the repeated drumbeat of "I have a dream," were inflected so uniquely and interpretatively that King seemed almost to be a singing rather than speaking. He performed every line dynamically, adding meaning and emotional gravity though oral emphasis and unexpected and unusually placed dramatic pauses. His delivery was reminiscent of the musical tradition of the blues. The coloration that King added to his words through their performance achieved the effect of the blues. Taylor Branch observes: "The slow determination of his cadence exposed all the more clearly the passion that overshadowed the content of the dream. It went beyond the limitations of language and culture to express something that was neither pure rage nor pure joy, but a universal transport of the kind that makes the blues sweet."[11] The lyricism of King's oratory was also punctuated by his quotations from song, including the counterpoise created by his quotation from "America the Beautiful"—"My country 'tis of thee, sweet land of liberty . . ." to his moving concluding quotation from a black spiritual: "Free at Last! Free at last/ Thank God Almighty, we are free at last!" This six second passage, which King delivered while slowly raising and panning his right arm in a final benediction to his audience, is as iconic an image of King as American Colonial painter Gilbert Stuart's unfinished portrait is of George Washington.

As Lincoln had not expected to deliver at Gettysburg what Gary Wills describes as the "words that remade America," King had not expected to make the most moving or memorable speech of the event, let alone of the American civil rights movement. He had written a text that fit roughly into the seven minute limit imposed by the organizers of the march, but with the sermon King extemporized, the speech grew not only in length but in historical proportion. In the aftermath of the event, King and other civil rights leaders were conveyed from the Lincoln Memorial to the White House, where they would meet the president. Kennedy, who had watched the speech on television, recognized that King's words had achieved a powerful effect. He commented spontaneously to a staffer: "He's damn good."[12] A student of oratory, Kennedy admired King's prowess and particularly his ability to extemporize. When the civil rights leaders entered the Oval Office, Kennedy greeted King by repeating the refrain that would endure in national memory—"I have a dream." Not everyone was as astute. While the *New York Times* used the line to headline its story, the *Washington Post* failed to mention King's speech, focusing instead on a speech delivered by A. Philip Randolph.[13]

King's message of nonviolence and social justice advanced the movement but failed to quell the murderous rage among its most militant white opponents. Violence erupted in Birmingham only a few weeks later. A bomb planted by the Ku Klux Klan killed four young girls in the Sixteenth Street Baptist Church in Birmingham. King memorialized the dead girls in a subdued eulogy free of condemnation for the terrorists. His mildness in this private setting underscored the pacifism he preached before the masses. The broad emotional sweeps of his civic oratory contrast with a compact and focused reflection on a loss borne most profoundly by four families and a community. "Good night sweet princesses, good night those who symbolize a new day," he said in a conclusion that revealed an indebtedness to Shakespeare. King, who earned a reputation as a spellbinding orator and social activist, was first a compassionate pastor and spiritual leader.

As he continued his fight for civil rights, King's rhetoric forged connections among various humanitarian causes; the same philosophy that anchored his fight for racial justice and equality would also inspire him to speak out against poverty, discrimination in housing and labor, and war. In 1964, the year that the Civil Rights Act was passed, King received the Nobel Peace Prize, becoming at age thirty-five the youngest man ever to be honored with the prestigious award. In 1968, after King had struggled for years on behalf of African Americans and a nation that needed to be reconciled with its own constitutional vision of equality, an assassin's bullet silenced his prophetic voice. He had propelled the nation forward philosophically, socially, and legally with the open hand of persuasion and the clenched fist of indomitable resolve. He invented and instilled a new self image for black American citizens. By preaching nonviolent action, of rising "to the majestic heights by meeting physical force with soul force," King led blacks to transcend both the lawless outrages and the sly paternalism to which they had been subject for generations. For this King deserves the enduring gratitude of all Americans whose dream was reinvigorated and reaffirmed by its extension to black Americans. His sermons, writings, and speeches, most memorably represented by his speech in Washington on a hot August day in Washington, DC, in 1963, constitute the central rhetorical legacy of the civil rights era.

I Have a Dream

August 28, 1963
Washington, DC

I am happy to join with you today in what will go down in history as the greatest demonstration for freedom in the history of our nation.

Five score years ago, a great American, in whose symbolic shadow we stand today, signed the Emancipation Proclamation. This momentous decree came as a great beacon light of hope for millions of Negro slaves who had been seared in the flames of withering injustice. It came as a joyous daybreak to end the long night of their captivity.

But one hundred years later, the Negro still is not free. One hundred years later, the life of the Negro is still sadly crippled by the manacles of segregation and the chains of discrimination. One hundred years later, the Negro lives on a lonely island of poverty in the midst of a vast ocean of material prosperity. One hundred years later, the Negro is still languished in the corners of American society and finds himself an exile in his own land.

So we have come here today to dramatize a shameful condition. In a sense we have come to our nation's capital to cash a check. When the architects of our republic wrote the magnificent words of the Constitution and the Declaration of Independence, they were signing a promissory note to which every American was to fall heir. This note was a promise that all men—yes black men as well as white men, would be guaranteed the unalienable rights of life, liberty, and the pursuit of happiness.

It is obvious today that America has defaulted on this promissory note in so far as her citizens of color are concerned. Instead of honoring this sacred obligation, America has given the Negro people a bad check; a check which has come back marked "insufficient funds." But we refuse to believe that the bank of justice is bankrupt. We refuse to believe that there are insufficient funds in the great vaults of opportunity of this nation. So we have come to cash this check—a check that will give us upon demand the riches of freedom and the security of justice.

We have also come to this hallowed spot to remind America of the fierce urgency of now. This is no time to engage in the luxury of cooling off or to take the tranquilizing drug of gradualism. Now is the time to make real the promises of democracy. Now is the time to rise from the dark and desolate valley of segregation to the sunlit path of racial justice. Now is the time to lift our nation from the quicksands of racial injustice to the solid rock of brotherhood. Now is the time to make justice a reality for all of God's children. It would be fatal for the nation to overlook the urgency of the moment. This sweltering summer of the Negro's legitimate discontent will not pass until there is an invigorating autumn of freedom and equality.[a]

Nineteen sixty-three is not an end, but a beginning. Those who hope that the Negro needed to blow off steam and will now be content, will have a rude awakening if the nation returns to business as usual. There will be neither rest nor tranquility in America until the Negro is granted his citizenship rights. The whirlwinds of revolt will continue to shake the foundations of our nation until the bright day of justice emerges.

But there is something that I must say to my people who stand on the warm threshold which leads into the palace of justice. In the process of gaining our rightful place we must not be guilty of wrongful deeds. Let us not seek to satisfy our thirst for freedom by drinking from the cup of bitterness and hatred. We must forever conduct our struggle on the high plane of dignity and discipline. We must not allow our creative protest to degenerate into physical violence. Again and again, we must rise to the majestic heights of meeting physical force with soul force.

The marvelous new militancy which has engulfed the Negro community must not lead us to a distrust of all white people, for many of our white brothers, as evidenced by their presence here today, have come to realize that their destiny is tied up with our destiny and their freedom is inextricably bound to our freedom. We cannot walk alone.

And as we walk, we must make the pledge that we shall march ahead. We cannot turn back. There are those who are asking the devotees of civil rights, "When will you be satisfied?" We can never be satisfied as long as the Negro

a. An allusion to William Shakespeare, *Richard III*, act 1, scene 1: "Now is the winter of our discontent made glorious summer . . . "

is the victim of the unspeakable horrors of police brutality. We can never be satisfied as long as our bodies, heavy with the fatigue of travel, cannot gain lodging in the motels of the highways and the hotels of the cities. We cannot be satisfied as long as the Negro's basic mobility is from a smaller ghetto to a larger one. We can never be satisfied as long as our children are stripped of their selfhood and robbed of their dignity by signs stating "For Whites Only." We can not be satisfied as long as a Negro in Mississippi cannot vote and a Negro in New York believes he has nothing for which to vote. No, we are not satisfied, and we will not be satisfied until justice rolls down like waters and righteousness like a mighty stream.[b]

I am not unmindful that some of you have come here out of excessive trials and tribulations. Some of you have come fresh from narrow jail cells. Some of you have come from areas where your quest for freedom left you battered by the storms of persecution and staggered by the winds of police brutality. You have been the veterans of creative suffering. Continue to work with the faith that unearned suffering is redemptive.

Go back to Mississippi; go back to Alabama; go back to South Carolina; go back to Georgia; go back to Louisiana; go back to the slums and ghettos of our northern cities, knowing that somehow this situation can and will be changed. Let us not wallow in the valley of despair.

I say to you, my friends, that even though we must face the difficulties of today and tomorrow, I still have a dream. It is a dream deeply rooted in the American dream. I have a dream that one day this nation will rise up, live out the true meaning of its creed—we hold these truths to be self-evident: that all men are created equal.

I have a dream that one day on the red hills of Georgia, sons of former slaves and the sons of former slave owners will be able to sit down together at the table of brotherhood.

I have a dream that one day, even the state of Mississippi, a desert state, a state sweltering with the heat of injustice, sweltering with the heat of oppression, will be transformed into an oasis of freedom and justice.

I have a dream that my four little children will one day live in a nation where they will not be judged by the color of their skin but by the content of their character. I have a dream today!

I have a dream that one day down in Alabama, with its vicious racists, with its governor having his lips dripping with the words of interposition

b. Amos 5:23–24.

and nullification, one day, right there in Alabama, little black boys and black girls will be able to join hands with little white boys and white girls as sisters and brothers. I have a dream today!

I have a dream that one day every valley shall be exalted, every hill and mountain shall be made low, the rough places will be made plain, and the crooked places will be made straight, and the glory of the Lord shall be revealed, and all flesh shall see it together.[c]

This is our hope. This is the faith that I go back to the South with.

With this faith we will be able to hew out of the mountain of despair a stone of hope. With this faith we will be able to transform the jangling discords of our nation into a beautiful symphony of brotherhood. With this faith we will be able to work together, to pray together, to struggle together, to go to jail together, to stand up for freedom together, knowing that we will be free one day. This will be the day when all of God's children will be able to sing with a new meaning—"My country, 'tis of thee, sweet land of liberty, of thee I sing. Land where my fathers died, land of the pilgrim's pride, from every mountainside, let freedom ring." And if America is to be a great nation, this must become true.

So let freedom ring from the prodigious hilltops of New Hampshire.

Let freedom ring from the mighty mountains of New York.

Let freedom ring from the heightening Alleghenies of Pennsylvania!

Let freedom ring from the snowcapped Rockies of Colorado!

Let freedom ring from the curvaceous slopes of California!

But not only that.

Let freedom ring from Stone Mountain of Georgia!

Let freedom ring from Lookout Mountain of Tennessee!

Let freedom ring from every hill and molehill of Mississippi. From every mountainside, let freedom ring.

And when we allow freedom to ring, when we let it ring from every village and every hamlet, from every state and every city, we will be able to speed up that day when all of God's children—black men and white men, Jews and Gentiles, Protestants and Catholics—will be able to join hands and sing in the words of the old Negro spiritual, "Free at last! free at last! thank God Almighty, we are free at last!"

c. Isaiah 40:4.

Malcolm X

The Ballot or the Bullet

Martin Luther King upheld the banner of nonviolent protest and envisaged "the dream" of African American equality but also foresaw, more ominously, that "the whirlwinds of revolt will continue to shake the foundations of our nation until the bright day of justice emerges." King offered Americans a choice between peaceful acquiescence to a reasonable demand for equal rights or sustained social turmoil as African Americans struggled for inclusion in the American dream. The appeal of Martin Luther King's idea of "meeting force with soul force" was increased by the prospect that some African Americans would choose violence, for in the background competing spokesmen such as Malcolm X proposed meeting physical force with physical force. It is difficult to account for the appeal of Martin Luther King's nonviolent civil rights rhetoric without reference to the contrasting voice of Malcolm X.

Their rhetoric was as different as their backgrounds. King was the heir to a three generation dynasty of Baptist preachers in Atlanta. He and his cohesive family were admired within a confident middle-class African American community. Great things were expected of King, and he achieved them. Malcolm Little, born in Omaha, Nebraska, in 1925, belonged to a family far less insulated from daily reminders of white racism, whose sting Malcolm felt throughout his life. His family did not put down generational roots in Omaha but was forced out by the Ku Klux Klan (KKK) and moved to Lansing, Michigan, only to have their house set ablaze by the Black Legionnaires, a white group with the same mission as the KKK. When Malcolm was only six, his father, Earl, an itinerant preacher who followed the black nationalist theology of Father Divine, was either accidentally killed by a streetcar or, as some people, including Malcolm, believed, through the nefarious work of the Black Legionnaires. Malcolm's mother, Louise, soldiered on raising eight children, but she ultimately succumbed to mental illness and was institutionalized in the State Mental Hospital in Kalamazoo, where she would remain for twenty-six years. The children were sent to live in different foster homes in Lansing.[1]

Abject poverty and privation had caused Malcolm to steal food while in Lansing, and his mother's insanity and institutionalization left him without a disciplinarian. Bad behavior at school resulted in his expulsion, and the authorities sent Malcolm from a foster home in Lansing to a "detention home" in nearby Mason, Michigan, which typically was the first step on the path to incarceration in a reform school. Fortunately, however, Malcolm was allowed to attend the local junior high school, where he quickly distinguished himself. He rose to be one of the three best students academically and in seventh grade was elected class president.[2] His election turned out to be a Pyrrhic victory. In a scene no doubt repeated many times between ambitious African American students and previously trusted teachers and guidance counselors, Malcolm was told indelicately that he should abandon his ambition to become a lawyer in favor of carpentry: "A lawyer—that's no realistic goal for a nigger."[3] Devastated by this unexpected verdict from an English teacher in whom Malcolm had confided, he turned his intelligence to pursuits he could achieve on the streets. After finishing eighth grade in Mason, Malcolm left the detention home to live with his half sister, Ella, in Roxbury, Massachusetts.[4] At a tender age, Malcolm, the street-wise "Detroit Red," developed as a hustler, with involvement in the sale of drugs, in prostitution, and in gambling rings, first in Boston and then in Harlem. In 1942, by the age of seventeen, he was fully launched on a career in crime, which was interrupted in 1946 by a conviction on a burglary charge and six years in prison.[5]

By force of will, Malcolm would emerge out of a cauldron of crime and imprisonment a redeemed man. While in the penitentiary, Malcolm read, studied, and argued philosophy and theology. He read widely—Kant, Schopenhauer, Nietzsche, Spinoza, Milton, Will Durant, H. G. Wells, and W. E. B. Du Bois. He was drawn to the prophetic religion of the Nation of Islam (NOI) and its founder, Elijah Muhammad, whom he credited with his transformation.[6] "It was right there in prison," he says, "that I made up my mind to devote the rest of my life to telling the white man about himself—or die."[7] After his parole, Malcolm, who abandoned his slave surname, Little, in favor of X, symbolizing an unknown African surname, worked in truck and automobile factories in Detroit before becoming an assistant pastor for Elijah Muhammad's Temple Number 1.[8] He rose quickly through the ranks and became the NOI's chief spokesman. Under Malcolm, the NOI flourished with thirty radio stations and forty new temples.[9]

Malcolm preached the gospel of the NOI faithfully, including the concept of black superiority and royal lineage, the evils of whites, the need for self-discipline and self-defense, and the careful regulation of Black Muslim women. He constructed a powerful rhetoric but, paradoxically, one upon which he could not act. The NOI prevented him from engaging in public acts of protest against racism. Learning of Elijah Muhammad's extramarital affairs and his unscrupulous use of the religion's funds disillusioned Malcolm. Muhammad ordered Malcolm's silence when, in January 1964, he said that John F. Kennedy's assassination signified "the chickens coming home to roost." After ninety days, on March 8, 1964, Malcolm broke his silence and his association with NOI, when he announced that he had formed the Muslim Mosque and a new political entity, the Organization of African American Unity.[10]

Malcolm X introduced the ideology of the Muslim Mosque, Inc., in four public rallies. He announced his plan to accept all speaking engagements, and to become politically active in the South. According to the *New York Times*: "He would seek to convert the Negro population from nonviolence to active self-defense against white supremacists in all parts of the country."[11] Malcolm also delivered speeches in several other American cities, including Boston, Cleveland, and Detroit. "The Ballot or the Bullet" was first presented on April 3, 1964, at Cleveland's Cory United Methodist Church, and served as the basis for later speeches until Malcolm's assassination in 1965. In Cleveland, Malcolm shared the stage with reporter and black activist Louis E. Lomax, at a meeting of the Congress of Racial Equality (CORE), the organization dedicated to nonviolent action such as the historic lunch-counter sit-ins of 1960.[12]

In the introduction of the speech, Malcolm struck an immediate note of irony and humor: "Mr. Moderator, Brother Lomax, brothers and sisters, friends and enemies: I just can't believe everyone in here is a friend and I don't want to leave anybody out." There were, undoubtedly, enemies there, namely, representatives of the NOI, as well as FBI agents assigned to file reports on Malcolm's activities.[13] The speech heralds Malcolm's new role as a civil rights activist, although affirming that he is still also a Muslim minister. He calls for unity with other civil rights activists to fight against the "political oppression," "economic exploitation," and "social degradation at the hands of the white man." Explaining the title of his speech, he declares that in the political year 1964, African Americans will be "forced either to use the ballot or the bullet." Later in the speech he advises: "If you're afraid to use an expression like that, you should get on out of the country, you should get back in the cotton patch, you should get back in the alley." The choice of the ballot or the bullet was both a threat to white racists and a challenge to politically indifferent blacks. Southern states denied African Americans the right to vote, while African Americans frequently did not exercise their right in those states where they could vote.

The speech develops the parallel themes that white politicians, including disingenuous white liberal politicians, should not be trusted and that, when confronted with violent oppression, African Americans should return like for like. The odds of winning in a physical confrontation might be against African Americans but, he notes wryly, that if drafted, they would fight eight hundred million Chinese in Korea. In fighting racism in the United States "you will at least know what you're fighting for." Imagery, irony, paradox, embarrassing truths, provocative observations, flashes of blistering invective, disarming frankness, and rational reasoning are hallmarks of Malcolm X's rhetoric.

One notable characteristic of Malcolm X's rhetoric is the utterance of a radical, hyperbolic, and sometimes apparently indefensible declaration, which is then clearly rationalized and explained. For example, early in the speech, Malcolm claims not to be an American. His logic, based upon definition, is impeccable. If he were an American, and therefore one who enjoyed all the rights of citizenship, what need is there for the Civil Rights Act of 1964? Malcolm goes on to criticize the ongoing Senate filibuster against the act led by Southern senators. The Democrats, he observes, nominally under the leadership of Lyndon Johnson, deceitfully hold out the promise of racial equality while conspiring with the Dixiecrats, the segregationist Southern wing of the Democratic Party. Malcolm pierces the logic of Lyndon Johnson's claim that as a Southerner he can better deal with Southern issues: "Let Eastland be president, he's from the South too."

Senator James Eastland, of Mississippi, the chair of the Senate Judiciary Committee, was a staunch opponent of the Civil Rights Act. He was one of the Southern Democrats whose seniority had led to powerful committee chairmanships. Ironically, these Democrats represented states that retained power by denying African Americans the right to vote through literacy tests and poll taxes. The Democrats held a majority in both the House and Senate, but the Southern Democrats arrayed against civil rights and voter rights legislation: "You and I in America are faced not with a segregationist conspiracy, we're faced with a government conspiracy. . . . The same government that you go abroad to fight for and die for is the government that is in a conspiracy to deprive you of your voting rights, deprive you of your economic opportunities, deprive you of decent housing, deprive you of a decent education."

Another characteristic of Malcolm's rhetoric is the interruption of a thought to express a note of irony or an emotional reaction to a prior comment. Take, for example, the image-laden sentence: "Uncle Sam's hands are dripping with blood, dripping with the blood of the black man in this country. He's the earth's number-one hypocrite. He has the audacity—yes, he has—imagine him posing as the leader of the free world. The free world! And you over here singing 'We shall Overcome.' Expand the civil-rights struggle to the level of human rights, take it into the United Nations . . ."

The phrase "the ballot or the bullet," which is used as a potent refrain in the speech, is not simply stylistic artifice—two instances of synecdoche, paired to create an antithesis. Rhetorical effectiveness compelled Malcolm X to make the threat of violence real. He speaks, for example, of black youth in Jacksonville, Mississippi, who threw Molotov cocktails. With rising anger he urges that when the police unlawfully put down antisegregation demonstrations, and use a police dog against the demonstrators, victims should "kill that dog. I say it, if they put me in jail tomorrow, kill—that—dog." He advises ominously that one should "die for what you believe in. But don't die alone. Let your dying be reciprocal." The message of reciprocal violence, of killing one's assailant, although not an immediate incitement to violence, is expressed in irony that is rhetorical bluster at one level, but beneath which there is also a dark threat. Malcolm repeats the symbolic threat of the bullet throughout the speech: "Let him know that it must be the ballot or the bullet." The choice between the ballot or the bullet is not for white Americans only. African Americans must also choose to accept the potency of the ballot: "Don't be throwing out any ballots. A ballot is like a bullet. You don't throw your ballots until you see a target, and if that target is not within your reach. Keep your ballot in your pocket."

Malcolm invites the audience to walk with him over a bed of burning embers. Although a Hotspur who does not hesitate to make a provocative threat, Malcolm does not engage in the kind of ranting diatribe that would close the ears of sympathetic whites. He moves quickly from topic to topic, from jabs at congressional Democrats and Lyndon Johnson to repeated incendiary suggestions of violent resistance. He peppers his speech with colorful epithets, "handkerchief-heads," "Uncle Tom," Polacks," "Hunkies," "this tricky, blue-eyed liberal [Lyndon Johnson]," "the enemy," and his favorite term "cracker," for example, "Old crackers," Northern crackers," "Southern crackers," "cracker Senators."

Regrettably there is no film record of Malcolm's speech in Cleveland and very little film footage of any of his speeches. The current generation's memory of Malcolm's delivery was etched by Denzel Washington's persuasive portrayal of the civil rights leader in the 1992 movie *X*. In a sense, Washington did not need to move too far from his oeuvre to develop the film character because Malcolm X, like Washington, was a consummate actor. He had an actor's bearing and a firebrand's charisma. His ramrod posture, textured baritone voice, and commanding gaze suggested the magnetic self-possession of one destined to lead. "As a man," remembered *New York Times* reporter M. S. Handler, "Malcolm X had the physical bearing and the inner self confidence of a born aristocrat."[14] The lean, handsome, and business-attired Malcolm X had a presence that filled a room. Malcolm X spoke extemporaneously, which both added authenticity to his message and contributed to the excitement of listening to a speaker who often said the unexpected and extreme. Another version of this speech, delivered in Detroit, makes the same points but with different phrasing.

The audio recordings of Malcolm X's speeches demonstrate how effectively he used delivery to complete the emotional evocations of his words: irony, humor, contempt, and anger, but also sincerity and commitment to cause, as well as empathy towards all victims of racism and oppression.[15] His voice became more forceful and his inflection more insistent as he drove home a repeated point. His statements and rhetorical questions usually involved anaphora, a repetition of word and phrase, which could be enhanced by increasing the volume and intensity of delivery. To give the audience an opportunity to respond verbally or with applause, he would stop speaking, and as some film footage reveals, dramatically rest his forefinger on his chin.[16] When he asked a rhetorical question meant to indict the opponents of civil rights, his oral phrasing gave the question a sharp edge. As with much African American oratory, influenced by a long history of spontaneous, vernacular preaching, Malcolm X's speeches invite a rhythmic increase in force and inflection, such as: "Let the world know how bloody his [Uncle Sam's] hands are. Let the world know the hypocrisy that's practiced over here. Let it be the ballot or the bullet. Let him know that it must be the ballot or the bullet."

Despite that his speech could be interpreted as a polarizing rhetoric of violent recrimination, Malcolm X talks of the importance of transcending the quest for civil rights with a quest for human rights. He speaks of the need to obtain allies in this cause, "Latin-Americans," Africans, Asians, and Chinese. Civil rights confines the quest to the United States, while human rights broadens the struggle so that, in an ideal world, the United Nations could adjudicate it. He also believes that the struggle of African Americans in the United States must be judged by the court of world public opinion: "Let the world know the hypocrisy that's practiced over here." In this speech, Malcolm pledges support for the political agenda of the civil rights movement, a departure from the inaction of Black Muslims in the Nation of Islam, from which he had recently separated. He offers his support in school desegregation, in rent strikes, in boycotts against segregated schools, and in voter registration drives.

Malcolm also appeals to black nationalism, urging Blacks to think of themselves as Africans rather than as "negroes." Whites have defined Africans in America as "negroes." Africans enjoy a status that "negroes" do not. He tells the poignant and paradoxical story of a very dark African American who wraps his head in a turban and enters a segregated restaurant in Atlanta. He is served, while the waitress later acknowledges that a "negro" would have been ejected. The themes of moral and economic uplift that Malcolm had developed while the NOI spokesman are expressed here as well—the admonition to blacks to free themselves of vices and "improve the moral fiber of our community," and the encouragement to African American ownership of businesses. Blacks, he argues, give their money to white businessmen, while they remain in ghettos: "Once you gain control of the economy of your own community, then you don't have to picket and boycott and beg some cracker downtown for a job in his business." Although he maintains that his newly formed Muslim Mosque, Inc., does not mix religion and politics, he suggests that black nationalism is the means by which to approach the civil rights movement. Drawing an invidious comparison between himself and

Billy Graham, he claims that Graham was preaching the gospel of "white nationalism," just as Malcolm was preaching the gospel of nationalism for his race. Black nationalism is, he argues, a superior alternative to the "compromising" and "pussy footing" of CORE or the National Association for the Advancement of Colored People (NAACP). Malcolm speaks of a planned black nationalist party convention and the creation, if necessary, of a black nationalist army, repeating his threat of armed action, couched in the language of Patrick Henry's apocryphal call to rebellion: "It'll be the ballot or the bullet. It'll be liberty or it'll be death."

Malcolm's threat of armed defense peppers the entire speech but is always matched with a more positive alternative—for example, with "the ballot," or "let the government do its job." He notes the constitutional right to bear arms but explains that he is not calling for armed battalions. He says ironically that compared with a multibillion-dollar defense budget, no one should begrudge African Americans "spending $12 or $15 for a single-shot, or double action [shotgun]" but then immediately adds the equivocation: "Don't go out shooting people, but . . . any time you and I sit around and read where they bomb a church and murder in cold blood, not some grownups, but four little girls while they are praying." The reference is to the bombing of the Sixteenth Street Baptist Church in Birmingham, Alabama, famously addressed by Martin Luther King in his eulogy of the four slain girls. Malcolm X's mention of armed response seems more realistic and biting here than in other references.

In some sections, the equivocal nature of the "bullet" is slyly ironic, oscillating between rhetorical hyperbole and an active intention. Malcolm capitalizes on the shock value of the "the ballot or the bullet" refrain to rally African American support while creating anxiety in the white community. The irony is more effective for its edge of earnestness; yet one is never sure to what extent the threat is real or pretended, expressive of frustration or contemplative of action. While on one hand, a threat to return violence with violence cannot be lightly taken, on the other, the hyperbole and even humor with which the threat is sometimes expressed makes it seem like verbal jousting. As a phrase, "the ballot or the bullet" appropriates the rhetorical contrast of "give me liberty or give me death," but not its conditional certainty or its melodramatic gravity. In part, this is because the threat is so frequently joined with a qualification. In part, it is because it is so often repeated, as if one utterance could not possibly be enough to convince the audience. The high-minded cause of racial justice also somehow contextually deprives the "bullet" of its violent intimations as does Malcolm's intelligence and religious commitment. Although Malcolm speaks relentlessly of the bullet, his commitments to join boycotts and voter registration drives seem more certain. Malcolm X's "bullet" is often more synecdochal than substantial, an expression of wrath and never an incitement to immediate violence, although the contemporary white community undoubtedly took the threat seriously.

The conclusion of the speech foreshadows Malcolm X's assassination only a few months later: "No if you never see me another time in your life, if I die in the morning, I'll die saying one thing: the ballot or the bullet, the ballot or the bullet." He says that a civil rights demonstration in 1964 would have an entirely different character than that of 1963, which featured the nonviolent Martin Luther King. It will be "non-nonviolent." Its participants are "not going with white friends" and they are not buying round trip tickets. To avoid the maelstrom, Lyndon Johnson must end the filibuster of the Civil Rights Act and "denounce the Southern branch of his party."

The editor of Malcolm X's speeches at Harvard University, Archie Epps, aptly states that "Malcolm X created, primarily with rhetoric, a radical view of the Negro experience in America."[17] Malcolm confronted white Americans with one of their worst forebodings, that African Americans could not be mollified indefinitely, and that their righteous rage might be vented on the nation. Although he claimed not to be an American, in a great American tradition Malcolm spoke truth to power and, like Martin Luther King, became a martyr to his cause. Feared and reviled by some, embraced and revered by others during his lifetime, historical reflection has legitimized his rhetoric and sanctified Malcolm X as a courageous voice in one of America's most turbulent eras.

The Ballot or the Bullet

April 3, 1964
Cleveland, Ohio

Mr. Moderator, Brother Lomax, brothers and sisters, friends and enemies: I just can't believe everyone in here is a friend and I don't want to leave anybody out. The question tonight, as I understand it, is "The Negro Revolt, and Where Do We Go from Here?" or "What Next?" In my little humble way of understanding it, it points toward either the ballot or the bullet.

Before we try and explain what is meant by the ballot or the bullet, I would like to clarify something concerning myself. I'm still a Muslim, my religion is still Islam. That's my personal belief. Just as Adam Clayton Powell is a Christian minister who heads the Abyssinian Baptist Church in New York, but at the same time takes part in the political struggles to try and bring about rights to the black people in this country; and Dr. Martin Luther King is a Christian minister down in Atlanta, Georgia, who heads another organization fighting for the civil rights of black people in this country; and Rev. Galamison, I guess you've heard of him, is another Christian minister in New York who has been deeply involved in the school boycotts to eliminate segregated education; well, I myself am a minister, not a Christian minister, but a Muslim minister; and I believe in action on all fronts by whatever means necessary.

Although I'm still a Muslim, I'm not here tonight to discuss my religion. I'm not here to try and change your religion. I'm not here to argue or discuss anything that we differ about, because it's time for us to submerge our differences and realize that it is best for us to first see that we have the same problem, a common problem—a problem that will make you catch hell whether you're a Baptist, or a Methodist, or a Muslim, or a nationalist.

Whether you're educated or illiterate, whether you live on the boulevard or in the alley, you're going to catch hell just like I am. We're all in the same boat and we all are going to catch the same hell from the same man. He just happens to be a white man. All of us have suffered here, in this country, political oppression at the hands of the white man, economic exploitation at the hands of the white man, and social degradation at the hands of the white man.

Now in speaking like this, it doesn't mean that we're anti-white, but it does mean we're anti-exploitation, we're anti-degradation, we're anti-oppression. And if the white man doesn't want us to be anti-him, let him stop oppressing and exploiting and degrading us. Whether we are Christians or Muslims or nationalists or agnostics or atheists, we must first learn to forget our differences. If we have differences, let us differ in the closet; when we come out in front, let us not have anything to argue about until we get finished arguing with the man. If the late President Kennedy could get together with Khrushchev and exchange some wheat, we certainly have more in common with each other than Kennedy and Khrushchev had with each other.

If we don't do something real soon, I think you'll have to agree that we're going to be forced either to use the ballot or the bullet. It's one or the other in 1964. It isn't that time is running out—time has run out! 1964 threatens to be the most explosive year America has ever witnessed. The most explosive year. Why? It's also a political year. It's the year when all of the white politicians will be back in the so-called Negro community jiving you and me for some votes. The year when all of the white political crooks will be right back in your and my community with their false promises, building up our hopes for a letdown, with their trickery and their treachery, with their false promises which they don't intend to keep. As they nourish these dissatisfactions, it can only lead to one thing, an explosion; and now we have the type of black man on the scene in America today—I'm sorry, Brother Lomax[a]—who just doesn't intend to turn the other cheek any longer.

Don't let anybody tell you anything about the odds are against you. If they draft you, they send you to Korea and make you face 800 million Chinese. If you can be brave over there, you can be brave right here. These odds aren't

a. Louis Lomax (1922–1970): Print and broadcast journalist, known as the first African American reporter on network television (CBS). Lomax was particularly influential in bringing Malcolm X to the attention of the American public, through television, documentary ("The Hate That Hate Produced," 1959, CBS), and print (*When the Word Is Given*, 1963).

as great as those odds. And if you fight here, you will at least know what you're fighting for.

I'm not a politician, not even a student of politics; in fact, I'm not a student of much of anything. I'm not a Democrat, I'm not a Republican, and I don't even consider myself an American. If you and I were Americans, there'd be no problem. Those Hunkies that just got off the boat, they're already Americans; Polacks are already Americans; the Italian refugees are already Americans. Everything that came out of Europe, every blue-eyed thing, is already an American. And as long as you and I have been over here, we aren't Americans yet.

Well, I am one who doesn't believe in deluding myself. I'm not going to sit at your table and watch you eat, with nothing on my plate, and call myself a diner. Sitting at the table doesn't make you a diner, unless you eat some of what's on that plate. Being here in America doesn't make you an American. Being born here in America doesn't make you an American. Why, if birth made you American, you wouldn't need any legislation, you wouldn't need any amendments to the Constitution, you wouldn't be faced with civil-rights filibustering in Washington, D.C., right now. They don't have to pass civil-rights legislation to make a Polack an American.

No, I'm not an American. I'm one of the 22 million black people who are the victims of Americanism. One of the 22 million black people who are the victims of democracy, nothing but disguised hypocrisy. So, I'm not standing here speaking to you as an American, or a patriot, or a flag-saluter, or a flag-waver—no, not I. I'm speaking as a victim of this American system. And I see America through the eyes of the victim. I don't see any American dream; I see an American nightmare.

These 22 million victims are waking up. Their eyes are coming open. They're beginning to see what they used to only look at. They're becoming politically mature. They are realizing that there are new political trends from coast to coast. As they see these new political trends, it's possible for them to see that every time there's an election the races are so close that they have to have a recount. They had to recount in Massachusetts to see who was going to be governor, it was so close. It was the same way in Rhode Island, in Minnesota, and in many other parts of the country. And the same with Kennedy and Nixon when they ran for president. It was so close they had to count all over again. Well, what does this mean? It means that when white people are evenly divided, and black people have a bloc of votes of their own, it is left up to them to determine who's going to sit in the White House and who's going to be in the dog house.

It was the black man's vote that put the present administration in Washington, D.C. Your vote, your dumb vote, your ignorant vote, your wasted vote put in an administration in Washington, D.C., that has seen fit to pass every kind of legislation imaginable, saving you until last, then filibustering on top of that. And your and my leaders have the audacity to run around clapping their hands and talk about how much progress we're making. And what a good president we have. If he wasn't good in Texas, he sure can't be good in Washington, D.C. Because Texas is a lynch state. It is in the same breath as Mississippi, no different; only they lynch you in Texas with a Texas accent and lynch you in Mississippi with a Mississippi accent. And these Negro leaders have the audacity to go and have some coffee in the White House with a Texan, a Southern cracker—that's all he is—and then come out and tell you and me that he's going to be better for us because, since he's from the South, he knows how to deal with the Southerners. What kind of logic is that? Let Eastland be president, he's from the South too. He should be better able to deal with them than Johnson.

In this present administration they have in the House of Representatives 257 Democrats to only 177 Republicans. They control two-thirds of the House vote. Why can't they pass something that will help you and me? In the Senate, there are 67 senators who are of the Democratic Party. Only 33 of them are Republicans. Why, the Democrats have got the government sewed up, and you're the one who sewed it up for them. And what have they given you for it? Four years in office, and just now getting around to some civil-rights legislation. Just now, after everything else is gone, out of the way, they're going to sit down now and play with you all summer long—the same old giant con game that they call filibuster. All those are in cahoots together. Don't you ever think they're not in cahoots together, for the man that is heading the civil-rights filibuster is a man from Georgia named Richard Russell. When Johnson became president, the first man he asked for when he got back to Washington, D.C., was "Dicky"—that's how tight they are. That's his boy, that's his pal, that's his buddy. But they're playing that old con game. One of them makes believe he's for you, and he's got it fixed where the other one is so tight against you, he never has to keep his promise.

So it's time in 1964 to wake up. And when you see them coming up with that kind of conspiracy, let them know your eyes are open. And let them know you got something else that's wide open too. It's got to be the ballot or the bullet. The ballot or the bullet. If you're afraid to use an expression like that, you should get on out of the country, you should get back in the cotton patch, you should get back in the alley. They get all the Negro vote, and after they get it, the Negro gets nothing in return. All they did when they got to Washington was give a few big Negroes big jobs. Those big Negroes didn't need big jobs, they already had jobs. That's camouflage, that's trickery, that's treachery, window-dressing. I'm not trying to knock out the Democrats for the Republicans, we'll get to them in a minute. But it is true—you put the Democrats first and the Democrats put you last.

Look at it the way it is. What alibis do they use, since they control Congress and the Senate? What alibi do they use when you and I ask, "Well, when are you going to keep your promise?" They blame the Dixiecrats. What is a Dixiecrat? A Democrat. A Dixiecrat is nothing but a Democrat in disguise. The titular head of the Democrats is also the head of the Dixiecrats, because the Dixiecrats are a part of the Democratic Party. The Democrats have never kicked the Dixiecrats out of the party. The Dixiecrats bolted themselves once, but the Democrats didn't put them out.[b] Imagine, these lowdown Southern segregationists put the Northern Democrats down. But the Northern Democrats have never put the Dixiecrats down. No, look at that thing the way it is. They have got a con game going on, a political con game, and you and I are in the middle. It's time for you and me to wake up and start looking at it like it is, and trying to understand it like it is; and then we can deal with it like it is.

The Dixiecrats in Washington, D.C., control the key committees that run the government. The only reason the Dixiecrats control these committees is because they have seniority. The only reason they have seniority is because they come from states where Negroes can't vote. This is not even a government that's based on democracy. It is not a government that is made up of representatives of the people. Half of the people in the South can't even vote. Eastland is not even supposed to be in Washington. Half of the senators and congressmen who occupy these key positions in Washington, D.C., are there illegally, are there unconstitutionally.

I was in Washington, D.C., a week ago Thursday, when they were debating whether or not they should let the bill come onto the floor. And in the back

b. In 1948, upset with President Truman's executive order to desegregate the army, a splinter group of Southern Democrats formed the States Rights Democratic Party and ran Strom Thurmond for president as a third party. The nickname "Dixiecrats" was coined during this election and continued to be used in the 1950s and 1960s to refer to the prosegregationist Democrats from the South.

of the room where the Senate meets, there's a huge map of the United States, and on that map it shows the location of Negroes throughout the country. And it shows that the Southern section of the country, the states that are most heavily concentrated with Negroes, are the ones that have senators and congressmen standing up filibustering and doing all other kinds of trickery to keep the Negro from being able to vote. This is pitiful. But it's not pitiful for us any longer; it's actually pitiful for the white man, because soon now, as the Negro awakens a little more and sees the vise that he's in, sees the bag that he's in, sees the real game that he's in, then the Negro's going to develop a new tactic.

These senators and congressmen actually violate the constitutional amendments that guarantee the people of that particular state or county the right to vote. And the Constitution itself has within it the machinery to expel any representative from a state where the voting rights of the people are violated. You don't even need new legislation. Any person in Congress right now, who is there from a state or a district where the voting rights of the people are violated, that particular person should be expelled from Congress. And when you expel him, you've removed one of the obstacles in the path of any real meaningful legislation in this country. In fact, when you expel them, you don't need new legislation, because they will be replaced by black representatives from counties and districts where the black man is in the majority, not in the minority.

If the black man in these Southern states had his full voting rights, the key Dixiecrats in Washington, D.C., which means the key Democrats in Washington, D.C., would lose their seats. The Democratic Party itself would lose its power. It would cease to be powerful as a party. When you see the amount of power that would be lost by the Democratic Party if it were to lose the Dixiecrat wing, or branch, or element, you can see where it's against the interests of the Democrats to give voting rights to Negroes in states where the Democrats have been in complete power and authority ever since the Civil War. You just can't belong to that Party without analyzing it.

I say again, I'm not anti-Democrat, I'm not anti-Republican, I'm not anti-anything. I'm just questioning their sincerity, and some of the strategy that they've been using on our people by promising them promises that they don't intend to keep. When you keep the Democrats in power, you're keeping the Dixiecrats in power. I doubt that my good Brother Lomax will deny that. A vote for a Democrat is a vote for a Dixiecrat. That's why, in 1964, it's time now for you and me to become more politically mature and realize what the ballot is for; what we're supposed to get when we cast a ballot; and that if we don't cast a ballot, it's going to end up in a situation where we're going to have to cast a bullet. It's either a ballot or a bullet.

In the North, they do it a different way. They have a system that's known as gerrymandering, whatever that means. It means when Negroes become too heavily concentrated in a certain area, and begin to gain too much political power, the white man comes along and changes the district lines. You may say, "Why do you keep saying white man?" Because it's the white man who does it. I haven't ever seen any Negro changing any lines. They don't let him get near the line. It's the white man who does this. And usually, it's the white man who grins at you the most, and pats you on the back, and is supposed to be your friend. He may be friendly, but he's not your friend.

So, what I'm trying to impress upon you, in essence, is this: You and I in America are faced not with a segregationist conspiracy, we're faced with a government conspiracy. Everyone who's filibustering is a senator—that's the government. Everyone who's finagling in Washington, D.C., is a congressman—that's the government. You don't have anybody putting blocks in your path but people who are a part of the government. The same government that you go abroad to fight for and die for is the government that is in a conspiracy to deprive you of your voting rights, deprive you of your economic opportunities, deprive you of decent housing, deprive you of decent education. You don't need to go to the employer alone, it is the government itself, the government of America, that is responsible for the oppression and exploitation and degradation of black people in this country. And you should drop it in their lap. This government has failed the Negro. This so-called democracy has failed the Negro. And all these white liberals have definitely failed the Negro.

So, where do we go from here? First, we need some friends. We need some new allies. The entire civil-rights struggle needs a new interpretation, a broader interpretation. We need to look at this civil-rights thing from another angle—from the inside as well as from the outside. To those of us whose philosophy is black nationalism, the only way you can get involved in the civil-rights struggle is give it a new interpretation. The old interpretation excluded us. It kept us out. So, we're giving a new interpretation to the civil-rights struggle, an interpretation that will enable us to come into it, take part in it. And these handkerchief-heads who have been dillydallying and pussy footing and compromising—we don't intend to let them pussyfoot and dillydally and compromise any longer.

How can you thank a man for giving you what's already yours? How then can you thank him for giving you only part of what's already yours? You haven't even made progress, if what's being given to you, you should have had already. That's not progress. And I love my Brother Lomax, the way he pointed out we're right back where we were in 1954. We're not even as far up as we were in 1954. We're behind where we were in 1954. There's more segregation now than there was in 1954. There's more racial animosity, more racial hatred, more racial violence today in 1964, than there was in 1954. Where is the progress?

And now you're facing a situation where the young Negro's coming up. They don't want to hear that "turn the-other-cheek" stuff, no. In Jacksonville, those were teenagers, they were throwing Molotov cocktails. Negroes have never done that before. But it shows you there's a new deal coming in. There's new thinking coming in. There's new strategy coming in. It'll be Molotov cocktails this month, hand grenades next month, and something else next month. It'll be ballots, or it'll be bullets. It'll be liberty, or it will be death. The only difference about this kind of death—it'll be reciprocal. You know what is meant by "reciprocal"? That's one of Brother Lomax's words, I stole it from him. I don't usually deal with those big words because I don't usually deal with big people. I deal with small people. I find you can get a whole lot of small people and whip hell out of a whole lot of big people. They haven't got anything to lose, and they've got everything to gain. And they'll let you know in a minute: "It takes two to tango; when I go, you go."

The black nationalists, those whose philosophy is black nationalism, in bringing about this new interpretation of the entire meaning of civil rights, look upon it as meaning, as Brother Lomax has pointed out, equality of opportunity. Well, we're justified in seeking civil rights, if it means equality of opportunity, because all we're doing there is trying to collect for our investment. Our mothers and fathers invested sweat and blood. Three hundred and ten years we worked in this country without a dime in return—I mean without a *dime* in return. You let the white man walk around here talking about how rich this country is, but you never stop to think how it got rich so quick. It got rich because you made it rich.

You take the people who are in this audience right now. They're poor, we're all poor as individuals. Our weekly salary individually amounts to hardly anything. But if you take the salary of everyone in here collectively it'll fill up a whole lot of baskets. It's a lot of wealth. If you can collect the wages of just these people right here for a year, you'll be rich—richer than rich.

When you look at it like that, think how rich Uncle Sam had to become, not with this handful, but millions of black people. Your and my mother and father, who didn't work an eight-hour shift, but worked from "can't see" in the morning until "can't see" at night, and worked for nothing, making the white man rich, making Uncle Sam rich.

This is our investment. This is our contribution—our blood. Not only did we give of our free labor, we gave of our blood. Every time he had a call to arms, we were the first ones in uniform. We died on every battlefield the white man had. We have made a greater sacrifice than anybody who's standing up in America today. We have made a greater contribution and have collected less. Civil rights for those of us whose philosophy is black nationalism, means: "Give it to us now. Don't wait for next year. Give it to us yesterday, and that's not fast enough."

I might stop right here to point out one thing. Whenever you're going after something that belongs to you, anyone who's depriving you of the right to have it is a "criminal." Understand that. Whenever you are going after something that is yours, you are within your legal rights to lay claim to it. And anyone who puts forth any effort to deprive you of that which is yours, is breaking the law, is a criminal. And this was pointed out by the Supreme Court decision. It outlawed segregation. Which means segregation is against the law. Which means a segregationist is breaking the law. A segregationist is a criminal. You can't label him as anything other than that. And when you demonstrate against segregation, the law is on your side. The Supreme Court is on your side.

Now, who is it that opposes you in carrying out the law? The police department itself. With police dogs and clubs. Whenever you demonstrate against segregation, whether it is segregated education, segregated housing, or anything else, the law is on your side, and anyone who stands in the way is not the law any longer. They are breaking the law, they are not representatives of the law. Any time you demonstrate against segregation and a man has the audacity to put a police dog on you, kill that dog, kill him, I'm telling you, kill that dog. I say it, if they put me in jail tomorrow, kill-that-dog. Then you'll put a stop to it. Now, if these white people in here don't want to see that kind of action, get down and tell the mayor to tell the police department to pull the dogs in. That's all you have to do. If you don't do it, someone else will.

If you don't take this kind of stand, your little children will grow up and look at you and think "shame." If you don't take an uncompromising stand—I don't mean go out and get violent; but at the same time you should never be nonviolent unless you run into some nonviolence. I'm nonviolent with those who are nonviolent with me. But when you drop that violence on me, then you've made me go insane, and I'm not responsible for what I do. And that's the way every Negro should get. Any time you know you're within the law, within your legal rights, within your moral rights, in accord with justice, then die for what you believe in. But don't die alone. Let your dying be reciprocal. This is what is meant by equality. What's good for the goose is good for the gander.

When we begin to get in this area, we need new friends, we need new allies. We need to expand the civil-rights struggle to a higher level—to the level of human rights. Whenever you are in a civil-rights struggle, whether you know it or not, you are confining yourself to the jurisdiction of Uncle Sam. No one from the outside world can speak out in your behalf as long as your struggle is a civil-rights struggle. Civil rights comes within the domestic affairs of this country. All of our African brothers and our Asian brothers and our Latin-American brothers cannot open their mouths and interfere in the domestic affairs of the United States. And as long as it's civil rights, this comes under the jurisdiction of Uncle Sam.

But the United Nations has what's known as the charter of human rights, it has a committee that deals in human rights. You may wonder why all of the atrocities that have been committed in Africa and in Hungary and in Asia and in Latin America are brought before the UN, and the Negro problem is never brought before the UN. This is part of the conspiracy. This old, tricky, blue-eyed liberal who is supposed to be your and my friend, supposed to be in our corner, supposed to be subsidizing our struggle, and supposed to be acting in the capacity of an adviser, never tells you anything about human rights. They keep you wrapped up in civil rights. And you spend so much time barking up the civil-rights tree, you don't even know there's a human-rights tree on the same floor.

When you expand the civil-rights struggle to the level of human rights, you can then take the case of the black man in this country before the nations in the UN. You can take it before the General Assembly. You can take Uncle Sam before a world court. But the only level you can do it on is the level of human rights. Civil rights keeps you under his restrictions, under his jurisdiction. Civil rights keeps you in his pocket. Civil rights means you're asking Uncle Sam to treat you right. Human rights are something you were born with. Human rights are your God given rights. Human rights are the rights that are recognized by all nations of this earth. And any time any one violates your human rights, you can take them to the world court. Uncle Sam's hands are dripping with blood, dripping with the blood of the black man in this country. He's the earth's number-one hypocrite. He has the audacity—yes, he has—imagine him posing as the leader of the free world. The free world! And you over here singing "We Shall Overcome." Expand the civil-rights struggle to the level of human rights, take it into the United Nations, where our African brothers can throw their weight on our side, where our Asian brothers can throw their weight on our side, where our Latin-American brothers can throw their weight on our side, and where 800 million Chinamen are sitting there waiting to throw their weight on our side.

Let the world know how bloody his hands are. Let the world know the hypocrisy that's practiced over here. Let it be the ballot or the bullet. Let him know that it must be the ballot or the bullet.

When you take your case to Washington, D.C., you're taking it to the criminal who's responsible; it's like running from the wolf to the fox. They're all in cahoots together. They all work political chicanery and make you look like a chump before the eyes of the world. Here you are walking around in America, getting ready to be drafted and sent abroad, like a tin soldier, and when you get over there, people ask you what are you fighting for, and you have to stick your tongue in your cheek. No, take Uncle Sam to court, take him before the world.

By ballot I only mean freedom. Don't you know—I disagree with Lomax on this issue—that the ballot is more important than the dollar? Can I prove it? Yes. Look in the UN. There are poor nations in the UN; yet those poor nations can get together with their voting power and keep the rich nations from making a move. They have one nation—one vote, everyone has an equal vote. And when those brothers from Asia, and Africa and the darker parts of this earth get together, their voting power is sufficient to hold Sam in check. Or Russia in check. Or some other section of the earth in check. So, the ballot is most important.

Right now, in this country, if you and I, 22 million African-Americans—that's what we are—Africans who are in America. You're nothing but Africans. Nothing but Africans. In fact, you'd get farther calling yourself African instead of Negro. Africans don't catch hell. You're the only one catching hell. They don't have to pass civil-rights bills for Africans. An African can go anywhere he wants right now. All you've got to do is tie your head up. That's right, go anywhere you want. Just stop being a Negro. Change your name to Hoogagagooba. That'll show you how silly the white man is. You're dealing with a silly man. A friend of mine who's very dark put a turban on his head and went into a restaurant in Atlanta before they called themselves desegregated. He went into a white restaurant, he sat down, they served him, and he said, "What would happen if a Negro came in here? And there he's sitting, black as night, but because he had his head wrapped up the waitress looked back at him and says, "Why, there wouldn't no nigger dare come in here."

So, you're dealing with a man whose bias and prejudice are making him lose his mind, his intelligence, every day. He's frightened. He looks around and sees what's taking place on this earth, and he sees that the pendulum of time is swinging in your direction. The dark people are waking up. They're losing their fear of the white man. No place where he's fighting right now is he winning. Everywhere he's fighting, he's fighting someone your and my complexion. And they're beating him. He can't win any more. He's won his last battle. He failed to win the Korean War. He couldn't win it. He had to sign a truce. That's a loss. Any time Uncle Sam, with all his machinery for warfare, is held to a draw by some rice eaters, he's lost the battle. He had to sign a truce. America's not supposed to sign a truce. She's supposed to be bad. But she's not bad any more. She's bad as long as she can use her hydrogen bomb, but she can't use hers for fear Russia might use hers. Russia can't use hers, for fear that Sam might use his. So, both of them are weaponless. They can't use the weapon because each's weapon nullifies the other's. So the only place where action can take place is on the ground. And the white man can't win another war fighting on the ground. Those days are over. The black man knows it, the brown man knows it, the red man knows it, and the yellow man knows it. So they engage him in guerrilla warfare. That's not his style. You've got to have heart to be a guerrilla warrior, and he hasn't got any heart. I'm telling you now.

I just want to give you a little briefing on guerrilla warfare because, before you know it, before you know it—It takes heart to be a guerrilla warrior because you're on your own. In conventional warfare you have tanks and a whole lot of other people with you to back you up, planes over your head and all that kind of stuff. But a guerrilla is on his own. All you have is a rifle, some sneakers and a bowl of rice, and that's all you need—and a lot of heart. The Japanese on some of those islands in the Pacific, when the American soldiers landed, one Japanese sometimes could hold the whole army off. He'd just wait until the sun went down, and when the sun went down they were all equal. He would take his little blade and slip from bush to bush, and from American to American. The white soldiers couldn't cope with that. Whenever you see a white soldier that fought in the Pacific, he has the shakes, he has a nervous condition, because they scared him to death.

The same thing happened to the French up in French Indochina. People who just a few years previously were rice farmers got together and ran the heavily-mechanized French army out of Indochina. You don't need it—modern warfare today won't work. This is the day of the guerrilla. They did the same thing in Algeria. Algerians, who were nothing but Bedouins, took a rifle and sneaked off to the hills, and de Gaulle and all of his highfalutin' war machinery couldn't defeat those guerrillas. Nowhere on this earth does the white man win in a guerrilla warfare. It's not his speed. Just as guerrilla warfare is prevailing in Asia and in parts of Africa and in parts of Latin America, you've got to be mighty naive, or you've got to play the black man cheap, if you don't think some day he's going to wake up and find that it's got to be the ballot or the bullet.

I would like to say, in closing, a few things concerning the Muslim Mosque, Inc., which we established recently in New York City. It's true we're Muslims and our religion is Islam, but we don't mix our religion with our politics and our economics and our social and civil activities—not any more. We keep our religion in our mosque. After our religious services are over, then as Muslims we become involved in political action, economic action and social and civic action. We become involved with anybody, anywhere, any time and in any manner that's designed to eliminate the evils, the political, economic and social evils that are afflicting the people of our community.

The political philosophy of black nationalism means that the black man should control the politics and the politicians in his own community; no more. The black man in the black community has to be re-educated into the science of politics so he will know what politics is supposed to bring him in return. Don't be throwing out any ballots. A ballot is like a bullet. You don't throw your ballots until you see a target, and if that target is not within your reach, keep your ballot in your pocket. The political philosophy of black nationalism is being taught in the Christian church. It's being taught in the NAACP.[c] It's being taught in CORE[d] meetings. It's being taught in SNCC[e] meetings. It's being taught in Muslim meetings. It's being taught

c. National Association for the Advancement of Colored People.
d. Congress of Racial Equality.
e. Student Nonviolent Coordinating Committee.

where nothing but atheists and agnostics come together. It's being taught everywhere. Black people are fed up with the dillydallying, pussyfooting, compromising approach that we've been using toward getting our freedom. We want freedom *now*, but we're not going to get it saying "We Shall Overcome." We've got to fight until we overcome.

The economic philosophy of black nationalism is pure and simple. It only means that we should control the economy of our community. Why should white people be running all the stores in our community? Why should white people be running the banks of our community? Why should the economy of our community be in the hands of the white man? Why? If a black man can't move his store into a white community, you tell me why a white man should move his store into a black community. The philosophy of black nationalism involves a re-education program in the black community in regards to economics. Our people have to be made to see that any time you take your dollar out of your community and spend it in a community where you don't live, the community where you live will get poorer and poorer, and the community where you spend your money will get richer and richer. Then you wonder why where you live is always a ghetto or a slum area. And where you and I are concerned, not only do we lose it when we spend it out of the community, but the white man has got all our stores in the community tied up; so that though we spend it in the community, at sundown the man who runs the store takes it over across town somewhere. He's got us in a vise.

So the economic philosophy of black nationalism means in every church, in every civic organization, in every fraternal order, it's time now for our people to become conscious of the importance of controlling the economy of our community. If we own the stores, if we operate the businesses, if we try and establish some industry in our own community, then we're developing to the position where we are creating employment for our own kind. Once you gain control of the economy of your own community, then you don't have to picket and boycott and beg some cracker downtown for a job in his business.

The social philosophy of black nationalism only means that we have to get together and remove the evils, the vices, alcoholism, drug addiction, and other evils that are destroying the moral fiber of our community. We ourselves have to lift the level of our community, the standard of our community to a higher level, make our own society beautiful so that we will be satisfied in our own social circles and won't be running around here trying to knock our way into a social circle where we're not wanted.

So I say, in spreading a gospel such as black nationalism, it is not designed to make the black man re-evaluate the white man—you know him already—but to make the black man re-evaluate himself. Don't change the white man's mind—you can't change his mind, and that whole thing about appealing to the moral conscience of America—America's conscience is bankrupt. She lost all conscience a long time ago. Uncle Sam has no conscience. They don't know what morals are. They don't try and eliminate an evil because it's evil, or because it's illegal, or because it's immoral; they eliminate it only when it threatens their existence. So you're wasting your time appealing to the moral conscience of a bankrupt man like Uncle Sam. If he had a conscience, he'd straighten this thing out with no more pressure being put upon him. So it is not necessary to change the white man's mind. We have to change our own mind. You can't change his mind about us. We've got to change our own minds about each other. We have to see each other with new eyes. We have to see each other as brothers and sisters. We have to come together with warmth so we can develop unity and harmony that's necessary to get this problem solved our selves. How can we do this? How can we avoid jealousy? How can we avoid the suspicion and the divisions that exist in the community? I'll tell you how.

I have watched how Billy Graham comes into a city, spreading what he calls the gospel of Christ, which is only white nationalism. That's what he is. Billy Graham is a white nationalist; I'm a black nationalist. But since it's the natural tendency for leaders to be jealous and look upon a powerful figure like Graham with suspicion and envy, how is it possible for him to come into a city and get all the cooperation of the church leaders? Don't think because they're church leaders that they don't have weaknesses that make them envious and jealous—no, everybody's got it. It's not an accident that when they want to choose a cardinal [as Pope] over there in Rome, they get in a closet so you can't hear them cussing and fighting and carrying on.

Billy Graham comes in preaching the gospel of Christ, he evangelizes the gospel, he stirs everybody up, but he never tries to start a church. If he came in trying to start a church, all the churches would be against him. So, he just comes in talking about Christ and tells everybody who gets Christ to go to any church where Christ is; and in this way the church cooperates with him. So we're going to take a page from his book.

Our gospel is black nationalism. We're not trying to threaten the existence of any organization, but we're spreading the gospel of black nationalism. Anywhere there's a church that is also preaching and practicing the gospel of black nationalism, join that church. If the NAACP is preaching and practicing the gospel of black nationalism, join the NAACP. If CORE is spreading and practicing the gospel of black nationalism, join CORE. Join any organization that has a gospel that's for the uplift of the black man. And when you get into it and see them pussyfooting or compromising, pull out of it because that's not black nationalism. We'll find another one.

And in this manner, the organizations will increase in number and in quantity and in quality, and by August, it is then our intention to have a black nationalist convention which will consist of delegates from all over the country who are interested in the political, economic and social philosophy of black nationalism. After these delegates convene, we will hold a seminar, we will hold discussions, we will listen to everyone. We want to hear new ideas and new solutions and new answers. And at that time, if we see fit then to form a black nationalist party, we'll form a black nationalist party. If it's necessary to form a black nationalist army, we'll form a black nationalist army. It'll be the ballot or the bullet. It'll be liberty or it'll be death.

It's time for you and me to stop sitting in this country, letting some cracker senators, Northern crackers and Southern crackers, sit there in Washington, D.C., and come to a conclusion in their mind that you and I are supposed to have civil rights. There's no white man going to tell me anything about *my* rights. Brothers and sisters, always remember, if it doesn't take senators and congressmen and presidential proclamations to give freedom to the white man, it is not necessary for legislation or proclamation or Supreme Court decisions to give freedom to the black man. You let that white man know, if this is a country of freedom, let it be a country of freedom; and if it's not a country of freedom, change it.

We will work with anybody, anywhere, at any time, who is genuinely interested in tackling the problem head-on, nonviolently as long as the enemy is nonviolent, but violent when the enemy gets violent. We'll work with you on the voter-registration drive, we'll work with you on rent strikes, we'll work with you on school boycotts—I don't believe in any kind of integration; I'm not even worried about it because I know you're not going to get it anyway; you're not going to get it because you're afraid to die; you've got to be ready to die if you try and force yourself on the white man, because he'll get just as violent as those crackers in Mississippi, right here in Cleveland. But we will still work with you on the school boycotts because we're against a segregated school system. A segregated school system produces children who, when they graduate, graduate with crippled minds. But this does not mean that a school is segregated because it's all black. A segregated school means a school that is controlled by people who have no real interest in it whatsoever.

Let me explain what I mean. A segregated district or community is a community in which people live, but outsiders control the politics and the economy of that community. They never refer to the white section as a segregated community. It's the all-Negro section that's a segregated community. Why? The white man controls his own school, his own bank, his own economy, his own politics, his own everything, his own community—but he also controls yours. When you're under someone else's control, you're segregated. They'll always give you the lowest or the worst that there is to offer, but it doesn't mean you're segregated just because you have your own. You've got to *control* your own. Just like the white man has control of his, you need to control yours.

You know the best way to get rid of segregation? The white man is more afraid of separation than he is of integration. Segregation means that he puts you away from him, but not far enough for you to be out of his jurisdiction; separation means you're gone. And the white man will integrate faster than he'll let you separate. So we will work with you against the segregated school system because it's criminal, because it is absolutely destructive, in every way imaginable, to the minds of the children who have to be exposed to that type of crippling education.

Last but not least, I must say this concerning the great controversy over rifles and shotguns. The only thing that I've ever said is that in areas where the government has proven itself either unwilling or unable to defend the lives and the property of Negroes, it's time for Negroes to defend themselves. Article number two of the constitutional amendments provides you and me the right to own a rifle or a shotgun. It is constitutionally legal to own a shotgun or a rifle. This doesn't mean you're going to get a rifle and form battalions and go out looking for white folks, although you'd be within your rights—I mean, you'd be justified; but that would be illegal and we don't do anything illegal. If the white man doesn't want the black man buying rifles and shotguns, then let the government do its job. That's all. And don't let the white man come to you and ask you what you think about what Malcolm says—why, you old Uncle Tom. He would never ask you if he thought you were going to say, "Amen!" No, he is making a Tom out of you.

So, this doesn't mean forming rifle clubs and going out looking for people, but it is time, in 1964, if you are a man, to let that man know. If he's not going to do his job in running the government and providing you and me with the protection that our taxes are supposed to be for, since he spends all those billions for his defense budget, he certainly can't begrudge you and me spending $12 or $15 for a single-shot, or double-action. I hope you understand. Don't go out shooting people, but any time, brothers and sisters, and especially the men in this audience—some of you wearing Congressional Medals of Honor, with shoulders this wide, chests this big, muscles that big—any time you and I sit around and read where they bomb a church and murder in cold blood, not some grownups, but four little girls while they were praying to the same God the white man taught them to pray to, and you and I see the government go down and can't find who did it.

Why, this man—he can find Eichmann hiding down in Argentina somewhere. Let two or three American soldiers, who are minding somebody else's business way over in South Vietnam, get killed, and he'll send battleships, sticking his nose in their business. He wanted to send troops down to Cuba and make them have what he calls free elections—this old cracker who doesn't have free elections in his own country. No, if you never see me another time in your life, if I die in the morning, I'll die saying one thing: the ballot or the bullet, the ballot or the bullet.

If a Negro in 1964 has to sit around and wait for some cracker senator to filibuster when it comes to the rights of black people, why, you and I should hang our heads in shame. You talk about a march on Washington in 1963, you haven't seen anything. There's some more going down in '64. And this time they're not going like they went last year. They're not going singing "We Shall Overcome." They're not going with white friends. They're not going with placards already painted for them. They're not going with round-trip tickets. They're going with one way tickets.

And if they don't want that non-nonviolent army going down there, tell them to bring the filibuster to a halt. The black nationalists aren't going to wait. Lyndon B. Johnson is the head of the Democratic Party. If he's for civil rights, let him go into the Senate next week and declare himself. Let him go in there right now and declare himself. Let him go in there and denounce the Southern branch of his party. Let him go in there right now and take a moral stand—right now, not later. Tell him, don't wait until election time. If he waits too long, brothers and sisters, he will be responsible for letting a condition develop in this country which will create a climate that will bring seeds up out of the ground with vegetation on the end of them looking like something these people never dreamed of. In 1964, it's the ballot or the bullet. Thank you.

Stokely Carmichael (Kwame Ture)

Black Power

Stokely Carmichael was among the most versatile speakers of the American civil rights movement. In his autobiography, he notes that he developed different styles of speaking "depending on audience and situation . . . standard-English speech reserved for the merely affluent and curious . . . more analytic, and ideological arguments for more serious political and intellectual forums, and . . . a down-home nitty-gritty idiom in a style I mostly borrowed from the Harlem street-corner nationalists and southern black preachers" reserved for "brothers and sisters on the block."[1] He organized uneducated and disenfranchised African Americans in Mississippi and published articles in the *New York Review of Books* and *Massachusetts Review*.[2] Still in the gristle during the height of the civil rights movement, Carmichael was only twenty-five when he delivered his address "Black Power" in Berkeley on October 29, 1966. Carmichael, just elected head of the Student Nonviolent Coordinating Committee (SNCC), had first used the term "Black Power" in a speech to six hundred people that June in Greenwood, Mississippi. He had drawn applause, voluble "amens," and foot stomping when he reflected on his twenty-seventh arrest that day: "I ain't going to jail no more . . . We been saying 'Freedom' for six years and we ain't got nothin.' What we gonna start saying now is Black Power!" The term percolated to the surface of the speech but had been brewing for several days in response to the slogan of the Southern Christian Leadership Conference's (SCLC), "Freedom Now." "That don't scare White folks," Carmichael later told journalist and fellow activist, Charlie Cobb, "The only thing that's gonna get us freedom is power."[3]

Carmichael had gone to Mississippi in 1964 as the SNCC project director for the Mississippi Delta. He had spent summers there throughout his college years at Howard University in Washington, DC, beginning in 1961. His goal was to register voters, but also to create a sense of confidence among African Americans, who made up two-thirds of the region's population.[4] Carmichael's activities in Mississippi as well as the speeches he gave across the country were closely followed by the national press. The "Black Power" comment that had ignited his audience in June quickly drew fire from both Martin Luther King and the head of the NAACP, Roy Wilkins. "Black supremacy," King warned, "would be equally as evil as white supremacy."[5] The *Saturday Evening Post* thought Carmichael's militant pronouncement in Greenwood important enough to declare ruefully: "We are all Mississippians."[6]

The idea of Black Power had not originated with Carmichael, nor was he its sole proponent, but Carmichael's speeches amplified the message so that no corner of American society failed to hear it.[7] Black Power was the counterpoise to nonviolent activism preached by Martin Luther King Jr., the SCLC, the NAACP, the Urban League, and other mainstream civil rights organizations.[8] It divided the civil rights movement, worrying King that it would precipitate tensions in urban areas with heavy concentration of African Americans.[9]

Carmichael was born on June 29, 1941, to Trinidadian parents in Port of Spain. His parents, neither of whom were high school graduates, immigrated to the United States a few years later, and Carmichael and other family members joined them in 1952. In New York City, Stokely's father, who dreamed of a better life for his family in America, worked as a carpenter by day and a taxi driver at night. He died in his forties, the victim, Stokely believed, of overwork. An honorable, hardworking, religious man, Stokely's father believed in education and had an ample collection of books.[10] Although in words Stokely rejected his father's embrace of "work and overcome," in actions he clearly profited from the model of hard work his father provided. He competed for a coveted seat in the Bronx High School of Science, where he distinguished himself. While in New York City, Carmichael kept the company of white leftists, became active in the Congress of Racial Equality (CORE), and participated in sit-ins in the South. Perhaps most importantly, he volunteered in the office of Bayard Rustin, an African American proponent of socialism, whom Carmichael did not meet until entering Howard University, but in whose footsteps he said he wanted to follow.[11] At Howard, which Cobb describes as a "vast bourgeois sea," Carmichael found "a tiny activist island."[12] He joined an organization called the Nonviolent Action Group (NAG) and participated in the summer of 1961 Freedom Ride, during which he entered a waiting room intended for whites only and was incarcerated for forty-nine days in Parchman Prison in Mississippi, where he suffered repeated beatings.[13]

Subsequently a member and then chairman of SNCC, in the early and mid-1960s, Carmichael was a much sought-after speaker at colleges throughout the nation. He ultimately severed his association with SNCC and in 1968, became the "Prime Minister of the Black Nation," in what Taylor Branch describes as a "fantasy merger between the remnants of SNCC and the Black Panther Party.[14] Carmichael's involvement with the Black Panther Party was brief, lasting about a year, but the party caught the attention of FBI director J. Edgar Hoover, who viewed the organization as "now the greatest threat to the internal security of country," and which COINTELPRO, a covert FBI operation, sought to destroy. After the death of Malcolm X, whom Hoover feared could become "a 'messiah' who would unify and electrify the militant black nationalist movement," Hoover saw the possibility that Malcolm X's mantle would fall upon either Martin Luther King Jr. or Stokely Carmichael.[15] Carmichael ultimately left the United States to live in Guinea with his wife, singer Miriam Makeba. Changing his name to Kwame Ture to honor two influential African mentors, he remained a popular speaker on behalf of the All African People's Revolutionary Party. He died of prostate cancer in 1988.[16]

Carmichael was invited to speak at Berkeley as part of a conference on Black Power that the Students for a Democratic Society (SDS) had organized. Among the purposes of the conference was raising money for SNCC, whose chairmanship Carmichael had assumed in May 1966.[17] The audience was a throng of ten thousand spectators, mostly whites, gathered in the Greek Theatre, a massive, raked outdoor amphitheatre with a broad stage in front of a classically columned facade. The number of people attending exceeded the eighty-five hundred seats in the theater, which on other occasions was used for music festivals and rock concerts.

Carmichael's speech was preceded by political wrangling among student organizations, apprehension by the university administration, and posturing by incumbent governor Pat Brown and his rival Ronald Reagan. The SDS had not invited the Afro-American Student Union (AASU) to attend, and the AASU, therefore, both boycotted the event and asked that Carmichael not speak at the conference. Carmichael met with leaders of the AASU on the morning before the speech and agreed not to speak of Black Power to a white audience.[18] Black Power was perceived to be an exhortation that should be reserved for black audiences. University administrators were concerned about Carmichael's speech for different reasons. The vice chancellor for student affairs feared that the speech would lead to an outbreak of violence as had happened when Carmichael spoke at a rally in Atlanta.[19] With the gubernatorial election close at hand, Republican candidate Ronald Reagan saw an opportunity to reassert his position against student protest. He sent a telegram to Carmichael asking him not to speak. For his part, incumbent Democratic governor Pat Brown flew to a meeting with police authorities in Oakland so that provisions would be made against any possibility of violence. Reagan called Brown's meeting a "grandstand stunt," and Brown made declarations against "those who are attempting to turn race against race—black power wielders and white supremacist shouters."[20] Clearly unimpressed by the symbolic attempts of both candidates, Carmichael observes in his speech that "You can't move morally against a man like Brown and Reagan. You've got to move politically to put them out of business."

Despite Carmichael's promises to avoid the subject of Black Power, the speech is a declaration of that doctrine. The lectern from which Carmichael spoke displayed a sign in red letters "Black Power and its Challenges." "Black Power" had become the bugbear of the civil rights movement, and a substantial portion of the speech is devoted to explaining the concept and defending it against the misinterpretations of critics. The term had come to mean much more than the "empowerment" of blacks, although its original and primary intent was to symbolize solidarity among African Americans and a racial identity distinct from that imposed by whites. Journalists frequently represented Black Power as symbolizing black racism and threatening a maelstrom of violence if not outright insurrection. They created unsubstantiated fears "that the Mau Maus were about to pillage suburbia."[21]

In the introduction, Carmichael makes reference to the dispute among whites about the meaning of Black Power as "intellectual masturbation" and reminds his "self-appointed white critics" that, in the words of George Bernard Shaw, "'All criticism is a[n] autobiography.' Dig yourself. OK." Throughout his speech, Carmichael elaborates on the meanings and definitions of words such as Black Power, integration, and civil rights. Like many African American activists of the era, and especially the Black Power advocates, Carmichael understood that controlling the language was the necessary first step to controlling one's political, economic, and social destiny. Thus, he immediately proposes in the speech that the fight for integration should be understood as a fight against white supremacy. Similarly, he redefines white liberal activism on behalf of civil rights as discriminatory and paternalistic, since whites cannot "give" African Americans a freedom; rather, it is the birthright of all Americans. Civil rights laws are written for whites, not African Americans, because African Americans knew that they had rights all along: "That [civil rights] bill was for white people. I know I can live anyplace I want to live. It is white people across this country who are incapable of allowing me to live where I want to live. You need a civil rights bill, not me." The campaign for integration, he says, is a misdirected effort that does nothing to solve the problem of "white supremacy." If there is integration it should cut both ways: "You can come live in Watts. . . . we're going to start adopting us some white people to live in our neighborhood."

Although Carmichael did not, as he had promised the AASU, avoid making a speech about Black Power; his address confronted and condemned his audience, including those who had invited him to speak. He terms Berkeley the "white intellectual ghetto of the West," tells the peace movement that it has been a "failure," and condemns the array of liberal altruistic projects such as Head Start, Upward Lift, Boot Strap and the Peace Corps. These last he terms "modern-day missionaries," a branch of imperialist capitalism designed to exploit persons of color at home and around the world. As he recounts: "The missionaries came [to Africa] with the Bible, and we had the land; when they left, they had the land, and we still have the Bible. That's been the rationalization for Western civilization as it moves across the world—stealing, plundering and raping everybody in its path." "You must start [your work] inside the white community," he tells his audience. Leave the African American community alone—it can take care of itself. But, he notes for his white activist audience, "the white activist has failed miserably to develop the movement inside of his community."

White activists have failed, he says, because they have not understood that the problem is an institutional, not a racist, one, and in this regard, he deviates from earlier militant speakers such as Malcolm X. For the latter, the fundamental issue was the world's racism. For Carmichael, racism is a tool used by imperialist capitalism to accumulate and preserve its wealth. The fundamental problem is "economic exploitation," and the fundamental question to white activists is, can they "tear down the institutions which have put us all in a trick bag we've been into for the last hundreds of years."

After observing that the United States is a "nation of thieves," Carmichael argues that unless America's very institutions are changed, a "color blind" society will be impossible: "Do you think you're capable of building those human relationships, as the country now stands? You're fooling yourself. It is impossible for white and black people to talk about building a relationship based on humanity when the country is the way it is, when institutions are clearly against us." "Poverty," he argues, "is well calculated in this country. It is well calculated and the reason why the poverty program won't work is because the calculators of poverty are administering it." The barrier to equality was institutional and systemic, and only a militant challenge such as that embodied in Black Power could alter it.

Carmichael's rhetorical treatment of the Vietnam War is consistent with his analysis of civil rights. The war is a device by which the imperialist capitalists could continue to exploit the persons of color in Vietnam. The war is "illegal and immoral" because, besides "killing babies, women, and children," the war is about getting the "American pie." Although Carmichael wants economic conditions for African Americans to change, he vows that he does "not want to be a part of the American pie," and African Americans do not "want to become a part of that society." The Vietnam War demonstrates America's racism in a second regard as well. In his autobiography, Carmichael writes that "sending young black men to be cannon fodder in the Vietnam atrocity. . . . was the crowning insult. The Vietnam War ain't nothing but white men sending black men to kill brown men to defend, so they claim, a country they stole from red men."[22] In the Berkeley speech, he plays fortissimo on this theme that the war was racist and immoral. African Americans, underrepresented in American universities, were not protected from the draft by 2S (student) deferments, and Carmichael had, in fact, the day before his speech at Berkeley, been detained by his draft board in New York City. "Black Power" in this arena meant refusing to fight in service of an oppressive society: "We will not allow them to make us hired killers. We will stand pat. We will not kill anybody they say [to] kill." Echoing a thought similarly expressed by Malcolm X, Carmichael said ominously that if blacks were to kill "we're going to decide who we [are] going to kill." Urging African Americans toward a nonviolent approach to social change is to Carmichael sheer hypocrisy in light of the violence inflicted by the Vietnam War and the ever-present fact of violence in urban ghettos.

Carmichael denies that the Black Power slogan advocates violence or that it is reverse racism, instead holding that they have "anti-racist racism," because they are bonding as blacks against the racism inherent in America's institutions. Whites' misperceptions of the intentions of Black Power stem from psychological projection and a phobia about the term "black." He observes ironically that neither "Negro power," nor "power for colored people" would engender the fear that Black Power engenders, presumably because "negro" and "colored" are terms applied by whites to African Americans while "black" is self-definition. The so-called Black Panther Party that Carmichael helped form became a similar bête noir, and his explanation of the genesis of the black panther symbol is replete with irony. While the real name of the organization was the "Lowndes County Freedom Organization," as a political party in Alabama, it required a visual symbol. Journalists referred to the party by the emblem rather than the name, but did not do the same for the "Alabama Democratic Party," whose symbol was a white rooster. "Our question is, Why don't they call the Alabama Democratic Party the 'White Cock Party'?"

Such sardonic commentary typifies Carmichael's style of speaking, a style sometimes termed "rapping" in the 1960s. As he recounted in his autobiography, this style of speaking grew out of African American traditions such as black preaching, and street-corner discourse such as "playing the dozens." The "rap" speech was marked by an extemporaneous delivery with an emphasis on rhythm, creative use of language, humor, irony, and audience interaction. Malcolm X, Eldridge Cleaver, and H. Rap Brown were all noted for their ability to speak in this style.

Carmichael's rapping style is "cool," as one critic has suggested.[23] In it he incorporates esoteric references to George Bernard Shaw, Jean Paul Sartre, and Albert Camus, mixing these with street jive: "If you play like Nazis, we playing back with you this time around. Get hip to that." His diction runs the gamut. Carmichael often forms his sentences with the punctilious grammatical refinement of a college professor. In addition to its grammatical purity, the following exemplary passage also enlists parallelism and the stylistic device of anaphora or repetition: "It is we who picked the cotton for nothing. It is we who are the maids in the kitchens of liberal white people. It is we who are the janitors, the porters, the elevator men; we who sweep up your college floors." At other turns, Carmichael unexpectedly breaks into the African American vernacular that he says he normally "reserves for 'brothers and sisters on the block,'" such as when he declaims, "We don't think the Democratic Party represents the needs of black people. We know it don't" or "We are called reverse racists. Ain't that a gas?" There is rhythmical repetition in the speech, as in: "This country told us that if we worked hard we could succeed, and if that were true we would own this country lock, stock, and barrel—lock, stock, and barrel—lock, stock and barrel." Extemporaneously responding to the audience's feedback—or inviting it—Carmichael frequently employs repetition of the last few words of a sentence: "[A]nd that's their problem, not mine—they're [*sic*] problem, they're problem," or "You can't move morally against a man like Brown and Reagan. You've got to move politically to put them out of business. You've got to move politically," or "God knows we need to be leaders today 'cause the men who run this country are sick, are sick," or "This country is a nation of thieves. It stands on the brink of becoming a nation of murderers. We must stop it. We must stop it. We must stop it. We must stop it."

Thus, Carmichael's speech is laden with sardonic epithets that emphasize wordplay, as when he castigates white activists as modern-day missionaries. African American soldiers in Vietnam are "black mercenaries" because they are fighting on behalf of imperialist capitalists, the secretary of state is "a fool named Rusk," Reagan and Brown are "clowns who waste time parrying with each other," and, evoking the story of Jesus in the temple, he says that America is a "a nation of thieves." In response to police precautions against African American violence in Oakland, the audience is told that they do not need "Gestapo troops, because this is not 1942, and if you play like Nazis, we playing back with you this time around." He also tells his white audience that, because very few African Americans will be admitted to Berkeley, they will have only a modest opportunity to tell themselves about their fellow students, "Well he's almost as good as we are; he's not like the others." To make the point that nonviolence should be taught to white racists not blacks, Carmichael asks sardonically: "Can you name me one black man today who's killed anybody white and is still alive?" Larry Robinson suggests that the mixture of sadness and laughter evoked by Carmichael's speeches is characteristic, "an oratorical version of the message of Negro spirituals and jazz blues.[24] Carmichael borrows from the oral tradition of song and preaching, and as Charles Stewart notes, he was "an actor-showman with a gift for histrionics."[25] Adept at mimicry and broad facial expressions that underscored his caustically witty remarks, Carmichael elicited abundant interaction with his audience, who responded with frequent laughter and applause. Although many of his comments are intended to evoke laughter, Carmichael's own countenance was stern, if not angry. His arms were in constant movement. He would raise one arm above his head and then bring it down dramatically to punctuate a thought. He sometimes circled his finger while unfolding a point, elevated a fist to chest height or raised both fists at the elbows as if lifting a barbell and then pumped his arms as a further means of marking a telling phrase.

Carmichael's rousing message and evocative delivery propelled him to celebrity status during the civil rights movement. His charismatic advocacy for Black Power made him immensely popular with militant black and white audiences but also caused him to be censured by less militant civil rights moderates, and to be feared by whites such as J. Edgar Hoover, who sought to discredit him. One could not be indifferent to Carmichael's speeches. His enthusiasm for and advocacy of fundamental social change never ebbed. In his later years, stricken with cancer, he continued to greet everyone with the ebullient slogan "ready for revolution."[26] According to Stewart, Black Power rhetoric created at least one revolutionary result: it "forever replaced 'Negro' with black and African-American."[27] Although Carmichael's eloquence is distinctly modern, it nevertheless exemplifies Cicero's ancient claim "that the orator's virtue is pre-eminently manifested either in rousing men's hearts to anger, hatred, or indignation or in recalling them from these same passions to mildness and mercy."[28]

Black Power

October, 1966
Oakland, California

Thank you very much. It's a privilege and an honor to be in the white intellectual ghetto of the West. This is a student conference, as it should be, held on a campus, and we'll never be caught up in intellectual masturbation on the question of Black Power. That's a function of the people who are advertisers but call themselves reporters. Incidentally, for my friends and members of the press, my self-appointed white critics, I was reading Mr. Bernard Shaw[a] two days ago, and I came across a very important quote that I think is most apropos to you. He says, "All criticism is a[n] autobiography." Dig yourself. OK.

The philosophers Camus[b] and Sartre[c] raise the question of whether or not a man can condemn himself. The black philosopher who is pragmatic, Frantz Fanon,[d] answered the question. He said that man could not. Camus and Sartre don't answer the question. We in SNCC[e] tend to agree with Fanon—a man cannot condemn himself. If he did, he would then have to inflict punishment upon himself. An example is the Nazis. Any of the Nazi prisoners who, after he was caught and incarcerated, admitted that he committed crimes, that he killed all the many people that he killed, had to commit

a. George Bernard Shaw (1856–1950): Irish playwright and literary critic, author of *Pygmalion*.
b. Albert Camus (1913–1960): Algerian-born French writer and existentialist philosopher, author of *The Stranger*.
c. Jean-Paul Sartre (1905–1980): French philosopher and playwright, author of *Being and Nothingness*, *The Flies*, and *No Exit*.
d. Frantz Fanon (1925–1961): Martinique-born psychiatrist and philosopher, author of *Black Skins, White Masks* and *The Wretched of the Earth*.
e. Student Nonviolent Coordinating Committee.

suicide. The only ones able to stay alive were the ones who never admitted that they committed a crime against people—that is, the ones who rationalized that Jews were not human beings and deserved to be killed, or that they were only following orders. There's another, more recent example provided by the officials and the population—the white population—of Neshoba County, Mississippi (that's where Philadelphia is). They could not condemn Sheriff Rainey,[f] his deputies, and the other fourteen men that killed three human beings. They could not because they elected Mr. Rainey to do precisely what he did; and condemning him would be condemning themselves.

In a much larger view, SNCC says that white America cannot condemn herself. So black people have done it—you stand condemned. The institutions that function in this country are clearly racist; they're built upon racism. The questions to be dealt with then are: How can black people inside this country move? How can white people who say they're not a part of those institutions begin to move? And how then do we begin to clear away the obstacles that we have in this society, to make us live like human beings?

Several people have been upset because we've said that integration was irrelevant when initiated by blacks, and that in fact it was an insidious subterfuge for the maintenance of white supremacy. In the past six years or so, this country has been feeding us a "thalidomide drug[g] of integration," and some negroes have been walking down a dream street talking about sitting next to white people. That does not begin to solve the problem. We didn't go to Mississippi to sit next to Ross Barnett[h]; we did not go to sit next to Jim Clark[i]; we went to get them out of our way. People ought to understand that; we were never fighting for the right to integrate, *we were fighting against white supremacy*. In order to understand white supremacy we must dismiss the fallacious notion that white people can give anybody their freedom. No man can give anybody his freedom. A man is born free. You may enslave a

f. Lawrence Rainey (1923–2002): Sheriff of Neshoba County implicated in the 1964 deaths of civil rights workers Schwerner, Chaney, and Goodman. Rainey was found not guilty of conspiracy to commit murder charges in 1967. He was also involved in several incidents prior to 1964, including the shooting death of an African American from Chicago who was visiting Philadelphia, Mississippi, in 1959 and the whipping with a leather belt of an African American man.

g. Thalidomide: A tranquilizer often prescribed in the late 1950s to alleviate morning sickness. The drug was discovered to cause severe birth defects.

h. Ross Barnett (1898–1987): Governor of Mississippi, 1960–1964, opposed the civil rights movement and the 1962 desegregation of the University of Mississippi.

i. Jim Clark (1922–2007): Sheriff of Dallas County, Alabama, 1955–1966, in which the town of Selma is located. Clark ordered his deputies to charge the civil rights marchers on the Edmund Pettus Bridge on 7 Mar. 1965, commonly known as "Bloody Sunday."

man after he is born free, and that is in fact what this country does. It enslaves blacks after they're born. The only thing white people can do is *stop denying black people their freedom.*

I maintain that every civil rights bill in this country was passed for white people, not for black people. For example, I am black. I know that. I also know that while I am black I am a human being. Therefore I have the right to go into any public place. White people didn't know that. Every time I tried to go into a place they stopped me. So some boys had to write a bill to tell that white man, "He's a human being; don't stop him." That bill was for that white man, not for me. I knew that I could vote all the time and that it wasn't a privilege but my right. Every time I tried I was shot, killed or jailed, beaten or economically deprived. So somebody had to write a bill to tell white people, "When a black man comes to vote, don't bother him." That bill was for white people. I know I can live anyplace I want to live. It is white people across this country who are incapable of allowing me to live where I want to live. You need a civil rights bill, not me. I know I can live where I want to live.

So that the failures to pass a civil rights bill isn't because of Black Power, isn't because of the Student Nonviolent Coordinating Committee; it's not because of the rebellions that are occurring in the major cities. It is incapability of whites to deal with their own problems inside their own communities. That is the problem of the failure of the civil rights bill.

And so in a sense we must then ask, How is it that black people move? And what do we do? But the question in a greater sense is, How can white people who are the majority—and who are responsible for making democracy work, make it work? They have failed miserably on this point. They have never made democracy work, be it inside the United States, Vietnam, South Africa, the Philippines, South America, Puerto Rico or wherever America has been. We not only condemn the country for what it has done internally, but we must condemn it for what it does externally. We see this country trying to rule the world, and someone must stand up and start articulating that this country is not God, and cannot rule the world.

The white supremacist attitude, which you have either consciously or subconsciously, is running rampant through the society today. For example, missionaries were sent to Africa with the attitude that blacks were automatically inferior. As a matter of fact, the first act the missionaries did when they got to Africa was to make us cover up our bodies, because they said it got them excited. We couldn't go bare-breasted any more because they got excited! When the missionaries came to civilize us because we were uncivilized, educate us because we were uneducated, and give us some literate studies because we were illiterate, they charged a price. The missionaries came with the Bible, and we had the land; when they left, they had the land, and we still have the Bible. That's been the rationalization for Western civilization as it moves across the world—stealing, plundering and raping everybody in its path. Their one rationalization is that the rest of the world is uncivilized and they are in fact civilized. But the West is un-civil-ized. And that runs on today, you see, because now we have "modern-day missionaries," and they come into our ghettos,—they Head Start, Upward Lift, Bootstrap, and Upward Bound us into white society. They don't want to face the real problem. A man is poor for one reason and one reason only—he does not have money. If you want to get rid of poverty, you give people money. And you ought not to tell me about people who don't work, and that you can't give people money without working, because if that were true, you'd have to start stopping Rockefeller, Kennedy, Lyndon Baines Johnson, Lady Bird Johnson, the whole of Standard Oil, the Gulf Corporation, all of them, including probably a large number of the board of trustees of this university. The question, then, is not whether or not one can work; it's *Who has power to make his or her acts legitimate?* That is all. In this country, that power is invested in the hands of white people, and they make their acts legitimate.

We are now engaged in a psychological struggle in this country, and that is whether or not black people will have the right to use the words they want to use without white people giving their sanction to it; and that we maintain, whether they like it or not, we gonna use the word "Black Power"—and let them address themselves to that; but that we are not going to wait for white people to sanction Black Power. We're tired waiting; every time black people move in this country, they're forced to defend their position before they move. It's time that the people who are supposed to be defending their position do that. That's white people. They ought to start defending themselves as to why they have oppressed and exploited us.

Now it is clear that when this country started to move in terms of slavery, the reason for a man being picked as a slave was one reason—because of the color of his skin. If one was black one was automatically inferior, inhuman, and therefore fit for slavery; so that the question of whether or not we are individually suppressed is nonsensical, and it's a downright lie. We are oppressed as a group because we are black, not because we are lazy, not because we're apathetic, not because we're stupid, not because we smell, not because we eat watermelon and have good rhythm. We are oppressed because we are black.

And in order to get out of that oppression one must wield the group power that one has, not the individual power which this country then sets the criteria under which a man may come into it. That is what is called in this country as integration: "You do what I tell you to do and then we'll let you sit at the table with us." And that we are saying that we have to be opposed to that. We must now set up criteria and that if there's going to be any integration, it's going to be a two-way thing. If you believe in integration, you can come live in Watts. You can send your children to the ghetto schools. Let's talk about that. If you believe in integration, then we're going to start adopting us some white people to live in our neighborhood.

So it is clear that the question is not one of integration or segregation. Integration is a man's ability to want to move in there by himself. If someone wants to live in a white neighborhood and he is black, that is his choice. It should be his rights. It is not because white people will not allow him. So vice versa: If a black man wants to live in the slums, that should be his right. Black people will let him. That is the difference. And it's a difference on which this country makes a number of logical mistakes when they begin to try to criticize the program articulated by SNCC.

Now we maintain that we cannot afford to be concerned about 6 percent of the children in this country, black children, who you allow to come into white schools. We have 94 percent who still live in shacks. We are going to be concerned about those 94 percent. You ought to be concerned about them too. The question is, Are we willing to be concerned about those 94 percent? Are we willing to be concerned about the black people who will never get to Berkeley, who will never get to Harvard, and cannot get an education, so you'll never get a chance to rub shoulders with them and say, "Well, he's almost as good as we are; he's not like the others"? The question is, How can white society begin to move to see black people as human beings? I am black, therefore I am; not that I am black and I must go to college to prove myself. I am black, therefore I am. And don't deprive me of anything and say to me that you must go to college before you gain access to X, Y, and Z. It is only a rationalization for one's oppression.

The political parties in this country do not meet the needs of people on a day-to-day basis. The question is, How can we build new political institutions that will become the political expressions of people on a day-to-day basis? The question is, How can you build political institutions that will begin to meet the needs of Oakland, California? And the needs of Oakland, California, is not 1,000 policemen with submachine guns. They don't need that. They need that least of all. The question is, How can we build institutions where those people can begin to function on a day-to-day basis, where they can get decent jobs, where they can get decent houses, and where they can begin to participate in the policy and major decisions that affect their lives? That's what they need, not Gestapo troops, because this is not 1942, and if you play like Nazis, we playing back with you this time around. Get hip to that.

The question then is, How can white people move to start making the major institutions that they have in this country function the way it is supposed to function? That is the real question. And can white people move inside their own community and start tearing down racism where in fact it does exist? Where it exists. It is you who live in Cicero[j] and stop us from living there. It is white people who stop us from moving into Grenada.[k] It is white people who make sure that we live in the ghettos of this country. It is white institutions that do that. They must change. In order—In order for America to really live on a basic principle of human relationships, a new society must be born. Racism must die, and the economic exploitation of this country of non-white peoples around the world must also die—must also die.

Now there are several programs that we have in the South, most in poor white communities. We're trying to organize poor whites on a base where they can begin to move around the question of economic exploitation and political disfranchisement. We know—we've heard the theory several times—but few people are willing to go into there. The question is, Can the white activist not try to be a Pepsi generation who comes alive in the black community, but can he be a man who's willing to move into the white community and start organizing where the organization is needed? Can he do that? The question is, Can the white society or the white activist disassociate himself with two clowns who waste time parrying with each other rather than talking about the problems that are facing people in this state? Can you dissociate yourself with those clowns and start to build new institutions that will eliminate all idiots like them.

---

j. Cicero, Illinois, is a suburb of Chicago and in late summer and early fall of 1966 was targeted by Martin Luther King Jr. for demonstrations against its closed housing policy. Several times the planned demonstrations were postponed.

k. Grenada County, Mississippi, was strongly segregationist. In the summer of 1966, it was the focus of civil rights activities.

And the question is, If we are going to do that when and where do we start, and how do we start? We maintain that we must start doing that inside the white community. Our own personal position politically is that we don't think the Democratic Party represents the needs of black people. We know it don't. And that if, in fact, white people really believe that, the question is, if they're going to move inside that structure, how are they going to organize around a concept of whiteness based on true brotherhood and based on stopping exploitation, economic exploitation, so that there will be a coalition base for black people to hook up with? You cannot form a coalition based on national sentiment. That is not a coalition. If you need a coalition to redress itself to real changes in this country, white people must start building those institutions inside the white community. And that is the real question, I think, facing the white activists today. Can they, in fact, begin to move into and tear down the institutions which have put us all in a trick bag that we've been into for the last hundred years?

I don't think that we should follow what many people say that we should fight to be leaders of tomorrow. Frederick Douglass said that the youth should fight to be leaders today. And God knows we need to be leaders today, 'cause the men who run this country are sick, are sick. So that can we on a larger sense begin now, today, to start building those institutions and to fight to articulate our position, to fight to be able to control our universities—We need to be able to do that—and to fight to control the basic institutions which perpetuate racism by destroying them and building new ones? That's the real question that faces us today, and it is a dilemma because most of us do not know how to work, and that the excuse that most white activists find is to run into the black community.

Now we maintain that we cannot have white people working in the black community, and we mean it on a psychological ground. The fact is that all black people often question whether or not they are equal to whites, because every time they start to do something, white people are around showing them how to do it. If we are going to eliminate that for the generation that comes after us, then black people must be seen in positions of power, doing and articulating for themselves, for themselves.

That is not to say that one is a reverse racist; it is to say that one is moving in a healthy ground; it is to say what the philosopher Sartre says: One is becoming an "antiracist racist." And this country can't understand that. Maybe it's because it's all caught up in racism. But I think what you have in SNCC is an anti-racist racism. We are against racists. Now if everybody who is white see themself [*sic*] as a racist and then see us against him, they're speaking from their own guilt position, not ours, not ours.

Now then, the question is, How can we move to begin to change what's going on in this country? I maintain, as we have in SNCC, that the war in Vietnam is an illegal and immoral war. And the question is, What can we do to stop that war? What can we do to stop the people who, in the name of our country, are killing babies, women, and children? What can we do to stop that? And I maintain that we do not have the power in our hands to change that institution, to begin to recreate it, so that they learn to leave the Vietnamese people alone, and that the only power we have is the power to say, "Hell no!" to the draft.

We have to say—We have to say to ourselves that there is a higher law than the law of a racist named McNamara.[l] There is a higher law than the law of a fool named Rusk.[m] And there's a higher law than the law of a buffoon named Johnson.[n] It's the law of each of us. It's the law of each of us. It is the law of each of us saying that we will not allow them to make us hired killers. We will stand pat. We will not kill anybody that they say kill. And if we decide to kill, we're going to decide who we going to kill. And this country will only be able to stop the war in Vietnam when the young men who are made to fight it begin to say, "Hell, no, we ain't going."

Now then, there's a failure because the Peace Movement has been unable to get off the college campuses where everybody has a 2S and not going to get drafted anyway. And the question is, How can you move out of that into the white ghettos of this country and begin to articulate a position for those white students who do not want to go. We cannot do that. It is something—sometimes ironic that many of the peace groups have beginning to call us violent and say they can no longer support us, and we are in fact the most militant organization [for] peace or civil rights or human rights against the war in Vietnam in this country today. There isn't one organization that has begun to meet our stance on the war in Vietnam, 'cause we not only say we are against the war in Vietnam; we are against the draft. We are against the draft. No man has the right to take a man for two years and train him to be a killer. A man should decide what he wants to do with his life.

---

l. Robert McNamara (1916–2009) was secretary of defense under Presidents Kennedy and Johnson, from 1961–1968.

m. Dean Rusk (1909–1994) was secretary of state under Presidents Kennedy and Johnson, from 1961–1969.

n. Lyndon Baines Johnson (1908–1973) was president of the United States from 1963 to 1969.

So the question then is it becomes crystal clear for black people because we can easily say that anyone fighting in the war in Vietnam is nothing but a black mercenary, and that's all he is. Any time a black man leaves the country where he can't vote to supposedly deliver the vote for somebody else, he's a black mercenary. Any time a—Any time a black man leaves this country, gets shot in Vietnam on foreign ground, and returns home and you won't give him a burial in his own homeland, he's a black mercenary, a black mercenary.

And that even if I were to believe the lies of Johnson, if I were to believe his lies that we're fighting to give democracy to the people in Vietnam, as a black man living in this country I wouldn't fight to give this to anybody. I wouldn't give it to anybody. So that we have to use our bodies and our minds in the only way that we see fit. We must begin like the philosopher Camus to come alive by saying "No!" That is the only act in which we begin to come alive, and we have to say "No!" to many, many things in this country. This country is a nation of thieves. It has stole everything it has, beginning with black people, beginning with black people. And that the question is, How can we move to start changing this country from what it is—a nation of thieves. This country cannot justify any longer its existence. We have become the policeman of the world. The marines are at our disposal to always bring democracy, and if the Vietnamese don't want democracy, well dammit, "We'll just wipe them the hell out, 'cause they don't deserve to live if they won't have our way of life."

There is then in a larger sense, What do you do on your university campus? Do you raise questions about the hundred black students who were kicked off campus a couple of weeks ago? Eight hundred? Eight hundred? And how does that question begin to move? Do you begin to relate to people outside of the ivory tower and university wall? Do you think you're capable of building those human relationships, as the country now stands? You're fooling yourself. It is impossible for white and black people to talk about building a relationship based on humanity when the country is the way it is, when the institutions are clearly against us.

We have taken all the myths of this country and we've found them to be nothing but downright lies. This country told us that if we worked hard we would succeed, and if that were true we would own this country lock, stock, and barrel—lock, stock, and barrel—lock, stock, and barrel. It is we who have picked the cotton for nothing. It is we who are the maids in the kitchens of liberal white people. It is we who are the janitors, the porters, the elevator men; we who sweep up your college floors. Yes, it is we who are the hardest workers and the lowest paid, and the lowest paid.

And that it is nonsensical for people to start talking about human relationships until they're willing to build new institutions. Black people are economically insecure. White liberals are economically secure. Can you begin to build an economic coalition? Are the liberals willing to share their salaries with the economically insecure black people they so much love? Then if you're not, are you willing to start building new institutions that will provide economic security for black people? That's the question we want to deal with. That's the question we want to deal with.

We have to seriously examine the histories that we have been told. But we have something more to do than that. American students are perhaps the most politically unsophisticated students in the world, in the world, in the world. Across every country in this world, while we were growing up, students were leading the major revolutions of their countries. We have not been able to do that. They have been politically aware of their existence. In South America our neighbors down below the border have one every 24 hours just to remind us that they're politically aware.

And we have been unable to grasp it because we've always moved in the field of morality and love while people have been politically jiving with our lives. And the question is, How do we now move politically and stop trying to move morally? You can't move morally against a man like Brown[o] and Reagan.[p] You've got to move politically to put them out of business. You've got to move politically.

You can't move morally against Lyndon Baines Johnson because he is an immoral man. He doesn't know what it's all about. So you've got to move politically. You've got to move politically. And that we have to begin to develop a political sophistication—which is not to be a parrot: "The two-party system is the best party in the world." There is a difference between being a parrot and being politically sophisticated.

We have to raise questions about whether or not we do need new types of political institutions in this country, and we in SNCC maintain that we need them now. We need new political institutions in this country. Any time—Any time Lyndon Baines Johnson can head a Party which has in it

o. Edmund G. Brown (1909–1996): Governor of California from 1959 to 1967. He was defeated in his 1966 campaign for reelection by Ronald Reagan.

p. Later president of the United States, Ronald Reagan (1911–2004) was governor of California from 1967 to 1975.

Bobby Kennedy,[q] Wayne Morse,[r] Eastland,[s] Wallace,[t] and all those other supposed-to-be-liberal cats, there's something wrong with that Party. They're moving politically, not morally. And that if that party refuses to seat black people from Mississippi and goes ahead and seats racists like Eastland and his clique, it is clear to me that they're moving politically, and that one cannot begin to talk morality to people like that.

We must begin to think politically and see if we can have the power to impose and keep the moral values that we hold high. We must question the values of this society, and I maintain that black people are the best people to do that because we have been excluded from that society. And the question is, we ought to think whether or not we want to become a part of that society. That's what we want to do.

And that that is precisely what it seems to me that the Student Nonviolent Coordinating Committee is doing. We are raising questions about this country. I do not want to be a part of the American pie. The American pie means raping South Africa, beating Vietnam, beating South America, raping the Philippines, raping every country you've been in. I don't want any of your blood money. I don't want it—don't want to be part of that system. And the question is, How do we raise those questions? How do we . . . How do we begin to raise them?

We have grown up and we are the generation that has found this country to be a world power, that has found this country to be the wealthiest country in the world. We must question how she got her wealth? That's what we're questioning, and whether or not we want this country to continue being the wealthiest country in the world at the price of raping every—everybody else across the world. That's what we must begin to question. And that because black people are saying we do not now want to become a part of you, we are called reverse racists. Ain't that a gas?

Now, then, we want to touch on nonviolence because we see that again as the failure of white society to make nonviolence work. I was always surprised

q. Robert F. Kennedy: Attorney general under President Kennedy and in 1964 elected a Democratic US senator from New York. Robert Kennedy was generally viewed as pro–civil rights.
r. Wayne Morse (1900–1974): US senator from Oregon. Initially elected as a Republican in 1944, Morse became a Democrat in 1955 and was one of only two senators who voted against the Gulf of Tonkin resolution, which authorized the Vietnam War. Morse was defeated for reelection in 1968.
s. James Eastland (1904–1986): US Democratic senator from Mississippi from 1943 to 1978; staunchly defended segregation and states' rights.
t. George C. Wallace (1919–1998) was Democratic governor of Alabama for four discontinuous terms (1963–1967, 1971–1979, and 1983–1987). In the 1960s, he was strongly segregationist, and widely known for his "stand in the schoolhouse door" at the University of Alabama.

at Quakers who came to Alabama and counseled me to be nonviolent, but didn't have the guts to start talking to James Clark to be nonviolent. That is where nonviolence needs to be preached—to Jim Clark, not to black people. They have already been nonviolent too many years. The question is, Can white people conduct their nonviolent schools in Cicero where they belong to be conducted, not among black people in Mississippi. Can they conduct it among the white people in Grenada?

Six-foot-two men who kick little black children—can you conduct nonviolent schools there? That is the question that we must raise, not that you conduct nonviolence among black people. Can you name me one black man today who's killed anybody white and is still alive? Even after rebellion, when some black brothers throw some bricks and bottles, ten thousand of them has to pay the crime, 'cause when the white policeman comes in, anybody who's black is arrested, "'cause we all look alike."

So that we have to raise those questions. We, the youth of this country, must begin to raise those questions. And we must begin to move to build new institutions that's going to speak to the needs of people who need it. We are going to have to speak to change the foreign policy of this country. One of the problems with the peace movement is that it's just too caught up in Vietnam, and that if we pulled out the troops from Vietnam this week, next week you'd have to get another peace movement for Santo Domingo. And the question is, How do you begin to articulate the need to change the foreign policy of this country—a policy that is decided upon race, a policy on which decisions are made upon getting economic wealth at any price, at any price.

Now we articulate that we therefore have to hook up with black people around the world; and that that hookup is not only psychological, but becomes very real. If South America today were to rebel, and black people were to shoot the hell out of all the white people there—as they should, as they should—then Standard Oil would crumble tomorrow. If South Africa were to go today, Chase Manhattan Bank would crumble tomorrow. If Zimbabwe, which is called Rhodesia by white people, were to go tomorrow, General Electric would cave in on the East Coast. The question is, How do we stop those institutions that are so willing to fight against "Communist aggression" but closes their eyes to racist oppression? That is the question that you raise. Can this country do that?

Now, many people talk about pulling out of Vietnam. What will happen? If we pull out of Vietnam, there will be one less aggressor in there—we won't be there, we won't be there. And so the question is, How do we articulate those positions? And we cannot begin to articulate them from the same assumptions that the people in the country speak, 'cause they speak from different assumptions than I assume what the youth in this country are talking about.

That we're not talking about a policy or aid or sending Peace Corps people in to teach people how to read and write and build houses while we steal their raw materials from them. Is that what we're talking about? 'Cause that's all we do. What underdeveloped countries need is—information on how to become industrialized, so they can keep their raw materials where they have it, produce them and sell it to this country for the price it's supposed to pay; not that we produce it and sell it back to them for a profit and keep sending our modern day missionaries in, calling them the sons of Kennedy. And that if the youth are going to participate in that program, how do you raise those questions where you begin to control that Peace Corps program? How do you begin to raise them?

How do we raise the questions of poverty? The assumptions of this country is that if someone is poor, they are poor because of their own individual blight, or they weren't born on the right side of town; they had too many children; they went in the army too early; or their father was a drunk, or they didn't care about school, or they made a mistake. That's a lot of nonsense. Poverty is well calculated in this country. It is well calculated, and the reason why the poverty program won't work is because the calculators of poverty are administering it. That's why it won't work.

So how can we, as the youth in the country, move to start tearing those things down? We must move into the white community. We are in the black community. We have developed a movement in the black community. The challenge is that the white activist has failed miserably to develop the movement inside of his community. And the question is, Can we find white people who are going to have the courage to go into white communities and start organizing them? Can we find them? Are they here and are they willing to do that? Those are the questions that we must raise for the white activist.

And we're never going to get caught up in questions about power. This country knows what power is. It knows it very well. And it knows what Black Power is 'cause it deprived black people of it for 400 years. So it knows what Black Power is. That the question of, Why do black people—Why do white people in this country associate Black Power with violence? And the question is because of their own inability to deal with "blackness." If we had said "Negro power" nobody would get scared. Everybody would support it.

Or if we said power for colored people, everybody'd be for that, but it is the word "black"—it is the word "black" that bothers people in this country, and that's their problem, not mine—they're [*sic*] problem, they're problem.

Now there's one modern day lie that we want to attack and then move on very quickly and that is the lie that says anything all black is bad. Now, you're all a college university crowd. You've taken your basic logic course. You know about a major premise and minor premise. So people have been telling me anything all black is bad. Let's make that our major premise.

Major premise: Anything all black is bad.

Minor premise or particular premise: I am all black.

Therefore . . .

I'm never going to be put in that trick bag; I am all black and I'm all good, dig it. Anything all black is not necessarily bad. Anything all black is only bad when you use force to keep whites out. Now that's what white people have done in this country, and they're projecting their same fears and guilt on us, and we won't have it, we won't have it. Let them handle their own fears and their own guilt. Let them find their own psychologists. We refuse to be the therapy for white society any longer. We have gone mad trying to do it. We have gone stark raving mad trying to do it.

I look at Dr. King on television every single day, and I say to myself: "Now there is a man who's desperately needed in this country. There is a man full of love. There is a man full of mercy. There is a man full of compassion." But every time I see Lyndon on television, I said, "Martin, baby, you got a long way to go."

So that the question stands as to what we are willing to do, how we are willing to say "No," to withdraw from that system and begin within our community to start to function and to build new institutions that will speak to our needs. In Lowndes County, we developed something called the *Lowndes County Freedom Organization*. It is a political party. The Alabama law says that if you have a Party you must have an emblem. We chose for the emblem a black panther, a beautiful black animal which symbolizes the strength and dignity of black people, an animal that never strikes back until he's back so far into the wall, he's got nothing to do but spring out. Yeah. And when he springs he does not stop.

Now there is a Party in Alabama called the *Alabama Democratic Party*. It is all white. It has as its emblem a white rooster and the words "white supremacy" for the write. Now the gentlemen of the Press, because they're advertisers, and because most of them are white, and because they're produced by that white institution, never called the *Lowndes County Freedom Organization* by its name, but rather they call it the Black Panther Party. Our question is, Why don't they call the Alabama Democratic Party the "White Cock Party"? (It's fair to us. . . . .) It is clear to me that that just points out America's problem with sex and color, not our problem, not our problem. And it is now white America that is going to deal with those problems of sex and color.

If we were to be real and to be honest, we would have to admit—we would have to admit that most people in this country see things black and white. We have to do that. All of us do. We live in a country that's geared that way. White people would have to admit that they are afraid to go into a black ghetto at night. They are afraid. That's a fact. They're afraid because they'd be "beat up," "lynched," "looted," "cut up," etcetera, etcetera. It happens to black people inside the ghetto every day, incidentally, and white people are afraid of that. So you get a man to do it for you—a policeman. And now you figure his mentality, when he's afraid of black people. The first time a black man jumps, that white man going to shoot him. He's going to shoot him. So police brutality is going to exist on that level because of the incapability of that white man to see black people come together and to live in the conditions. This country is too hypocritical and that we cannot adjust ourselves to its hypocrisy.

The only time I hear people talk about nonviolence is when black people move to defend themselves against white people. Black people cut themselves every night in the ghetto—Don't anybody talk about nonviolence. Lyndon Baines Johnson is busy bombing the hell of out Vietnam—Don't nobody talk about nonviolence. White people beat up black people every day—Don't nobody talk about nonviolence. But as soon as black people start to move, the double standard comes into being.

You can't defend yourself. That's what you're saying, 'cause you show me a man who—who would advocate aggressive violence that would be able to live in this country. Show him to me. The double standards again come into itself. Isn't it ludicrous and hypocritical for the political chameleon who calls himself a Vice President in this country to—to stand up before this country and say, "Looting never got anybody anywhere"? Isn't it hypocritical for Lyndon to talk about looting, that you can't accomplish anything by looting and you must accomplish it by the legal ways? What does he know about legality? Ask Ho Chi Minh, he'll tell you.[u]

u. Ho Chi Minh (1890–1969): President of the (Communist) Democratic Republic of Vietnam (North Vietnam) from 1945 until his death in 1969.

So that in conclusion we want to say that number one, it is clear to me that we have to wage a psychological battle on the right for black people to define their own terms, define themselves as they see fit, and organize themselves as they see it. Now the question is, How is the white community going to begin to allow for that organizing, because once they start to do that, they will also allow for the organizing that they want to do inside their community. It doesn't make a difference, 'cause we're going to organize our way anyway. We're going to do it. The question is, How are we going to facilitate those matters, whether it's going to be done with a thousand policemen with submachine guns, or whether or not it's going to be done in a context where it is allowed to be done by white people warding off those policemen. That is the question.

And the question is, How are white people who call themselves activists ready to start move into the white communities on two counts: on building new political institutions to destroy the old ones that we have? And to move around the concept of white youth refusing to go into the army? So that we can start, then, to build a new world. It is ironic to talk about civilization in this country. This country is uncivilized. It needs to be civilized. It needs to be civilized.

And that we must begin to raise those questions of civilization: What it is? And who do it? And so we must urge you to fight now to be the leaders of today, not tomorrow. We've got to be the leaders of today. This country—This country is a nation of thieves. It stands on the brink of becoming a nation of murderers. We must stop it. We must stop it. We must stop it. We must stop it.

And then, therefore, in a larger sense there's the question of black people. We are on the move for our liberation. We have been tired of trying to prove things to white people. We are tired of trying to explain to white people that we're not going to hurt them. We are concerned with getting the things we want, the things that we have to have to be able to function. The question is, Can white people allow for that in this country? The question is, Will white people overcome their racism and allow for that to happen in this country? If that does not happen, brothers and sisters, we have no choice but to say very clearly, "Move over, or we're going to move on over you."

Thank you.

Martin Luther King Jr.

A Time to Break Silence

Martin Luther King, Jr. had begun to criticize America's involvement in the Vietnam War two years before this landmark speech at Riverside Church. At a Howard University address in 1965, he said that the war was "accomplishing nothing," and at that year's Southern Christian Leadership Conference (SCLC) annual meeting, he argued that the United States must negotiate with the Viet Cong and that it must halt the bombing. His antiwar stance at this point was not radical, however; he also declared that there should be no unilateral US withdrawal. Still, he was heavily criticized for his stand. Benjamin Hooks warned King against going "too far in the international arena." The SCLC dissociated itself from King's antiwar comments. Many black leaders argued that King's antiwar stance would hurt the cause of civil rights, even as that cause was gaining real legislative success. In addition to such criticism by black leaders and the black press, King was attacked by many white leaders and the white press. *U.S. News and World Report* asked, "Is Vietnam to Become a 'Civil Rights' Issue?" *Time* also signaled its disapproval in its headline: "Confusing the Cause." Both *Time* and *U.S. News and World Report* quoted the NAACP's Roy Wilkins as saying, "I don't believe civil rights groups have enough information on Viet Nam, or foreign policy, to make it their cause." The white establishment clearly agreed with Wilkins. By fall of 1965, emotionally fatigued from fighting the criticism and with the press of other issues such as the Watts riot, King returned his focus to civil rights.[1]

Events, however, caught up with him. In the summer of 1966, the Office of Economic Opportunity, the primary agency for Johnson's Great Society programs, had its budget cut by one-third in order to support the growing defense appropriations. In a very real sense, the poor were funding the war. African Americans were also shouldering a disproportionate share of the combat duty. As early as 1964, only 18.8 percent of eligible whites were drafted as compared to 30.2 percent of eligible blacks. By 1967, fueled by the troop buildup in Vietnam, 31 percent of eligible whites were being drafted compared to 67 percent of eligible blacks. Moreover, while 13 percent of the military was African American, they drew 28 percent of the combat assignments. Yet as late as 1967, although most blacks favored a cease-fire or some lessening of hostilities, only 25 percent were opposed to US involvement in Vietnam, compared with 15 percent of white Americans. The majority of African American antiwar sentiment was found in the young, the urban, and the poor.[2]

Indeed, in 1966, King rallied the SCLC to his position, and some of its leadership, such as Hosea Williams and Ralph Abernathy, began to speak out actively against the war. Throughout the year, King, too, briefly addressed the war in sermons and speeches, but not until the spring of 1967 did he begin to deliver speeches devoted solely to the antiwar cause. The first such speech was at a forum sponsored by the *Nation* on February 25, 1967. However, his most compelling speech, and the one that drew the greatest national attention, was his address at the Riverside Church before a meeting sponsored by the Clergy and Laymen Concerned about Vietnam. Speaking to an audience of about three thousand, King explained his antiwar position in New York, on April 4, 1967, exactly one year before his assassination.[3]

According to communication scholar Michael Eric Dyson, "A Time to Break Silence" was originally drafted by Vincent Harding, revised by King, and then delivered largely extemporaneously at the Riverside Church. Harding, a minister and professor at Spelman College in Atlanta, had a specific agenda for the speech. He wanted it to be a strong statement against the war, he wanted the antiwar argument to be grounded in King's role as a religious leader for peace and freedom, and he wanted King to express solidarity with the Vietnamese people. In this speech, King accomplished all three goals.[4]

As with many of King's speeches, a striking feature of "A Time to Break Silence" was its careful organization. He began the speech on a highly personal note, speaking of the "betrayal of my own silences," and the "burnings of my own heart," remarking that "many persons have questioned the wisdom" of speaking out against the Vietnam War. He enunciated the objections of his critics in a series of rhetorical questions, and then enumerated seven reasons why he opposed the Vietnam War. Importantly, he arranged these in an ascending order of importance. He began with the more practical concerns: the war drained funds from the antipoverty program, it disproportionately sent young poor men to combat, and any support of the war on his part eroded his support of nonviolent protests at home. The next three reasons were more philosophical, drawn from his position as a religious leader concerned about human rights. The civil rights movement had always been about more than just the procurement of legal changes, King said, and he quoted the motto of the SCLC: "To save the soul of America." As a recipient of the Nobel Peace Prize, King declared that he felt a responsibility to speak on behalf of peace whenever appropriate. Finally, the cause of peace was the cause of Christ, and as a minister, he could not remain silent about the war.

The speech then made an interesting transition as King moved to the seventh reason. Indeed, if one were not counting, it could go unnoticed that this *was* the seventh reason for opposing the war, because in length and tone it differed markedly from the first six. Basically, King argued that in pursuing the war, Americans were ignoring the irreparable harms they were inflicting upon the Vietnamese people. In this section, and it was fundamentally a section unto itself, King recounted the history of the Vietnam War. He described the post–World War II French efforts to recolonize Vietnam, the 1954 Geneva agreements that temporarily split Vietnam into two nations, and the increasing commitment of American troops in the 1960s. He invited his audience to see the history through the eyes of the Vietnamese people. "They must see Americans as strange liberators," he said, as "they watch as we poison their water, as we kill a million acres of their crops. They must weep as the bulldozers roar through their areas preparing to destroy their precious trees. . . . What do the peasants think as we ally ourselves with the landlords and as we refuse to put any action into our many words concerning land reform? . . . We must speak for them and raise the questions they cannot raise. These too are our brothers." But King did not stop by identifying the concerns of the Vietnamese people. His perspective—his looking at the war through the eyes of others—continued through three other groups: the National Liberation Front (NLF) or Viet Cong, the North Vietnamese, and the American soldier. His transition from talking about the Vietnamese to discussing the American soldier captured the larger point he was making in this portion of the speech. "At this point, I should make it clear that while I have tried in these last few minutes to give a voice to the voiceless of Vietnam and to understand the arguments of those who are called enemy,

I am as deeply concerned about our own troops there as anything else. For it occurs to me that what we are submitting them to in Vietnam is not simply the brutalizing process that goes on in any war where armies face each other and seek to destroy. We are adding cynicism to the process of death, for they must know after a short period there that none of the things we claim to be fighting for are really involved." His reference to the American soldier was short, however, as he quickly thereafter announced the thesis of his speech: that this "madness must cease" and that "the initiative to stop [the war] must be ours." Using religious language, King called for five concrete actions that the government must undertake:

1. End all bombing.
2. Declare a unilateral cease-fire.
3. Curtail the military buildup in Thailand and interference in Laos.
4. Include the NLF in the peace talks.
5. Set a date for the removal of all foreign troops from Vietnam.

King had called for the first and fourth of these two actions years prior to his speech. The other three, and especially the last, however, were newer proposals and indicated an increasingly radical antiwar stand.

After enumerating these policy proposals the government should enact, King turned to the audience, the ministers and laymen present at the meeting and those who later read the speech. He called for their actions to match their words in "seeking out every creative means of protest possible," language he had often used in his civil rights discourse. "We must all protest," he told his audience. Specifically, however, he urged the ministers to counsel young men to resist the draft by registering as conscientious objectors. This was a truly radical call, because to qualify as a conscientious objector one needed to document an objection to *all* war, not simply *some* wars. King, however, suggested a different kind of conscientious objection, one more akin to civil disobedience. He wanted potential draftees to help clarify "our nation's role in Vietnam," and thus he urged them to conscientiously object to the morality of this war in particular. However, one could also read King's message as an endorsement of pacifism, that is, a radical call to nonviolence as a way of life, not simply a method of protest. While Coretta Scott King had earlier embraced this more pacifist approach, Martin Luther King Jr. had not. Even King's categorical call to resist the draft by registering as conscientious objectors did not fully clarify the extent of his pacifism, perhaps purposely so.[5]

In the final portion of the speech, King once again grounded his antiwar stand in the larger question of human rights. There was a worldwide revolution occurring, he said, of which Vietnam was a part. Countries in Asia, Africa, and Latin America were throwing off the chains of colonialism; the causes of peace, justice, and compassion were being advanced around the globe. America's reactionary and de facto colonization of South Vietnam was another facet of racial injustice. "These are revolutionary times," King concluded; "all over the globe men are revolting against old systems of exploitation and oppression, and out of the wounds of a frail world, new systems of justice and equality are being born." To protest US involvement in Vietnam was to be part of that revolution. In language reminiscent of his civil rights rhetoric, he summoned the audience: "Now let us begin. Now let us rededicate ourselves to the long and bitter—but beautiful—struggle for a new world. This is the calling of the sons of God, and our brothers wait eagerly for our response."

Thus, the arrangement and arguments of the speech were aimed to achieve the goals Harding had outlined. King began by announcing his motives for taking on the issue of Vietnam, and those motives were grounded pragmatically and philosophically in his position as a civil rights leader and as a leader in the global movement for peace and justice. His motive was to support the Vietnamese people. Then after clearly and categorically announcing the policies he supported for the government and for himself, including draft resistance, King returned to the image of the global, revolutionary movement. In his arguments and organization, King had portrayed Vietnam through the prism of civil rights.

King's choice of language accomplished the same purpose. This discourse did not contain the eloquence of King's "I Have a Dream" speech, his sermons, or many other of his civil rights speeches, but then this speech had a different purpose. Although the audience at the church was predominantly opposed to the war, this was a speech designed for a larger audience—to justify King's strong antiwar stance and to persuade them to join the cause. He was not seeking to inspire in the way the Dream speech did; he was seeking to convert. Although the language did not soar, as noted above it still echoed much of his civil rights discourse. He had, for example, many axiomatic references to peace, justice, and nonviolence, such as "social change comes most meaningfully through nonviolent action," "this kind of positive revolution of our values is our best defense against communism," and "we must not engage in a negative anti-communism, but rather in a positive thrust for democracy." Also, his language represented him as a loyal critic of the government, just as he had done in the civil rights movement: "I come to this platform to make a passionate plea to my beloved nation," and "it should be incandescently clear that no one who has any concern for the integrity and life of America today can ignore the present war." Finally, much of the word choice and phrasing was quintessentially Martin Luther King Jr.: "incandescently," "languish under our bombs," "a symptom of a far deeper malady within the American spirit," and "every creative means of protest possible." King thus made effective use of his language. It did not risk alienating the unconverted with florid language and sweeping generalizations, yet it still contained some rhetorical flourishes. More than that, it was true to his civil rights style of discourse and thus indicated that this issue, too, was cut from the same cloth.

Yet while King's language was effective overall, there were several passages that were especially noteworthy for their condemnation of America's involvement in the war and for the language in which King couches those condemnations. The first condemnation came in the opening section, as King argued that he could not condemn the violence of rioting if he did not also condemn the American violence in Vietnam. Using a rhetorical formulation common to Stokely Carmichael and other Black Power advocates, King declared that "I knew that I could never again raise my voice against the violence of the oppressed in the ghettos without having first spoken clearly to the greatest purveyor of violence in the world today—my own government." The second condemnation came shortly after the first, just as King had transitioned to the philosophical motives for condemning the war. As he noted, the SCLC's motto was to "save the soul of America," but, he said, the war in Vietnam threatens that soul. Using a vivid metaphor, King concluded: "if America's soul becomes totally poisoned, part of the autopsy must read 'Vietnam.' It can never be saved so long as it destroys the deepest hopes of men the world over."

He condemned America for a third time late in the speech, as he discussed the global revolution. In the middle of discussing the revolution against injustice he wove a summary of America's sin of Vietnam, a review of the indictments made in the opening portion of the speech: "This business of burning human beings with napalm, of filling our nation's homes with orphans and widows, of injecting poisonous drugs of hate into the veins of peoples normally humane, of sending men home from dark and bloody battlefields physically handicapped and psychologically deranged, cannot be reconciled with wisdom, justice, and love. A nation that continues year after year to spend more money on military defense than on programs of social uplift is approaching spiritual death." When combined with his clarion call to resist the draft, this stylish language condemning America helped create a radical tenor. Harding wanted a strong condemnation of the war. King's speech delivered, with reasons clearly ordered and language insightfully chosen.

It was a testament to the rhetorical power of this speech that, whenever Martin Luther King Jr.'s stand on Vietnam was discussed, it was this speech that was referenced, and not his February 25 speech nor his April 15 speech delivered at the United Nations as a part of Spring Mobilization Day. The reaction of the mainstream white press to the speech was overwhelmingly negative. *Time*'s report was typical, except that it combined the story of the Riverside Church speech with that of the Spring Mobilization Day. Of the April 4 speech, its first and, in this case only, direct quotation taken from the speech was that King had called America "the greatest purveyor of violence in the world." Every mainstream white press article included that as the first direct quotation from the speech. Even the *New York Times* story, one of the few written rather dispassionately, quoted the line in its lead paragraph. In the conservatively leaning *Time* magazine, the second reference made to the content of the speech was to say that King had "compared its [America's] use of new weapons in Vietnam to Nazi medical experiments." King had in fact made that analogy, in a single sentence in the middle of a paragraph: "What do they think as we test out our latest weapons on them, just as the Germans tested out new medicine and new tortures in the concentration camps of Europe?" *Time*, *Life*, *Newsweek*, and the *New York Times* all mentioned that evocative comparison in their reports. *Time* concluded its review of the speech by quoting several black leaders who condemned or seemed to condemn King's stand: Ralph Bunche, Whitney Young, Bayard Rustin, and the NAACP. The magazine could thus ominously suggest that King had perhaps "reneged . . . on the entire cause of nonviolent Negro advancement."[6]

Life magazine labeled its editorial "Dr. King's Disservice to His Cause." Besides claiming that King came "close to betraying the cause for which he has worked so long," *Life* charged him with "going off on a tangent." "By characterizing" Vietnam as a colonialist war, *Life* argued, he introduced matters "that have nothing to do with the legitimate battle for equal rights here in America." It approvingly quoted the NAACP's resolution that rejected the "attempt to merge the civil rights movement with the peace movement." *Newsweek* was nearly as condemnatory, but, like *Time*, it criticized him in a straight news article rather than an editorial. *Newsweek* allowed that "King was at his most compelling when he decried the war's drain on domestic poverty programs," but "when he plunged into geopolitics, he seemed to be in over his head." His speech mixed "evangelical passion with simplistic political judgment." "The speech drew standing ovations from King's peace-conscious audience," *Newsweek* duly noted, "but the elders of the civil-rights movement, hawks and doves alike, still thought that King ought to stick to the unfinished business of the Negro revolt—and their reaction, accordingly, was mainly embarrassed silence." An opinion piece by Kenneth Crawford accompanied the "straight" news account. Referring to two unspecified speeches "addressed to Negroes," Crawford reported King as saying that "since the war is taking attention from the civil-rights movement . . . it must be stopped by application of the principles of passive resistance." King had thus "advised Negroes to seek exemption from the draft as conscientious objectors." These speeches were, Crawford believed, "shocking for their demagoguery and reckless distortions of fact." Although he may not have been referring to the Riverside Church speech, the fact that the column ran next to the "news" account of the April 4 address implied that Crawford's criticisms applied to that speech as well. Yet King had not singled out African Americans as qualifying as the only conscientious objectors. Although he did object to the war disproportionately affecting the poor and the black, his call to resist was not specific in regard to race. King had also objected to the war on humanitarian and Christian grounds, but those reasons went unreported in *Newsweek*.

The African American press was no kinder. Carl Rowan's denunciation of King in the pages of the *Reader's Digest* was the most famous. Entitled "Martin Luther King's Tragic Decision," Rowan criticized King for having placed the civil rights movement in jeopardy, for having alienated Lyndon Johnson, whom Rowan believed had been the strongest presidential supporter of civil rights in American history, and for having handed the opponents of civil rights some inflammatory ammunition about King being a communist supporter. Rowan opened his article with many of the same quotations of King's speech found in the white press accounts: that the United States was the greatest purveyor of violence, that it had poisoned the Vietnamese water, that US troops had killed a million Vietnamese civilians, mostly children, that American use of new weapons was akin to the Germans testing new tortures, and that young men should register as conscientious objectors. The article recounted the biography of King and some of the context in which the decision to announce against the war was made. Rowan largely ignored the opening of King's speech, in which King had explained his motives for declaring against the war. As had the representatives of the white press, Rowan reported the negative reactions among black leaders, citing Wilkins, Young, and Rustin, and here insinuating that perhaps King's ego had caused him to reject their advice to stick with civil rights. Emphasizing practical politics, Rowan concluded: "Martin Luther King has alienated many of the Negro's friends and armed the Negro's foes, in both parties, by creating the lasting impression that the Negro is disloyal. By urging Negroes not to respond to the draft or to fight in Vietnam, he has taken a tack that many Americans of all races consider utterly irresponsible."[7]

Ebony's response to the speech was particularly intriguing. In its May issue, which was already on the newsstands as King spoke at Riverside, the magazine had an impressive photo layout of King's retreat in Jamaica the preceding winter. The coverage was positive: the world acclaimed leader had taken a two-month sabbatical in order to plot the next development for the civil rights struggle. In June, however, the magazine had no notable coverage of King's speech. There was, however, an article on Private First Class Ulysses C. Kendall of Chicago, who was an infantryman stationed in Vietnam, with accompanying photographs. Embedded in the story was a single, telling reference to King: "Despite the example set by heavyweight champion Muhammad Ali who refused to take the oath after being drafted and despite the preachings of Stokely Carmichael and Dr. Martin Luther King against any involvement in the Viet Nam war, most Negro youths do what their fathers have done before them—they sign up, go into the forces and, as Department of Defense records can well attest, serve bravely and with honor wherever they are sent." There was no doubt where *Ebony* stood on the issue of Martin Luther King Jr. and the Vietnam War.[8]

The only favorable press coverage came from those outlets that were already antiwar in outlook. The *Christian Century*, for example, wrote that "King speaks for peace." The editorial reversed King's arrangement, beginning with the five governmental actions that he had demanded, and then reporting his reasons for being antiwar. Missing from the article were the more inflammatory comments: America as the greatest purveyor of violence, American soldiers killing a million civilians, and the analogy of America's weapons testing in Vietnam to German concentration camps. The editorial did repeat the image of the autopsy, but within the context of King's reasons for opposing the war. The editorial concluded that "King's plea was a magnificent blend of eloquence and raw fact, of searing denunciation and tender wooing, of political sagacity and Christian insight, of tough realism and infinite compassion."[9]

Martin Luther King Jr.'s "A Time to Break the Silence" certainly moved the already converted. The *New York Times* reported that he received a standing ovation from the crowd of three thousand packed into Riverside Church. He did not, however, succeed in converting those who opposed him or who were afraid that the cause of Vietnam would detract from the movement for civil rights. Yet could any single speech have been effective in that way? King had put the problem eloquently, he had developed a strong rationale for opposing the war, he had made clear proposals for policy, and he had appealed for American empathy for the Vietnamese people. Whether or not the speech was immediately effective in changing people's opinions, it certainly ranks as one of the most eloquent pieces of antiwar discourse as well as one of the most famous.

A Time to Break Silence

April 4, 1967
New York, New York

I come to this magnificent house of worship tonight because my conscience leaves me no other choice. I join you in this meeting because I am in deepest agreement with the aims and work of the organization which has brought us together: Clergy and Laymen Concerned about Vietnam. The recent statements of your executive committee are the sentiments of my own heart, and I found myself in full accord when I read its opening lines: "A time comes when silence is betrayal." And that time has come for us in relation to Vietnam.

The truth of these words is beyond doubt, but the mission to which they call us is a most difficult one. Even when pressed by the demands of inner truth, men do not easily assume the task of opposing their government's policy, especially in time of war. Nor does the human spirit move without great difficulty against all the apathy of conformist thought within one's own bosom and in the surrounding world. Moreover, when the issues at hand seem as perplexed as they often do in the case of this dreadful conflict, we are always on the verge of being mesmerized by uncertainty; but we must move on.

And some of us who have already begun to break the silence of the night have found that the calling to speak is often a vocation of agony, but we must speak. We must speak with all the humility that is appropriate to our limited vision, but we must speak. And we must rejoice as well, for surely this is the first time in our nation's history that a significant number of its religious leaders have chosen to move beyond the prophesying of smooth patriotism to the high grounds of a firm dissent based upon the mandates of conscience and the reading of history. Perhaps a new spirit is rising among us. If it is, let us trace its movements and pray that our own inner being may be sensitive to its guidance, for we are deeply in need of a new way beyond the darkness that seems so close around us.

Over the past two years, as I have moved to break the betrayal of my own silences and to speak from the burnings of my own heart, as I have called for radical departures from the destruction of Vietnam, many persons have questioned me about the wisdom of my path. At the heart of their concerns this query has often loomed large and loud: Why are *you* speaking about the war, Dr. King? Why are *you* joining the voices of dissent? Peace and civil rights don't mix, they say. Aren't you hurting the cause of your people, they ask? And when I hear them, though I often understand the source of their concern, I am nevertheless greatly saddened, for such questions mean that the inquirers have not really known me, my commitment or my calling. Indeed, their questions suggest that they do not know the world in which they live.

In the light of such tragic misunderstandings, I deem it of signal importance to try to state clearly, and I trust concisely, why I believe that the path from Dexter Avenue Baptist Church—the church in Montgomery, Alabama, where I began my pastorate—leads clearly to this sanctuary tonight.

I come to this platform tonight to make a passionate plea to my beloved nation. This speech is not addressed to Hanoi or to the National Liberation Front.[a] It is not addressed to China or to Russia.

Nor is it an attempt to overlook the ambiguity of the total situation and the need for a collective solution to the tragedy of Vietnam. Neither is it an attempt to make North Vietnam or the National Liberation Front paragons of virtue, nor to overlook the role they must play in the successful resolution of the problem. While they both may have justifiable reasons to be suspicious of the good faith of the United States, life and history give eloquent testimony to the fact that conflicts are never resolved without trustful give and take on both sides.

Tonight, however, I wish not to speak with Hanoi and the National Liberation Front, but rather to my fellow Americans, who, with me, bear the greatest responsibility in ending a conflict that has exacted a heavy price on both continents.

a. Hanoi was the capital of North Vietnam. The National Liberation Front was the official name for the South Vietnamese communists (also called Viet Cong) who were fighting against the government of South Vietnam with the support of the communist North Vietnamese.

Importance of Vietnam

Since I am a preacher by trade, I suppose it is not surprising that I have seven major reasons for bringing Vietnam into the field of my moral vision. There is at the outset a very obvious and almost facile connection between the war in Vietnam and the struggle I, and others, have been waging in America. A few years ago there was a shining moment in that struggle. It seemed as if there was a real promise of hope for the poor—both black and white—through the poverty program. There were experiments, hopes, new beginnings. Then came the buildup in Vietnam, and I watched the program broken and eviscerated, as if it were some idle political plaything of a society gone mad on war, and I knew that America would never invest the necessary funds or energies in rehabilitation of its poor so long as adventures like Vietnam continued to draw men and skills and money like some demonic destructive suction tube. So, I was increasingly compelled to see the war as an enemy of the poor and to attack it as such.

Perhaps the more tragic recognition of reality took place when it became clear to me that the war was doing far more than devastating the hopes of the poor at home. It was sending their sons and their brothers and their husbands to fight and to die in extraordinarily high proportions relative to the rest of the population. We were taking the black young men who had been crippled by our society and sending them eight thousand miles away to guarantee liberties in Southeast Asia which they had not found in southwest Georgia and East Harlem. So we have been repeatedly faced with the cruel irony of watching Negro and white boys on TV screens as they kill and die together for a nation that has been unable to seat them together in the same schools. So we watch them in brutal solidarity burning the huts of a poor village, but we realize that they would hardly live on the same block in Detroit. I could not be silent in the face of such cruel manipulation of the poor.

My third reason moves to an even deeper level of awareness, for it grows out of my experience in the ghettoes of the North over the last three years—especially the last three summers. As I have walked among the desperate, rejected, and angry young men, I have told them that Molotov cocktails and rifles would not solve their problems. I have tried to offer them my deepest compassion while maintaining my conviction that social change comes most meaningfully through nonviolent action. But they ask—and rightly so—what about Vietnam? They ask if our own nation wasn't using massive doses of violence to solve its problems, to bring about the changes it wanted. Their questions hit home, and I knew that I could never again raise my voice against the violence of the oppressed in the ghettos without having first spoken clearly to the greatest purveyor of violence in the world today—my own government. For the sake of those boys, for the sake of this government, for the sake of the hundreds of thousands trembling under our violence, I cannot be silent.

For those who ask the question, "Aren't you a civil rights leader?" and thereby mean to exclude me from the movement for peace, I have this further answer. In 1957 when a group of us formed the Southern Christian Leadership Conference, we chose as our motto: "To save the soul of America." We were convinced that we could not limit our vision to certain rights for black people, but instead affirmed the conviction that America would never be free or saved from itself until the descendants of its slaves were loosed completely from the shackles they still wear. In a way we were agreeing with Langston Hughes, that black bard of Harlem, who had written earlier:

> O, yes,
> I say it plain,
> America never was America to me,
> And yet I swear this oath—
> America will be![b]

Now, it should be incandescently clear that no one who has any concern for the integrity and life of America today can ignore the present war. If America's soul becomes totally poisoned, part of the autopsy must read Vietnam. It can never be saved so long as it destroys the deepest hopes of men the world over. So it is that those of us who are yet determined that America *will* be led down the path of protest and dissent, working for the health of our land.

As if the weight of such a commitment to the life and health of America were not enough, another burden of responsibility was placed upon me in 1964; and I cannot forget that the Nobel Prize for Peace was also a commission—a commission to work harder than I had ever worked before for "the brotherhood of man." This is a calling that takes me beyond national allegiances, but even if it were not present I would yet have to live with the meaning of my commitment to the ministry of Jesus Christ. To me the relationship of this ministry to the making of peace is so obvious that I

b. Langston Hughes, "Let America Be America Again."

sometimes marvel at those who ask me why I'm speaking against the war. Could it be that they do not know that the good news was meant for all men—for Communist and capitalist, for their children and ours, for black and for white, for revolutionary and conservative? Have they forgotten that my ministry is in obedience to the one who loved his enemies so fully that he died for them? What then can I say to the Vietcong or to Castro[c] or to Mao[d] as a faithful minister of this one? Can I threaten them with death or must I not share with them my life?

And finally, as I try to explain for you and for myself the road that leads from Montgomery to this place I would have offered all that was most valid if I simply said that I must be true to my conviction that I share with all men the calling to be a son of the living God. Beyond the calling of race or nation or creed is this vocation of sonship and brotherhood, and because I believe that the Father is deeply concerned especially for his suffering and helpless and outcast children, I come tonight to speak for them. This I believe to be the privilege and the burden of all of us who deem ourselves bound by allegiances and loyalties which are broader and deeper than nationalism and which go beyond our nation's self-defined goals and positions. We are called to speak for the weak, for the voiceless, for the victims of our nation and for those it calls "enemy," for no document from human hands can make these humans any less our brothers.

And as I ponder the madness of Vietnam and search within myself for ways to understand and respond in compassion, my mind goes constantly to the people of that peninsula. I speak now not of the soldiers of each side, not of the ideologies of the Liberation Front, not of the junta in Saigon, but simply of the people who have been living under the curse of war for almost three continuous decades now. I think of them, too, because it is clear to me that there will be no meaningful solution there until some attempt is made to know them and hear their broken cries.

They must see Americans as strange liberators. The Vietnamese people proclaimed their own independence in 1945 after a combined French and Japanese occupation and before the Communist revolution in China. They were led by Ho Chi Minh. Even though they quoted the American Declaration of Independence in their own document of freedom, we refused to

c. Fidel Castro (b. 1926): Communist leader of Cuba since 1959.
d. Mao Tse Tung (1893–1976): Communist leader of the People's Republic of China from 1949 until his death.

recognize them. Instead, we decided to support France in its reconquest of her former colony.

Our government felt then that the Vietnamese people were not ready for independence, and we again fell victim to the deadly Western arrogance that has poisoned the international atmosphere for so long. With that tragic decision we rejected a revolutionary government seeking self-determination and a government that had been established not by China (for whom the Vietnamese have no great love) but by clearly indigenous forces that included some communists. For the peasants this new government meant real land reform, one of the most important needs in their lives.

For nine years following 1945 we denied the people of Vietnam the right of independence. For nine years we vigorously supported the French in their abortive effort to recolonize Vietnam.

Before the end of the war we were meeting eighty percent of the French war costs. Even before the French were defeated at Dien Bien Phu,[e] they began to despair of their reckless action, but we did not. We encouraged them with our huge financial and military supplies to continue the war even after they had lost the will. Soon we would be paying almost the full costs of this tragic attempt at recolonization.

After the French were defeated, it looked as if independence and land reform would come again through the Geneva Agreement.[f] But instead there came the United States, determined that Ho should not unify the temporarily divided nation, and the peasants watched again as we supported one of the most vicious modern dictators, our chosen man, Premier Diem.[g] The peasants watched and cringed as Diem ruthlessly rooted out all opposition, supported their extortionist landlords, and refused even to discuss reunification with the North. The peasants watched as all this was presided over by U.S. influence and then by increasing numbers of U.S. troops who came to help quell the insurgency that Diem's methods had aroused. When Diem

---

e. Dien Bien Phu: A climactic battle in spring 1954 in which the Vietnamese Communist forces (Viet Minh) defeated the French. Shortly after, the French and Viet Minh signed the 1954 Geneva Accords.

f. The Geneva agreement, or Geneva Accords, instituted a cease-fire between the Viet Minh and French. The accords temporarily divided Vietnam into two halves, designed to be reunified after free elections decided who would govern. Subsequent referenda were controversial, and the country was not reunified until 1975, after the Vietnam War.

g. Ngo Dinh Diem (1901–1963): Prime minister and later president of South Vietnam from 1954 until his assassination during a 1963 coup d'etat. Diem's rule was widely considered corrupt and nepotistic, and for the ruthless means he employed to stamp out any opposition.

was overthrown they may have been happy, but the long line of military dictators seemed to offer no real change—especially in terms of their need for land and peace.

The only change came from America, as we increased our troop commitments in support of governments which were singularly corrupt, inept, and without popular support. All the while the people read our leaflets and received the regular promises of peace and democracy—and land reform. Now they languish under our bombs and consider us—not their fellow Vietnamese—the real enemy. They move sadly and apathetically as we herd them off the land of their fathers into concentration camps where minimal social needs are rarely met. They know they must move on or be destroyed by our bombs. So they go—primarily women and children and the aged.

They watch as we poison their water, as we kill a million acres of their crops. They must weep as the bulldozers roar through their areas preparing to destroy the precious trees. They wander into the hospitals with at least twenty casualties from American firepower for one "Vietcong"-inflicted injury. So far we may have killed a million of them—mostly children. They wander into the towns and see thousands of the children, homeless, without clothes, running in packs on the streets like animals. They see the children degraded by our soldiers as they beg for food. They see the children selling their sisters to our soldiers, soliciting for their mothers.

What do the peasants think as we ally ourselves with the landlords and as we refuse to put any action into our many words concerning land reform? What do they think as we test out our latest weapons on them, just as the Germans tested out new medicine and new tortures in the concentration camps of Europe? Where are the roots of the independent Vietnam we claim to be building? Is it among these voiceless ones?

We have destroyed their two most cherished institutions: the family and the village. We have destroyed their land and their crops. We have cooperated in the crushing of the nation's only noncommunist revolutionary political force—the unified Buddhist Church. We have supported the enemies of the peasants of Saigon. We have corrupted their women and children and killed their men. What liberators!

Now there is little left to build on—save bitterness. Soon the only solid physical foundations remaining will be found at our military bases and in the concrete of the concentration camps we call fortified hamlets. The peasants may well wonder if we plan to build our new Vietnam on such grounds as these. Could we blame them for such thoughts? We must speak for them and raise the questions they cannot raise. These too are our brothers.

Perhaps a more difficult but no less necessary task is to speak for those who have been designated as our enemies. What of the National Liberation Front, that strangely anonymous group we call "VC" or "communists"? What must they think of the United States of America when they realize that we permitted the repression and cruelty of Diem, which helped to bring them into being as a resistance group in the South? What do they think of our condoning the violence which led to their own taking up of arms? How can they believe in our integrity when now we speak of "aggression from the North" as if there were nothing more essential to the war? How can they trust us when now we charge them with violence after the murderous reign of Diem and charge them with violence while we pour every new weapon of death into their land? Surely we must understand their feelings, even if we do not condone their actions. Surely we must see that the men we supported pressed them to their violence. Surely we must see that our own computerized plans of destruction simply dwarf their greatest acts.

How do they judge us when our officials know that their membership is less than twenty-five percent Communist, and yet insist on giving them the blanket name? What must they be thinking when they know that we are aware of their control of major sections of Vietnam, and yet we appear ready to allow national elections in which this highly organized political parallel government will not have a part? They ask how we can speak of free elections when the Saigon press is censored and controlled by the military junta. And they are surely right to wonder what kind of new government we plan to help form without them—the only party in real touch with the peasants. They question our political goals and they deny the reality of a peace settlement from which they will be excluded. Their questions are frighteningly relevant. Is our nation planning to build on political myth again, and then shore it up upon the power of new violence?

Here is the true meaning and value of compassion and nonviolence, when it helps us to see the enemy's point of view, to hear his questions, to know his assessment of ourselves. For from his view we may indeed see the basic weaknesses of our own condition, and if we are mature, we may learn and grow and profit from the wisdom of the brothers who are called the opposition.

So, too, with Hanoi. In the north, where our bombs now pummel the land, and our mines endanger the waterways, we are met by a deep but understandable mistrust. To speak for them is to explain this lack of confidence in Western words, and especially their distrust of American intentions now. In Hanoi are the men who led the nation to independence against the Japanese and the French, the men who sought membership in the French Commonwealth and were betrayed by the weakness of Paris and the willfulness of the colonial armies. It was they who led a second struggle against French domination at tremendous costs, and then were persuaded to give up the land they controlled between the thirteenth and seventeenth parallel as a temporary measure at Geneva. After 1954 they watched us conspire with Diem to prevent elections which could have surely brought Ho Chi Minh to power over a united Vietnam, and they realized they had been betrayed again.

When we ask why they do not leap to negotiate, these things must be remembered. Also, it must be clear that the leaders of Hanoi considered the presence of American troops in support of the Diem regime to have been the initial military breach of the Geneva Agreement concerning foreign troops. They remind us that they did not begin to send troops in large numbers and even supplies into the South until American forces had moved into the tens of thousands.

Hanoi remembers how our leaders refused to tell us the truth about the earlier North Vietnamese overtures for peace, how the president claimed that none existed when they had clearly been made. Ho Chi Minh has watched as America has spoken of peace and built up its forces, and now he has surely heard the increasing international rumors of American plans for an invasion of the North. He knows the bombing and shelling and mining we are doing are part of traditional pre-invasion strategy. Perhaps only his sense of humor and of irony can save him when he hears the most powerful nation of the world speaking of aggression as it drops thousands of bombs on a poor, weak nation more than eight thousand miles away from its shores. At this point I should make it clear that while I have tried in these last few minutes to give a voice to the voiceless in Vietnam and to understand the arguments of those who are called "enemy," I am as deeply concerned about our own troops there as anything else. For it occurs to me that what we are submitting them to in Vietnam is not simply the brutalizing process that goes on in any war where armies face each other and seek to destroy. We are adding cynicism to the process of death, for they must know after a short period there that none of the things we claim to be fighting for are really involved. Before long they must know that their government has sent them into a struggle among Vietnamese, and the more sophisticated surely realize that we are on the side of the wealthy, and the secure, while we create a hell for the poor.

Somehow this madness must cease. We must stop now. I speak as a child of God and brother to the suffering poor of Vietnam. I speak for those whose land is being laid waste, whose homes are being destroyed, whose culture is being subverted. I speak for the poor of America who are paying the double price of smashed hopes at home, and death and corruption in Vietnam. I speak as a citizen of the world, for the world as it stands aghast at the path we have taken. I speak as one who loves America, to the leaders of our own nation: The great initiative in this war is ours. The initiative to stop it must be ours.

This is the message of the great Buddhist leaders of Vietnam. Recently one of them wrote these words: *Each day the war goes on the hatred increases in the heart of the Vietnamese and in the hearts of those of humanitarian instinct. The Americans are forcing even their friends into becoming their enemies. It is curious that the Americans, who calculate so carefully on the possibilities of military victory, do not realize that in the process they are incurring deep psychological and political defeat. The image of America will never again be the image of revolution, freedom, and democracy, but the image of violence and militarism.*

If we continue, there will be no doubt in my mind and in the mind of the world that we have no honorable intentions in Vietnam. If we do not stop our war against the people of Vietnam immediately, the world will be left with no other alternative than to see this as some horrible, clumsy, and deadly game we have decided to play.

The world now demands a maturity of America that we may not be able to achieve. It demands that we admit that we have been wrong from the beginning of our adventure in Vietnam, that we have been detrimental to the life of the Vietnamese people. The situation is one in which we must be ready to turn sharply from our present ways.

In order to atone for our sins and errors in Vietnam, we should take the initiative in bringing a halt to this tragic war. I would like to suggest five concrete things that our government should do immediately to begin the long and difficult process of extricating ourselves from this nightmarish conflict:

1. *End all bombing in North and South Vietnam.*
2. *Declare a unilateral cease-fire in the hope that such action will create the atmosphere for negotiation.*

3. *Take immediate steps to prevent other battlegrounds in Southeast Asia by curtailing our military buildup in Thailand and our interference in Laos.*
4. *Realistically accept the fact that the National Liberation Front has substantial support in South Vietnam and must thereby play a role in any meaningful negotiations and any future Vietnam government.*
5. *Set a date that we will remove all foreign troops from Vietnam in accordance with the 1954 Geneva Agreement.*

Part of our ongoing commitment might well express itself in an offer to grant asylum to any Vietnamese who fears for his life under a new regime which included the Liberation Front. Then we must make what reparations we can for the damage we have done. We must provide the medical aid that is badly needed, making it available in this country, if necessary.

Protesting the War

Meanwhile, we in the churches and synagogues have a continuing task while we urge our government to disengage itself from a disgraceful commitment. We must continue to raise our voices and our lives if our nation persists in its perverse ways in Vietnam. We must be prepared to match actions with words by seeking out every creative method of protest possible.

As we counsel young men concerning military service, we must clarify for them our nation's role in Vietnam and challenge them with the alternative of conscientious objection. I am pleased to say that this is a path now chosen by more than seventy students at my own alma mater, Morehouse College, and I recommend it to all who find the American course in Vietnam a dishonorable and unjust one. Moreover, I would encourage all ministers of draft age to give up their ministerial exemptions and seek status as conscientious objectors. These are the times for real choices and not false ones. We are at the moment when our lives must be placed on the line if our nation is to survive its own folly. Every man of humane convictions must decide on the protest that best suits his convictions, but we must all protest.

There is something seductively tempting about stopping there and sending us all off on what in some circles has become a popular crusade against the war in Vietnam. I say we must enter that struggle, but I wish to go on now to say something even more disturbing. The war in Vietnam is but a symptom of a far deeper malady within the American spirit, and if we ignore this sobering reality we will find ourselves organizing clergy and laymen-concerned committees for the next generation. They will be concerned about Guatemala and Peru. They will be concerned about Thailand and Cambodia. They will be concerned about Mozambique and South Africa. We will be marching for these and a dozen other names and attending rallies without end, unless there is a significant and profound change in American life and policy. Such thoughts take us beyond Vietnam, but not beyond our calling as sons of the living God.

In 1957, a sensitive American official overseas said that it seemed to him that our nation was on the wrong side of a world revolution. During the past ten years, we have seen emerge a pattern of suppression which has now justified the presence of U.S. military "advisors" in Venezuela. This need to maintain social stability for our investments accounts for the counter-revolutionary action of American forces in Guatemala. It tells why American helicopters are being used against guerrillas in Colombia and why American napalm and Green Beret forces have already been active against rebels in Peru. It is with such activity in mind that the words of the late John F. Kennedy come back to haunt us. Five years ago he said, "Those who make peaceful revolution impossible will make violent revolution inevitable."[h]

Increasingly, by choice or by accident, this is the role our nation has taken—the role of those who make peaceful revolution impossible by refusing to give up the privileges and the pleasures that come from the immense profits of overseas investment.

I am convinced that if we are to get on the right side of the world revolution, we as a nation must undergo a radical revolution of values. We must rapidly begin the shift from a "thing-oriented" society to a "person-oriented" society. When machines and computers, profit motives and property rights, are considered more important than people, the giant triplets of racism, extreme materialism, and militarism are incapable of being conquered.

A true revolution of values will soon cause us to question the fairness and justice of many of our past and present policies. On the one hand, we are called to play the Good Samaritan on life's roadside, but that will be only an initial act. One day we must come to see that the whole Jericho Road must be transformed so that men and women will not be constantly beaten and robbed as they make their journey on life's highway. True compassion is more than flinging a coin to a beggar. It comes to see that an edifice which

h. John F. Kennedy, "Address on the First Anniversary of the Alliance for Progress," 13 Mar. 1962.

produces beggars needs restructuring. A true revolution of values will soon look uneasily on the glaring contrast of poverty and wealth. With righteous indignation, it will look across the seas and see individual capitalists of the West investing huge sums of money in Asia, Africa, and South America, only to take the profits out with no concern for the social betterment of the countries, and say, "This is not just." It will look at our alliance with the landed gentry of Latin America and say, "This is not just." The Western arrogance of feeling that it has everything to teach others and nothing to learn from them is not just. A true revolution of values will lay hand on the world order and say of war, "This way of settling differences is not just." This business of burning human beings with napalm, of filling our nation's homes with orphans and widows, of injecting poisonous drugs of hate into the veins of peoples normally humane, of sending men home from dark and bloody battlefields physically handicapped and psychologically deranged, cannot be reconciled with wisdom, justice, and love. A nation that continues year after year to spend more money on military defense than on programs of social uplift is approaching spiritual death.

America, the richest and most powerful nation in the world, can well lead the way in this revolution of values. There is nothing except a tragic death wish to prevent us from reordering our priorities so that the pursuit of peace will take precedence over the pursuit of war. There is nothing to keep us from molding a recalcitrant status quo with bruised hands until we have fashioned it into a brotherhood.

This kind of positive revolution of values is our best defense against communism. War is not the answer. Communism will never be defeated by the use of atomic bombs or nuclear weapons. Let us not join those who shout war and, through their misguided passions, urge the United States to relinquish its participation in the United Nations. These are days which demand wise restraint and calm reasonableness. We must not engage in a negative anticommunism, but rather in a positive thrust for democracy, realizing that our greatest defense against communism is to take offensive action in behalf of justice. We must with positive action seek to remove those conditions of poverty, insecurity, and injustice, which are the fertile soil in which the seed of communism grows and develops.

The People Are Important

These are revolutionary times. All over the globe men are revolting against old systems of exploitation and oppression, and out of the wounds of a frail world, new systems of justice and equality are being born. The shirtless and barefoot people of the land are rising up as never before. The people who sat in darkness have seen a great light. We in the West must support these revolutions. It is a sad fact that, because of comfort, complacency, a morbid fear of communism, and our proneness to adjust to injustice, the Western nations that initiated so much of the revolutionary spirit of the modern world have now become the arch anti-revolutionaries. This has driven many to feel that only Marxism has a revolutionary spirit. Therefore, communism is a judgment against our failure to make democracy real and follow through on the revolutions that we initiated. Our only hope today lies in our ability to recapture the revolutionary spirit and go out into a sometimes hostile world declaring eternal hostility to poverty, racism, and militarism. With this powerful commitment we shall boldly challenge the status quo and unjust mores, and thereby speed the day when "every valley shall be exalted, and every mountain and hill shall be made low, and the crooked shall be made straight, and the rough places plain."[i]

A genuine revolution of values means in the final analysis that our loyalties must become ecumenical rather than sectional. Every nation must now develop an overriding loyalty to mankind as a whole in order to preserve the best in their individual societies.

This call for a world-wide fellowship that lifts neighborly concern beyond one's tribe, race, class, and nation is in reality a call for an all-embracing and unconditional love for all mankind. This oft misunderstood, this oft misinterpreted concept—so readily dismissed by the Nietzsches[j] of the world as a weak and cowardly force—has now become an absolute necessity for the survival of man. When I speak of love I am not speaking of some sentimental and weak response. I am not speaking of that force which is just emotional bosh. I am speaking of that force which all of the great religions have seen as the supreme unifying principle of life. Love is somehow the key that unlocks the door which leads to ultimate reality. This Hindu-Muslim-Christian-Jewish-Buddhist belief about ultimate reality is beautifully summed up in the first epistle of Saint John: "Let us love one another, for love is God. And every one that loveth is born of God and knoweth God. He that loveth not knoweth not

i. Isaiah 40:4. King also references this passage in "I Have a Dream."

j. Friedrich Nietzsche (1844–1900): Noted German philosopher identified with nihilism and existentialism.

God, for God is love. If we love one another, God dwelleth in us and his love is perfected in us."[k]

Let us hope that this spirit will become the order of the day. We can no longer afford to worship the god of hate or bow before the altar of retaliation. The oceans of history are made turbulent by the ever-rising tides of hate. And history is cluttered with the wreckage of nations and individuals that pursued this self-defeating path of hate. As Arnold Toynbee says: "Love is the ultimate force that makes for the saving choice of life and good against the damning choice of death and evil. Therefore the first hope in our inventory must be the hope that love is going to have the last word."[l]

We are now faced with the fact that tomorrow is today. We are confronted with the fierce urgency of now. In this unfolding conundrum of life and history, there is such a thing as being too late. Procrastination is still the thief of time. Life often leaves us standing bare, naked, and dejected with a lost opportunity. The "tide in the affairs of men"[m] does not remain at flood; it ebbs. We may cry out desperately for time to pause in her passage, but time is adamant to every plea and rushes on. Over the bleached bones and jumbled residues of numerous civilizations are written the pathetic words, "Too late." There is an invisible book of life that faithfully records our vigilance or our neglect. "The moving finger writes, and having writ moves on. . . ."[n] We still have a choice today; nonviolent coexistence or violent co-annihilation.

We must move past indecision to action. We must find new ways to speak for peace in Vietnam and justice throughout the developing world, a world that borders on our doors. If we do not act, we shall surely be dragged down the long, dark, and shameful corridors of time reserved for those who possess power without compassion, might without morality, and strength without sight.

Now let us begin. Now let us rededicate ourselves to the long and bitter—but beautiful—struggle for a new world. This is the calling of the sons of God, and our brothers wait eagerly for our response. Shall we say the odds are too great? Shall we tell them the struggle is too hard? Will our message be that the forces of American life militate against their arrival as full men, and we send our deepest regrets? Or will there be another message—of

k. 1 John 4:7–8, 12. King also cites these passages from the First Letter of John in his Nobel Peace Prize acceptance speech.

l. Arnold Toynbee (1889–1975): British historian and author of *A Study of History*. King also references this quotation in his Nobel Peace Prize acceptance speech.

m. Shakespeare, *Julius Caesar* 4:3.

n. Omar Khayyam, *Rubaiyat of Omar Khayyam*, quatrain 71.

longing, of hope, of solidarity with their yearnings, of commitment to their cause, whatever the cost? The choice is ours, and though we might prefer it otherwise, we must choose in this crucial moment of human history.

As that noble bard of yesterday, James Russell Lowell, eloquently stated:

Once to every man and nation comes a moment to decide,
In the strife of Truth and Falsehood, for the good or evil side;
Some great cause, God's new Messiah offering each the bloom or blight,
And the choice goes by forever 'twixt that darkness and that light.
Though the cause of evil prosper, yet 'tis truth alone is strong
Though her portions be the scaffold, and upon the throne be wrong
Yet that scaffold sways the future, and behind the dim unknown
Standeth God within the shadow, keeping watch above his own.[o]

o. James Russell Lowell, "The Present Crisis."

Shirley Anita St. Hill Chisholm

It Is Time to Reassess Our National Priorities

As the first African American woman to be elected to Congress and, at the time, only one of nine African American members of Congress, Shirley Chisholm became a national celebrity overnight. Her office was deluged with calls from African American citizens from all corners of the country. She was, furthermore, in constant demand as a speaker, especially since her sharp and often stinging oratory was considered the sine qua non of her success in politics. Although already a presence on the national stage, a spotlight shone upon Chisholm when she ran for the Democratic nomination for president in 1972. No one, including Chisholm, expected that she would win the nomination, and one of Chisholm's largest obstacles was persuading people that her candidacy was not merely symbolic.[1] She wanted to prove that she could poll votes in the state primaries in which she intended to run. Her candidacy would also affect the chances of the white male Democrats she was running against, such as John Lindsay, Edmund Muskie, and George McGovern, whose campaign she ultimately supported. Although her particular strength could be seen as coalescing African American voters, Chisholm focused on issues associated with her gender more than with her race.[2] Chisholm often stated that being a female created more difficulties in her career than being African American.[3]

Shirley Chisholm was born in Brooklyn, the daughter of Charles St. Hill and Ruby Seale, who had come to New York separately from the British island of Barbados. Her father, an unskilled laborer, and her mother, a seamstress, made too little money during the 1920s to ensure the family's success. Her mother took Shirley, then three years old, and her two younger sisters to live with their grandmother in Barbados, where they remained for seven years. Chisholm credits her facility with the spoken and written word to the strict, British primary education she received in Barbados.[4]

In 1934, the St. Hills brought Shirley and her sisters back to the Brownsville neighborhood of Brooklyn, where they lived in an unheated, cold-water flat. Shirley idolized her father, a handsome, intelligent man who was an "omnivorous reader" and a devotee of Marcus Garvey, the black separatist from Jamaica.[5] In Brownsville, most of Chisholm's neighbors and friends were white and Jewish. When the family moved to Brooklyn's Bedford-Stuyvesant district, half of the population was black. There Shirley was exposed to racial slurs derogating African Americans and Jews that she had not experienced in Brownsville.[6] She distinguished herself at Girls' High School in Brooklyn and was offered scholarships at Vassar and Oberlin. Unable to afford room and board at these institutions, she attended Brooklyn College, where she majored in sociology, yet planned a career in teaching.[7] A successful student, she joined the recently inaugurated Harriet Tubman Society for African American students and also started an African American sorority. The Tubman Society undertook to expose the discriminatory practices of the all white student clubs, including the white sororities. The Brooklyn College Debating Society became the activity group she most enjoyed, particularly when the debates dealt with issues of discrimination and prejudice.[8] After graduating cum laude, Shirley landed a job working at a child-care center in Harlem and started on a master's degree in early childhood education at Columbia University. She would ultimately become the director of a private nursery school and then of a large child-care center.[9]

After learning that her fiancé had a wife in his native Jamaica and was involved in an "immigration fraud racket," Shirley was reunited with an old friend from college, another Jamaican, Conrad Chisholm, a private detective, whom she married. She had been active in organizations such as the Urban League and NAACP since college and became interested in local Brooklyn politics, which had been controlled by an ineffectual white political machine. She ultimately ran for the state assembly and won, the only African American woman then in the legislature and only the second to serve in the history of New York.[10]

In 1968, Chisholm ran for Congress from the twelfth congressional district, which had been redrawn to incorporate the predominantly African American and Puerto Rican Bedford-Stuyvesant area. The reapportionment plan was intended to enable a nonwhite to win the congressional seat from the previously gerrymandered district. Although the Democratic party leaders in Brooklyn worried about Chisholm's outspoken independence and tacitly supported the candidacy of state senator William Thompson, they did not openly endorse either candidate in the primaries. Chisholm devised the slogan "Fighting Shirley Chisholm—Unbought and Unbossed" and ran on it. She won the nomination and faced James Farmer, one of the founders and past chairman of the Congress of Racial Equality (CORE), in the general election. Farmer, a liberal who did not support the Nixon/Agnew ticket, ran as a Republican. In her autobiography, Chisholm criticized Farmer for running a campaign that emphasized gender—"He toured the district with sound trucks manned by young dudes with Afros, beating tom-toms: the big, black male image" and claimed in printed campaign material that his constituents needed a "strong male image and "a man's voice" in Congress.[11] Although Farmer enjoyed a high national profile as a civil rights leader, Chisholm had a number of advantages in the campaign. She could fluently address the Puerto Rican residents of Bedford-Stuyvesant in Spanish, their native language. She was a Brooklyn native, while Farmer, who lived in Manhattan, had merely rented an apartment in Brooklyn. Equally important was the fact that registered female voters outnumbered registered males by 2.5 to 1 in the newly redrawn twelfth district. Chisholm came to realize that Farmer's gender, which he had attempted to exploit in the campaign, was in fact "his Achilles heel."[12] She won election by a two-and-a-half-to-one margin.[13]

Yet another contest waited for Chisholm in Washington. Party leaders ignored her request for a seat on the Education Committee and appointed her to the House Farm and Agriculture Committee and the Subcommittee on Forestry and Rural Villages. Chisholm courageously lodged an objection with the committee of Democrats that had made the appointment, saying acerbically that "apparently all they know here in Washington about Brooklyn is that a tree grew there."[14] One senior Democrat told her that she had "committed political suicide," but she did succeed in having her committee assignment changed to veterans' affairs. Not content with this first foray against the House establishment, Chisholm volubly criticized the seniority system in Congress, which on the Democratic side bestowed substantial legislative control to the long-serving Southern white Democratic congressmen.[15] Chisholm's congressional career of seven terms spanned from 1968 to 1983. Upon her retirement, she accepted an endowed chair at Mount Holyoke

College and campaigned for Jesse Jackson in the presidential campaigns of 1984 and 1988.[16] She passed away on January 1, 2005.

Chisholm spoke with great earnestness and with what Charlayne Hunter aptly described as "nettling candor."[17] Her quickly paced, unhesitant, forceful delivery was also characterized by a slight lisp and the remnants of a Barbados accent that had fused with a Brooklyn accent. Chisholm, who enjoyed music and dancing, moved her slim five-foot-four frame dynamically to the cadence of her words.[18] Adding to her delivery were her straight posture and well-orchestrated facial expressions and gestures. She emphasized the most imperative of her declarations by pointing her index finger upward or outward toward her audience. Remembering her debates with her congressional opponent James Farmer, Chisholm reflected that, while Farmer might have expected a schoolteacher, he got something much different: "When I get on the platform," said Chisholm, "I am transformed; I have even been called Messianic!"[19]

Chisholm's maiden speech to Congress was no less of an auspicious beginning to her career than had been her committee assignment objections. It was one of many antiwar speeches delivered by House Democrats on the floor that day in a sustained oratorical volley that lasted for four hours. Outside was a demonstration by several hundred women marching to the Capitol, many dressed in black and carrying suspended black balloons in what the *New York Times* described as the "first sizeable demonstration since President Nixon's inauguration."[20] Chisholm's speech, although short, minced no words about the stark contrast between the money spent on defense and that spent on social programs, and between what Richard Nixon had said about the need for educational funding and what, as president, he was doing for education. It was a classic "guns or butter" speech that sounded a theme often heard in anti–Vietnam War rhetoric of that era. Chisholm began with two representative anecdotes: the president's support for a nine-billion-dollar missile-defense system, and the reduction in the Washington, DC, Head Start program, meant to improve educational opportunity for poor, disadvantaged, and minority children.

Although the speech has the force of an invective, it achieves restraint by being closely reasoned and carefully supported with examples, statistics, and quotations—precisely what one would expect from a woman skilled in the rapier-like thrusts of debate. Her target is the new president and his administration. She says, perhaps with only feigned optimism, that she had hoped for a different course than the one the president was pursuing. As she later notes, the new president had succeeded Lyndon Johnson, who had decided not to run for reelection because of the Vietnam War. While Nixon had spoken earlier of the need for urban renewal and the folly of reducing the education budget, his words had not been followed by his actions. She quotes Maurice Stans, the secretary of commerce, as saying that stopping inflation made it necessary to delay "major social objectives," and the secretary of health, education and welfare, Robert Finch, as saying that the war in Vietnam prevented the administration from spending the needed funding for education. In both instances, the credibility of her argument is enhanced by the reluctant witness principle, that is, using her opponents' own statements against them. She then rebuffs the administration's philosophy with a statement of a fellow congresswoman to express the alternative view that "Unless we can meet the crisis in education, we really can't afford the war."

In contrast to the temporizing of Secretaries Stans and Finch, Secretary of Defense Melvin Laird had recently spoken to the Senate about the need for what Chisholm describes as the "antiballistic missile insanity," and of the likelihood that the nation would remain involved in Vietnam for at least two more years. Chisholm's response is explosive: "Two more years. Two more years of hunger for Americans, of death for our best young men, of children here at home suffering the lifelong handicap of not having a good education when they are young. . . . Two more years of too little being done to fight our greatest enemies—poverty, prejudice and neglect—here in our own country. . . . It must stop this year—now." The accumulated force created by the repetition of "two more years" adds to the clarity and decisiveness of her position. As a debater, Chisholm understood the importance of creating "clash" between her arguments and those of her opponents, both through her declarations and through her evidence.

Chisholm employs similar arguments of contrast throughout the speech. She compares, for example, the billions spent on "impractical, inefficient, unsatisfactory, even worthless" defense programs, which had been subjected to little government oversight, with the Jobs Corps and its miniscule budget that had been "mercilessly exposed and criticized." Another organization, Pride Inc., run by young African American men with the help of a million-dollar federal grant, had been assigned six auditors from the General Accounting Office, while only five auditors had been assigned to investigate all the negotiated contracts of the Department of Defense.[21] As with America's current wars in Iraq and Afghanistan, the massive expenditures for the

Vietnam War gave liberal critics such as Chisholm an opportunity to take aim at a government focused on creating freedom abroad while hypocritically allowing "poverty and racism" in the United States. Like Iraq, and to a lesser extent Afghanistan, Vietnam was seen by critics such as Chisholm as "unnecessary," an "optional" war. The necessary war lay at home in places such as inner-city slums, which, she argues, were built through "prejudice and hatred." Chisholm, the practiced debater, documents this assertion by citing the Kerner Commission report, which she said her opponents were unwilling to accept.

Although early in the speech Chisholm speaks of herself as "a teacher, and as a woman," who therefore has special sympathy for the children who are denied the benefits of the Head Start program, she also later denies that she is pacifist, a position that might weaken her ethos. She repeats the point in her autobiography: "I am not a pacifist. Our country must be ready to protect itself when necessary, and its citizens must be ready to give their lives for it, in a just and unavoidable conflict."[22] It would have been somewhat paradoxical that a woman whose slogan was "Fighting Shirley Chisholm" to also declare herself to be a pacifist.[23] She is not opposed to war in the abstract, but adamantly criticizes the United States' involvement in the Vietnam War in particular. Although she says she has many reasons for opposing the Vietnam War, the one she emphasizes in this speech is the need for the resources to be spent at home.

Chisholm's conclusion powerfully expresses the logical inference of her carefully presented evidence and argument: that the administration has made the Vietnam War its priority to the exclusion of the essential war on poverty and racism that must be fought at home. "Our children, our jobless men, our deprived, rejected and starving fellow citizens must come first," she tells Congress. Because redressing poverty is our first priority, she vows to vote against all defense appropriations until the nation uses "its strength, its tremendous resources, for people and peace, not for profits and war." The direct beneficiaries of war are defense contractors who would undertake programs such as the nine billion dollar antiballistic missile initiative that President Nixon supported. Chisholm reminds the audience of the magnitude of the imbalance of defense spending, which saps two thirds of all federal tax receipts. In all, it was difficult to deny the logic of Chisholm's crisply articulated conclusion: While President Calvin Coolidge had said that the "'business of America is business,' . . . [at] this time, gentlemen, the business of America is war, and it is time for a change."

Lester Thonssen, who anthologized Chisholm's speech in the 1968–69 volume *Representative American Speeches*, noted that it was one of two celebrated maiden speeches of 1969, the other being an impassioned plea to end violence in Northern Ireland delivered by twenty-one-year old-Bernadette Devlin in the House of Commons.[24] Chisholm, who earlier expressed doubt about how much a freshman representative to Congress could accomplish, proved not only that her voice was equal in every way to those of her more senior colleagues, but that she would be heard, not just in Congress, but across the nation.[25]

It Is Time to Reassess Our National Priorities

March 26, 1969
Washington, DC

Mr. Speaker, on the same day President Nixon announced he had decided the United States will not be safe unless we start to build a defense system against missiles, the Head Start program[a] in the District of Columbia was cut back for the lack of money.

As a teacher, and as a woman, I do not think I will ever understand what kind of values can be involved in spending $9 billion—and more, I am sure—on elaborate, unnecessary, and impractical weapons when several thousand disadvantaged children in the nation's capital get nothing.

When the new administration took office, I was one of the many Americans who hoped it would mean that our country would benefit from the fresh perspectives, the new ideas, the different priorities of a leader who had no part in the mistakes of the past. Mr. Nixon had said things like this. "If our cities are to be livable for the next generation, we can delay no longer in launching new approaches to the problems that beset them and to the tensions that tear them apart." And he said, "When you cut expenditures for education, what you are doing is shortchanging the American future."

But frankly, I have never cared too much what people say. What I am interested in is what they do. We have waited to see what the new administration is going to do. The pattern is now becoming clear. Apparently launching those new programs can be delayed for a while, after all. It seems we have to get some missiles launched first. Recently the new secretary of

a. Federal program begun in 1965 to provide educational and health services to low-income preschool children. A major feature of the program is mandatory parental involvement.

commerce spelled it out. The secretary, Mr. Stans,[b] told a reporter that the new administration is "pretty well agreed it must take time out from major social objectives" until it can stop inflation.

The new secretary of health, education, and welfare, Robert Finch,[c] came to the Hill to tell the House Education and Labor Committee that he thinks we should spend more on education, particularly in city schools. But, he said, unfortunately we cannot "afford" to, until we have reached some kind of honorable solution to the Vietnam War. I was glad to read that the distinguished Member from Oregon [Mrs. Green] asked Mr. Finch this: "With the crisis we have in education, and the crisis in our cities, can we wait to settle the war? Shouldn't it be the other way around? Unless we can meet the crisis in education, we really can't afford the war."

Secretary of Defense Melvin Laird[d] came to Capitol Hill, too. His mission was to sell the antiballistic missile insanity to the Senate. He was asked what the new administration is doing about the war. To hear him, one would have thought it was 1968, that the former secretary of state[e] was defending the former policies, that nothing had ever happened, a president had never decided not to run because he knew the nation would reject him in despair over this tragic war we have blundered into. Mr. Laird talked of being prepared to spend at least two more years in Vietnam.

Two more years. Two more years of hunger for Americans, of death for our best young men, of children here at home suffering the lifelong handicap of not having a good education when they are young. Two more years of high taxes collected to feed the cancerous growth of a Defense Department budget that now consumes two-thirds of our federal income.

Two more years of too little being done to fight our greatest enemies—poverty, prejudice, and neglect—here in our own country. Two more years of fantastic waste in the Defense Department and of penny pinching on social programs. Our country cannot survive two more years, or four, of these kinds of policies. It must stop this year—now.

b. Maurice Stans (1908–1998): Secretary of commerce for President Nixon from 1969 to 1972.

c. Robert Finch (1925–1995) : served as campaign manager for Richard Nixon's 1960 presidential campaign, as lieutenant governor of California under Ronald Reagan from 1967 to 1969, as secretary of health, education and welfare under President Nixon from 1969 to 1970, and from 1970 to 1973 was on the White House staff as counselor to the president.

d. Melvin Laird (b. 1922): Republican representative from 1952 to 1969; secretary of defense for President Nixon from 1969 to 1973.

e. Refers to Dean Rusk, secretary of state under Lyndon Johnson, and closely connected with defending the war in Vietnam.

Now, I am not a pacifist. I am deeply, unalterably opposed to this war in Vietnam. Apart from all other considerations—and they are many—the main fact is that we cannot squander the lives, the money, the energy that we need desperately here, in our cities, in our schools.

I wonder whether we cannot reverse our whole approach to spending. For years, we have given the military, the defense industry, a blank check. New weapons systems are dreamed up, billions are spent, and many times they are found to be impractical, inefficient, unsatisfactory, even worthless. What do we do then? We spend more money on them. But with social programs, what do we do? Take the Job Corps. Its failure has been mercilessly exposed and criticized. If it had been a military research and development project, they would have been covered up or explained away, and Congress would have been ready to pour more billions after those that had been wasted on it.

The case of Pride, Inc., is interesting. This vigorous, successful black organization here in Washington, conceived and built by young, inner-city men, has been ruthlessly attacked by its enemies in the government, in this Congress. At least six auditors from the General Accounting Office were put to work investigating Pride. They worked seven months and spent more than $100,000. They uncovered a fraud. It was something less than $2,100. Meanwhile, millions of dollars—billions of dollars, in fact—were being spent by the Department of Defense, and how many auditors and investigators were checking into their negotiated contracts? Five.

We Americans have come to feel that it is our mission to make the world free. We believe that we are the good guys everywhere—in Vietnam, in Latin America, wherever we go. We believe that we are the good guys at home, too. When the Kerner Commission[f] told white America what black America had always known, that prejudice and hatred built the nation's slums, maintain them, and profit by them, white America would not believe it. But it is true. Unless we start to fight and defeat the enemies of poverty and racism in our own country and make our talk of equality and opportunity ring true, we are exposed as hypocrites in the eyes of the world when we talk about making other people free.

I am deeply disappointed at the clear evidence that the number-one priority of the new administration is to buy more and more weapons of war, to

f. Commissioned by President Johnson and led by former Illinois governor Otto Kerner, the Kerner Commission investigated the causes of the urban riots of the 1960s. Their major finding was that until economic conditions and opportunities for African Americans were changed, civil unrest would continue and probably escalate.

return to the era of the Cold War, to ignore the war we must fight here—the war that is not optional. There is only one way, I believe, to turn these policies around. The Congress can respond to the mandate that the American people have clearly expressed. They have said, "End this war. Stop the waste. Stop the killing. Do something for your own people first." We must find the money to "launch the new approaches," as Mr. Nixon said. We must force the administration to rethink its distorted, unreal scale of priorities. Our children, our jobless men, our deprived, rejected, and starving fellow citizens must come first.

For this reason, I intend to vote "No" on every money bill that comes to the floor of this House that provides any funds for the Department of Defense—any bill whatsoever—until the time comes when our values and priorities have been turned right side up again, until the monstrous waste and the shocking profits in the defense budget have been eliminated and our country starts to use its strength, its tremendous resources, for people and peace, not for profits and war.

It was Calvin Coolidge, I believe, who made the comment that "the business of America is business." We are now spending $80 billion a year on defense. That is two-thirds of every tax dollar. At this time, gentlemen, the business of America is war, and it is time for a change.

Barbara Charline Jordan

Speech on Watergate to the House Judiciary Committee

In July 1974, Barbara Jordan was a freshman representative from Texas, a junior member on what had, in that session, turned out to be the most important committee in Congress: the House Judiciary Committee. Since May 1974, the committee had been holding closed hearings on the subject of Richard Nixon's impeachment. As a junior member, Jordan consciously sought to avoid having the hearing turn into a partisan brawl. She had rarely spoken, and when she did, it was usually to summarize the discussion and get the committee on to the next issue. Hoping to create an environment for rational discussion, Jordan opposed the idea of beginning the hearings with opening statements from the committee members, preferring to concentrate on the substance of the matter at hand. Most members wanted to declare their position on impeachment before a national television audience, however, and on July 24, the committee began its public hearings with each member allowed a fifteen-minute statement. As one of the most junior members of the committee, Barbara Jordan spoke towards the end of the roll, on July 25. As it occurred, her speech was delivered around nine o'clock in the evening, eastern time, affording her a prime-time audience. *Newsweek* summarized the national response to Jordan's speech the following November: It was "the most memorable indictment of Richard Nixon to emerge from the House impeachment hearings." Out of two days of generally eloquent, impassioned, and moving speeches, Barbara Jordan's is the one that is still remembered.[1]

Born in Houston, Texas, in 1936, Barbara was the youngest of three daughters. Her father, Ben Jordan, had attended Tuskegee and worked in Houston as a union steward, warehouseman, and preacher. Her mother, Arlyne Patten Jordan, worked as a maid and, in her youth, had often spoken at revivals and church meetings. The Jordans drew upon traditional values in rearing their children, and Good Hope Missionary Baptist Church was the central institution in their social lives. Taught early that she should let nothing restrict her personal development, in 1952 Barbara entered Texas Southern University, an all-black university established in 1947 to delay racial integration among the Texas public universities. At TSU, she joined the speech and debate team, traveling nationally to compete against speakers from schools such as Harvard, New York University, and the University of Chicago. On the debate circuit, TSU soon acquired a national reputation, and her debate partner, Otis King, recalled that Barbara "was the absolute best orator we ever had." After graduation, she attended Boston University, where she earned a law degree. She returned to Houston to practice law and quickly became active in Democratic Party politics. In 1962 and 1964, she ran unsuccessfully for a seat in the Texas statehouse. In 1965, a Supreme Court decision ordered Texas to abandon its at-large method of districting and apportion legislative seats evenly on the basis of population. In 1966, Barbara Jordan won election in the newly created state senate district 11, encompassing most of Houston. She became the first black person elected to the Texas State Senate since 1883, and the first black female ever elected to the state legislature.[2]

In the all-male, all-white Texas State Senate, Jordan quickly established a reputation for practical politics. She worked tirelessly for her constituents' interests, and although idealistic, she also understood the role of compromise in politics and grew adept at the art of deal-making. Among her many admirers was President Lyndon Johnson. Johnson recognized in the young state senator the ability to enter the national political arena, and, with his support, in 1972, Jordan won a seat in the US House of Representatives. Johnson also influenced Jordan's appointment to the prestigious House Judiciary Committee, where she could have an impact on civil rights legislation. In the House, she became known as an effective legislator of unmatched integrity. To the nation, however, she was largely unknown except for her election "firsts" in Texas and for her election as the first African American female to Congress from the South. Her Watergate speech changed that literally overnight.[3]

Her speech was largely composed during the dinner break on the evening of July 25. She had been compiling notes on impeachment for some time.

During the dinner hour, she directed her secretary, Marian Ricks, to stay overtime to type the speech. Biographer Mary Beth Rogers recounts the scene: "Jordan began to jot down sentences in longhand and sent each page out to Ricks to type. She already had Bob Alcock prepare parallel statements on impeachment—historical documents, Constitutions of the Confederacy, wherever 'impeachment had been talked about'—against some for the Nixon offenses that had been detailed in that committee. 'So I had that chart, that comparison about what had been said and what it was that Richard Nixon had done.'" When the typing was finally complete, Bud Myers rushed to get Jordan to the hearing room before [Chairman Peter] Rodino gaveled the meeting to order." Representative Walter Flowers had earlier opened his statement with a reference to the Constitution's preamble—"We, the People"—and many others had naturally invoked the Constitution. "It occurred to me," Jordan recalled, "that not one of them had mentioned that back then the Preamble was not talking about *all* the people. So I said: 'Well, I'll just start with that.'" As Rogers summarizes it, "Jordan's lifetime experiences and her months of serious study had by now convinced her that the Constitution was a 'living' document—not something static, or delivered whole. 'We, the people,' are always becoming a people—a whole people—one people. The process goes on and on and must be protected. That is what she wanted to convey." Jordan's speech conveys exactly that. In ringing tones, with her strong voice and distinct enunciation, Jordan opens her speech unequivocally endorsing the Constitution. After defining it as a living document, she declares that "my faith in the Constitution is whole, it is complete, it is total," and with an authoritative delivery that extinguishes all doubt, she announces that "I am not going to sit here and be an idle spectator to the diminution, the subversion, the destruction of the Constitution." That introduction, or proem (overture, "before the song") as the Greeks termed it, enunciates her theme and sets the mood for the entire speech. With the exception of the short middle section of the speech, in which Jordan argues that there is no cause to delay voting, references to the Constitution are woven throughout the speech. Indeed, the matters of Watergate and the president are not mentioned until almost halfway through the speech.[4]

The first section of Jordan's speech focuses solely on the "nature of impeachment," laying the groundwork for the later parts. In this opening portion of the body of the speech, she seeks to accomplish three goals. First, she wants to establish the appropriate standard of evidence. To vote for impeachment, she reminds her colleagues and the nation, is not tantamount to pronouncing the president's guilt and the necessity of his removal from office. Rather, voting for impeachment means that the member of Congress believes that a trial should be held. The House is assigned the role of the accuser, Jordan points out; the Senate would be the jury. However, even as she addresses the issue of evidentiary requirements, Jordan foreshadows the next, more important point. By noting the separation of powers that exists between the House and the Senate, and observing that the "Framers of this constitution were very astute" in making it so, Jordan prepares the audience for this longer discussion of impeachment. Impeachment, she says, is also about the separation of powers, but now she is talking about the separation between the executive and the legislative branches. It is a "narrowly channeled exception" to the separation of powers, designed to "'bridle' the Executive if he engages in excesses." It is an important exception, however, because it places upon the legislature the *responsibility* to act as a check on the executive branch. Her quotation taken from the Virginia Ratification Convention is significant: "We do not trust our liberty to a particular branch. We need one branch to check the other." By implication, if Congress fails to impeach a president who deserves impeachment, it fails to live up to *its* constitutional duties just as surely as has that president, and such failure of responsibility would place the liberty of the nation in jeopardy. This explains the "solemnness" Jordan declares in the introduction that she feels, as she contemplates her *duty* as a guardian of the Constitution and of the nation's liberty.

Then Jordan moves to the third point she wishes to make in the opening section: that her vote will be made as a legislator, not as a Democrat. She makes that argument first by continuing to draw quotations from constitutional experts. Citing first Alexander Hamilton and then Woodrow Wilson, Jordan states that "indignation so great as to overgrow party interest *may* secure a conviction, but nothing else can." She follows this appeal to authority with a logical appeal to a universal principle: that "common sense would be revolted if we engaged upon this process for petty reasons." Jordan implies, in other words, that she and her party acknowledge that if politics is perceived as the chief motivation for pursuing impeachment they would suffer an angry political backlash. Because they had weighed the political consequences of seeking an impeachment, they were not acting rashly or irresponsibly. There were legitimate grounds for impeachment, and constitutionally they were discharging their duty in seeking it. In their role as guardians of the Constitution they were all acting not as Democrats but as legislators. Had there not been Republicans who had already given opening statements in which they had reluctantly declared for impeachment, Jordan's argument might not have been as persuasive. Because of the situation, however, the appeal became a powerful constitutional statement.

Jordan then moves to the one section of the speech that is not focused on the Constitution, as she advances a rebuttal to Republican arguments designed to delay the hearings. Again in a neatly organized fashion, Jordan argues first that there is indeed sufficient evidence to proceed with a decision on impeachment, and second that no reason had presented itself as to why the committee should wait for additional evidence. Generally, Jordan's tone towards the president is restrained. She had, in fact, refused to declare how she would vote on impeachment until this opening statement, and in the hearings had usually refrained from questioning the witnesses, preferring to listen and focus on the merits of the case. In this speech, Jordan never refers to the president by name, using only the title of his office. That she disapproves of his actions is clear in the tenor of the speech and the passionate tone of her voice, but she avoids any obvious emotional appeals or any references to Nixon's character. In responding to the Republican argument that the committee should wait to see if the president might supply further evidence, Jordan's disdain seems to boil just below the surface. She summarily dismisses the appeal to wait, noting forcefully that "there has not even been an obfuscated indication that this committee would receive any additional materials from the President. The committee subpoena is outstanding and if the President wants to supply that material, the committee sits here."[5]

All of this, however, is prefatory material that anticipates the heart of the speech: the argument that Richard Nixon should be impeached. Jordan's speech now imitates the notes she had made to herself, as she juxtaposes criteria for impeachment with actions of the president. The organization of this section is salient. There are four criteria advanced: if the president be connected in any suspicious manner with any person, if the president threatened the people's rights or liberties, if the president behaved amiss or betrayed the public trust, and if the president subverted the Constitution. The effect of ordering the criteria in this fashion is climactic. Jordan begins with the least serious charge first: connection with suspicious persons. While less psychologically serious than betraying liberties or subverting the Constitution, this criterion has the advantage of specificity. Here she can note that the president had met with Henry Peterson twenty-seven times. She refers to the payment of money to the defendants. Although the evidence is circumstantial, it is also specific.

The next criterion put forward is to protect our rights and rescue our liberties. Although this criteria sounds larger and more important than the next—to betray the public trust—the evidence supporting it is more narrowly defined. Specifically, she refers to the break-in of Daniel Ellsberg's psychiatrist's office. What the evidence gains in specificity, however, it potentially loses in psychological power. Still, it goes beyond the circumstantial even while maintaining specificity. The third impeachment criteria becomes larger still because the charge now affects the entire country. The president has betrayed the public trust by attempting, through public statements and actions, to "thwart the lawful investigation by government prosecutors." Not only is the effect of the charge serious—to thwart a lawful investigation—but these deceptive public statements, these lies, had been made to the entire American public. Jordan here exploits the outrage Americans had felt as they had discovered that Nixon had known since at least June 23 what had happened the week before at the Watergate Building, his many protestations afterward notwithstanding.

Finally, Jordan reaches the climax of the charges: that Nixon had subverted the Constitution. This is the apex of the argument, as she had foreshadowed in the introduction and the first section of the speech discussing the constitutional responsibility of the House. The effect of the section is climactic as well because the list of charges here is lengthier than the earlier evidence and more sweeping in scope. The president, Jordan charged, had "counseled his aides to commit perjury, willfully disregard[ed] the secrecy of grand jury proceedings, concealed surreptitious entry, [and] attempt[ed] to compromise a federal judge." A president is impeachable, she says, if he has subverted the Constitution.

What makes this section of the speech most noteworthy, however, is its use of syllogistic form and a "sandwich" structure. For each charge, Jordan supplies two parts of the traditional syllogism: the major and minor premises. The major premise, or generalization, is the impeachment criterion. Each section begins with a precise quotation of the criterion and the prestigious writer who had defined it. The criterion operate as a major premise; for example, a president is impeachable if he subverts the Constitution. Then

Jordan outlines the charges; that is, what the president is alleged to have done. These charges implicitly constitute the minor premise, but Jordan never explicitly draws the conclusion implied by the major and minor premises taken together, that the president had violated the impeachment criteria. In each case, she leaves it to the audience to decide whether the actions illustrate a violation. She never states the conclusion of the syllogism. Each time, Jordan refuses to pronounce the judgment that Nixon had committed impeachable offenses, even though that is the logical conclusion to her premises. Four times she repeats this pattern, and each time the audience is left tacitly to conclude Nixon's guilt. Each time, the audience anticipates that Jordan will finally declare openly that Nixon is guilty, but she does not do so. Instead, she accentuates the audience's anticipation and participation by repeating, at the end of each section, the impeachment criterion. Thus the audience hears the major premise, has the minor premise outlined for them, and then hears the major premise again. The conclusion that is logically inescapable becomes psychologically inescapable as well, made more powerful by virtue of being unexpressed.

Jordan finally provides the answer the audience anticipates, but even here she finds an artful way to say that Nixon is impeachable without actually saying it. Once more, she makes the audience a partner in her communication: "If the impeachment provision in the Constitution of the United States will not reach the offenses charged here, then perhaps that 18th century Constitution should be abandoned to a 20th century paper shredder." In this vivid antithesis, Jordan indicates her unequivocal support for impeachment by suggesting her willingness to abandon the Constitution as unworkable if it cannot impeach the president. The depth of her commitment is unmistakably communicated through the contrast of this conclusion with her introduction, where she declares that she will not be an "idle spectator to the diminution, the subversion, the destruction of the Constitution."

With some irony, Jordan concludes that it is "reason, not passion" that must "guide our deliberations." Barbara Jordan's passion for her subject is evident, yet hers is a philosophical passion for the Constitution and for upholding the Constitution. Her passion is distinct from the partisan and political emotions that surrounded the moment, and that is her point. She has argued with reason, citing only the best constitutional authorities, but her oration has also flowed from a deep-seated commitment to the Constitution as a living document that protects liberty and preserves rights. The highest elected officer of the land had, she believes, violated that document, and he deserves to be called into account.

Barbara Jordan did not immediately know how her speech had been received by the American public. On television, CBS reporter Bruce Morton stated that she had the "best mind on the committee," but inside the committee room, even applause had not been allowed. She learned quickly, however, that the American public approved. A crowd had gathered to cheer her upon her departure from the Rayburn Building. Telegrams and letters began arriving immediately. As might be expected, some were negative and vituperative.

> You should beg God to forgive you for your part in attempting to destroy a great man. As for the truth of what you say, your arrogance is exceeded only by your ignorance.

> I sincerely hope that when many of you politicians in Washington, D.C., finish that we will still have something left of our government; the Communists must laugh with joy at what is taking place, and the American taxpayers are picking up the tab.

Overwhelmingly, however, the responses were positive and often moving. They represented a cross section of America, both economically and geographically, and some seem all the more sincere because of their faulty grammar and misspelled words.

> I am not from Texas, nor am I black. . . . Eloquence, forthrightness, incisive rationality, and dignity are rare qualities. Yet you, as a black woman from the South, vividly displayed these qualities. That a black woman from the South should have these qualities is no surprise; that the American political process should have progressed far enough to allow you to display these qualities to the entire country is a surprise.

> Madam, after Listen to you in Impeachment Committee which you speak so eloquence made me Happy. Because I was Born in Texas in 1874, 9 of June, I know you had some Bad Days to make it where you are to Day. Since we are so far apart I am asking you to send me one of your poto that I mite keep it the Rest of My Life.

> Your fifteen-minute statement to the committee was a literary masterpiece in my estimation.

> I followed the televised Judiciary Committee hearings very closely and was most impressed with your cogency, articulation, and probity. You simply made me proud to be an American. . . . I was very moved by your opening remarks . . . quite to tears. Run for President someday and I shall be there with you!

> I loved to here you speak. You are a Beautiful Woman, we watch on TV. . . . I am 74 years old and my husband is 83 and I work every day. But we want to thank all of you good people for our good USA. I am a white lady that love you all.

> This white, Yankee Republican would be honored at some future date to campaign for our 1st black, 1st woman President. If you were the candidate.

> You have changed the minds of myself, my wife, our relatives, and all our friends, for the good of our country, as before we watched you on T.V. we thought only a man should be the President but all of us will vote for you or any black man or lady.

> When you speak of that great Document the "Constitution of our beloved United States" it brings tears to my eyes. You see I am European born and a citizen by "choice." I pledged to protect and allegiance to it, not to the President, whoever he may be. Your vote is not against a President but Richard M. Nixon who consorts with the enemy of the Constitution, which spells Treason in any language.

> Your scholarship was breathtaking tonight; your logic convincing; your sincerity unimpeachable; your power and beauty and dignity overwhelming. When you run for President, you can count on my vote.

Barbara Jordan's "hymn to the Constitution," as *Newsweek* termed it, was indeed the "most memorable indictment of Richard Nixon to emerge from the House hearings." Her reason and passion had combined to make it eloquent beyond the moment.[6]

After the speech, Barbara Jordan was asked to be one of two keynoters at the 1976 Democratic convention, and she was often mentioned as a possible vice presidential candidate or Supreme Court justice. The progressive deterioration caused by multiple sclerosis, with which she was afflicted shortly after she had come to Congress in 1973, forced her into retirement from professional politics. In her remaining years, she taught at the University of Texas at Austin and promoted a variety of political causes, and in 1992, she returned to speak to the Democratic National Convention. After battling declining health for many years, Barbara Jordan passed away in January 1996. Her "hymn to the Constitution," however, lives on in the history of the discordant period in which she served as a US congresswoman.

Speech on Watergate to the House Judiciary Committee

July 25, 1974
Washington, DC

Mr. Chairman, I join my colleague, Mr. Rangel, in thanking you for giving the junior members of this Committee the glorious opportunity of sharing the pain of this inquiry. Mr. Chairman, you are a strong man and it has not been easy, but we have tried as best we can to give you as much assistance as possible.

Earlier today, we heard the beginning of the Preamble to the Constitution of the United States. "We, the People." It's a very eloquent beginning. But, when that document was completed on the 17th of September in 1787, I was not included in that "We, the People." I felt somehow for many years that George Washington and Alexander Hamilton just left me out by mistake. But through the process of amendment, interpretation and court decision, I have finally been included in "We, the People."

Today, I am an inquisitor. And hyperbole would not be fictional and would not overstate the solemnness that I feel right now. My faith in the Constitution is whole, it is complete, it is total. And I am not going to sit here and be an idle spectator to the diminution, the subversion, the destruction of the Constitution.

"Who can so properly be the inquisitors for the nation as the representatives of the nation themselves?"[a] The subjects of its jurisdiction are those offenses which proceed from the misconduct of public men. And that's what we're talking about. In other words, from the abuse or violation of some public trust. It is wrong, I suggest, it is a misreading of the Constitution

a. Federalist Papers, no. 65.

for any member here to assert that for a Member to vote for an Article of Impeachment means that that member must be convinced that the President should be removed from office. The Constitution doesn't say that. The powers relating to impeachment are an essential check in the hands of this body, the legislature, against and upon the encroachments of the Executive. The division between the two branches of the legislature, the House and the Senate, assigning to the one the right to accuse and to the other the right to judge, the Framers of this Constitution were very astute. They did not make the accusers and the judges, and the judges, the same person.

We know the nature of impeachment. We have been talking about it awhile now. "It is chiefly designed for the President and his high ministers" to somehow be called into account. It is designed to "bridle" the Executive if he engages in excesses. "It is designed as a method of national inquest into the conduct of public men."[b] The Framers confined in the Congress the power, if need be, to remove the President in order to strike a delicate balance between a President swollen with power and grown tyrannical, and the preservation of the independence of the Executive. The nature of impeachment; a narrowly channeled exception to the separation of powers maxim, the Federal Convention of 1787 said that. It limited impeachment to high crimes and misdemeanors and discounted and opposed the term "maladministration." It is to be used only for "great misdemeanors," so it was said in the North Carolina Ratification Convention. And in the Virginia Ratification Convention: "We do not trust our liberty to a particular branch. We need one branch to check the other."

"No one need be afraid," the North Carolina Ratification Convention, "no one need be afraid that officers who commit oppression will pass with immunity."

"Prosecutions of impeachments will seldom fail to agitate the passions of the whole community," said Hamilton in the Federalist Papers No. 65. "We divide into parties, more or less friendly or inimical to the accused." I do not mean political parties in that sense. The drawing of political lines goes to the motivation behind impeachment; but impeachment must proceed within the confines of the constitutional term, "high crime and misdemeanors."

Of the impeachment process, it was Woodrow Wilson who said that "nothing short of the grossest offenses against the plain law of the land

b. Federalist Papers, no. 65.

will suffice to give them speed and effectiveness. Indignation so great as to overgrow party interest *may* secure a conviction, but nothing else can."

Common sense would be revolted if we engaged upon this process for petty reasons. Congress has a lot to do. Appropriations, tax reform, health insurance, campaign finance reform, housing, environmental protection, energy sufficiency, mass transportation. Pettiness cannot be allowed to stand in the face of such overwhelming problems. So, today, we are not being petty. We are trying to be big because the task we have before us is a big one.

This morning in a discussion of the evidence we are told that the evidence which purports to support the allegations of misuse of the CIA by the President is thin. We are told that that evidence is insufficient. What that recital of the evidence this morning did not include is what the President *did* know on June the 23rd, 1972. The President *did* know that it was Republican money, that it was money from the Committee for the Re-election of the President, which was found in the possession of one of the burglars arrested on June the 17th.

What the President *did* know on the 23rd of June was the prior activities of E. Howard Hunt, which included his participation in the break-in of Daniel Ellsberg's psychiatrist, which included Howard Hunt's participation in the Dita Beard–ITT affair, which included Howard Hunt's fabrication of cables designed to discredit the Kennedy Administration.

We were further cautioned today that perhaps these proceedings ought to be delayed because certainly there would be new evidence forthcoming from the President of the United States. There has not even been an obfuscated indication that this committee would receive any additional materials from the President. The committee subpoena is outstanding and if the President wants to supply that material, the committee sits here.

The fact is that on yesterday, the American people waited with great anxiety for eight hours, not knowing whether their President would obey an order of the Supreme court of the United States.

At this point, I would like to juxtapose a few of the impeachment criteria with some of the actions the President has engaged in.

Impeachment criteria: James Madison, from the Virginia Ratification Convention: "If the President be connected in any suspicious manner with any person and there be grounds to believe that he will shelter him, he may be impeached."

We have heard time and time again that the evidence reflects the payment to defendants money. The President had knowledge that these funds were being paid and these were funds collected for the 1972 presidential campaign. We know that the President met with Mr. Henry Peterson 27 times to discuss matters related to Watergate and immediately thereafter met with the very persons who were implicated in the information Mr. Peterson was receiving. The words are, "if the President is connected in any suspicious manner with any person and there be grounds to believe that he will shelter that person, he may be impeached."

Justice Story: "Impeachment is intended, is intended for occasional and extraordinary cases where a superior power acting for the whole people is put into operation to protect their rights and rescue their liberties from violations."

We know about the Houston Plan. We know about the break-in of the psychiatrist's office. We know that there were absolute complete direction on September 3rd when the President indicated that a surreptitious entry had been made into Dr. Fielding's office after having met with Mr. Ehrlichman and Mr. Young. "Protect their rights." "Rescue their liberties from violation."

The Carolina Ratification Convention impeachment criteria: Those are impeachable "who behave amiss or betray the public trust."

Beginning shortly after the Watergate break-in and continuing to the present time the President has engaged in a series of public statements and actions designed to thwart the lawful investigation by government prosecutors. Moreover the President has made public announcements and assertions bearing on the Watergate case which the evidence will show he knew to be false. These assertions, false assertions, impeachable, those who misbehave. Those who "behave amiss or betray the public trust."

James Madison again at the Constitutional Convention: "A President is impeachable if he attempts to subvert the Constitution."

The Constitution charges the President with the task of taking care that the laws be faithfully executed, and yet the President has counseled his aides to commit perjury, willfully disregard the secrecy of grand jury proceedings, conceal surreptitious entry, attempt to compromise a federal judge, while publicly displaying his cooperation with the processes of criminal justice. "A President is impeachable if he attempts to subvert the Constitution."

If the impeachment provision in the Constitution of the United States will not reach the offenses charged here, then perhaps that 18th century Constitution should be abandoned to a 20th century paper shredder. Has the President committed offenses, planned and directed and acquiesced in a course of conduct which the Constitution will not tolerate? That is the question. We know that. We know the question. We should now forthwith proceed to answer the question. It is reason, and not passion, which must guide our deliberations, guide our debate, and guide our decision.

I yield back the balance of my time, Mr. Chairman.

Jesse Louis Jackson

Speech to the Democratic National Convention
(The Rainbow Coalition)

Few modern speakers compare in the power of their eloquence with the Reverend Jesse Jackson. After the assassination of Martin Luther King, Jesse Jackson's community organizing and public speaking propelled him to the forefront of the public's consciousness. Whether involved with a domestic civil rights issue or travelling internationally, his rhetorical presence cannot be ignored. Arguably, the strong, credible campaigns he conducted for the Democratic presidential nomination in 1984 and 1988 paved the way for Barack Obama's nomination and election in 2008. His 1984 speech to the Democratic National Convention was especially compelling, providing him with a large, national audience, most of whom had never heard him deliver a speech in its entirety. Although Jesse Jackson was already a household name, the speech catapulted him to a level of political importance never before experienced by an African American.

Jesse Louis Burns was born on October 8, 1941, in Greenville, South Carolina, to Helen Burns, then still a student in high school. Jesse's father was Noah Robinson, a married, relatively wealthy African American who lived next door to Helen and her mother, who worked as a maid to a white family in town. According to Jackson, growing up illegitimate in a segregated Southern city, unacknowledged by his biological father, was deeply affecting. So, too, was the love and care he experienced from his mother and grandmother, and Helen's marriage to Charles Jackson, a janitor, who adopted him in 1957.[1] Of Charles, Jackson said "he gave me his name, his love, his encouragement, discipline and a high sense of self respect."[2] Jesse was a talented athlete and an able student, who upon graduation in 1959 accepted a football scholarship from the University of Illinois. He was disappointed to discover that discrimination and prejudice were as pervasive in the North as they had been in South Carolina, and for his sophomore year, he transferred to North Carolina A&T College in Greensboro, North Carolina, a historically black college.[3] Jackson arrived at A&T after the famed Woolworth sit-in of February 1960, but he quickly became involved in other civil rights activities at the school. As student body president, he helped organize similar protests and in June 1963 was arrested at one of those demonstrations. The previous December he had married Lavinia Brown, and in May 1964 he graduated from A&T with a degree in sociology.[4]

Upon graduation, Jackson enrolled in Chicago Theological Seminary, but the following spring he travelled south to meet Martin Luther King Jr. and ask for work with King's Southern Christian Leadership Conference (SCLC). In early 1966, Jackson was appointed to lead Operation Breadbasket for the SCLC's Chicago chapter.[5] Operation Breadbasket, a program intended to expand the civil rights movement, focused on improving economic opportunities for African Americans. Jackson became embroiled in some controversy following Dr. King's assassination in 1968. Interviewed on national television, Jackson described himself as the last person to be with King as he lay shot on the balcony of the Lorraine Hotel in Memphis. Telegenic, charismatic, and a successful community activist in Chicago, Jackson attracted considerable media attention, although his story about the assassination was disputed by other SCLC leaders. A struggle over leadership of the SCLC ensued, and in 1971, Jackson was forced out of the SCLC.[6] Remaining in Chicago, Jackson founded Operation People United to Save Humanity (PUSH), an organization patterned largely after Operation Breadbasket. In addition to this community-based activist work, in the 1970s, Jackson became known for his positive self-improvement speeches aimed at disadvantaged youth, centered on the phrase, "I am somebody." In 1976, he created PUSH-Excel, a branch of the PUSH organization focused on youth.[7]

During the 1970s and early 1980s, Jackson's political activities became increasingly important. In 1979, he traveled to South Africa, where he vehemently denounced the system of apartheid. He later journeyed to the Middle East, and during that trip he controversially embraced Yasir Arafat, the exiled leader of the Palestinian Liberation Organization. In 1983, he campaigned energetically for Harold Washington's election as mayor of Chicago. Not only did Washington become the first African American mayor of that city, but during the course of the campaign, Jackson's organization helped register one hundred thousand new African American voters. In late 1983 and early 1984, Jackson negotiated the release of Lt. Robert Goodman, an African American Navy fighter pilot shot down and captured in Syria. Much criticism ensued, however, for Jackson had met as a private American citizen with Syrian president Hafez Assad in order to effect Goodman's release.[8]

On November 3, 1983, Jackson declared his candidacy for the Democratic presidential nomination. Calling his supporters a "rainbow coalition"—a term he had also employed when announcing the formation of PUSH in 1971—Jackson pledged to speak on behalf of the disenfranchised. As a political novice and an African American, Jackson's candidacy was initially dismissed by the media. His campaign registered two million new voters, however, and he won five primaries and over 20 percent of the popular vote. Controversy continued to surround Jackson. In January 1984, in a conversation with *Washington Post* reporter Milton Coleman, himself an African American, that Jackson clearly believed was off-the-record, the candidate referred to New York as "Hymietown." Already wary of Jackson due to his public appearances with Arafat and Assad, many Jewish leaders were vocally critical. Jackson apologized for his remarks, but mutual suspicion between Jewish voters and Jackson's campaign persisted. The Rainbow Coalition's perceptions that it was being marginalized by the media and the Democratic establishment carried over into the Democratic National Convention, when Jackson's 20 percent of the popular vote translated into only eight percent of the delegates and when, initially, the party Brahmins appeared likely to prevent Jackson's delegates from raising certain issues during the platform hearings. Ultimately, his delegates were included in the hearings, although they lost three out of the four specific plank fights. Jackson was, however, provided with a prime speaking time on Tuesday evening, the second night of the convention.[9]

Delivered to an estimated audience of thirty-three million television viewers, Jackson's speech was part apologia, part speech of reconciliation, and part stump speech.[10] Its style was vintage Jackson—filled with parallel structure, repetition, rhyme, vivid metaphors, irony, and minihomilies. Even more than King's "I Have a Dream" speech twenty-one years earlier, Jackson's fifty-one-minute-long "Rainbow Coalition" address provided many white Americans with their first exposure to the black Baptist style of preaching. Jackson's address was not simply a political speech; it was a spiritual speech as well.

The speech unfolds naturally, much as a sermon might. There is a logical progression and organization to the speech, but the transitions between sections are subtle. Jackson begins with a call for unity, grounded in his "faith in a mighty God, . . . genuine respect and love for our country, and inheriting the legacy of a great party, the Democratic party." Although broad from one point of view, his call also speaks directly to the specific situation. The campaign had been hotly and, at times, irritably contested. The platform battles to which Jackson alludes later in the speech had also been contentious. A major media "subplot" to the convention was whether Jackson would warmly endorse Mondale, a question fueled in part by the Mondale-Jackson battle but also in part by Ted Kennedy's tepid support of Jimmy Carter's reelection campaign four years earlier. From this situation-specific call for unity, Jackson then moves to his apologia. Still seeking to close the rift between African Americans and Jews, he casts himself as a "public servant," and "not a perfect servant," asking those whom he might have offended to "please forgive me," for that was not "my truest self."

After completing these two situation-specific introductory sections, Jackson shifts to content drawn from his campaign stump speech. He draws from his introductory remarks; combining the themes of unity and forgiveness, he forwards the metaphor of America as a quilt. The "quilt" allows unity in its diversity, and the unity is preserved as individuals "forgive" the disagreements that inevitably arise when individuals speak their conscience. Here Jackson reviews his Rainbow Coalition's agenda, with the metaphor of the "rainbow" operating very similarly to that of the patchwork quilt. After advancing that agenda, Jackson attacks the Reagan administration with rhetoric taken from his standard stump speech. Then, in contrast to the Reagan administration's harmful policies, Jackson discerns that the Democratic Party, with its diverse constituent members raising "the right issues," provides a "way out." Walter Mondale is the right candidate for President, because the Democratic Party is the right party and Mondale is the Democratic nominee. Jackson concludes with a "message for our youth," a peroration drawn from his youth-oriented motivational speeches, but nicely blended with his portrayal of the Democratic Party as the positive alternative to Reagan.

While his organization is subtle, Jackson's style is flashy. As is typical of his speaking, his 1984 address is filled with parallel structure accentuated by rhyme, alliteration, and vivid imagery. Through parallel structure, Jackson calls attention to points of comparison and contrast. His anaphora (repeated beginning) of "The Rainbow Coalition," for example, suggests the common interests that unite seemingly diverse and differentiated communities, such as Arab Americans and small farmers: "The Rainbow Coalition is making room for Arab Americans. . . . The Rainbow Coalition is making room for Hispanic Americans. . . . The Rainbow is making room for the Native American. . . . The Rainbow Coalition includes Asian Americans. . . . The Rainbow is making room for the young Americans. . . . The Rainbow includes disabled veterans. . . . The Rainbow is making room for small farmers." Jackson's use of parallel structure to sharpen his messages of contrast is even more frequent and pronounced. Referring to the disabled veterans, Jackson employs antimetabole, a parallel reversal that repeats common terms: "The disabled have their handicap revealed and their genius concealed; while the able-bodied have their genius revealed and their disability concealed." He places this abstract contrast into concrete terms when he concludes, yet again in parallel structure, that he would "rather have Roosevelt in a wheelchair than Reagan on a horse."

The idea of contrast, delivered through parallel structure, reinforces several key messages in Jackson's speech. The errors for which he apologizes, for example, do not truly reflect his nature as a human being: "Charge [my low points] to my head and not to my heart. My head—so limited in its finitude; my heart, which is boundless in its love for the human family." Jackson also contrasts the unimportant controversies that have distracted the party with the important differences in policy between the Democrats and Republicans: "We must turn from finger pointing to clasped hands. . . . We must turn to each other and not on each other and choose higher ground." And Reagan's record should be judged in comparison with those principles: "We must not measure greatness from the mansion down, but the manger up."

The sharpest, most sustained parallel contrasts occur in the last quarter of the speech, as Jackson builds to an emotional climax. Contrast helps celebrate what his campaign and his supporters had accomplished: "We could afford to lose the vote (on platform planks); issues are nonnegotiable. . . . Our heads are perhaps bloody, but not bowed. . . . When we think, on this journey from slave-ship to championship, that we have gone from the planks of the Boardwalk in Atlantic City in 1964 to fighting to help write the planks in the platform in San Francisco in '84, there is a deep and abiding sense of joy in our souls in spite of the tears in our eyes. Though there are missing planks, there is a solid foundation upon which to build." Such structure also serves to contrast the Democratic alternative to the Republican's Reagan. "Our foreign policy," Jackson says, "must be characterized by mutual respect, not by gunboat diplomacy. . . . Our nation at its best feeds the hungry. Our nation at its worst, at its worst, will mine the harbors of Nicaragua." Our Middle East foreign policy is characterized by "too many interests and too few friends." Parallel structure of contrast figures prominently in Jackson's closing message to youth, as he repetitively contrasts the "slummy side" with the "sunny side": "When I see a missing door—that's the slummy side. Train some youth to become a carpenter—that's the sunny side." Resonating with echoes of Dr. King, Jackson's "dream" section is fully structured in parallel contrasts—"Dream of lawyers . . . . Dream of doctors . . . . Dream of preachers and priests . . . ."—and his concluding paragraph contains parallel comparisons of policies whose "time" has come as well as contrasts between what is and what should be: "We come from disgrace to amazing grace."

As with his "slummy side/sunny side" and "disgrace to amazing grace" contrasts, Jackson makes common use of alliteration and rhyme to accentuate his parallel constructions, and thereby infuse the speech with the high style of a Sunday sermon. His constituency, he tells his audience, are the "desperate, the damned, the disinherited, the disrespected, and the despised." Similar uses of alliteration abound. He has watched his opponents contend with the "crosswinds and cross-fires" of the campaign; he apologizes for any errors of "temper, taste, or tone"; after the platform fight "our heads are perhaps bloody, but not bowed"; and he urges his audience to "dream of lawyers more concerned about justice than a judgeship" and then to "dream of preachers and priests who will prophesy and not just profiteer." Rhyme is likewise employed liberally. Referring to the Democratic party, he argues that "the team that got us here must be expanded, not abandoned." In the middle of his alliterative imperatives to dream about lawyers, preachers, and priests who will do good, he tells his audience in rhyme to "dream of doctors more concerned about public health than personal wealth."

Repetition is yet another rhetorical flourish Jackson uses that echoes the style of African American preaching. In general, he repeats phrases as a part of the call-and-response motif, reiterating a message to which the audience has audibly responded.[11] Summarizing a colloquial example, Jackson observes that "you cannot hold someone in the ditch unless you linger there with them. Unless you linger there." Most typically the repeated segment is an imperative. "We've got to make a judgment," he tells the audience, "We've got to make a judgment." Or, later in the speech, he urges them that "We must all come up together. We must come up together." His closing refrain, "Our time has come," is both a declaration and an imperative and brings the speech to an emotional crescendo.

Jackson's use of vivid imagery and irony are two additional noteworthy features of his speech and, again, typify his preaching style of address. Contrasting Roosevelt in a wheelchair to Reagan on a horse, or the description of the slummy and sunny sides of the ghetto—replete with images of broken windows, missing doors, and vulgar graffiti—represent his appeal to the visual. What is perhaps the most salient passage of the speech is also an exemplar of Jackson's preaching style of address. Evoking Reagan's stand on school prayer, Jackson begins by noting that "Mr. Reagan will ask us to pray, and I believe in prayer." Jackson then juxtaposes Reagan's stand on prayer with his policies as they affect the poor: "He cuts energy assistance to the poor, cuts breakfast programs from children, cuts lunch programs from children, cuts job training from children, and then says to an empty table, 'Let us pray.'" Jackson then makes clear the irony, with a modestly humorous observation: "Apparently, he is not familiar with the structure of a prayer. You thank the Lord for the food that you are about to receive, not the food that just left. I think that we should pray, but don't pray for the food that left. Pray for the man that took the food to leave."

As the preceding passage from the speech suggests, Jackson's speech also sounds like a sermon because he is comfortable with discussing political issues in the context of spiritual concerns. He frames the success of the Democratic Party, for example, in terms of how well it meets the challenge of the Gospel of Matthew that "whatever you do for the least of these, you do unto me."[12] Similarly, he allows his supporters to move from opposing Walter Mondale to supporting him by grounding the change in the well-known verse from Ecclesiastes. Just as there is a "time to sow and a time to reap," there is a "time to compete and a time to cooperate." In a similar way, Jackson references Isaiah that we are all precious in God's sight and the Synoptic Gospels in reference to pouring new wine into old wineskins.[13] The Gospel of John—"And I, if I be lifted up"—is featured prominently in the closing portion of Jackson's address.[14] Beyond grounding many of his arguments in biblical principles, however, Jackson shows also his comfort talking about religion in ways that most politicians, who broadly invoke "God" and "faith in God" but rarely go further, do not. He invokes the commonality of the Reverend King and Rabbi Abraham Heschel, for example, and makes a definitive claim of common heritage for "these three great religions—Judaism, Christianity and Islam." When, then, Jackson condemns the United States' tolerance of apartheid as a "moral disgrace," his spiritual charge is literal.

As with all good sermons, the concluding paragraph is the most heavily laden with Jackson's moral message. It opens with a quintessentially Christian philosophical statement summarizing the relationship between faith and life itself: "Suffering breeds character. Character breeds faith. In the end, faith will not disappoint." He then paraphrases the apostle Paul when he says that if his audience is true to these principles, "our faith, hope and dreams will prevail." Echoing the Passion and Resurrection of Christ in his description of the transition from wrong to right, Jackson says that "weeping has endured for nights, but now joy cometh in the morning. Our time has come. No grave can hold our body down." He then concludes with a call to make the transition, to "leave racial battle ground and come to economic common ground and moral higher ground." He finishes with a rhetorical nod to America's secular faith—drawing from Emma Lazarus's famous poem "The New Colossus," inscribed at the base of the Statue of Liberty: "Give me your tired, give me your poor, your huddled masses who yearn to breathe free and come November, there will be a change because our time has come." Although literally a portion of America's secular, political culture, the cited portion of Lazarus's poem echoes Christ's message in the Gospel of Matthew with which Jackson had begun his speech—to feed the hungry, clothe the naked, and shelter the homeless.

Contemporary accounts concur that Jackson's speech electrified the convention audience and was widely well received. While many of the convention's speeches were praised, especially Mario Cuomo's keynote address on the night preceding Jackson's speech, most of the media agreed with *Newsweek*'s assessment that "it was Jackson's speech that brought a new music to the mainstream of American oratory."[15] *Time* magazine called it a "stem-winder" and a "sweaty, moving 51-minute tour-de-force."[16] Biographer Matthew Frady records that, according to reports, during the course of Jackson's speech the television audience *grew*, as viewers called their friends and families to turn on their sets, until the number of viewers totaled thirty-three million. Many delegates, white and black, wept from emotion.[17] Florida governor Bob Graham was famously quoted as saying, immediately after the speech, "If you are a human being, and weren't affected by what you just heard, you may be beyond redemption."[18] In the *New York Times*, reporter John Russel wrote that the speech produced "genuine unity" at the convention, and marked the "re-emergence of the political speech as something to be proud of."[19]

Jackson's speech, however, was not a "political speech" in the modern sense. Graham's reference to "beyond redemption" comes closer to the religious heart of the address. Both the media and the convention audience recognized the speech as a sermon delivered within a secular political context. *Time* called it a "revival meeting," while *Newsweek* said that it had a "perfect preacher's pitch."[20] The *Nation* termed it a "spellbinding sermon."[21] Audio recordings of the speech provide evidence of the audience's interpretation that this is indeed a sermon in the convention hall. From the very beginning, even before Jackson begins to speak, there are calls of encouragement to him in the hall, as one might hear from an African American congregation as it urges its preacher on. The call-and-response motif, by which the preacher invites the audience to respond, is also present throughout Jackson's "stem-winder."

The historic impact of Jackson's speech, and his preceding campaign, is undeniable. Many African Americans saw in Jackson's speech a kind of coming-of-age, as first his campaign and then his convention address certified that an African American could be a legitimate contender for the presidency. Frady quotes the novelist James Baldwin as saying of Jackson's speech: "Nothing will ever again be what it was before. It changes the way the boy on the street and the boy on Death Row and his mother and his father and his sweetheart and his sister think about themselves. . . . And no one will ever forget this moment, no matter what happens now."[22] Lee Atwater, the Republican strategist, credited Jackson's presidential campaign for the Democratic congressional gains in the 1986 elections.[23] Certainly the speech and his campaign provided the momentum for his 1988 run for the Democratic presidential nomination, an effort in which he doubled his primary vote totals from 3.5 million in 1984 to 7 million. In 1988, Jackson placed first or second in forty-six of the fifty-four contests.[24] In 1984, his was an "African American" campaign. While many African Americans—especially Democratic Party regulars—did not support him, overwhelmingly his backers in this first campaign were African American.[25] Although he still had difficulty attracting white voters in 1988, his support did increase and broaden in that campaign over the 1984 effort.[26]

While most African Americans greeted the speaker and the speech with enthusiasm, some were disappointed, feeling that he had been too apologetic and not aggressive enough in putting forth the Rainbow Coalition's agenda.[27]

Ernest House, in *Jesse Jackson and the Politics of Charisma*, is especially critical, claiming that the speech brought "the whites to tears and the blacks to anger," and that "many of Jackson's black supporters were extremely disappointed in the actual speech, thinking it far too conciliatory."[28] House recognizes the speech as a "powerful one," however, but criticizes it as a speech of "unification rather than one of castigation as [Jackson's] followers had wanted."[29] Still, he credits the stump speech portion of the address—attacking Reagan and advancing the Rainbow Coalition's agenda—as an important statement that demonstrated "that Jackson could handle sophisticated economic issues that embraced the welfare of the entire nation."[30]

In 2008, Senator Barack Obama broke new ground first when he received the Democrats' nomination for president, and then again when he won the general election. He did so in large part because many voters of all races perceived that an African American could be a legitimate contender for the American presidency. Many African Americans had helped prepare the way for Senator Obama—especially politicians such as Mayor Bradley of Los Angeles and Governor Wilder of Virginia, who had proved that African Americans could garner broad support for their campaigns and their policies. Jesse Jackson, with his two landmark campaigns of 1984 and 1988, and his two dynamic convention speeches, "Rainbow Coalition" in 1984 and "Common Ground and Common Sense" in 1988, was especially instrumental in making Obama's successes possible. Delivered with the cadence, style, and imagery rooted in his black Baptist background, his religiously themed rhetoric spoke movingly to a national audience.

Speech to the Democratic National Convention

(The Rainbow Coalition)

July 18, 1984
San Francisco, California

Thank you very much.

Tonight we come together bound by our faith in a mighty God, with genuine respect and love for our country, and inheriting the legacy of a great party, the Democratic Party, which is the best hope for redirecting our nation on a more humane, just, and peaceful course.

This is not a perfect party. We are not a perfect people. Yet, we are called to a perfect mission. Our mission: to feed the hungry; to clothe the naked; to house the homeless; to teach the illiterate; to provide jobs for the jobless[a]; and to choose the human race over the nuclear race.

We are gathered here this week to nominate a candidate and adopt a platform which will expand, unify, direct, and inspire our party and the nation to fulfill this mission. My constituency is the desperate, the damned, the disinherited, the disrespected, and the despised. They are restless and seek relief. They have voted in record numbers. They have invested the faith, hope, and trust that they have in us. The Democratic Party must send them a signal that we care. I pledge my best not to let them down.

There is the call of conscience, redemption, expansion, healing, and unity. Leadership must heed the call of conscience, redemption, expansion, healing, and unity, for they are the key to achieving our mission. Time is neutral and does not change things. With courage and initiative, leaders change things. No generation can choose the age or circumstance in which it is born, but through leadership it can choose to make the age in which it is born an age of

a. Refers to Matthew 25: 34–45: "For I was hungry and you gave me food."

enlightenment, an age of jobs, and peace, and justice. Only leadership—that intangible combination of gifts, the discipline, information, circumstance, courage, timing, will, and divine inspiration—can lead us out of the crisis in which we find ourselves. Leadership can mitigate the misery of our nation. Leadership can part the waters and lead our nation in the direction of the Promised Land. Leadership can lift the boats stuck at the bottom.

I have had the rare opportunity to watch seven men, and then two, pour out their souls, offer their service, and heal and heed the call of duty to direct the course of our nation.[b] There is a proper season for everything. There is a time to sow and a time to reap.[c] There's a time to compete and a time to cooperate. I ask for your vote on the first ballot as a vote for a new direction for this party and this nation—a vote of conviction, a vote of conscience. But I will be proud to support the nominee of this convention for the presidency of the United States of America. Thank you.

I have watched the leadership of our party develop and grow. My respect for both Mr. Mondale and Mr. Hart is great. I have watched them struggle with the crosswinds and cross-fires of being public servants, and I believe they will both continue to try to serve us faithfully.

I am elated by the knowledge that for the first time in our history a woman, Geraldine Ferraro, will be recommended to share our ticket.[d]

Throughout this campaign, I've tried to offer leadership to the Democratic Party and the nation. If, in my high moments, I have done some good, offered some service, shed some light, healed some wounds, rekindled some hope, or stirred someone from apathy and indifference, or in any way along the way helped somebody, then this campaign has not been in vain.

For friends who loved and cared for me, and for a God who spared me, and for a family who understood, I am eternally grateful.

If, in my low moments, in word, deed, or attitude, through some error of temper, taste, or tone, I have caused anyone discomfort, created pain, or revived someone's fears, that was not my truest self. If there were occasions when my grape turned into a raisin and my joy bell lost its resonance, please forgive me. Charge it to my head and not to my heart. My head—so limited in its finitude; my heart, which is boundless in its love for the

b. Jackson is referring here to the seven contenders for the 1984 Democratic presidential nomination: Walter Mondale (ultimately the nominee), Senators Gary Hart, John Glenn, Alan Cranston, and Ernest Hollings, former senator George McGovern, and Jackson himself.

c. Ecclesiastes, 3:1–8: "For everything there is a season, . . . a time to plant, and a time to pluck up what is planted."

d. Representative Geraldine Ferraro (1935–2011): Democratic vice presidential nominee in 1984.

human family. I am not a perfect servant. I am a public servant doing my best against the odds. As I develop and serve, be patient: God is not finished with me yet.

This campaign has taught me much; that leaders must be tough enough to fight, tender enough to cry, human enough to make mistakes, humble enough to admit them, strong enough to absorb the pain, and resilient enough to bounce back and keep on moving.

For leaders, the pain is often intense. But you must smile through your tears and keep moving with the faith that there is a brighter side somewhere.

I went to see Hubert Humphrey three days before he died.[e] He had just called Richard Nixon from his dying bed, and many people wondered why. And I asked him. He said, "Jesse, from this vantage point, the sun is setting in my life, all of the speeches, the political conventions, the crowds, and the great fights are behind me now. At a time like this you are forced to deal with your irreducible essence, forced to grapple with that which is really important to you. And what I've concluded about life," Hubert Humphrey said, "When all is said and done, we must forgive each other, and redeem each other, and move on."

Our party is emerging from one of its most hard fought battles for the Democratic Party's presidential nomination in our history. But our healthy competition should make us better, not bitter. We must use the insight, wisdom, and experience of the late Hubert Humphrey as a balm for the wounds in our party, this nation, and the world. We must forgive each other, redeem each other, regroup, and move on. Our flag is red, white, and blue, but our nation is a rainbow—red, yellow, brown, black, and white—and we're all precious in God's sight.[f]

America is not like a blanket—one piece of unbroken cloth, the same color, the same texture, the same size. America is more like a quilt: many patches, many pieces, many colors, many sizes, all woven and held together by a common thread. The white, the Hispanic, the black, the Arab, the Jew, the woman, the native American, the small farmer, the businessperson, the environmentalist, the peace activist, the young, the old, the lesbian, the gay, and the disabled make up the American quilt.

---

e. Hubert Humphrey (1911–1978): US senator (1948–1964), vice president (1964–1968), and Democratic presidential nominee running against Richard Nixon in 1968. Humphrey was widely recognized for his strong support of civil rights as early as the 1948 Democratic Convention.

f. Isaiah 43:4: "because you are precious in my sight."

Even in our fractured state, all of us count and fit somewhere. We have proven that we can survive without each other. But we have not proven that we can win and make progress without each other. We must come together.

From Fannie Lou Hamer[g] in Atlantic City in 1964 to the Rainbow Coalition in San Francisco today; from the Atlantic to the Pacific, we have experienced pain but progress, as we ended American apartheid laws. We got public accommodations. We secured voting rights. We obtained open housing, as young people got the right to vote. We lost Malcolm, Martin, Medgar, Bobby, John, and Viola.[h] The team that got us here must be expanded, not abandoned.

Twenty years ago, tears welled up in our eyes as the bodies of Schwerner, Goodman, and Chaney were dredged from the depths of a river in Mississippi.[i] Twenty years later, our communities, black and Jewish, are in anguish, anger, and pain. Feelings have been hurt on both sides. There is a crisis in communications. Confusion is in the air. But we cannot afford to lose our way. We may agree to agree; or agree to disagree on issues; we must bring back civility to these tensions.

We are copartners in a long and rich religious history—the Judeo-Christian traditions. Many blacks and Jews have a shared passion for social justice at home and peace abroad. We must seek a revival of the spirit, inspired by a new vision and new possibilities. We must return to higher ground. We are bound by Moses and Jesus but also connected with Islam and Mohammed. These three great religions, Judaism, Christianity, and Islam, were all born in the revered and holy city of Jerusalem.

We are bound by Dr. Martin Luther King Jr. and Rabbi Abraham Heschel,[j] crying out from their graves for us to reach common ground. We are bound by shared blood and shared sacrifices. We are much too intelligent, much

g. Fannie Lou Hamer (1917–1977): Vice chair of the Mississippi Freedom Democratic Party, which unsuccessfully sought to have its delegates seated at the 1964 Democratic National Convention. Ms. Hamer is widely known for her speech to the Credentials Committee at that convention.

h. Jackson is probably referring here to Malcolm X, Martin Luther King Jr., Medgar Evers, Bobby Kennedy, John F. Kennedy, and Viola Liuzzo. Evers (1925–1963) was an NAACP field secretary in Mississippi who was murdered during the voting rights campaign there. Liuzzo (1935–1965) was shot and killed by Klansmen after participating in a voting rights march in Alabama.

i. Michael Schwerner, Andrew Goodman, and John Chaney were civil rights workers in Mississippi during "Freedom Summer." They were slain there on 12 June 1964.

j. Rabbi Abraham Heschel (1907–1972): A highly regarded Jewish theologian born in Warsaw, Poland, who narrowly escaped from Nazi-occupied Poland during World War II. He participated in the 1965 Selma civil rights march with Dr. Martin Luther King Jr.

too bound by our Judeo-Christian heritage, much too victimized by racism, sexism, militarism, and anti-Semitism, much too threatened as historical scapegoats to go on divided one from another. We must turn from finger pointing to clasped hands. We must share our burdens and our joys with each other once again. We must turn to each other and not on each other and choose higher ground.

Twenty years later, we cannot be satisfied by just restoring the old coalition. Old wine skins must make room for new wine. We must heal and expand. The Rainbow Coalition is making room for Arab Americans. They, too, know the pain and hurt of racial and religious rejection. They must not continue to be made pariahs. The Rainbow Coalition is making room for Hispanic Americans who this very night are living under the threat of the Simpson-Mazzoli bill[k]; and farm workers from Ohio who are fighting the Campbell Soup Company with a boycott to achieve legitimate workers' rights.

The Rainbow is making room for the Native American, the most exploited people of all, a people with the greatest moral claim amongst us. We support them as they seek the restoration of their ancient land and claim amongst us. We support them as they seek the restoration of land and water rights, as they seek to preserve their ancestral homeland and the beauty of a land that was once all theirs. They can never receive a fair share for all they have given us. They must finally have a fair chance to develop their great resources and to preserve their people and their culture.

The Rainbow Coalition includes Asian Americans, now being killed in our streets—scapegoats for the failures of corporate, industrial, and economic policies.

The Rainbow is making room for the young Americans. Twenty years ago, our young people were dying in a war for which they could not even vote. Twenty years later, young America has the power to stop a war in Central America and the responsibility to vote in great numbers. Young America must be politically active in 1984. The choice is war or peace. We must make room for young America.

The Rainbow includes disabled veterans. The color scheme fits in the Rainbow. The disabled have their handicap revealed and their genius concealed; while the able-bodied have their genius revealed and their disability

k. An immigration reform bill that required documentation of worker's legal status in the United States. The original bill was attacked by civil rights activists who believed it could be used to discriminate against Hispanics.

concealed. But ultimately, we must judge people by their values and their contribution. Don't leave anybody out. I would rather have Roosevelt in a wheelchair than Reagan on a horse.

The Rainbow is making room for small farmers. They have suffered tremendously under the Reagan regime. They will either receive 90 percent parity or 100 percent charity. We must address their concerns and make room for them. The Rainbow includes lesbians and gays. No American citizen ought be denied equal protection from the law.

We must be unusually committed and caring as we expand our family to include new members. All of us must be tolerant and understanding as the fears and anxieties of the rejected and the party leadership express themselves in many different ways. Too often what we call hate—as if it were some deeply-rooted philosophy or strategy—is simply ignorance, anxiety, paranoia, fear, and insecurity. To be strong leaders, we must be long-suffering as we seek to right the wrongs of our party and our nation. We must expand our party, heal our party, and unify our arty. That is our mission in 1984.

We are often reminded that we live in a great nation—and we do. But it can be greater still. The Rainbow is mandating a new definition of greatness. We must not measure greatness from the mansion down, but the manger up. Jesus said that we should not be judged by the bark we wear but by the fruit that we bear. Jesus said that we must measure greatness by how we treat the least of these.

President Reagan says the nation is in recovery. Those ninety thousand corporations that made a profit last year but paid no federal taxes are recovering. The thirty-seven thousand military contractors who have benefited from Reagan's more than doubling of the military budget in peacetime, surely they are recovering. The big corporations and rich individuals who received the bulk of a three-year, multibillion tax cut from Mr. Reagan are recovering. But no such recovery is under way for the least of these.

Rising tides don't lift all boats, particularly those stuck at the bottom. For the boats stuck at the bottom there's a misery index. This administration has made life more miserable for the poor. Its attitude has been contemptuous. Its policies and programs have been cruel and unfair to working people. They must be held accountable in November for increasing infant mortality among the poor. In Detroit, one of the great cities of the western world, babies are dying at the same rate as [in] Honduras, the most underdeveloped nation in our hemisphere. This administration must be held accountable for policies that have contributed to the growing poverty in America. There are now thirty-four million people in poverty, 15 percent of our nation. Twenty-three million are white; eleven million black, Hispanic, Asian, and others—mostly women and children. By the end of this year, there will be forty-one million people in poverty. We cannot stand idly by. We must fight for a change now.

Under this regime we look at Social Security. The '81 budget cuts included nine permanent Social Security benefit cuts totaling $20 billion over five years. Small businesses have suffered under Reagan tax cuts. Only 18 percent of total business tax cuts went to them; 82 percent to big businesses. Health care under Mr. Reagan has already been sharply cut. Education under Mr. Reagan has been cut 25 percent. Under Mr. Reagan, there are now 9.7 million female head families. They represent 16 percent of all families. Half of all of them are poor. Seventy percent of all poor children live in a house headed by a woman, where there is no man. Under Mr. Reagan, the administration has cleaned up only 6 of 546 priority toxic waste dumps. Farmers' real net income was only about half its level in 1979.

Many say that the race in November will be decided in the South. President Reagan is depending on the conservative South to return him to office. But the South, I tell you, is unnaturally conservative. The South is the poorest region in our nation and, therefore, [has] the least to conserve. In his appeal to the South, Mr. Reagan is trying to substitute flags and prayer cloths for food, and clothing, and education, health care, and housing.

Mr. Reagan will ask us to pray, and I believe in prayer. I have come to this way by the power of prayer. But then, we must watch false prophecy. He cuts energy assistance to the poor, cuts breakfast programs from children, cuts lunch programs from children, cuts job training from children, and then says to an empty table, "Let us pray." Apparently, he is not familiar with the structure of a prayer. You thank the Lord for the food that you are about to receive, not the food that just left. I think that we should pray, but don't pray for the food that left. Pray for the man that took the food to leave. We need a change. We need a change in November.

Under Mr. Reagan, the misery index has risen for the poor. The danger index has risen for everybody. Under this administration, we've lost the lives of our boys in Central America and Honduras, in Grenada, in Lebanon, in nuclear standoff in Europe. Under this administration, one-third of our children believe they will die in a nuclear war. The danger index is increasing in this world. All the talk about the defense against Russia: the Russian submarines are closer, and their missiles are more accurate. We live in a world tonight more miserable and a world more dangerous.

While Reaganomics and Reaganism is talked about often, so often we miss the real meaning. Reaganism is a spirit, and Reaganomics represents the real economic facts of life. In 1980, Mr. George Bush, a man with reasonable access to Mr. Reagan, did an analysis of Mr. Reagan's economic plan. Mr. George Bush concluded that Reagan's plan was "voodoo economics." He was right. Third-party candidate John Anderson said, "a combination of military spending, tax cuts, and a balanced budget by '84 would be accomplished with blue smoke and mirrors." They were both right.

Mr. Reagan talks about a dynamic recovery. There's some measure of recovery. Three and a half years later, unemployment has inched just below where it was when he took office in 1981. There are still 8.1 million people officially unemployed; 11 million working only part-time. Inflation has come down, but let's analyze for a moment who has paid the price for this superficial economic recovery.

Mr. Reagan curbed inflation by cutting consumer demand. He cut consumer demand with conscious and callous fiscal and monetary policies. He used the federal budget to deliberately induce unemployment and curb social spending. He then weighed and supported tight monetary policies of the Federal Reserve Board to deliberately drive up interest rates, again to curb consumer demand created through borrowing. Unemployment reached 10.7 percent. We experienced skyrocketing interest rates. Our dollar inflated abroad. There were record bank failures, record farm foreclosures, record business bankruptcies; record budget deficits, record trade deficits.

Mr. Reagan brought inflation down by destabilizing our economy and disrupting family life. He promised—he promised in 1980 a balanced budget. But instead we now have a record $200 billion budget deficit. Under Mr. Reagan, the cumulative budget deficit for his four years is more than the sum total of deficits from George Washington to Jimmy Carter combined. I tell you, we need a change.

How is he paying for these short-term jobs? Reagan's economic recovery is being financed by deficit spending—$200 billion a year. Military spending, a major cause of this deficit, is projected over the next five years to be nearly $2 trillion, and will cost about $40,000 for every taxpaying family. When the government borrows $200 billion annually to finance the deficit, this encourages the private sector to make its money off of interest rates as opposed to development and economic growth.

Even money abroad—we don't have enough money domestically to finance the debt, so we are now borrowing money abroad, from foreign banks, governments, and financial institutions: $40 billion in 1983; $70 to $80 billion in 1984—40 percent of our total; over $100 billion—50 percent of our total—in 1985. By 1989, it is projected that 50 percent of all individual income taxes will be going just to pay for interest on that debt. The United States used to be the largest exporter of capital, but under Mr. Reagan, we will quite likely become the largest debtor nation.

About two weeks ago, on July the 4th, we celebrated our Declaration of Independence, yet every day supply-side economics is making our nation more economically dependent and less economically free. Five to 6 percent of our gross national product is now being eaten up with President Reagan's budget deficits. To depend on foreign military powers to protect our national security would be foolish, making us dependent and less secure. Yet, Reaganomics has us increasingly dependent on foreign economic sources. This consumer-led but deficit-financed recovery is unbalanced and artificial. We have a challenge as Democrats to point a way out.

Democracy guarantees opportunity, not success.

Democracy guarantees the right to participate, not a license for either a majority or a minority to dominate.

The victory for the Rainbow Coalition in the platform debates today was not whether we won or lost, but that we raised the right issues. We could afford to lose the vote; issues are nonnegotiable. We could not afford to avoid raising the right questions. Our self-respect and our moral integrity were at stake. Our heads are perhaps bloody, but not bowed. Our back is straight. We can go home and face our people. Our vision is clear.

When we think, on this journey from slave-ship to championship, that we have gone from the planks of the boardwalk in Atlantic City in 1964 to fighting to help write the planks in the platform in San Francisco in '84, there is a deep and abiding sense of joy in our souls in spite of the tears in our eyes. Though there are missing planks, there is a solid foundation upon which to build. Our party can win, but we must provide hope which will inspire people to struggle and achieve; provide a plan that shows a way out of our dilemma and then lead the way.

In 1984, my heart is made to feel glad because I know there is a way out—justice. The requirement for rebuilding America is justice. The linchpin of progressive politics in our nation will not come from the North; they, in fact, will come from the South. That is why I argue over and over again. We look from Virginia around to Texas, there's only one black congressperson out of 115. Nineteen years later, we're locked out of the Congress, the Senate and the Governor's Mansion. What does this large black vote mean? Why do I fight to win second primaries and fight gerrymandering and annexation and at-large [elections]? Why do we fight over that? Because I tell you, you cannot hold someone in the ditch unless you linger there with them. Unless you linger there.

If you want a change in this nation, you enforce that Voting Rights Act. We'll get twelve to twenty black, Hispanics, female, and progressive congresspersons from the South. We can save the cotton, but we've got to fight the boll weevils. We've got to make a judgment. We've got to make a judgment.

It is not enough to hope ERA will pass.[1] How can we pass ERA? If blacks vote in great numbers, progressive whites win. It's the only way progressive whites win. If blacks vote in great numbers, Hispanics win. When blacks, Hispanics, and progressive whites vote, women win. When women win, children win. When women and children win, workers win. We must all come up together. We must come up together.

Thank you.

For all of our joy and excitement, we must not save the world and lose our souls. We should never short-circuit enforcing the Voting Rights Act at every level. When one of us rise[s], all of us will rise. Justice is the way out. Peace is the way out. We should not act as if nuclear weaponry is negotiable and debatable.

In this world in which we live, we dropped the bomb on Japan and felt guilty, but in 1984, other folks [have] also got bombs. This time, if we drop the bomb, six minutes later, we too will be destroyed. It's not about dropping the bomb on somebody. It is about dropping the bomb on everybody. We must choose to develop minds over guided missiles, and think it out, and not fight it out. It's time for a change.

Our foreign policy must be characterized by mutual respect, not by gunboat diplomacy, big stick diplomacy, and threats. Our nation at its best feeds the hungry. Our nation at its worst, at its worst, will mine the harbors of Nicaragua, at its worst will try to overthrow their government, at its worst will cut aid to American education and increase the aid to El Salvador; at its worst, our nation will have partnerships with South Africa. That's a moral disgrace. It's a moral disgrace. It's a moral disgrace.

1. ERA: The Equal Rights Amendment.

We look at Africa. We cannot just focus on apartheid in southern Africa. We must fight for trade with Africa, and not just aid to Africa. We cannot stand idly by and say we will not relate to Nicaragua unless they have elections there, and then embrace military regimes in Africa overthrowing democratic governments in Nigeria and Liberia and Ghana. We must fight for democracy all around the world and play the game by one set of rules.

Peace in this world. Our present formula for peace in the Middle East is inadequate. It will not work. There are twenty-two nations in the Middle East. Our nation must be able to talk and act and influence all of them. We must build upon Camp David, and measure human rights by one yardstick. In that region we have too many interests and too few friends.

There is a way out—jobs. Put America back to work. When I was a child growing up in Greenville, South Carolina, the Reverend Sample used to preach every so often a sermon relating to Jesus. And he said, "If I be lifted up, I'll draw all men unto me."[m] I didn't quite understand what he meant as a child growing up, but I understand a little better now. If you raise up truth, it's magnetic. It has a way of drawing people.

With all this confusion in this convention, the bright lights and parties and big fun, we must raise up the simple proposition: If we lift up a program to feed the hungry, they'll come running; if we lift up a program to study war no more, our youth will come running; if we lift up a program to put America back to work, and an alternative to welfare and despair, they will come working.

If we cut that military budget without cutting our defense, and use that money to rebuild bridges and put steel workers back to work, and use that money and provide jobs for our cities, and use that money to build schools and pay teachers and educate our children and build hospitals and train doctors and train nurses, the whole nation will come running to us.

As I leave you now, we vote in this convention and get ready to go back across this nation in a couple of days. In this campaign, I've tried to be faithful to my promise. I lived in old barrios, ghettos, and reservations and housing projects. I have a message for our youth. I challenge them to put hope in their brains and not dope in their veins. I told them that like Jesus, I, too, was born in the slum. But just because you're born in the slum does not mean the slum is born in you, and you can rise above it if your mind is made up. I told them in every slum there are two sides. When I see a broken

m. John 12:32.

window—that's the slummy side. Train some youth to become a glazier—that's the sunny side. When I see a missing brick—that's the slummy side. Let that child in the union and become a brick mason and build—that's the sunny side. When I see a missing door—that's the slummy side. Train some youth to become a carpenter—that's the sunny side. And when I see the vulgar words and hieroglyphics of destitution on the walls—that's the slummy side. Train some youth to become a painter, an artist—that's the sunny side.

We leave this place looking for the sunny side because there's a brighter side somewhere. I'm more convinced than ever that we can win. We will vault up the rough side of the mountain. We can win. I just want young America to do me one favor, just one favor. Exercise the right to dream. You must face reality—that which is. But then dream of a reality that ought to be—that must be. Live beyond the pain of reality with the dream of a bright tomorrow. Use hope and imagination as weapons of survival and progress. Use love to motivate you and obligate you to serve the human family.

Young America, dream. Choose the human race over the nuclear race. Bury the weapons and don't burn the people. Dream—dream of a new value system. Teachers who teach for life and not just for a living; teach because they can't help it. Dream of lawyers more concerned about justice than a judgeship. Dream of doctors more concerned about public health than personal wealth. Dream of preachers and priests who will prophesy and not just profiteer. Preach and dream!

Our time has come. Our time has come. Suffering breeds character. Character breeds faith. In the end, faith will not disappoint. Our time has come. Our faith, hope, and dreams will prevail. Our time has come. Weeping has endured for nights, but now joy cometh in the morning. Our time has come. No grave can hold our body down. Our time has come. No lie can live forever. Our time has come. We must leave racial battleground and come to economic common ground and moral higher ground. America, our time has come. We come from disgrace to amazing grace. Our time has come. Give me your tired, give me your poor, your huddled masses who yearn to breathe free, and come November, there will be a change because our time has come.

Marian Wright Edelman

Children's Legislative Issues
(Speech to the National Education Association)

Born and raised in rural South Carolina, Marian Wright Edelman has become the consummate political reformer at the national level. After receiving on-the-ground field experience in the 1960s with the famed Legal Defense and Education Fund of the National Association for the Advancement of Colored People (NAACP), in 1973, Marian Wright Edelman founded the Children's Defense Fund (CDF). From that position she has campaigned tirelessly on behalf of national and state legislation to benefit children. She speaks frequently, and her addresses are uniformly filled with facts, figures, examples, and specific policy proposals for which she advocates. Her 1985 keynote to the National Education Association's annual conference is characteristic of her speaking. Her address is policy oriented—sharply and specifically contrasting her vision of America with that of President Ronald Reagan—yet also a speech in which, at turns, Edelman talks directly and plainly with her audience.

Marian Wright was born in 1939 in Bennettsville, South Carolina, to Arthur and Maggie Bowen Wright. Her father was a Baptist minister who believed that his work in service of his community must extend beyond the confines of the church sanctuary.[1] Parks, lunch counters, and nursing homes were not available to African Americans. So on the church grounds, the Reverend Wright built a playground for African American youth; he installed a grill to serve inexpensive food; and he established the Wright House for the Aged. Marian's childhood was consumed with school, church, and helping with the family's extended social services ventures. Her father died in 1954, but her mother continued to help run the Wright House for the Aged and in her widowhood, took in foster children as well.[2]

In 1956, Marian left to attend Spelman College in Atlanta. There she participated in sit-ins and civil rights demonstrations and served as president of the student body. She graduated from Spelman in 1960 and in 1963, earned her law degree at Yale University. Throughout her undergraduate and graduate work, Marian acquired extensive international experience. She studied at the University of Paris and in Switzerland during her junior year at Spelman and participated in another exchange study tour that took her to eastern Europe and the USSR. In the summer of 1962, after her second year of law school, she worked in the Ivory Coast of Africa for Crossroads Africa, a community development program established in 1958 on which John F. Kennedy's Peace Corps was modeled.[3]

After graduating from Yale, Marian joined the NAACP as a staff attorney. In 1964, she worked with the Mississippi Summer Project voting drive, helping African Americans recognize and exercise their legal rights. Her work, there, however, brought back to the surface her family's deep roots in social services. As she later recalled: "The people they'd tried to register to vote didn't have anything to eat, didn't have a place to live. That made the first real point to me—that without social and economic underpinnings, the right to vote does not mean as much as it need be."[4] Her first major battle was to bring the Head Start program to Mississippi when the state government refused to apply for the federal program. That campaign blended grassroots organizing with court battles and congressional lobbying—a blueprint for what Edelman would later undertake with the CDF.[5]

In 1967, Marian organized Senator Robert F. Kennedy's famous tour of the Mississippi Delta, a widely televised visit that demonstrated the depth of poverty experienced in portions of America. During the tour, she met Peter Edelman, a legislative assistant to Senator Kennedy. In 1968 they married, one of the first interracial marriages in Virginia after its legal ban on such marriages had been overturned. In 1968, Marian Wright Edelman established a local branch of the NAACP Legal Defense and Educational Fund in Jackson, Mississippi. That arm of the NAACP focused directly on helping individual African Americans improve their lives. In that capacity, Edelman continued the work she had begun in Mississippi in 1964.[6]

Since the beginning of her time at work in Mississippi, Edelman had observed the deep poverty and harsh living conditions experienced by many, and particularly children. By 1973, she decided to redirect her efforts from the battle for increased legal rights to the cause of improving the lives of poor and neglected children and so founded the Children's Defense Fund. Modeled after the NAACP Legal Defense and Educational Fund, the CDF had as its mission the tangible improvement of poor children's lives.[7]

Marian Wright Edelman has spent much of her adult life lobbying on behalf of legislation to benefit children, and her public speaking is a model for lobbyist oratory. Her rhetoric is marked by an attention to detail: what policy she is proposing, what problem the proposed policy is targeting, what costs and benefits will result from the policy, and what will happen if the policy is or is not adopted. The level of analysis and detail in her speeches could almost be characterized as "wonkish"—a charge sometimes leveled at the public speaking of Bill Clinton (especially in his early years) and of Barack Obama. However, interspersed with the policy details, Edelman includes language that speaks directly to the audience, engaging them as cooperative partners and keeping their focus on the fundamental goal to which anyone can relate: helping disadvantaged children have better lives. The result is an address that is very substantive, yet one in which she speaks with the audience rather than at or down to them.

"Children's Legislative Issues" begins immediately with a biting analysis of the problem: the Reagan administration's cuts in federal programs that benefit children. Edelman introduces the discussion with a quotation from Martin Luther King Jr.'s "A Time to Break Silence," a quotation that reflects on the moral decline of a nation that invests heavily in its military but shortchanges its own people. After establishing that framework, Edelman scathingly indicts the Reagan administration's budget as a "moral travesty." She interweaves statistics that testify to the declining well-being of children, contrasting the rates of death caused by poverty with those caused by the more commonly expected circumstances, such as traffic accidents or cancer. She follows that stark depiction with the Reagan proposal to cut "5.2 billion . . . from poor children and families' programs" while increasing the military budget by thirty-two billion dollars. She concludes her statement of contrast in direct fashion: the children of America need less protection from "external enemies" and more spent on protection from internal "enemies."

After contrasting Reagan's extravagant spending on the military with the paucity of spending on the problem of poverty, Edelman continues the remainder of the opening half of her speech with a series of parallel charges against the Reagan administration. She turns first to the problem of infant mortality, followed by the issues of childhood vaccinations, child abuse, homelessness, youth unemployment, and the increasing tax burden on the poor. Until she comes to the issue of the tax burden on the working poor, Edelman consistently casts each problem in contrast to Reagan's military spending. While he is spending billions on defense to protect the nation's children from military attack, she observes that "American children need protection, as you know, against growing child abuse," and "American children need to be protected against the enemy of homelessness." Each problem she enunciates is again supported with a plethora of statistical evidence. While we are building seventeen thousand new nuclear weapons, two million fewer children will receive federally supported vaccinations next year; two hundred thousand more children were reported abused last year; the Reagan administration is cutting a twenty-five million dollar training program that helps child-care workers detect and help abused children; 22 percent of homeless shelter occupants are children; AFDC recipients have had their funding cut by 1.7 billion dollars since Reagan took office; and 160 million dollars will be trimmed from the summer youth employment program.

The final problem articulated in this opening half of the speech is the increasing tax burden on the working poor. Here, instead of contrasting the children's problem with Reagan's military spending, she focuses on the tax breaks the government provides to corporations and the wealthy. The contrast, then, lies with the Reagan administration's highly publicized campaign to "lower taxes," a campaign that benefits the rich but not the poor. Again, Edelman supports her argument very specifically. "The amount of Federal tax," she tells her audience, "paid by those with incomes below the Federal poverty line increased 58 percent from 1980 to 1982 alone." While a working mother of three with an income of $10,500 would pay $1,186 in taxes in 1984, well-known companies such as DuPont, Texaco, and AT&T had paid no federal income taxes.

After concluding her indictment of the Reagan administration with a brief passage on deficit reduction, Edelman turns to the Children's Survival Bill. As she characterizes this move in her transition, the CDF believes strongly that "you can't beat something with nothing." The Children's Survival Bill serves as a synecdochic frame, an easily remembered title for a variety of programs for which the CDF is lobbying. From among the various proposals that comprise the bill, Edelman strategically selects two initiatives to discuss that are especially appropriate to an audience of teachers—teen pregnancy prevention and teen health and prenatal care. Both initiatives include community- and school-based programs that would appeal to, and benefit from the assistance of, her audience.

As with the first half of her speech, her exposition of these two initiatives is buttressed with abundant supporting material that incorporates both statistics and examples. Thus, she notes of the problem of teen pregnancy, "In 1983, 523,000 babies were born to teen mothers. Ten thousand of these babies were born to girls fourteen and under." Regarding prenatal care and counseling, she observes that "one out of every three teens who have a first child, get pregnant again within two years." Community-based programs can work to solve such problems, she argues, as "in St. Paul, and in Houston, and a few other cities . . . they have been able to reduce the teen repeat pregnancy rate to almost nothing." Prenatal care pays off, she notes, because "it costs us $600 to give prenatal care, including vitamins and nutritional supplements to women, . . . [but] about $20,000 to care for a premature infant just in the first twenty days of life."

If not carefully employed, Edelman's voluminous use of evidence, especially statistical, could easily overwhelm the hearer. In addition to speaking very distinctly and using repetition to emphasize the point she is making, at key junctures in the speech Edelman includes language and appeals that serve to actively engage the audience in the subject of her talk.

In her language, for example, Edelman is often reflexive, "thinking out loud" and so inviting her listeners to be partners in a collaborative process. As she works through the litany of societal ills that have been exacerbated by the Reagan administration's policies, for example, she mentions that the audience had "talked about education already, so I will skip that, because you know more about that than I do." "Too often we start off on welfare," she confides to them, "and then we all end up fighting each other." "I think we should ask," and "I think it could make a difference," she tells them, and "this annoys me greatly." "We have tried to pick prenatal care as the first action issue on which we will all try to work together on teen pregnancy," she says conspiratorially, revealing to the audience the CDF's lobbying strategy.

Edelman also explicitly requests her listeners' participation. "I hope that we can get your help," she tells them plainly; "in looking at those provisions of the Children's Survival Bill, a number of them are school-related. . . . And I would hope that you all might look at that school-based clinic, comprehensive clinic notion, and find that that might be one among many that you might support." "I think we, who care about people, and decency, and fairness, have got to say that they should first convince President Reagan,

Defense Secretary Weinberger, and the powerful special interest beneficiaries of defense and tax largesse, to make deficit reduction their first priority before sending poor, handicapped and homeless children again to the front lines of a deficit reduction war no one else is fighting. And we've got to make that clear." Through such direct appeals as well as her use of first person plural pronouns, she attempts to mold the audience and herself into a collective "we."

In a rhetorically astute move, Edelman also combines the two styles in order to move the audience from hearers to doers. After disclosing to her audience her thoughts and feelings about a problem that children face, she consistently asks for their participation: "What do we do about all this?" Her discussion of the CDF's lobbying approach during the first two years of the Reagan administration is representative. In that section she walks the audience through the CDF's thinking and asks them to reason the problem through with her: "In the first two years, as you know, with the avalanche of Reagan cuts we were told that there was no way we could stop the absolute across the board repeal, as he attempted to do, of virtually every Federal program serving children. Our first priority, therefore, was to stop the repeal effort, to keep the framework of the laws in place, because if we lost the laws, we figured we might never get them back. And so we said lose the money, but try to keep the things intact. And we think, with the help of NEA and many others, [we] have succeeded in keeping the Federal framework of protections for handicapped children, for children who are without homes, in education, in health, intact." The audience begins as a third-party, "omniscient" observer of the CDF and its decision-making process: "we were told," "our first priority," "and so we said lose the money, but try to keep the things intact." Ultimately, however, the audience and Edelman become united as "we": "we think, with the help of NEA and others, [we] have succeeded." Consistently throughout the speech, Edelman thus takes the audience into her confidence—"In the second two years, we said it's time to try to get some of our money back, and we drafted a Children's Survival Bill which was used as a basis for beginning to get specific restorations"—and then rhetorically converts them to partners: "And we always have to remember that while we got some money back, we are about 20 percent back towards where we started in 1980."

Despite the heavy statistical evidence, Edelman also keeps the speech conversational through language that conveys her thoughts very plainly. She characterizes the connection between teenage pregnancies and premature births and infant mortality as "like night follows the day." Preventing teen pregnancy is critical because "children having children is like an engine that is driving new generations of poor children." Babies born to teen mothers need good prenatal care because "these children are born with enough things stacked against them. They don't need a birth defect or other things, too." Edelman recounts asking her budget director to help her "laymanize" the notion of $3.2 trillion, and they do so by characterizing it in terms of "since Jesus Christ was born." Her story illustrating the issue of teen mothers producing generation after generation of teen mothers is representative: "In 1983, 523,000 babies were born to teen mothers. Ten thousand of these babies were born to girls fourteen and under. Last week I heard from a big city, which I will leave unnamed, about a twelve year old who had a child, whose mother was twenty-two. And I sort of said, I've seen thirty year old grandmothers, and forty year old grandmothers, but when you get to grandmothers in the twenties, you've just gotten me. I mean, that's really a bit much." Edelman begins with the statistics that verify the extent of the problem, but follows those statistics with the story of the twenty-two year old grandmother. She then summarizes the point with a reflexive comment that colloquially shares her view with her audience: "I mean, that's really a bit much."

Edelman's story of the Grace Commission and the W. R. Grace Company is similarly constructed and again exemplifies her deft rhetorical touch. Statistical evidence that formally communicates the extent of the issue is interspersed throughout her discussion: "fifty-eight percent," "annual income of 10,500 dollars," "1,186 dollars in taxes," "13.7 billion dollars in profits," "684 million dollars in profits," "got back twelve and a half million dollars in negative tax rebates." Edelman uses very direct language to summarize the problem: "While the President claims to want the poor to work, he has penalized their work with higher taxes." By the end of the section, Edelman has cut through to the heart of the problem and exposed the irony of the situation in unmistakable terms: "Something is wrong about that [the Grace company's receiving negative tax rebates]. If we just brought the W. R. Grace's tax rate, Federal tax rate, up to zero, [Laughter] we could pay for nine million school lunches that the President has cut."

Marian Wright Edelman thus constructs a speech of consummate lobbying rhetoric. She clearly indicts the status quo, contrasting what is with what should be. Her policy proposals are specific without losing her audience in the details. Her support for her points is both formal—usually statistical—and informal. Her direct language clearly defines and evaluates even as it invites the audience into a collaborative conversation. She talks with her audience and consistently asks them to become "we" with her and the CDF. Her speeches do not "soar;" they are instead businesslike even as they are interesting, entertaining, educational, and, for many, effective. Thirty-six years after its founding, the CDF remains a vibrant advocacy organization and it still has Marian Wright Edelman as its president.

Since 1985, Edelman has continued to give voice to the problems discussed in her speech to the NEA. She has lobbied, spoken, raised money, authored articles, given interviews, and published books, such as the *New York Times* best seller *The Measure of Success: A Letter to My Children and Yours* (1992).[8] She has received the Presidential Medal of Freedom and the Robert F. Kennedy Lifetime Achievement Award.[9] While *The Measure of Success* addressed the individual's responsibility to self as well as society, in 2008, Edelman authored a book comprised of myriad letters. *The Sea Is So Wide and My Boat Is So Small* is addressed to a wide range of audiences whom she feels have the power to change America's care of its children.[10] An interview she gave upon the publication of the volume echoes her NEA speech from two and a half decades earlier: "'I am grandmother,' she said proudly. 'And I've been radicalized all over again, thinking about the kind of world that we are leaving my grandchildren. It's less safe; it's less just. I worry. I think the responsibility of adults is to leave the next generation a better world than we found it. I do worry about adults coming in and not providing the guidance that our children need.'"[11]

Children's Legislative Issues

(Speech to the National Education Association)

February 22, 1985
Washington, DC

Martin Luther King said, in the middle of the Vietnam War, that a nation that continues year after year to spend more money on military defense than on programs of social uplift is approaching spiritual death. If we look at the President's[a] fiscal 1986 budget, you will see and I feel, that it is a moral travesty. Although more children die each year from poverty than from traffic fatalities and suicide combined, twice more children die from poverty than die from heart disease and cancer combined, [the]President's new budget for the fifth consecutive year in a row, attempts to cut billions from children. Specifically it seeks to cut 5.2 billion dollars in fiscal '86 from poor children and families' programs on top of the ten billion dollars a year in cut-backs made in these programs since 1980. The military will gain 32 billion dollars in fiscal '86, on top of a 178 billion in increases they have been given since 1980. If President Reagan's budget priorities succeed, by 1990 every American will be spending 19 percent less on poor children and families, and 86 percent more on defense. Over a five year period, more American children die from poverty, than the total number of American battle deaths in the Vietnam War. Yet President seeks a 239 percent increase by 1990 to make our children more secure from external enemies. Our leaders dream about a new multibillion dollar Star Wars[b] system to make our defenses impenetrable against enemy missiles. It would be nice if they could dream of a smaller, achievable war against the internal enemy of child poverty, a war that saves

a. President Ronald Reagan, 1981–1989.

b. The Strategic Defense Initiative, nicknamed "Star Wars," proposed building an antimissile system in space.

and enhances rather than takes and threatens human life. [Applause] Every poor American child could be lifted out of poverty in 1986 for less than half of the proposed defense spending increase in that one year alone.

We need to tell the American People, and President Reagan and the Congress that American children not only need defense against poverty, but against preventable infant mortality and birth defects. By 1990, 22,000 American babies are going to die, primarily because of low birth weight. We can prevent at least one in eight of these infant deaths and thousands of handicapping conditions simply by providing their mothers prenatal care. For 7 percent, or twenty-five days, of the defense budget increase, again, just next year, every poor mother and baby could be provided Medicaid, and thus prenatal care coverage. Instead, the Reagan budget proposes to cut Medicaid again by six billion dollars over the next three years, although 700,000 children have already lost their Medicaid cards or benefits because of AFDC[c] cutbacks and eligibility changes. We're also at the lowest point in over a decade in the number of poor children who participate in Medicaid even though we have had a dramatic increase in the number of children who fall into poverty. Since 1979 we've had 3.3 million new children becoming poor. If these new Medicaid cuts take place, an additional ten million children will be at risk of losing some Medicaid benefits or eligibility. I think we should ask, how many four pound babies will it take to balance the Federal budget?

In the Reagan decade, we are building 17,000 new nuclear weapons at an estimated cost of 71 billion dollars. The new Reagan budget allows only enough money to stockpile one month of vaccination serum for children. As a result, two million fewer children will be able to be immunized next year over last year if the Reagan budget request prevails. And this is at a time when half of all black preschool children are not fully immunized against DPT and polio.

American children need protection, as you know, against growing child abuse. An estimated 1.5 million children were reported abused and neglected in 1983, an increase of 200,000 over the previous year. Yet the Reagan administration is cutting child abuse programs. We were able to get in a new 25 million dollar training fund for child care workers to try to respond to the allegations of child abuse last year, and he is proposing to abolish that 25 million dollar program.

c. Aid to Families with Dependent Children. The Federal program most commonly considered "welfare" when the Federal government is discussed.

American children need to be protected against the enemy of homelessness. According to a new 1984 HUD[d] study, 22 percent of the homeless in shelters, not including runaway shelters, are children under 18 years of age. Conservatively, over 66,000 children are currently living without permanent shelter. But the President's budget seeks to emasculate low income housing programs and to rip another 325 million dollar hole in the already tattered survival net of Aid to Families with Dependent Children—AFDC—the favorite whipping boy of everybody. AFDC recipients, 66 percent of whom are children, have already been cut by 1.7 billion dollars since 1980. They receive an average daily benefit of three dollars and sixty-seven cents. There is not a lot of fat left there to cut. In addition, the President's budget proposes to take another 650 million dollars from child nutrition programs, although five billion have already been cut from these programs. That means that several million additional children will lose school lunches under this proposal, and children and family day care homes will lose the bulk of their Federal child care food support, and this Federal child care food program has been our one handle to try to get some regulation or control over the quality of what so many millions of children receive in family day care.

Talked about education already, so I will skip that, because you know more about that than I do. A hundred and sixty million dollars are proposed to be cut from the summer youth program. A hundred million dollars previously appropriated for fiscal '85 and another sixty million is proposed to be cut in fiscal '86. This is 20 percent cut and, as a result, 1.7 million fewer youths will be provided summer employment. This annoys me greatly because I, in looking at some of the tax breaks, realize that about a third, it's over ten million, baseball and hockey tickets are bought each year under the business deduction allowance for corporate pleasure outings at an estimated cost of about 80 million dollars, and it seems to me that we should much better support jobs for young people in the summer than hockey games for corporate executives.

He's proposing to eliminate the Juvenile Justice and Delinquency Prevention Program, a 70 million dollar preventive effort which helps troubled youth and avoids costly incarceration. He's proposing to freeze the Title XX social services block grant, which is the main Federal source of child care for working parents. He would freeze it at 2.7 billion, which is 200 million dollars below the fiscal 1981 level, even though we know about the increasing

d. Department of Housing and Urban Development.

needs for child care and one of the things that we are seeking in our new Children's Survival Bill, which I will talk about briefly, is a 980 million dollar increase in Title XX, because if we are going to deal with the problems of child care it seems that the way you do so is to improve the quality and to improve the training, and you have to have money to do that.

But while decimating Federal programs for needy families and children, the new Reagan budget also ignores the skyrocketing tax burden, the Federal tax burden on the working poor, while as you know the taxes of the rich have been cut. While the President claims to want the poor to work, he has penalized their work with higher taxes. The amount of Federal tax paid by those with incomes below the Federal poverty line increased 58 percent from 1980 to 1982 alone. In 1984, a working single mother, with three children, and a below poverty level income of 10,500 dollars, paid 1,186 dollars in taxes, this is the combined Federal payroll and Social Security taxes. This almost 1200 dollar tax bill that this poor mother paid was more than Boeing, General Electric, Dupont, Texaco, Mobil and AT&T altogether paid in 1983, although these huge corporations earned 13.7 billion dollars in profits. And we've heard a lot about the Grace Commission.[e] And Peter Grace is talking about the need for more program cuts in social welfare programs, and waste and fraud and abuse. But we have not heard about is the fact that Peter Grace's company, the W. R. Grace Company, earned 684 million dollars in profits from 1981 to 1983, paid no net Federal income tax, and actually got back twelve and a half million dollars from the government in negative tax rebates to the sale of excess tax benefits. Something is wrong about that. If we just brought the W. R. Grace's tax rate, Federal tax rate, up to zero, [Laughter] we could pay for nine million school lunches that the President has cut. [Applause]

Now you know you've heard a lot, talking about how in the Congress, many in the Congress, say that deficit reduction, which we must all be concerned about, that they say it must be the first priority. I think we, who care about people, and decency, and fairness, have got to say that they should first convince President Reagan, Defense Secretary Weinberger, and the powerful special interest beneficiaries of defense and tax largesse, to make

e. In 1982, President Reagan formed the Private Sector Survey on Cost Control to study waste in the federal government. Chaired by businessman J. Peter Grace, the Grace Commission issued its report in Jan. 1984. The commission claimed that, if the recommendations in its report were followed, almost $500 million per year could be saved. The report, and its claimed savings, were highly controversial.

deficit reduction *their* first priority before sending poor, handicapped and homeless children again to the front lines of a deficit reduction war no one else is fighting. And we've got to make that clear. [Applause] And secondly it does seem to me that in a decent country, a democratic country, that deficit reduction should take second seat to death reduction and poverty reduction among our most vulnerable children.

What do we do about all this? One, I think clearly is to inform ourselves, but secondly, because we really feel strongly at CDF[f] that you can't beat something with nothing we have for the last two or three years tried always to put before the Congress an affirmative vision of what it is the Federal Government ought to be doing to invest preventively in children. We call it the Children's Survival Bill. And while it is not acted upon as an overall bill, many of its provisions have been a basis for restorations of millions of dollars to children's programs. In the first two years, as you know, with the avalanche of Reagan cuts we were told that there was no way we could stop the absolute across the board repeal, as he attempted to do, of virtually every Federal program serving children. Our first priority, therefore, was to stop the repeal effort, to keep the framework of the laws in place, because if we lost the laws, we figured we might never get them back. And so we said lose the money, but try to keep the things intact. And we think, with the help of NEA[g] and many others, have succeeded in keeping the Federal framework of protections for handicapped children, for children who are without homes, in education, in health, intact. I mean the chimney's had a few bricks knocked off of it, and the paint's kind of been scraped off in some corners, but the foundation is there.

In the second two years, we said it's time to try to get some of our money back, and we drafted a Children's Survival Bill which was used as a basis for beginning to get specific restorations. And the Congress over the last two years has given back about two and a half billion dollars in specific program restorations. For things like WIC,[h] and some of the other child nutrition programs, some of the child care programs, and last year actually expanded Medicaid services for a half million mothers and poor children. This year we have drafted a new Children's Survival Bill which tries to lay out a blueprint for Federal investment in preventive and youth self-sufficiency steps that

f. Children's Defense Fund.

g. National Education Association.

h. Women, Infants, Children: A federally funded program with the purpose of improving the health and nutrition of women and their dependent children.

can restore more of the ten billion dollars that was taken in 1980. And we always have to remember that while we got some money back, we are about 20 percent back towards where we started in 1980.

So that we are trying to get back to where we were, but more importantly we are trying to take the initiative to say that it is time for the nation to undertake a range of specific steps to give young people skills and employment opportunities to enable them to contribute to, rather than depend on, the community. We're putting special emphasis on adolescent pregnancy prevention. Tax fairness for the poor and single families of the kind that I've talked about here, is a strong priority. The overall Bill this year costs 14 billion dollars. We offer 40 billion dollars offsetting provisions for cutting which could pay for these 14 billion dollars in programs for children and which could leave 25 billion dollars to reduce the Federal deficit. I hope that we can get your help in looking at those provisions of the Children's Survival Bill, a number of them are school-related. And I want to talk about two other companion pieces, because I think while it is critically important to give young people healthy beginnings, it is equally important that we talk about now building into our young people from the beginning all the steps which will leave them at eighteen on a self-sufficient basis. For the two companion priorities will be our big theme for the next several years.

The first is testing of a range of community and policy making strategies designed to prevent teen pregnancy and to build self-sufficient youth. In 1983, 523,000 babies were born to teen mothers. Ten thousand of these babies were born to girls fourteen and under. Last week I heard from a big city, which I will leave unnamed, about a twelve year old who had a child, whose mother was twenty-two. And I sort of said, I've seen thirty year old grandmothers, and forty year old grandmothers, but when you get to grandmothers in the twenties, you've just gotten me. I mean, that's really a bit much. But over 300,000 of the teens who give birth annually, have not completed high school. Thirty-six thousand of these children having children have not completed the eighth grade. Thirty-one percent of all babies born to teens are paid for by Medicaid at an annual cost of 200 million dollars and sixty percent of all AFDC mothers had their first child as a teen. We need to deal with this as a major issue because children having children is like an engine that is driving new generations of poor children. And if we are serious about trying to talk about healthy and stable families, and preventing child poverty, trying to intervene in this critical area is important. And I think we've got to talk about how we reach our children younger and younger. Most of our sex education is too little, too late. We've got to deal with our media, which sells our children sex without consequence. I have just in the last few years, having adolescent sons, have begun to listen to the lyrics of rock music. It's outrageous. They are sold sex every time they go to the movies, cut on the TV sets, see Brooke Shields commercials,[i] and it seems to me that all of us—I don't want to sound like Jerry Falwell[j] [Laughter]—but at least, you know, it seems to me that we are going to have to deal with the atmosphere—it's very hard, and easy for people to say "let the parents teach their kids the right values"—but you know the whole society makes it very difficult for parents to set their children's values alone. And we have got to deal with the external forces as well as try to strengthen our families and their control over their children.

The second piece of the teen pregnancy campaign, because so much of our ability to succeed, it seems to me, will depend on our attitudes, on our not moralizing. The key to the teen pregnancy issue, I am convinced, and I have two years of homework, and I don't pretend to know all the answers, but a key thing is giving young people hope, is having them have a stake in the future, having a sense that they're going somewhere, that there is a job there. That they can read and they can write, and they've got some skills and they feel respected, and have a basis for demanding that respect. And I suspect that we can do all the sex education in the world, but if young people don't feel wanted and have a place in the society, it's going to have a minimal impact. [Applause]

But the second area [interrupted by applause]. And obviously schools are critical institutions for having an impact on this issue, and I'm going to come back to that very briefly and then sit down. The other piece that we want to start with, because too often we start off on welfare and then we all end up fighting each other, we have tried to pick prenatal care as the first action issue on which we will all try to work together on teen pregnancy. The need is overwhelming. Infant mortality rates, I'm afraid, are going to begin to show a new increase if we do not deal with the erosion in access to prenatal care which we have been seeing on a nationwide basis in our country for the last several years, particularly among minority women.

i. In the early 1980s, at age fourteen, model and actress Brooke Shields was featured in a set of controversial ads for Calvin Klein jeans. In the television version, Shields struck provocative poses and asked, "You want to know what comes between me and my Calvins?—Nothing."
j. Rev. Jerry Falwell: Senior minister of Lynchburg Baptist Church.

And like night follows the day, you are going to see the mortality following that. The number of low birth weight babies among teens is unacceptably high, and it seems to me in terms of the cost atmosphere in this nation right now, that by getting the nation to invest in prenatal care we can not only reach some of the young people we need to reach, get them into the health care system, avoid as many premature babies as we can, therefore low birth weight babies, because these children are born with enough things stacked against them. They don't need a birth defect or other things, too. But secondly, if we can get them into the health care system, perhaps we can counsel them and give them the help they need to avoid that second child. And one out of every three teens who have a first child, get pregnant again within two years.

And if we can begin to prevent these second children—again, one of the few models, and in the Children's Survival Bill we have built in a model demonstration program for about a hundred million dollars, that is a school-based model where there's been significant success—in school-based comprehensive health clinics that have provided a range of health services to teens including prenatal care, but gives immunizations, it gives all the athletic check-ups. But in St. Paul, and in Houston, and a few other cities—St. Paul particularly has the best evaluated program—they have been able to reduce the teen repeat pregnancy rate to almost nothing, and more important they have kept those young women in school. I think one of the things that's clear that you're going to have to go where teenagers—put the services where the teens are—rather than waiting for the teens to find a way, to find the services. And I would hope that you all might look at that school-based clinic, comprehensive clinic notion, and find that that might be one among many that you might support, among the provisions in the Children's Survival Bill. I think it could make a difference.

And secondly, we can make a very strong case that for every dollar you spend on prenatal care, it costs us $600 to give prenatal care, including vitamins and nutritional supplements to women, it can save an awful lot of money. It costs about $20,000 to care for a premature infant just in the first twenty days of life.

I hope we can get you, if you only buy one thing from CDF this year, you can take it, xerox it, plagiarize it, but please, the budget won't be out in final copy—we have a pre-release copy—but it will be out next week, but there are order forms out there—But I wish you would help us begin to get the message around about the misguided budget priorities, and how they affect children, and to see that some provisions of the Children's Survival Bill don't make sense in your community.

Lastly, I just guess I hope—and the NEA has been strong—we will simply not let our morale flag. You know, I think that while we are trying to get the Congress to do what is right by children, it is so important that we begin to launch community-based programs, and teen pregnancy prevention. We have a number of materials that are available to help you. There's an Adolescent Pregnancy Child Watch Manual and Project that we have launched with the National Council of Negro Women, and the Junior Leagues, and the March of Dimes, and about forty communities in twenty states. We will have available next week a comprehensive prenatal care kit and how you can launch a prenatal care campaign in your community, with state-based data on teen pregnancy by race, on all your health care issues by race and age. And I really hope that you might find a way to begin to get involved on teen pregnancy and premature baby prevention efforts in your own community. But lastly, I just hope that we will keep our spirits up, and fight back, and fight affirmatively. And the person this year who I have sort of re-discovered is Benjamin Mays,[k] whom I know you all know of, who was the former president of Morehouse College, and who died. And I guess I think we all need, from time to time, because we seem to be fighting negative battles, just need to sort of remind ourselves of the importance, and of privilege we have, with the cause that we have. And the need to continue to try to aim high. To be confident that we can win for children. And to keep at it. Because I think that we are awfully blessed, to have such a challenging and worthwhile cause to believe in and serve.

President Reagan wants to invest 3.2 trillion dollars over this decade in the military and our new weapons of death, which are of no use at all to the hungry children in this world. And I didn't even know how much a trillion dollars was, before Mr. Reagan took office with his defense stuff. [Laughter] And when I asked my budget director, research director, give me a way of laymanizing, and I haven't found a better way to explain it, and he said, "If you had spent a million dollars a day, every day since Jesus Christ was born, you would still be spending less than half of what the President wants the American people to believe the Defense Department can spend efficiently over the next decade." Three point two trillion dollars.

k. Dr. Benjamin E. Mays (1894–1984): President of Morehouse College, 1940–1967.

We're trying to invest 14 billion dollars in new weapons of life, and education, and health care. We should not be defensive or take "no" from anybody on the right to have this 14 billion dollars invested in children this year. We have the money. [Applause] And we should not be intimidated by anybody into lowering our goals or of giving in to the politics of the moment.

Dr. Mays said—and I am going to sit down now—I think he summed up our message and our mission. He said, "It must be borne in mind, that the tragedy in life doesn't lie in not reaching your goal. The tragedy lies in having no goal to reach. It isn't a calamity to die with dreams unfulfilled, but it is a calamity not to dream. It's not a disaster to be unable to capture your ideal, but it is a disaster to have no ideal to catch." Finally, he says, "it is not a disgrace not to reach the stars, but it is a disgrace to have no stars to reach. Not failure, but low aim, is sin." And I hope that of all the things that will go on this year, at least those of us who care about children will keep our aim high. That is the least we can do for them. Thank you. [Applause]

Barack Hussein Obama

Inaugural Address

An invitation to deliver the keynote address at the Democratic National Convention (DNC) in 2004 gave Barack Obama a platform upon which to forge a national identity.[1] He could not claim to be the first African American to deliver the convention keynote address. That honor belonged to Barbara Jordan, who realized that her selection as a keynote speaker in 1976 was its own powerful rhetorical message: "There is something different tonight," she had said. "I, Barbara Jordan, am a keynote speaker." Jordan had already come to national attention as the tenacious chair of the famous televised Watergate hearings. Barack Obama, by contrast, was an Illinois state senator, relatively unknown outside of his state, although after an unsuccessful run for a congressional seat, Obama had already announced his plans on running for a seat in the US Senate.[2] Both Jordan and Obama left a deep impression on the American public through their oratory and their personal stories of challenge and accomplishment. Obama took a page from Jordan in declaring that "tonight is a particular honor for me because, let's face it, my presence on this stage is pretty unlikely." Before turning to the defects of the Bush administration and the promise of a Kerry/Edwards ticket, Obama offered an autobiographical sketch. His father, Barack Sr., was a black Kenyan who came to the United States as a college student. *His* father had been a domestic servant and cook in Kenya. The younger Barack's Caucasian mother was born in Kansas, and her father had suffered through the Depression working on oil rigs until the Second World War, when he enlisted in the army, took advantage of the GI bill, sought an education, and partook of the American dream. The *New York Times* reported that Obama's "words of unity and hope brought some to tears and many to loud and long cheers."[3]

Looking back upon a successful journey to the Oval Office, a single speech is sometimes recognizable as igniting a politician's ascent to the nation's highest office: the "Happy Warrior" speech of Franklin Delano Roosevelt (FDR), nominating Alf Landon as the Democratic presidential nominee; Ronald Reagan's televised appeal on behalf of Barry Goldwater; and Abraham Lincoln's fabled "Cooper Union Address," decrying slavery, are three well-known examples. Obama's odyssey began in earnest with a speech in which he would articulate the theme of his own campaign for the presidency in 2008: "Hope in the face of difficulty, hope in the face of uncertainty, the audacity of hope."

Obama was an "unlikely" DNC keynote speaker, not only because of the racial identity about which he had mused in his 1995 book, *Dreams of My Father*, written at the urging of a publisher impressed with his selection as the first African American editor of the *Harvard Law Review*.[4] "My story," Obama said in his keynote address, "is part of the larger American story." The White House Web page distills this idea down to the frank declaration that: "His [the president's] story is the American story," although this is true only by a reflective interpretation that recognizes broad demographic diversity as the norm.[5] His father, Barack Sr., graduated Phi Beta Kappa from the University of Hawaii and completed a master's degree in economics at Harvard. His mother, Anne Dunham, divorced her husband before he left to return to his homeland, eventually to work as a senior economist at the Kenyan Ministry of Finance.

Anne and her son's lives were complicated by Anne's separation from Barack Sr. and subsequent marriage to an Indonesian graduate student in Hawaii. While her first husband pursued a master's degree in economics at Harvard, Anne took care of Barack while she attended the University of Washington in Seattle. After divorcing Barack Sr., Anne met and married Lolo Soetoro while finishing her BA at the University of Hawaii. Years later, she earned a PhD in anthropology from the same institution. Barack went with his mother and stepfather to live in Indonesia for four years, where he attended Catholic and Muslim schools, each for two years, then went back to live with his maternal grandparents in Hawaii so that he could enroll in a highly regarded private preparatory school, Punahou.[6] One of the few African Americans at the school, Obama made friends easily, played basketball, and sang in the choir, but an interior adolescent quest to find his moorings as a biracial youth with an absent father led him, for a time, to alcohol, marijuana, and, on occasion, cocaine. Despite what his mother described as "slipping grades," he was accepted at Occidental College in California and after two years transferred to Columbia University, where he received a BA in 1983.[7] Immediately after graduation, he decided to seek employment as a community organizer, wrote letters to potential employers across the country, but received no responses.[8] After a year working for a consulting firm in Manhattan, he found a job in Chicago more in line with his original aspirations. Accepting a meager salary of $10,000 in the first year, Obama worked for an organization sponsored by a number of churches seeking to improve the lives of South Side residents beset by a panoply of problems, including unemployment, shoddy schools, crime, and deteriorating neighborhoods and public housing.[9]

He left Chicago in 1988 to attend law school at Harvard, received his degree in 1991, and returned to Chicago, taught constitutional law part-time at the University of Chicago, organized a voter registration drive, and won election to the Illinois State Senate in 1996.[10] In the senate, he advocated ethics reform, death penalty process reform, early childhood education, enhanced health care for the poor, and requiring videotaping of interrogations in capital murder cases.[11] In 2000, he ran unsuccessfully for a congressional seat but was roundly defeated in the primary election, which was won by incumbent Bobby Rush, a former Black Panther.[12] Obama's successful run for the US Senate took a surprising turn. A scandal involving the Republican nominee, Jack Ryan, resulted in Ryan's withdrawal. Alan Keyes, an articulate, bombastic African American talk show host who had previously run for the Republican presidential nomination, was quickly selected to run against Obama but lost to Obama in a landslide. The election was historic because there had only been two previous African American senators since Reconstruction.[13] In the US Senate, Obama worked on behalf of lobbying reform, arms control, and transparency in federal spending.[14] After only three years in the Senate, Obama sought the nation's highest office, won a hotly contested primary race in a field that narrowed to Obama and Hillary Clinton, and then won the general election against Arizona senator John McCain.

In his inaugural address, President Obama spoke "in person" to 1.8 million people, an audience that began in front of the Capitol, where the speech was delivered, and extended for a distance of two miles, down the Washington Mall, past the Washington Monument, to the Lincoln Memorial.[15] More people attended the inauguration on that clear, cold day than had attended any other event in Washington, DC, history. Thirty-eight million others watched the inauguration ceremony on television.[16] The fact that the Obama inauguration was more widely watched than any other since Ronald Reagan's might suggest more than Obama's and Reagan's popularity. Both presidents took office during economic recessions, although some regarded the recession that began in 2008 as the worst to have occurred since the Great Depression.[17] The public looked to the new president for words that would help restore confidence. Expectations ran high, both because of the nation's economic travail and because of Obama's reputation as an orator. The "gathering clouds and raging storms" that Obama mentions in his introduction prominently included both an economic crisis and lingering wars in Iraq and Afghanistan, but the inaugural also encompassed other problems that Obama had addressed during his campaign such as improving health care and education and turning the nation to alternative sources of energy. A Canadian journalist who criticized the address as "a clichéd dud," nevertheless insightfully stated that: "An Inaugural Address worthy of its occasion winds history into every sentence. Echo and allusion, direct quotation, bind the day to the great words and deeds of all the days before it."[18] It is difficult to write an inaugural address that satisfies these criteria without also inviting the criticism that it is laden with what sound like shibboleths and platitudes. The mention of words and events held fast in cultural memory are necessarily part of every American presidential inaugural. Obama's speech was rich in "echo and allusion" that stretched across both time and place, but it also achieved a distinctively modern quality—spare and simple but conveying sincerity and determination.

The speech was a call to a "new generation of Americans," as Kennedy had said in his inaugural, but the generation was not, like Kennedy's, the Cold War generation, but the *post*–Cold War generation that George W. Bush had also addressed in his two inaugurals, from the opposite side of the political divide. Surely part of the enthusiasm and anticipation for Obama's inaugural derived from the sense that, after eight years, a liberal voice of a generation had taken command of the microphone. As historian Allen Weinstein observes, two quite different segments of the post–Cold War generation exulted in George W. Bush's and Barack Obama's ascensions to power and the inaugural words that formally marked those ascents, just as different segments of the Cold War generation had responded differently to Kennedy's and then Nixon's inaugurations.[19]

In the Obama inaugural, the resonances of FDR's first inaugural are unmistakable, such as Obama's criticism of "greed and irresponsibility" and praise of previous generations who struggled against the adversity common to all and the extraordinary burdens of the slave and the soldier. Like FDR, Obama acknowledges that America was "in the midst of crisis"—"Homes have been lost, jobs shed, businesses shuttered." Both presidents expressly rejected "fear," and promised that America would return to prosperity. FDR had blamed "the practices of the unscrupulously moneychangers" for the nation's ills, while Obama less antagonistically blames the "greed and irresponsibility on the part of some" for the economic collapse. Both praised work in contrast to wealth. While FDR had advised that "The joy, the moral stimulation, of work no longer must be forgotten in the mad chase of evanescent profits; Obama notes that "there is nothing so satisfying to the spirit, so defining of our character as giving our all to a difficult task." The new president reflects that the nation's journey toward greatness is not "for those that prefer leisure over work, or seek only the pleasures of riches and fame," and praises "the doers, the makers of things"—implicitly indicting those whose fortunes had come from the manipulation of money. FDR criticized "a generation of self-seekers," while Obama ruminates that our forebears "saw America as bigger than the sum of individual ambitions." FDR had offered consolation in the fact that "our common difficulties . . . concern, thank God, only material things"; Obama in the fact that the United States remains "the most prosperous, powerful nation on Earth."

FDR spoke of the "perils which our forefather's conquered" and invoked "the American spirit of the pioneer," while Obama reminds his audience of the "sacrifices borne by our ancestors" and recalls "the perils" the Founding Fathers faced in drafting "the charter to assure the rule of law and the rights of man." Both saw the importance of action—"This nation is asking for action and action now," Roosevelt had declared, while Obama echoes: "The state of our economy calls for action, bold and swift." War and terrorism ("a far-reaching network of violence and hatred") were additional challenges that Obama acknowledges and, because of the wars in Iraq and Afghanistan, the examples of the sacrifices made by prior generations necessarily include those made on the battlefield: "Concord and Gettysburg; Normandy and Khe Sanh." Obama deftly fuses the themes of persevering against military and economic travails at the end of his speech by quoting a passage from Thomas Paine's pamphlet, "The American Crisis," which George Washington had ordered be read to his troops at the lowest point of the Revolutionary War: "Let it be told to the future world . . . that in the depth of winter, when nothing but hope and virtue could survive . . . that the city and the country, alarmed at one common danger, came forth to meet [it]."

In 1933, Americans sought redemption for greedily participating in stock market and real estate speculation fueled by debts incurred "with an entire abandon of common sense."[20] Roosevelt offered a means of redemption through a "restoration of the ancient truths" to the "temple of civilization." It is less clear that the hard times of the recent recession produced an equally rueful public, although Obama offers redemption in the same form as Roosevelt, the embrace of the creed of equality, liberty, and the pursuit of happiness and of recommitment to the "old" national values—"honesty and hard work, courage and fair play, tolerance and curiosity, loyalty and patriotism." "What is demanded," he says, "is a return to these truths." The evils from which Obama believes Americans need to be delivered included the "childish things" the Christian Bible proposed one should "set aside," which, in the full compass of the president's criticism, includes not only materialism, but "petty grievances and false promises, [and the] worn out dogmas."

The notable similarity between FDR's first inaugural and Obama's inaugural is rooted in their response to crisis with a form of discourse known as a jeremiad, once used by Puritan colonial leaders to exhort their brethren to depart from evil and cleave to religious truths that would restore them to the path of a God-given destiny. Richard Johannesen notes that even in the seventeenth and eighteenth centuries, the "progress of the American nation" was fused with the "progress of the Kingdom of God." Modern secular jeremiads used by American political leaders emphasize the "American Dream," and the belief in America as the "Promised Land."[21] Religious jeremiads take their name from the prophet Jeremiah, who exhorted fallen-away Jews to return to their beliefs, urged repentance, and envisioned a better future. Falls from grace in secular jeremiads involve departures from principles embodied in the America's founding documents and in "the words and actions of the Founding Fathers."[22] Although many inaugural addresses also remind their audience of the principles upon which the nation is founded, Obama's address incorporates a lamentation of the evils of greed, irresponsibility, and selfishness and calls for a renewal of progress toward the ideals embodied in the Constitution. "Expanded by the blood of generations . . . those ideals," the new president says, in a phrase alluding to a similar declaration made in JFK's inaugural, "still light the world, and we will not give them up for expedience sake."

The jeremiad fits within the genre of epideictic oratory, which Aristotle defined as speech of praise or blame. The jeremiad does both, lamenting the evils that characterized the past and praising ideals and the consequences of hewing to these ideals. But Obama's inaugural is not only concerned with recommitting citizens to founding principles; it sets the stage for policies and, therefore, also belongs to the deliberative genre of rhetoric. One of the potential impediments of the jeremiad is that it can become a substitute for action, but both FDR and Obama vigorously call for action.[23] FDR discusses a litany of government programs, of "greatly needed projects," which ultimately would constitute the New Deal and lead to national recovery. Obama touches more briefly on the need for programs to develop the nation's infrastructure, improve health care, develop alternative sources of energy, and improve education and muses abstractly about the systemic evils of an economy that "favors only the prosperous," arguing for the importance of expanding "the reach of our prosperity" and extending "opportunity to every willing heart." Obama's rhetoric, in turns moralistic and policy oriented, led the writer of George Bush's two inaugural addresses, Michael Gersen, to reflect that "Like Lincoln or Martin Luther King, Jr., Obama positioned himself as a conservative revolutionary—attempting to re-create our country by asserting the traditional principles that gave it birth."[24] Obama's progressivism is also reminiscent of Teddy Roosevelt (TR), who similarly saw the moral and practical implications of concentrated wealth as well as the means by which the federal government could expand the material blessings of liberty and equality. Both TR and Obama realized the rhetorical value in advocating for progressive programs by appealing to conservative values.

Obama also invokes moralistic and philosophical principles in addressing the problems of confronting terrorism and ending two protracted wars. One principle he enunciates suggests a razor sharp criticism of the Bush/Cheney administration: "As for our common defense, we reject as false the choice between our safety and our ideals." Members of the Bush administration expressed indignation at the implicit criticism of the former president's policies to combat terrorism, such as the restraints on personal freedom imposed by the Patriot Act and the detention of prisoners without due process in Guantanamo Bay, Cuba, about which Democrats had long complained.[25] In asserting the nation's readiness "to lead once more," Obama further underscores his differences with the Bush administration's leadership in the world, particularly in noting that the nation's power "grows through its prudent use; our security emanates from the justness of our cause, the force of our example, the tempering qualities of humility and restraint," and proposing that America should be "guided by these principles once more." Such rhetoric prepares the ground for the president's statement that, consistent with his campaign promises, the United States would "begin to responsibly leave Iraq to its own people and forge a hard-earned peace in Afghanistan."[26] As a counterbalance to this moral criticism of recent US foreign policy, Obama proclaims: "We will not apologize for our way of life, nor will we waver in its defense." And to terrorists, he boldly declares: "our spirit is stronger and cannot be broken—you cannot outlast us, and we will defeat you." The ringing clarity and strength of these proclamations expressed upon the world stage matched the pledge of John Kennedy's inaugural address to accept of the responsibility of "defending freedom in its hour of maximum danger."

Obama accepts the mantle not just of the US presidency but of leadership in a world beset by terrorism, totalitarianism, and tribal animus. He carried forward the role of the United States not simply as a superpower, but as what Dante Germino has described as a "supernation," responsible for the welfare of other nations, initially against the threats of the Cold War and now, in the post–Cold War era, against terrorism, a threat less apocalyptic, but no less of the "long twilight struggle" that Kennedy describes.[27] Although other presidential inaugurals, notably Kennedy's, have offered pledges to people in other corners of the world, in the current era of global interconnectedness, Obama's inaugural is the first to acknowledge that others besides Americans were expressly part of the audience: "And so, to all the other peoples and government who are watching today, from the grandest capitals to the small village where my father was born, know that America is a friend to each nation."[28] In a particularly forceful, though paradoxical, portion of his inaugural, the president notes that "America is a nation of Christians and Muslims, Jews and Hindus, and non-believers" and tells the Muslim world that "we seek a new way forward," while firmly criticizing those who blame the West for their ills: "Know that your people will judge you on what you can build, not what you destroy." Obama is conciliatory to Middle Eastern dictators, such as those in Iran and Syria. Though judging "that you are on the wrong side of history," he offers to "extend a hand if you are willing to unclench your fist." American presidential inaugurals typically mention God, earlier inaugurals often using literary synonyms, and quote or paraphrase the Bible, as does Obama in referring to Paul's advice to the Corinthians, "It is time to set aside childish things," as support for putting an end to political dogmatism.[29] No other inaugural has characterized the United States as multireligious, multiethnic, and multilinguistic, but never before has the need been so great to blunt Middle Eastern extremist propaganda that scapegoats America as a determined foe of Muslim religion and culture. Obama's inaugural is unique among inaugurals not only in its description of American ecumenicalism, but in the very use of the word "Muslim," as Nicholas Kristof also notes.[30]

It would have been difficult for the president to deliver a speech as historic as the event it memorialized—the inauguration of the first African American president. David Sanger of the *New York Times* encapsulated the paradox: "Mr. Obama's ascendance was so historic that the address became larger than its own language, more imbued with meaning than anything he could say."[31] Commentators throughout the world registered varying degrees of satisfaction and disappointment. Some criticized the speech as platitudinous, or "surprisingly flat," while others thought it was wholly equal to both the occasion and Obama's reputation as a speaker or rated it more cautiously as a "very fine speech, without being, perhaps, one for the ages."[32] Compared to Obama's rousing stump speeches and his brilliant speech on race, occasioned by criticisms of remarks made by his pastor the Reverend Jeremiah Wright, the inaugural was somber and restrained, appropriate both to the occasion and the perils of the accelerating economic decline and two protracted wars.[33] Its brevity—about twenty-four hundred words—rivaled FDR's first inaugural, similarly brief—fewer than two thousand words—delivered in another hour of crisis that required clear and decisive language to quell public anxiety.

It was a speech about grave national problems that touched only lightly on the issue of race in American life. Toward the end of the speech, Obama reflected briefly that the creed of equality is "why a man whose father less than 60 years ago might not have been served in a local restaurant can now stand before you to take a most sacred oath." He did not need to dwell further on the significance of the passage of power to the son of a black African that brought tears of joy to the eyes of many observers. At least one critic would have liked Obama to seal the occasion with a direct reference to Martin Luther King Jr. and the civil rights movement, which had made his ascent possible.[34] He had done just that in the conclusion of the Democratic Party nomination acceptance speech delivered on the forty-fifth anniversary of the slain civil rights leader's "I Have a Dream" speech. In his first speech as president, Obama chose a less personal path, rekindling a memory, not of 1963 and "the summer of the Negro's legitimate discontent" about which Martin Luther King Jr. had spoken, but of 1778 and "our common danger, in this winter of our hardship." The "timeless words" that Obama chose to remember were not King's "I have a dream," reflecting a struggle with which Obama was closely identified, but Thomas Paine's "honor and virtue," values associated with the more fundamental struggle of the nation's birth. The outward focus of the speech is further supported by the fact that "we" is used sixty times and "our" fifty-six times, while "I" is used only twice and "me" not at all. Eliminating the first person singular was a piece of advice that John Kennedy had given his inaugural address collaborator, Theodore Sorenson, perhaps in tacit homage to Abraham Lincoln, who, in his celebrated Second Inaugural Address, scrupulously avoided self-reference, incorporating the words "I" and "myself" only one time each.[35]

Like Sorenson, Jon Favreau, chief White House speechwriter and lead writer of the inaugural, was the president's alter ego, having learned to write in a voice indistinguishable from the president's. Before the event, Favreau remarked that the task of writing the speech was complicated by the need to include historical allusions while also crafting the speech in language that was "right for the times."[36] It is easy to inflate language when affirming founding principles and when referencing passionately remembered historical events. Indeed, the speech, although rich in metaphor and symbolism, is notable for its simple language, which suits both the president's conversational style of oratory and the sense of intimacy that the electronic media create. Most of the words in the speech do not exceed two syllables, and one of the longer sentences in the speech is a mere eighty-five words, a far cry from the 732-word sentence John Adams felt a need to include in his inaugural. Favreau had met with the president for an hour to discuss the speech and was assisted by a speechwriting staff that searched for historical material to incorporate, including responses to national crises. Favreau contemplated recordings of past inaugurals and consulted Peggy Noonan, who had written lyrical speeches for Ronald Reagan as well as George H. W. Bush's inaugural. Obama shared in the writing process with several opportunities to read and edit successive drafts of the speech.[37]

The delivery of the speech was Obama's responsibility alone. John Kennedy, who excelled in debate, interviews, and press conferences, was a slightly stiff platform speaker who needed to be coached to deliver his inaugural effectively. Barack Obama, by contrast, delivers speeches with an effortless grace, a nonchalance that was not sabotaged even by the misquotation of the oath of office by Chief Justice Roberts during the swearing-in ceremony moments prior to the address. London's *Daily Telegraph* described Obama as "one of the most gifted orators of his generation," a sentiment that is widely shared.[38] Like Ronald Reagan, he delivers his speeches so naturally and effortlessly that the fact that he is reading from a teleprompter, rather than phrasing his thoughts spontaneously, is easily forgotten. Obama undoubtedly learned much about shaping words and phrases for the ear by listening to the rhapsodic sermons of African American preachers such as the Reverend Wright, and about connecting intimately with an audience from his experiences as a community organizer and law-school lecturer. His oral phrasing, inflections, pauses, and emphasis, all achieved with his rich baritone voice, contributed to the effectiveness of an artful oral performance that betrayed not a hint of artifice. If, as Phillip Collins, one of Tony Blair's speechwriters, remarked, Obama's speeches are "about the tune, not the lyrics," he sang the tune as well as any American president in recent memory.[39] Abraham Lincoln predicted that his Second Inaugural Address would "wear well."[40] How well President Obama's inaugural address "wears" will surely depend on the success of his presidency as much as the historic achievement of his election.

Inaugural Address

January 20, 2009
Washington, DC

My fellow citizens: I stand here today humbled by the task before us, grateful for the trust you've bestowed, mindful of the sacrifices borne by our ancestors.

I thank President Bush for his service to our nation, as well as the generosity and cooperation he has shown throughout this transition.

Forty-four Americans have now taken the presidential oath. The words have been spoken during rising tides of prosperity and the still waters of peace. Yet, every so often, the oath is taken amidst gathering clouds and raging storms. At these moments, America has carried on not simply because of the skill or vision of those in high office, but because we, the people, have remained faithful to the ideals of our forebears and true to our founding documents.

So it has been; so it must be with this generation of Americans.

That we are in the midst of crisis is now well understood. Our nation is at war against a far-reaching network of violence and hatred. Our economy is badly weakened, a consequence of greed and irresponsibility on the part of some, but also our collective failure to make hard choices and prepare the nation for a new age. Homes have been lost, jobs shed, businesses shuttered. Our health care is too costly, our schools fail too many, and each day brings further evidence that the ways we use energy strengthen our adversaries and threaten our planet.

These are the indicators of crisis, subject to data and statistics. Less measurable, but no less profound, is a sapping of confidence across our land; a nagging fear that America's decline is inevitable, that the next generation must lower its sights.

Today I say to you that the challenges we face are real. They are serious and they are many. They will not be met easily or in a short span of time. But know this America: They will be met.

On this day, we gather because we have chosen hope over fear, unity of purpose over conflict and discord. On this day, we come to proclaim an end to the petty grievances and false promises, the recriminations and worn-out dogmas that for far too long have strangled our politics. We remain a young nation. But in the words of Scripture, the time has come to set aside childish things. The time has come to reaffirm our enduring spirit; to choose our better history; to carry forward that precious gift, that noble idea passed on from generation to generation: the God-given promise that all are equal, all are free, and all deserve a chance to pursue their full measure of happiness.

In reaffirming the greatness of our nation we understand that greatness is never a given. It must be earned. Our journey has never been one of short-cuts or settling for less. It has not been the path for the faint-hearted, for those that prefer leisure over work, or seek only the pleasures of riches and fame. Rather, it has been the risk-takers, the doers, the makers of things—some celebrated, but more often men and women obscure in their labor—who have carried us up the long rugged path towards prosperity and freedom.

For us, they packed up their few worldly possessions and traveled across oceans in search of a new life. For us, they toiled in sweatshops, and settled the West, endured the lash of the whip, and plowed the hard earth. For us, they fought and died in places like Concord and Gettysburg, Normandy and Khe Sahn.[a]

Time and again these men and women struggled and sacrificed and worked till their hands were raw so that we might live a better life. They saw America as bigger than the sum of our individual ambitions, greater than all the differences of birth or wealth or faction.

This is the journey we continue today. We remain the most prosperous, powerful nation on Earth. Our workers are no less productive than when this crisis began. Our minds are no less inventive, our goods and services no less needed than they were last week, or last month, or last year. Our capacity remains undiminished. But our time of standing pat, of protecting

a. Battle of Concord during the American Revolution, 19 Apr. 1775; battle of Gettysburg during the Civil War, 1–3 July 1863; invasion of Normandy (D-Day) during World War II, 6 June 1944; and battle of Khe Sahn during the Vietnam War, primarily conducted between 21 Jan. and 8 Apr. 1968.

narrow interests and putting off unpleasant decisions—that time has surely passed. Starting today, we must pick ourselves up, dust ourselves off, and begin again the work of remaking America.

For everywhere we look, there is work to be done. The state of our economy calls for action, bold and swift. And we will act, not only to create new jobs, but to lay a new foundation for growth. We will build the roads and bridges, the electric grids and digital lines that feed our commerce and bind us together. We'll restore science to its rightful place, and wield technology's wonders to raise health care's quality and lower its cost. We will harness the sun and the winds and the soil to fuel our cars and run our factories. And we will transform our schools and colleges and universities to meet the demands of a new age. All this we can do. All this we will do.

Now, there are some who question the scale of our ambitions, who suggest that our system cannot tolerate too many big plans. Their memories are short, for they have forgotten what this country has already done, what free men and women can achieve when imagination is joined to common purpose, and necessity to courage. What the cynics fail to understand is that the ground has shifted beneath them, that the stale political arguments that have consumed us for so long no longer apply.

The question we ask today is not whether our government is too big or too small, but whether it works—whether it helps families find jobs at a decent wage, care they can afford, a retirement that is dignified. Where the answer is yes, we intend to move forward. Where the answer is no, programs will end. And those of us who manage the public's dollars will be held to account, to spend wisely, reform bad habits, and do our business in the light of day, because only then can we restore the vital trust between a people and their government.

Nor is the question before us whether the market is a force for good or ill. Its power to generate wealth and expand freedom is unmatched. But this crisis has reminded us that without a watchful eye, the market can spin out of control. The nation cannot prosper long when it favors only the prosperous. The success of our economy has always depended not just on the size of our gross domestic product, but on the reach of our prosperity, on the ability to extend opportunity to every willing heart—not out of charity, but because it is the surest route to our common good.

As for our common defense, we reject as false the choice between our safety and our ideals. Our Founding Fathers—our Founding Fathers, faced with perils that we can scarcely imagine, drafted a charter to assure the rule of law and the rights of man—a charter expanded by the blood of generations. Those ideals still light the world, and we will not give them up for expedience sake.

And so, to all the other peoples and governments who are watching today, from the grandest capitals to the small village where my father was born, know that America is a friend of each nation, and every man, woman and child who seeks a future of peace and dignity. And we are ready to lead once more.

Recall that earlier generations faced down fascism and communism not just with missiles and tanks, but with the sturdy alliances and enduring convictions. They understood that our power alone cannot protect us, nor does it entitle us to do as we please. Instead they knew that our power grows through its prudent use; our security emanates from the justness of our cause, the force of our example, the tempering qualities of humility and restraint.

We are the keepers of this legacy. Guided by these principles once more we can meet those new threats that demand even greater effort, even greater cooperation and understanding between nations. We will begin to responsibly leave Iraq to its people and forge a hard-earned peace in Afghanistan. With old friends and former foes, we'll work tirelessly to lessen the nuclear threat, and roll back the specter of a warming planet.

We will not apologize for our way of life, nor will we waver in its defense. And for those who seek to advance their aims by inducing terror and slaughtering innocents, we say to you now that our spirit is stronger and cannot be broken—you cannot outlast us, and we will defeat you.

For we know that our patchwork heritage is a strength, not a weakness. We are a nation of Christians and Muslims, Jews and Hindus, and nonbelievers. We are shaped by every language and culture, drawn from every end of this Earth; and because we have tasted the bitter swill of civil war and segregation, and emerged from that dark chapter stronger and more united, we cannot help but believe that the old hatreds shall someday pass; that the lines of tribe shall soon dissolve; that as the world grows smaller, our common humanity shall reveal itself; and that America must play its role in ushering in a new era of peace.

To the Muslim world, we seek a new way forward, based on mutual interest and mutual respect. To those leaders around the globe who seek to sow conflict, or blame their society's ills on the West, know that your people will judge you on what you can build, not what you destroy.

To those who cling to power through corruption and deceit and the silencing of dissent, know that you are on the wrong side of history, but that we will extend a hand if you are willing to unclench your fist.

To the people of poor nations, we pledge to work alongside you to make your farms flourish and let clean waters flow; to nourish starved bodies and feed hungry minds. And to those nations like ours that enjoy relative plenty, we say we can no longer afford indifference to the suffering outside our borders, nor can we consume the world's resources without regard to effect. For the world has changed, and we must change with it.

As we consider the role that unfolds before us, we remember with humble gratitude those brave Americans who at this very hour patrol far-off deserts and distant mountains. They have something to tell us, just as the fallen heroes who lie in Arlington[b] whisper through the ages.

We honor them not only because they are the guardians of our liberty, but because they embody the spirit of service—a willingness to find meaning in something greater than themselves.

And yet at this moment, a moment that will define a generation, it is precisely this spirit that must inhabit us all. For as much as government can do, and must do, it is ultimately the faith and determination of the American people upon which this nation relies. It is the kindness to take in a stranger when the levees break, the selflessness of workers who would rather cut their hours than see a friend lose their job which sees us through our darkest hours. It is the firefighter's courage to storm a stairway filled with smoke, but also a parent's willingness to nurture a child that finally decides our fate.

Our challenges may be new. The instruments with which we meet them may be new. But those values upon which our success depends—honesty and hard work, courage and fair play, tolerance and curiosity, loyalty and patriotism—these things are old. These things are true. They have been the quiet force of progress throughout our history.

What is demanded, then, is a return to these truths. What is required of us now is a new era of responsibility—a recognition on the part of every American that we have duties to ourselves, our nation and the world; duties that we do not grudgingly accept, but rather seize gladly, firm in the knowledge that there is nothing so satisfying to the spirit, so defining of our character than giving our all to a difficult task.

---

b. Arlington National Cemetery: One of two national cemeteries administered by the United States Army.

This is the price and the promise of citizenship. This is the source of our confidence—the knowledge that God calls on us to shape an uncertain destiny. This is the meaning of our liberty and our creed, why men and women and children of every race and every faith can join in celebration across this magnificent mall; and why a man whose father less than 60 years ago might not have been served in a local restaurant can now stand before you to take a most sacred oath.

So let us mark this day with remembrance of who we are and how far we have traveled. In the year of America's birth, in the coldest of months, a small band of patriots huddled by dying campfires on the shores of an icy river. The capital was abandoned. The enemy was advancing. The snow was stained with blood. At the moment when the outcome of our revolution was most in doubt, the father of our nation ordered these words to be read to the people:

"Let it be told to the future world . . . that in the depth of winter, when nothing but hope and virtue could survive . . . that the city and the country, alarmed at one common danger, came forth to meet [it]."[c]

America: In the face of our common dangers, in this winter of our hardship, let us remember these timeless words. With hope and virtue, let us brave once more the icy currents, and endure what storms may come. Let it be said by our children's children that when we were tested we refused to let this journey end, that we did not turn back nor did we falter; and with eyes fixed on the horizon and God's grace upon us, we carried forth that great gift of freedom and delivered it safely to future generations.

Thank you. God bless you. And God bless the United States of America.

c. The quotation is from Thomas Paine, *The American Crisis*. George Washington ordered the quotation to be read to the American troops in Dec. 1776, shortly before the battle of Trenton.

Notes · Sources · Index

Notes

Introduction

1. Cicero, *De Oratore I* 2:5–8, 10–12.
2. Taylor Branch, *Parting of the Waters: America in the King Years, 1954–63* (New York: Simon and Schuster, 1988), 882.
3. Henry Louis Gates Jr. and Nellie Y. McKay, eds., *The Norton Anthology of African American Literature*, 2nd ed. (W. W. Norton and Company, 2004), 4.
4. Gunnar Myrdal, *An American Dilemma: The Negro Problem and Modern Democracy* (New York: Harper and Brothers, 1944).

Maria W. Miller Stewart, Lecture, Delivered at the Franklin Hall

1. Marilyn Richardson and Maria W. Stewart, *America's First Black Woman Political Writer: Essays and Speeches* (Bloomington: Indiana University Press, 1987), 45.
2. See Richardson, xiii; Shirley J. Yee, *Black Women Abolitionists: A Study in Activism, 1828–1860* (Knoxville: University of Tennessee Press, 1992), 26; and Karlyn Kohrs Campbell, *Man Cannot Speak for Her* (New York: Praeger Publishing, 1989), 2:2.
3. Campbell, 2:2.
4. A notable exception is Sojourner Truth, who seems to have drawn far more heavily on stories from the New Testament for her biblical referents.
5. Psalm 69:4, 12.
6. Psalm 69:32–33, 35–36.
7. Refers to laments found in Psalm 13, Psalm 35, Psalm 94, Habakkuk 1:2, and Revelation 6:10.
8. Acts 10:34; Romans 2:11. Modern translations are often "God shows no partiality"; the phrasing "no respecter of persons" is from the King James Version.
9. Maria W. Stewart, *Productions of Maria W. Stewart* (Boston: Friends of Freedom and Virtue, 1835), 63–72 and 72–82.
10. Although Yee indicates that it was an 1831 speech, there is no record that Stewart delivered any lectures as early as 1831. The Feb. 1833 speech is the oration that most strongly takes African American men to task. See Yee, 115.
11. Stewart, *Productions*, 81.
12. Karlyn Kohrs Campbell, *Man Cannot Speak for Her*, vol. 1 (New York: Praeger Publishing, 1989), 19.
13. Yee, 26.
14. Campbell, 1:18.

Henry Highland Garnet, An Address to the Slaves of the United States of America

1. Martin B. Pasternak, *Rise Now and Fly to Arms: The Life of Henry Highland Garnet* (New York: Garland, 1995), 3–15.

2. Pasternak, 25–32.
3. Pasternak, 28–30, 45.
4. Pasternak, 45–46.
5. Antithesis is the placing of contrasting thoughts in parallel structure ("judged not by the color of their skin but by the content of their character"); hyperbole is deliberate exaggeration; synecdoche is the use of a part to represent the whole, often a phrase that is either created or borrowed, so that the phrase represents the larger piece of discourse ("I have a dream today").
6. All as quoted in Pasternak, 47.

Sojourner Truth, A'n't I a Woman?

1. Nell Irvin Painter, *Sojourner Truth: A Life, a Symbol* (New York: W. W. Norton, 1996), 11.
2. Painter, 13–14
3. [Olive Gilbert and Frances Titus], *Narrative of Sojourner Truth: A Bondswoman of Olden Time, Emancipated by the New York State Legislature in the Early Part of the Present Century; with a History of Her Labors and Correspondence Drawn from Her "Book of Life"* (1887; rpt. Salem, NH.: Ayer Company, 1990), 16–17.
4. Painter, 21–24.
5. Painter, 23–25.
6. Painter, 30–31.
7. Painter, 79.
8. Painter, 75–76.
9. Painter, 103.
10. Gage says that reading novelist Harriet Beecher Stowe's *Atlantic Monthly* article on Truth led her to publish the story of Truth's speech in Akron. Carleton Mabee, *Sojourner Truth: Slave, Prophet, Legend.* (New York: New York University Press, 1993), 68–69. Painter argues that Stowe's description of Truth also helped to shape her report of the speech.
11. Mabee, 68.
12. Gilbert and Titus, 133; Mabee, 69–70, 73; Painter 169.
13. Mabee, 69.
14. Mabee, 70; Painter, 171.
15. Painter, 170.
16. Mabee, 78–80.
17. Gilbert and Titus, 135.
18. Painter, 171.
19. Mabee, 71–74.
20. Suzanne Pullon Fitch and Roseann M. Mandziuk, *Sojourner Truth as Orator; Wit, Story, and Song* (Westport, CT: Greenwood Press, 1997), 74.
21. Mabee, 75–76.
22. Quoted in Painter, 98.
23. Painter relates several poignant stories of history students and professional historians preferring the Gage version to that which she and Mabee had carefully documented. See 281–85.

Frederick Douglass, What to the American Slave Is the Fourth of July?

1. Gregory P. Lampe, *Frederick Douglass: Freedom's Voice, 1818–1845* (East Lansing: Michigan State University Press, 1998), 9–13; and Waldo E. Martin Jr., *The Mind of Frederick Douglass* (Chapel Hill: University of North Carolina Press, 1984), 139–40.

2. Kevin McClure, "Frederick Douglass's Use of Comparison in His Fourth of July Oration: A Textual Analysis," *Western Communication Journal* 64 (2000): 428–29.
3. John Lucaites, "The Irony of 'Equality' in Black Abolitionist Discourse: The Case of Frederick Douglass's 'What to the Slave Is the Fourth of July?'" in *Rhetoric and Political Culture in Nineteenth-Century America*, ed. Thomas W. Benson. (East Lansing: Michigan State University Press, 1997), 55.
4. McClure, 428–29.
5. Lampe, 80–81.
6. Martin, 140–42; and Gerald Fulkerson, "Frederick Douglass 1818–1895: Abolitionist, Reformer," in *African-American Orators: A BioCritical Sourcebook*, ed. Richard W. Leeman (Westport, CT: Greenwood Press, 1996), 82–83.
7. Fulkerson, 90–91; David Blight, "What to the Slave Is the Fourth of July," *Time*, 27 June 2005. <http:/www.time.com/time/nation/article/0.8599.1077058.00html>. Accessed on 24 Apr. 2008.
8. Blight.
9. John W. Blassingame, ed., *The Frederick Douglass Papers Series One: Speeches, Debates, and Interviews* (New Haven: Yale University Press, 1979), 1:xxxiii.
10. Blassingame, 1:xxxviii.
11. Blassingame, 1:xxxvii.
12. David W. Chesebrough, *Frederick Douglass: Oratory from Slavery*. (Westport, CT: Greenwood Press, 1998), 45.
13. James Jasinski interprets this complex and ambiguous metaphor somewhat differently. "Rearticulating History in Epideictic Discourse: Frederick Douglass's 'The Meaning of the Fourth of July to the American Negro,'" in *Rhetoric and Political Culture in Nineteenth-Century America*, ed. Thomas W. Benson (East Lansing: Michigan State University Press, 1997), 80–82.
14. Lucaites, 55–56.
15. See also Robert E. Terrill, "Irony, Silence, and Time: Frederick Douglass on the Fifth of July," *Quarterly Journal of Speech* 89 (2003): 224–25.
16. Chesebrough, 40–41.
17. Chesebrough, 39.
18. McClure, 428–29; Lucaites, 55.

Henry McNeal Turner, I Claim the Rights of a Man

1. John Dittmer, "The Education of Henry McNeal Turner," *Black Leaders of the Nineteenth Century*, ed. Leon Litwack and August Meier (Urbana: University of Illinois Press, 1988), 258.
2. E.g., see Stephen Ward Angell, *Bishop Henry McNeal Turner and African-America Religion in the South* (Knoxville: University of Tennessee Press, 1992), 1, 88; and Philip S. Foner, *The Voice of Black America, 1797–1971* (New York: Simon and Shuster, 1972).
3. Melbourne S. Cummings, "The Rhetoric of Bishop Henry McNeal Turner," *Journal of Black Studies* 12 (1982): 459.
4. Cummings, 460.
5. Dittmer, 255.
6. Dittmer, 255.
7. Dittmer, 255–58.
8. Mark 6:11: "And whoever will not receive you nor hear you, when you depart from there, shake off the dust under your feet as a testimony against them."

9. Edwin S. Redkey, *Black Exodus: Black Nationalist and Back-to-Africa Movements 1890–1910* (New Haven: Yale University Press, 1969), 24–26; 170–74.
10. Henry McNeal Turner, "Will It Be Possible for the Negro to Attain, in This Country, unto the American Type of Civilization?," *Twentieth Century Negro Literature*, ed. D. W. Culp (1902, rpt. New York: Arno, 1969), 45.

Frederick Douglass, Oration on the Occasion of the Dedication of the Lincoln Monument

1. "The Lincoln Monument," *New York Times*, 15 Apr. 1876, 1.
2. Philip S. Foner, *Frederick Douglass: A Biography* (New York: Citadel Press, 1964), 184–85.
3. Foner, 191–207.
4. Foner, 203–7
5. Foner, 209–15.
6. Douglass's quotation is a close though not exact paraphrase of Lincoln's Second Inaugural Address, in which he said: "Fondly do we hope, fervently do we pray, that this mighty scourge of war may speedily pass away. Yet, if God wills that it continue until all the wealth piled by the bondsman's two hundred and fifty years of unrequited toil shall be sunk, and until every drop of blood drawn with the lash shall be paid by another drawn with the sword, as was said three thousand years ago, so still it must be said 'the judgments of the Lord are true and righteous altogether.'"
7. "The Lincoln Monument," *New York Times*, 5 Apr. 1876, 1; and "Douglass on Lincoln," *New York Times*, 22 Apr. 1876, 3.
8. *Oration Delivered by Frederick Douglass on the Occasion of the Unveiling of the Freedmen's Monument in Honor of Abraham Lincoln* (Washington, DC: Gibson Brothers, 1876).
9. See Tom O'Brien, "Douglass Shines at Lincoln Statue Unveiling," 17 Apr. 2004, as retrieved from <www.washingtontimes.com/civilwar/20040416-090928-7018r.htm>. Accessed on 3 May 2007; Rep. Joe Pitts, "Abe Lincoln and Frederick Douglass: Giants in the Cause of Freedom," 20 Feb. 2001, press commentary, as retrieved from <www.house.gov/pitts/press/commentary/022001c-lincolndouglass.htm>. Accessed on 18 July 2011.

Frances Ellen Watkins Harper, Duty to Dependent Races

1. William H. Robinson, *Early Black American Poets* (Dubuque, IA: Wm. C. Brown, Publishers, 1969), 3.
2. Frances Smith Foster, *A Brighter Coming Day: A Frances Ellen Watkins Harper Reader* (New York: Feminist Press at the City University of New York, 1990), 5–18.
3. William Still, *The Underground Rail Road* (Philadelphia: Porters and Coates, 1872), 790.
4. Foster, 18.
5. Foster, 18–21. For an analysis of Harper's legacy as a poet, see Maryemma Graham, "Introduction," *Complete Poems of Frances E. W. Harper* (New York: Oxford University Press, 1988), xxxiii–lvii.
6. Foster, 20–23.
7. That is, the first antithesis contrasts how the "man" mocks one for having A when he is the one who took the A, while in the next antithesis the man who took the B mocks one for having B.
8. Richard W. Leeman, *"Do Everything" Reform: The Oratory of Frances E. Willard* (Westport, CT: Greenwood Press, 1992), 90.

Ida B. Wells-Barnett, Lynch Law in All Its Phases

1. Linda O. McMurray, *To Keep the Waters Troubled: The Life of Ida B. Wells* (New York: Oxford University Press, 1998), 3–16; and Patricia A. Schechter, *Ida B. Wells-Barnett and American Reform, 1880–1930* (Chapel Hill: University of North Carolina Press, 2001), 11–2.
2. McMurray, 24–31.
3. McMurray, drawing upon Wells's autobiography, discusses a third apparent lesson learned—that Wells felt abandoned by some in the African American community who believed that she was, especially for a woman, too outspoken and controversial (30).
4. McMurray, 76–113; 118–19.
5. Wells's article is quoted in part in Ida B. Wells-Barnett, *Selected Works of Ida B. Wells-Barnett*, ed. Trudier Harris (New York: Oxford University Press, 1991), 16–17.
6. Ida B. Wells, *Crusade for Justice*; McMurray, 130–68; Schechter, 75–88.
7. McMurray, 178–81.
8. *American Citizen*, 24 Feb. 1893.
9. *American Citizen*, 21 Oct. 1892.
10. *Washington Bee*, 29 Oct. 1892.
11. Frederick Douglass, "Hon. Fred. Douglass's Letter," in Ida B. Wells, *Southern Horrors: Lynch Law in All Its Phases* (New York: *New York Age* Print, 1892). Rpt. in Harris, 15.
12. *Liverpool Daily Post*, 23 Mar. 1894.
13. *Christian Register*, 12 Apr. 1894.
14. *Manchester Guardian*, 30 Mar. 1894.
15. *New York Sun*, 30 July 1894.
16. *Memphis Commercial*, 15 Dec. 1892.
17. *Memphis Appeal-Avalanche*, 23 May 1893.
18. *Washington Post*, 31 May 1893.
19. McMurray, 168.

Booker T. Washington, Atlanta Exposition Address

1. Andrew King, "Booker T. Washington and the Myth of Heroic Materialism," *Quarterly Journal of Speech* 60 (1974): 323–27.
2. See, for example, Booker T. Washington, "A Speech Delivered before the Women's New England Club" (27 Jan. 1890), *The Booker T. Washington Papers*, ed. Louis R. Harlan, Stuart B. Kaufman, and Raymond W. Smock (Champaign: University of Illinois Press, 1974), 3:25–26; and Booker T. Washington, "A Speech before the New York Congregational Club" (16 Jan. 1893), Harlan, et al., 3:282.
3. Among those in attendance that day were the mayor of Atlanta and the president of the Southern Railroad. Booker T. Washington, *Up from Slavery: An Autobiography*, (Williamstown, Mass.: Corner House, 1989).
4. James Creelman, "South's New Epoch," *New York World*, 19 Sept. 1895, in Harlan, et al., 4:3.
5. Creelman, 9.
6. Clark Howell, writing to the *New York World*, 19 Sept. 1895: 2, quoted in Harlan, et al., 4:17.
7. William Still to Washington, 19 Sept. 1895, in Harlan, et al., 4:18.
8. Rev. Burwell T. Harvey to Washington, 25 Sept. 1895, in Harlan, et al., 4:29.
9. Du Bois to Washington, 24 Sept. 1895, in Harlan, et al., 4:26. There are many letters from contemporaries in the Booker T. Washington Papers, vol. 4, that offer general praise of his speech.
10. As quoted in Louis R. Harlan, *Booker T. Washington: The Making of a Black Leader* (New York: Oxford University Press, 1972), 227.

11. As quoted in Harlan, 225–56.
12. As quoted in Harlan, 226.
13. W. E. B. Du Bois, *The Souls of Black Folk* (Chicago: A. C. McClurg, 1903).
14. King, 323.
15. Washington, *Up from Slavery*, 211–12.
16. As quoted in Harlan, 216, 217.
17. Washington, *Up from Slavery*, 230.
18. Washington, *Up from Slavery*, 230.
19. Harlan, 227.
20. Creelman, 9.
21. Creelman, 10.
22. "The Atlanta Exposition," *New York Times*, 19 Sept. 1895, 1.
23. Washington, *Up from Slavery*, 235.

Mary Church Terrell, What It Means to Be Colored in the Capital of the United States

1. Beverly Washington Jones, *Quest for Equality: The Life and Writings of Mary Eliza Church Terrell, 1863–1954* (Brooklyn: Carlson Publishing, 1990), 6–8.
2. Mary Church Terrell, *A Colored Woman in a White World* (Salem, NH: Ayer Company, 1940, 1986), 10–11.
3. Jones, 11–12; and Terrell, 659–60.
4. Jones, 12–14; and Terrell, 62–104.
5. Terrell, 383.
6. Campbell Gibson and Kay Jung, *Historical Census Statistics on Population Totals by Race, 1790 to 1990, and by Hispanic Origin, 1970 to 1990, for the United States, Regions, Divisions, and States* (Washington, DC: Census Bureau, 2002), Working Paper Series, no. 56.
7. See, for example, Karyln Kohrs Campbell, "Style and Content in the Rhetoric of Early Afro-American Feminists," *Quarterly Journal of Speech* 72 (1986): 441–43; and Ruth Leon W. Butler and A. Cheree Carlson, "Mary Eliza Church Terrell," *African-American Orators: A BioCritical Sourcebook*, ed. Richard W. Leeman (Westport, CT: Greenwood Press, 1996), 326–27.
8. Cynthia P. King, "Recrimination and Respectability in Mary Church Terrell's 'What It Means to Be Colored in the Capital of the U.S.,'" in *Voices of Democracy* (online journal), forthcoming.
9. Mary Church Terrell, "First Presidential Address to the National Association of Colored Women," Jones, 133–38; and "Service Which Should Be Rendered the South," *Voice of the Negro*, Feb. 1905, 182–86, rpt. in Jones, 205–11.
10. Other examples of methods for employing enumeration would be (1) to arrange the stories from longest to shortest, so that the "pace" of the stories accelerates, as if they are "rushing" at the listener; or (2) to arrange them from least to most questionable, so that the earlier examples establish a pattern of audience agreement with the speaker and gradually the examples become more questionable, but less likely to be questioned.
11. Jones, 6–8.
12. Jones, 17–81; and Terrell, 127–88, 221–37, and 354–59.

William Edward Burghardt Du Bois, Disfranchisement

1. David Levering Lewis, *W. E. B. Du Bois: Biography of a Race, 1868–1919* (New York: Henry Holt, 1993), 11–26; and Francis L. Broderick, *W. E. B. Du Bois: Negro Leader in a Time of Crisis* (Stanford: Stanford University Press, 1959), 1–2.

2. W. E. B. Du Bois, *The Souls of Black Folks: Essays and Sketches* (New York: A. C. McLurg, 1903).
3. Lewis, 309, 315–30.
4. Lewis, 333. Similar race riots of the era would include the Wilmington riot of 1898, the Chicago riot of 1919, and the Tulsa riot of 1921.
5. W. E. B. Du Bois, *The Autobiography of W. E. B. Du Bois* (New York: International Publishers, 1968), 213.
6. Lewis, 385.
7. Stacy L. Smith and Martha Solomon Watson, "William Edward Burghardt Du Bois," *African-American Orators: A BioCritical Sourcebook*, ed. Richard W. Leeman (Westport, CT: Greenwood Press, 1996), 99.
8. Suzanne M. Marilley, *Woman Suffrage and the Origins of Liberal Feminism in the United States, 1820–1920* (Cambridge: Harvard University Press, 1996), 72–73.
9. Marilley, 73–80.
10. Marilley, 124–25. Also 14 and 168.
11. Sara Hunter Graham, *Woman Suffrage and the New Democracy* (New Haven: Yale University Press, 1996), 9 and 23–25.
12. Lewis, 417.
13. As quoted in Lewis, 419.
14. Beth M. Waggenspack, *The Search for Self-Sovereignty: The Oratory of Elizabeth Cady Stanton* (Westport, CT: Greenwood Press, 1989), 82.
15. Waggenspack, 159.
16. Waggenspack, 161, 162, and 164.
17. Graham, 110, 149.

Marcus Mosiah Garvey, The Principles of the Universal Negro Improvement Association

1. Tony Martin, *Race First: The Ideological and Organizational Struggles of Marcus Garvey and the Universal Negro Improvement Association* (Westport, CT: Greenwood Press, 1976), 3–4; and Edmund David Cronon, *Black Moses: The Story of Marcus Garvey and the Universal Negro Improvement Association* (Madison: University of Wisconsin Press, 1969), 4–14.
2. Cronon, 15–19.
3. It is not clear whether Booker T. Washington was genuinely offering to support Garvey's tour of America, or whether his response was merely one of politeness. Cronon, 19.
4. Cronon, 19–20, 39–45.
5. Martin, 13.
6. Martin, 151–67; Stein, 61–107; and Cronon, 50–60.
7. Cronon, 45.
8. Consuelo C. Young, "A Study of Reader Attitudes toward the Negro Press," *Journalism Quarterly* 21 (1944): 148–52.
9. Cronon, 45–49.
10. Stein, 159–70; Cronon, 105–12.
11. Stein, 186–208; Cronon, 318.
12. Woodrow Wilson, "An Address to a Joint Session of Congress (January 8, 1918)." Arthur S. Link, ed., *The Papers of Woodrow Wilson*, vol. 45. (Princeton, NJ: Princeton University Press, 1984): 534–39.
13. "Cheering Negroes Hail Black Nation," *New York Times*, 3 Aug. 1920, 7.

14. As quoted in Martin, 101.
15. As quoted in Martin, 102.
16. Martin, 14–19.
17. Cronon, 222.
18. Stein, 274–75.

Vernon Johns, Rock Foundations

1. Many of Johns's later sermons were dictated to and typed by his children, such as Altona. She recalls, however, that he always left the manuscript in his study and recited the sermon from memory (e-mail correspondence with Altona Adelaide Johns Anderson, 23 Oct. 2008). Some that had appeared in pamphlet form were reprinted in Samuel Lucius Gandy, ed., *Human Possibilities: A Vernon Johns Reader* (Washington, DC: Hoffman Press, 1977). One Vernon Johns scholar, Ralph E. Luker, warns, however, that the Gandy volume includes a number of transcription errors (personal interview 22 Sept. 2008).
2. Taylor Branch, *Parting the Waters* (New York: Simon and Schuster, 1988), 7.
3. Branch, 7–8.
4. Branch, 8.
5. Branch, 9.
6. Branch, 9–11.
7. Branch, 11–25.

Martin Luther King Jr., I Have a Dream

1. Richard Lischer, *The Preacher King: Martin Luther King, Jr., and the Word that Moved America* (Oxford: Oxford University Press, 1995), 41–43.
2. Stephen B. Oates, *Let the Trumpet Sound: The Life of Martin Luther King, Jr.* (New York: Harper and Row, 1982), 31–33.
3. Oates, 54–57.
4. See S. Jonathan Bass, *Blessed Are the Peacemakers: Martin Luther King, Jr., Eight White Religious Leaders, and the "Letter from Birmingham Jail"* (Baton Rouge: Louisiana State University Press, 2001).
5. Martin Luther King, Jr., "If the Negro Wins, Labor Wins," *A Testament of Hope: The Essential Writings and Speeches of Martin Luther King, Jr.*, ed. James M. Washington (New York: HarperCollins, 1986, 1991), 201–7.
6. Bernard K. Duffy and Richard D. Besel, "Martin Luther King Jr.'s 'I Have a Dream' and the Politics of Cultural Memory: An Apostil". *ANQ: A Quarterly Journal of Short Articles, Notes and Reviews* 23.3 (2010): 184–91.7. Lischer, 43.
8. See J. Robert Cox, "The Fulfillment of Time: King's 'I Have a Dream' Speech (August 28, 1963)," *Texts in Context: Critical Dialogues on Significant Episodes in American Political Rhetoric*, ed. Michael C. Leff and Fred J. Kauffeld (Davis, CA: Hermagoras Press, 1989), 181–204.
9. David J. Garrow, *Bearing the Cross: Martin Luther King, Jr., and the Southern Christian Leadership Conference* (New York: William Morrow, 1986), 283.
10. Taylor Branch, *Parting the Waters: America in the King Years, 1954–63* (New York: Simon and Schuster, 1988), 881–82.
11. Branch, 882.
12. Branch, 883.
13. Branch, 883, 886.

Malcolm X, The Ballot or the Bullet

1. Clayborne Carson, *Malcolm X: The FBI File* (New York: Carroll and Graf Publishers, 1991), 20–22; Michael Eric Dyson, *Making Malcolm: The Myth and Meaning of Malcolm X* (New York: Oxford University Press, 1995), 3–5; Malcolm X with the assistance of Alex Haley, *The Autobiography of Malcolm X* (New York: Grove Press, 1964), 18–21, 24–25.
2. Malcolm X, 14, 18–21, 25, 28, 31.
3. Malcolm X, 37.
4. Malcolm X, 33, 38.
5. Malcolm X, 40–153.
6. Malcolm X, 176, 181, 187.
7. Malcolm X, 186.
8. Malcolm X, 201.
9. Dyson, 7.
10. Dyson, 11–12; Malcolm X, 289, 299, 321; Gertrude Samuels, "Feud within the Black Muslims," *New York Times Sunday Magazine*, 22 Mar. 1964, 17 ff; see also M. S. Handler, "Malcolm Splits with Muhammad," *New York Times*, 9 Mar. 1964, 1.
11. Handler, 1.
12. Malcolm X, *Malcolm X Speaks*, ed. George Breitman (New York: Merit Publishers, 1955), 23.
13. Carson. According to Carson, "In the view of FBI leaders, the danger posed by Malcolm X was not simply that he was a black nationalist but that he had been a potential 'messiah' who could unify, and electrify, the militant black nationalist movement" (45).
14. Handler, introduction, *The Autobiography of Malcolm X*, ix.
15. AmericanRhetoric.com has an audio recording of the Detroit version of the speech delivered on 12 Apr. 1964.
16. See video recording of Malcolm X's speech, "Police Violence," available in Roger Cook, Edward Roehling, and Lloyd Earl Rohler, *Great Speeches*, vol. 16 (Greenwood, IN: Educational Video Group, 2001).
17. Malcolm X., *The Speeches of Malcolm X at Harvard*, edited with an introductory essay by Archie Epps (New York: William Morrow, 1968), 7.

Stokely Carmichael (Kwame Ture), Black Power

1. Stokely Carmichael with Ekwueme Michael Thelwell, *Ready for Revolution: The Life and Struggles of Stokely Carmichael (Kwame Ture)* (New York: Scribner, 2003), 546.
2. Stokely Carmichael, "Speech at Morgan State College," in *The Rhetoric the Civil-Rights Movement*, ed. Haig A. Bosmajian and Hamida Bosmajian (New York: Random House, 1969), 109.
3. Charlie Cobb, "Revolution: From Stokely Carmichael to Kwame Ture, *Black Scholar* 27, no. 3–4 (1997): 32; Taylor Branch, *At Canaan's Edge: America in the King Years* (New York: Simon and Shuster, 2006), 486.
4. Cobb, 34–35
5. "Dr. King Deplores 'Black Power' Bid," *New York Times*, 21 June 1966, 30.
6. Cobb, 33.
7. Cobb, 32.
8. Cobb, 33; Simon Hall, "The NAACP, Black Power, and the African American Freedom Struggle, 1966–1969," *Historian* 69, no. 1 (2007): 50.
9. "Dr. King Deplores," 30.

10. Cobb, 34; Robert E. Terrill, "Stokely Carmichael (Kwame Ture): African American Civil Rights Leader," in *American Voices: An Encyclopedia of Contemporary Orators*, ed. Bernard K. Duffy and Richard W. Leeman (Westport, CT: Greenwood Press, 2005), 46.
11. Terrill, 46; Cobb, 34.
12. Cobb, 34.
13. Terrill, 46; Cobb, 35.
14. Branch, 703; Terrill, 47; and Carmichael and Thelwell, 588.
15. Carmichael and Thelwell, 664–65, 669.
16. Terrill, 47.
17. Terrill, 47.
18. Lawrence E. Davies, "Carmichael Asks Draft's Defiance," *New York Times* 30 Oct. 1966, 62; Victoria J. Gallagher, "Black Power in Berkeley: Postmodern Constructions in the Rhetoric of Stokely Carmichael," *Quarterly Journal of Speech* 87, no. 2 (May 2001): 144.
19. Gallagher, 145.
20. Davies, 62.
21. William L. Van Deburg, *New Day in Babylon: The Black Power Movement and American Culture, 1965–1975* (Chicago: University of Chicago Press, 1992), 21; also 16–19. The Mau Maus were a faction of the Kikuyu tribe in Kenya that fought against British colonial rule in the 1950s.
22. Carmichael and Thelwell, 546.
23. Pat Jefferson, "'Stokely's Cool': Style," *Today's Speech* 16, no. 3 (1968): 19.
24. Larry S. Richardson, "Stokely Carmichael: Jazz Artist," *Western Speech* 34 (1970): 213–14.
25. Charles J. Stewart. "The Evolution of a Revolution: Stokely Carmichael and the Rhetoric of Black Power," *Quarterly Journal of Speech* 83 (1997): 435.
26. Cobb, 32.
27. Stewart, 443. One could also argue that the Black Power rhetors' merging of militancy with demands for fundamental economic change contributed to the adoption of affirmative action as an energetic federal policy to redress the situation. The 1968 Kerner Commission, studying the urban riots of 1967, proposed policies that would seek to redress past economic wrongs, rather than those that simply removed discriminatory barriers. See John David Skrentny, *The Ironies of Affirmative Action: Politics, Culture, and Justice in America* (Chicago: University of Chicago Press, 1996), 92–110.
28. Cicero, Marcus Tullius, *De Oratore I.*, trans. E. W. Sutton and H. Rackham. (Cambridge, MA: Harvard University Press, 1942), 1:xii, 53.

Martin Luther King Jr., A Time to Break Silence

1. Michael Eric Dyson, *I May Not Get There with You* (New York: Free Press, 2000), 54–58; "Is Vietnam to Become a 'Civil Rights' Issue?" *U.S. News and World Report*, 19 July 1965, 12; "Confusing the Cause," *Time*, 16 July 1965, 20.
2. Dyson, 58, 60, 61.
3. Dyson, 59–60.
4. Dyson, 67–68.
5. Dyson, 52–54.
6. "The Nation," *Time*, 21 Apr. 1967, 21–22; "Dr. King's Disservice to His Cause," *Life*, 21 Apr. 1967, 4; "Civil Rights: Lord of the Doves," *Newsweek*, 17 Apr. 1967, 44–45; Douglas Robinson, "Dr. King Proposes a boycott of War," *New York Times*, 5 Apr. 1967, 1–2.
7. Carl T. Rowan, "Martin Luther King's Tragic Decision," *Reader's Digest*, Sept. 1967, 37–42.

8. *Ebony*, June 1967.
9. “King Speaks for Peace,” *The Christian Century*, 19 Apr. 1967, 492–93.

***Shirley Anita St. Hill Chisholm,* It Is Time to Reassess Our National Priorities**

1. Nichola D. Gutgold, *Paving the Way for Madam President* (Lanham, MD: Lexington Books, 2006), 52, 66.
2. Ernest B. Ferguson, “Mrs. Chisholm President? Don’t Take Her Too Lightly,” *Los Angeles Times*, 1 Oct. 1971, B7.
3. Chisholm, xii; Dorothy Townsend, “Women’s ‘Lib’ Groups Plan Nationwide Strike,” *Los Angeles Times*, 23 Aug. 1970, B1.
4. Chisholm, 3–8.
5. Chisholm, 11–14.
6. Chisholm, 12, 18.
7. Chisholm, 20–21; James Haskins, *Fighting Shirley Chisholm* (New York: Dial Press 1975), 57.
8. Haskins, 68, 59.
9. Chisholm, 28, 43.
10. Chisholm, 44–47, 54.
11. Chisholm, 71; John Kifner “Farmer and Woman in Lively Bedford-Stuyvesant Race,” *New York Times*, 26 Oct. 1968, 22.
12. Chisholm, 75.
13. Judy Klemesrud, “1968: For Women, It Was a Year Marked by Numerous ‘Firsts,’” *New York Times*, 1 Jan. 1969, 25; Chisholm, 77.
14. Richard L Madden, “Mrs. Chisholm Gets off House Farm Committee,” *New York Times*, 30 Jan. 1969, 1.
15. Chisholm, 85–86.
16. “AVoice: African American Voices in Congress.” <http://www.avoiceonline.org/cbc women/chisholm.html.> Accessed on 15 July 2011.
17. Review of *Unbought and Unbossed* by Shirley Chisholm, *New York Times*, 1 Nov. 1970, Proquest Historical Newspapers, 289.
18. Haskins, “Negro Woman to Speak Out in Congress,” *Los Angeles Times*, 1 Jan. 1969, 14.
19. Chisholm, 77.
20. Marjorie Hunter, “White House Pickets, House Speakers Score War,” *New York Times*, 27 Mar. 1969, 4.
21. Chisholm, 95.
22. Chisholm, 96.
23. Chisholm, 69.
24. *Representative American Speeches: 1968–1969*, ed. Lester Thonssen (New York: H. W. Wilson Company, 1969), 68.
25. Haskins, 14.

***Barbara Charline Jordan,* Speech on Watergate to the House Judiciary Committee**

1. Mary Beth Rogers, *Barbara Jordan: American Hero* (New York: Bantam, 1998), 205–13; “Jordan: Seeking the Power Points,” *Newsweek*, 4 Nov. 1974, 22; Anthony Lewis, “Debaters Ask: What Warrants Impeachment? What Is Proof?” *New York Times*, 28 July 1974, 157.
2. Rogers, 48–50, 53–57, 74–106.
3. Rogers, 109–59.
4. Rogers, 213.

5. Rogers, 206, 210.
6. Rogers, 217; and Barbara Jordan and Shelby Hearon, *Barbara Jordan: A Self-Portrait* (Garden City, NY: Doubleday, 1979), 193–99; and "Jordan: Seeking," 22.

Jesse Louis Jackson, Speech to the Democratic National Convention

1. Matthew Frady, *Jesse: The Life and Pilgrimage of Jesse Jackson* (New York: Random House, 1996), 75–96.
2. Lyndrey A. Niles and Carlos Morrison, "Jesse Louis Jackson," *African-American Orators: A BioCritical Sourcebook*, ed. Richard W. Leeman (Westport, CT: Greenwood Press, 1996), 192.
3. Frady, 116–42.
4. Frady, 169–81.
5. Frady, 185–207.
6. David B. McLennan, "Jesse Louis Jackson," *American Voices: An Encyclopedia of Contemporary Orators*, ed. Bernard K. Duffy and Richard W. Leeman (Westport, CT: Greenwood Press, 2005), 193; Frady, 208–57; and Niles and Morrison, 193–94.
7. Frady, 262–98.
8. McLennan, 193–94; Frady, 298–343.
9. Frady, 332–74; McLennan, 194; "Let the Joy Bell Ring," *Newsweek*, 30 July 1984, 22–23; and "Now to the Real Fight," *Time*, 30 July 1984, 19–26.
10. Frady, 367.
11. Jack Daniel and Geneva Smitherman, "How I Got Over: Communication Dynamics in the Black Community," *Quarterly Journal of Speech* 62 (1976): 26–39.
12. Matthew 25:40.
13. Isaiah 43:4; and Matthew 9:17, Mark 2:22, and Luke 5:37–39.
14. John 12:32.
15. "Let the Joy Bell Ring," 23.
16. "Now to the Real Fight," 19, and "Drama and Passion Galore," *Time*, 30 July 1984, 24.
17. "Drama and Passion Galore," 26; and Frady, 367.
18. "Let the Joy Bell Ring," 23. Also Frady, 367, and McLennan, 194.
19. John Russel, "Golden Tongues Return to the Land," *New York Times*, 19 July 1984, A18.
20. "Drama and Passion Galore," 24; and "Let the Joy Bell Ring," 22.
21. "After San Francisco," *Nation*, 4–11 Aug. 1984, 67.
22. Frady, 370.
23. Frady, 369.
24. McLennan, 194.
25. Frady, 332–407. Roger D. Hatch and Frank E. Watkins point out that, according to polls, 21 percent of Jackson's support was "nonblack," but then 79 percent of his supporters in 1984 were African Americans. *Straight from the Heart* (Philadelphia: Fortress Press, 1987), xiii.
26. Jon Cohen, "Obama 2008 vs. Jackson 1988," *Washington Post Online*, 28 Jan. 2008. <http://blog.washingtonpost.com/behind-the-numbers/2008/01/obama_2008_vs_jackson_1988.html>. Accessed on 12 Dec. 2009.
27. Frady, 370.
28. Ernest R. House, *Jesse Jackson and the Politics of Charisma* (Boulder, CO: Westview Press, 1988), 179.
29. House, 180.
30. House, 181.

Marian Wright Edelman, Children's Legislative Issues

1. Cheryl Goodman, "Marian Wright Edelman: I Know Why I've Been Put on Earth," *Crisis*, Mar./Apr. 1999, 14
2. Beth Waggenspack, "Marian Wright Edelman," in *African-American Orators: A Bio-Critical Sourcebook*, ed. Richard W. Leeman (Westport, CT: Greenwood Press, 1996), 110–11.
3. Waggenspack, 111.
4. Arthur Jones, "A Voice for the Poor in D.C.," *National Catholic Reporter*, 24 Mar. 2000, 4.
5. Jones, 4.
6. Suzanne Selinger, "Giving Life to Meaning," *Christian Century*, 17 May 2000, 573–74.
7. Arthur Jones, "Get Out of the Way," *National Catholic Reporter*, 24 Mar. 2000, 3.
8. Marian Wright Edelman, *The Measure of Success: A Letter to My Children and Yours* (Boston: Beacon Press, 1992).
9. Cyril Josh Barker, "Marian Wright Edelman: Plugging the Prison Pipeline," *New York Amsterdam News*, 20–26 Nov. 2008, 44.
10. Marian Wright Edelman, *The Sea Is So Wide and My Boat Is So Small: Charting a Course for the Next Generation* (New York: Hyperion Books, 2008).
11. Barker, 44.

Barack Hussein Obama, Inaugural Address

1. For scholarly discussions of this speech see: David A. Frank and Mark Lawrence McPhail, "Barack Obama's Address to the 2004 National Convention: Trauma, Compromise, Consilience, and the (Im)possibility of Racial Reconciliation," *Rhetoric and Public Affairs* 8 (2005): 571–94; and Robert C. Rowland and John M. Jones, "Recasting the American Dream and American Politics: Barack Obama's Keynote Address to the 2004 Democratic National Convention," *Quarterly Journal of Speech* 93 (2007): 425–48.
2. Garrett M. Graff, "The Legend of Barack Obama," <www.washingtonian.com>, 1 Nov. 2006: 1. Accessed on 12 Aug. 2009.
3. Randal C. Archibald, "Day After: Keynote Speaker Finds Admirers Everywhere." *New York Times*, 29 July 2004, 6.
4. Barack Obama, *Dreams from My Father: A Story of Race and Inheritance* (New York: Crown, 1995), xiii.
5. "The Administration: President Barack Obama," <www.whitehouse.gov>. Accessed on 12 Aug. 2009.
6. Obama, 154; Brian Charlton, "Obama Had Multiethnic Existence in Hawaii," *Washington Post*, 6 Feb. 2007. <www.washingtonpost.com>. Accessed on 12 Aug. 2009.
7. Obama, 92–96; Brian Charlton; "Meet the Candidate," <www.barackobama.com/about/>. Accessed on 12 Aug. 2009.
8. Obama, 133–35.
9. Obama, 164.
10. Glen Johnson, "Harvard Experiences Sculpt Obama Appeal," *Washington Post*, 26 Jan. 2007, <www.washingtonpost.com>. Accessed on 6 Sept. 2009; "Meet the Candidate"; Graff, 2.
11. Graff, 2.
12. Monica Davey, "A Surprise Senate Contender Reaches His Biggest Stage Yet," *New York Times*, 26 July 2004, A1, 6; Graff, 3.
13. Robin Toner and Katherine Q. Seelye, "Republicans Add Seats in South; Obama Wins," *New York Times*, 3 Nov. 2004, A1.
14. "The Administration: President Barack Obama," <www.whitehouse.gov>.

15. Although there was an audience of 1.8 million people at the mall, many of those physically present observed the speech, paradoxically, on giant television screens placed around the grounds.
16. Scott Helman and Michael Kranish, "The Time Has Come": Before Vast Crowd, Obama Takes Office with Call to Remake Nation," *Boston Globe*, 21 Jan. 2009, <www.boston.com>. Accessed on 10 Aug. 2009; "Inaugural Crowd Size Reportedly D.C. Record," *Boston Globe*, 22 Jan. 2009, <www.boston.com>. Accessed on 10 Aug. 2009.
17. Helman and Kranish.
18. Rex Murphy, "Obama's Speech a Clichéd Dud," *Globe and Mail* (Canada), 24 Jan. 2009, A19.
19. Allen Weinstein, "A Bridge, Poetry, Prose." *USA Today*, 20 Jan. 2009, 12A.
20. James Truslow Adams, *The Epic of America* (Boston: Little, Brown, and Company, 1934), 403.
21. Richard L. Johannesen, "The Jeremiad and Jenkin Lloyd Jones," *Communication Monographs* 52 (June 1985): 159–60.
22. Johannesen, 160.
23. Johannesen, 159–60; see also John M. Murphy "'A Time of Shame and Sorrow': Robert F. Kennedy and the American Jeremiad," *Quarterly Journal of Speech* 76 (1990): 404.
24. Michael Gerson, "The Conservative Revolutionary," *Washington Post*, 21 Jan. 2009, A11; "What They're Saying about Obama's Inaugural Address," *St. Petersburg Times* (4 State/Sun Coast edition), 21 Jan. 2009, 6A.
25. That the president had detention camps such as Guantanamo in mind when he declared in the inaugural "We reject as false the choice between our safety and our ideals" is also the interpretation of the editors of *Commonweal*. On the very evening of the inauguration, "President Obama ordered the suspension of military tribunals at Guantanamo Bay. This order and those issued in the following days, took the first steps toward closing the notorious prison. "Remaking America," *Commonweal*, 13 Feb. 2009, 5.
26. Peter Baker "Where Obama's Speech Got Harsh Reviews," *New York Times*, 23 Jan. 2009, 18.
27. Dante Germino, *The Inaugural Addresses of American Presidents: The Public Philosophy and Rhetoric* (Lanham, MD.: University Press of America, 1984), 19.
28. Anne Appelbaum, "Remaking America; We Are Ready to Lead the World Once More, President Tells His Adoring Nation," *Daily Telegraph*, 21 Jan. 2009, 1.
29. Ted Widmer, "So Help Me God," *The American Scholar*, <www.theamericanscholar.org>, 6. Accessed on 18 July 2011.
30. N. D. Kristof, "The Remaking of America" *New York Times*, 22 Jan. 2009, 33.
31. David E. Sanger, "Rejecting Bush Era, Reclaiming Older Values," *New York Times*, 21 Jan. 2009, 1.
32. Father Raymond J. DeSouza, "Strong Symbols, Weak Speech," *National Post* (Canada), 21 Jan. 2009, A10; "Paul Bedard, "President Barack Obama's Inaugural Address Scores High," *U.S. News and World Report*, 23 Jan. 2009, <www.infoweb.newsbank.com>. Accessed on 4 Aug. 2009; Michael Fullilove, "Fine Speech for an Extraordinary Historical Moment," *Sydney Morning Herald*, 22 Jan. 2009, 7.
33. For a discussion of Obama's speech concerning the Reverend Wright controversy see: David A. Frank, "The Prophetic Voice and the Face of the Other in Barack Obama's 'A More Perfect Union,' Address," 18 Mar. 2008, *Rhetoric and Public Affairs* 12 (2009), 167–94.
34. Murphy.

35. Denise Lavoie, “Exhibit Highlights Kennedy Inaugural,” *Boston Globe*, 9 Jan. 2009, <www.boston.com>. Accessed on 10 Aug. 2009.
36. Charles P. Pierce, “Just Words,” *Boston Globe*, 11 Jan. 2009. <www.boston.com>. Accessed on 10 Aug. 2009.
37. Widmer, 4; Ed Pilkington, “Barrack Obama’s Inauguration Speech . . . Crafted by 27 Year Old in Starbucks,” *Guardian* (London), 20 Jan. 2009. <www.guardian.co.uk>. Accessed on 31 Aug. 2009; Eli Saslow, “Helping to Write History,” *Washington Post*, 18 Dec. 2008, A1.
38. Appelbaum, 1.
39. Quoted in Henry Allen, “His Way with Words: Cadence and Credibility,” *Washington Post*, 20 Jan. 2009, AA23.
40. Waldo W. Braden, “Abraham Lincoln,” in *American Orators before 1900*, ed. Bernard K. Duffy and Halford Ryan (New York: Greenwood Press, 1987), 267.

Sources

Maria W. Miller Stewart, "Lecture, Delivered at Franklin Hall" (1832). Text taken from Maria W. Stewart, *Productions of Maria W. Stewart* (Boston: Friends of Freedom and Virtue, 1835), 51–56.

Henry Highland Garnet, "An Address to the Slaves of the United States of America" (1843). Text taken from Henry Highland Garnet, *A Memorial Discourse* (Philadelphia: Joseph M. Wilson, 1865), 44–51.

Sojourner Truth, "A'n't I a Woman?" (1851). Salem (OH) *Anti-Slavery Bugle* version: Text taken from the *Anti-Slavery Bugle* (Salem, OH), 21 June 1851. *History of Woman Suffrage* version: Text taken from *History of Woman Suffrage*, ed. Elizabeth Cady Stanton, Susan B. Anthony, and Matilda Joslyn Gage (New York: Fowler and Wells, Publishers, 1881), 1:116.

Frederick Douglass, "What to the American Slave Is the Fourth of July" (1852). Text taken from Frederick Douglass, *Oration, Delivered in Corinthian Hall, Rochester* (Rochester, NY: Lee, Mann, and Company, 1852).

Henry McNeal Turner, "I Claim the Rights of a Man" (1868). Text taken from Ethel Maude Christler, "Participation of Negroes in the Government of Georgia, 1867–1870." MA thesis, University of Georgia, 1932. Ms. Christler reprinted the text from a pamphlet supplied her by Bishop J. S. Flipper of Atlanta, GA.

Frederick Douglass, "Oration on the Occasion of the Dedication of the Lincoln Monument" (1876). Text taken from Frederick Douglass, *Oration Delivered by Frederick Douglass on the Occasion of the Unveiling of the Freedmen's Monument in Honor of Abraham Lincoln* (Washington, DC: Gibson Brothers, 1876).

Frances Ellen Watkins Harper, "Duty to Dependent Races" (1891). Text taken from Rachel Foster Avery, *Transactions of the National Council of Women of the United States* (Philadelphia: J. B. Lippincott and Co., 1891), 86–91.

Ida B. Wells-Barnett, "Lynch Law in All Its Phases" (1893). Text taken from Ida B. Wells, "Lynch Law in All Its Phases," *Our Day*, May 1893, 333–37.

Booker T. Washington, "Atlanta Exposition Address" (1895). Text taken from Booker T. Washington, *Up from Slavery* (Garden City, NY: Doubleday and Company, 1901), 218–25.

Mary Church Terrell, "What It Means to Be Colored in the Capital of the United States" (1906). Text taken from "What It Means to Be Colored in the Capital of the United States, *Independent*, 24 Jan. 1907, 181–86. There is no author credited by the *Independent*, but a handwritten version of the piece was discovered in Terrell's papers.

William Edward Burghardt Du Bois, "Disfranchisement (1912). Text taken from W. E. B. Du Bois, *Disfranchisement* (New York: National American Woman Suffrage Association, 1912).

Marcus Mosiah Garvey, "The Principles of the Universal Negro Improvement Association" (1922). Text taken from Marcus Garvey, *Philosophy and Opinions of Marcus Garvey or Africa for the Africans*, ed. Amy Jacques-Garvey (New York: Universal Publishing House, 1925), 2:93–100.

Vernon Johns, "Rock Foundations" (1926). Text taken from *Human Possibilities: A Vernon Johns Reader*, ed. Samuel Gandy (Washington, DC: Hoffman Press, 1977).

Martin Luther King Jr., "I Have a Dream" (1963). Text taken from Martin Luther King, Jr., *A Testament of Hope*, ed. James M. Washington (New York: HarperCollins), 217–21.

Malcolm X, "The Ballot or the Bullet" (1964). Text taken from Malcolm X, *Malcolm X Speaks: Selected Speeches and Statements*, ed. George Breitman (New York: Pathfinder, 1965, 1989), 23–44.

Stokely Carmichael (Kwame Ture), "Black Power" (1966). Text taken from *Stokely Speaks: Black Power to Pan-Africanism* (New York: Random House, 1971), 45–60.

Martin Luther King Jr., "A Time to Break Silence" (1967). Text taken from Martin Luther King Jr., *A Testament of Hope: The Essential Writings and Speeches of Martin Luther King, Jr.*, ed. James M. Washington (New York: Harper Collins, 1986), 231–44.

Shirley Anita St. Hill Chisholm, "It Is Time to Reassess Our National Priorities" (1969). Text taken from *Congressional Record* (Washington, DC: Government Printing Office, 1969), 115:7765.

Barbara Jordan, "Speech on Watergate to the House Judiciary Committee" (1974). Text taken from *House Committee on the Judiciary Hearings* (Washington, DC: Government Printing Office, 1974).

Jesse Louis Jackson, "Speech to the Democratic National Convention" (1984). Text transcribed from videotape by the editors. Video recording of the speech may be found at *Great Speeches*, vol. 3. Educational Video Group, 2004. <www.evgonline.com>.

Marian Wright Edelman, "Children's Legislative Issues" (1985). Speech by Marian Wright Edelman delivered to the National Education Association's Twenty-Third Annual Conference on Human and Civil Rights in Education on 22 Feb. 1985. Text transcribed from audiotape in *Critical Issues in Education* (Washington, DC: National Education Association, 1985).

Barack Hussein Obama, "Inaugural Address" (2009). Text taken from Barack Obama, "Inaugural Address," *Weekly Compilation of Presidential Documents* 45, no. 2 (2009): 1–4.

Index

Richard W. Leeman is professor of communication studies at the University of North Carolina at Charlotte, where he teaches classes in African American oratory, rhetorical theory, and political communication. He is the author or editor of five previous books, including *African-American Orators: A BioCritical Sourcebook*, *The Rhetoric of Terrorism and Counterterrorism*, *"Do Everything" Reform: The Oratory of Frances E. Willard*, and *American Voices: An Encyclopedia of Contemporary Orators*. He is the recipient of several scholarly awards, including the American Forensic Association Daniel Rohrer Award for Best Forensic Research Article.

Bernard K. Duffy is professor of communication studies at California Polytechnic State University at San Luis Obispo, where he teaches classes in rhetorical theory, persuasion, and American public address. He is the author or editor of six previous books, including *The Politics of Rhetoric: Richard M. Weaver and the Conservative Tradition*, *Douglas MacArthur: Warrior as Wordsmith*, *Health Communication: Developments and Directions* and *American Voices: An Encyclopedia of Contemporary Orators*. He is the recipient of the University Distinguished Teaching Award, the College of Liberal Arts Richard K. Simon Award for Outstanding Teaching, and the College of Liberal Arts Award for Outstanding Scholarship.